THE AMERICANS
WITH DISABILITIES ACT

THE AMERICANS WITH DISABILITIES ACT

From Policy to Practice

Edited by
Jane West

MILBANK MEMORIAL FUND
New York

Milbank Memorial Fund
1 East 75th Street
New York, N.Y. 10021

Printed in the United States of America

1 2 3 4 5 6 7 8 9 10
Library of Congress Catalog Card Number: 91-62005
ISBN 0-9629870-0-X

Table of Contents

Preface   vii

Acknowledgments   ix

Introduction — Implementing the Act:
  Where We Begin
  Jane West   xi

I. Getting Oriented

  The Social and Policy Context of the Act
    Jane West   3

  Essential Requirements of the Act:
    A Short History and Overview
    Nancy Lee Jones   25

  The Demographics of Disability
    Mitchell P. LaPlante   55

II. Employment: The Heart of Independence

  Employment Protections
    Chai R. Feldblum   81

  Employment Strategies for People with Disabilities:
    A Prescription for Change
    Paul G. Hearne   111

v

The Recent History and Immediate
Future of Employment among Persons
with Disabilities
Edward H. Yelin   129

The Economics of Employment
Thomas N. Chirikos   150

III. An Inclusive Infrastructure

Equal Access to Public Accommodations
Robert L. Burgdorf Jr.   183

Transportation Policy
Robert A. Katzmann   214

Implementing the Telecommunications
Provisions
Karen Peltz Strauss   238

Public Health Powers: The Imminence
of Radical Change
Lawrence O. Gostin   268

IV. Reinforcements for the Mandate

Tax Incentives
Daniel C. Schaffer   293

The Role of Technology in Removing Barriers
John C. DeWitt   313

Summing Up: Opportunities of Implementation
Jane West   333

Appendices

A: ADA Implementation Dates   337

B: Resource Organizations   340

Index   353

Preface

Since its inception in 1905 the purposes of the Milbank Memorial Fund have included "improv[ing] the physical, mental and moral condition of humanity." In 1991 we interpret these words to mean informing public and private decision makers about research-based knowledge in two areas. The first area is the prevention of disease and disability. The second is the allocation of resources for health care. The goals of the Americans with Disabilities Act (ADA), fostering the inclusion and independence of persons with disabilities, exemplify the purposes of the Fund.

This book was conceived early in 1990 during a conversation among board and staff members of the Milbank Memorial Fund and the JM Foundation. The ADA was then in the final stages of congressional debate. The participants in the conversation agreed that it would be useful to synthesize and make broadly available results of research and analysis that could assist people in the private and public sectors to implement the Act. The Fund, the J.M. Foundation, and the Dole Foundation for the Employment of Persons with Disabilities then convened a meeting of researchers and public officials who were closely involved with the ADA. The result of that meeting was a recommendation that the articles in this book should be commissioned, reviewed by peers, and then published.

We are grateful to our partner foundations, to the authors, to the advisory committee, and to the members of the staff of the Fund who edited the book and managed its production. We hope it helps in the implementation of the most comprehensive statement to date of national policy for persons with disabilities.

Samuel L. Milbank
Chairman

Daniel M. Fox
President

April 1991

Acknowledgements

I am grateful to the many people who contributed their time and talent to shaping this project. Without their generous assistance, the book would not reflect the breadth and depth it does today. The advisory group diligently reviewed papers, provided the authors with feedback, and helped in molding and directing this volume. Their time and invaluable suggestions are most appreciated. They are Chris Olander, Linda Morra, Nancy Jones, Lani Florian, Robert Burgdorf, Paul Hearne, Robert Katzmann, and Irving Zola.

In addition, a number of experts, some of them our own authors, reviewed various papers. I appreciate their time and thoughts. They are Kate Seelman, Clyde Behney, John Leslie, Larry Scadden, Lee Ruck, Carol Cohen, Larry Gostin, Chai Feldblum, Daniel Schaffer, Thomas Chirikos, and Edward Yelin.

For suggestions in organizing the volume, I am grateful to Ray Rist. For contributing their expertise and access to private collections of papers and reports, I extend thanks to Dave Capozzi, John Doyle, Malcolm Morrison, and Jean Argoff. For her administrative assistance, I thank Sandy Cawley.

Jane West
Washington, D.C.

Introduction—Implementing the Act: Where We Begin

Jane West

Americans with disabilities are the largest, poorest, least employed, and least educated minority in America. The Americans with Disabilities Act (ADA) is a bold and comprehensive mandate intended to eliminate one of the key barriers to independent living in the mainstream of American life for persons with disabilities: discrimination. This book presents a synthesis of what we know as a result of research and analysis about establishing and maintaining an accessible and inclusive world for people with disabilities. The audience for this book is made up of people concerned about public policy in general and the ADA in particular—at the federal, state, and local levels in the public sector, and in the for-profit and nonprofit arenas of the private sector.

Although many policies have been initiated in the past 15 years to promote the independence, productivity, and inclusion of persons with disabilities, the accomplishments have been modest. The ADA is a policy with ambitious goals. It is a policy that requires us to change our thinking about people with disabilities. The ADA demands that we focus on *people*, not on *disabilities*; that we focus on what they *can* do, not on what they *cannot* do. It is a policy that proclaims independence for people with disabilities—economic, social, and personal. The Act says participation in the mainstream of daily life is an American right.

The policy represents the culmination of years of progressive and

proactive efforts of persons with disabilities, the disability-rights movement, dedicated professionals, committed legislators and government
leaders, service providers whose programs have demonstrated outcomes
of independence for persons with disabilities, and visionaries in the
private sector who have seen beyond disabilities to abilities. The ADA
is a law supported by almost two decades of statutory, legal, and programmatic building blocks. For the first time, our nation has one
overarching policy that provides a framework for reshaping related policies and programs and a standard against which to measure those policies and programs.

The ADA was initiated and drafted in 1988 by the National Council
on Disability, an independent federal agency composed of 15 members
appointed by the President. The law is a comprehensive antidiscrimination mandate for persons with disabilities extending to virtually all
sectors of society and every aspect of daily living — work, leisure, travel,
communications. It provides civil-rights protections to persons with
disabilities that are comparable to those in force for women and minorities. Physical and communication barriers must be removed and discriminatory practices and procedures are to be eliminated. Reasonable
accommodations must be made for persons with disabilities, including
the provision of auxiliary aids and services. The ADA authorizes the
federal government to enforce the standards outlined in the Act.

This volume is a contribution to the effective implementation of the
ADA. As a synthesis of knowledge resulting from efforts to date to
ensure full participation in society by persons with disabilities, it is
intended to be a knowledge base for technical assistance efforts related
to ADA. Its goal is to provide information that will illuminate the
route from mandate to practice.

THE TARGET AUDIENCE

The broadness of the ADA mandate necessitates a large audience for
this book. One of our key motivations for undertaking a synthesis of
current knowledge about the independence, productivity, and inclusion of persons with disabilities is the fact that disability is a relatively
new area of social policy, and the broad sweep of the ADA mandate
requires that a broader range of implementors be involved than ever
before. Individuals who are skilled and knowledgeable in discrete areas

of public policy, such as employment or transportation, will need to expand their knowledge bases to include disability policy. Individuals who have dedicated their lives and careers to one area of disability policy and services, such as supported employment or special education, will need to learn about the full gamut of disability policy. Similarly, researchers from different disciplines, such as law and economics, will have to adopt an interdisciplinary perspective.

The ADA will be administered by four key federal agencies: the Department of Justice, the Equal Employment Opportunity Commission, the Department of Transportation, and the Federal Communications Commission. Technical-assistance efforts will be funded through the Department of Justice, the Equal Employment Opportunity Commission, and the Department of Education's National Institute on Disability and Rehabilitation Research. Other federal agencies will be involved in implementing the ADA by issuing guidelines, developing informational materials, providing technical assistance, and assessing the implementation of the law. This book is intended to be a resource for individuals in those agencies as well as federal grantees and contractors who will be providing technical assistance around the country.

The book is also directed to state and local government officials who are required to comply with the law themselves, but who will also undoubtedly be called upon by their constituents to provide information. We designed it to serve as a resource in the business of assessing the implications of the ADA for policies, practices, programs, and funding in individual communities.

Businesses and industry in the private sector, both small and large, are another targeted audience. Personnel directors and human-resources specialists must be informed about the requirements of the ADA and must have an understanding of the expertise available to facilitate compliance. As consumers of the products of the human-resources industry, they will have to assess both their own needs and the efficacy of the technical assistance available to them. This book is intended to address those concerns.

The private nonprofit sector has been actively organizing to contribute to the implementation effort. Under the leadership of some 15 major national grantmakers, a Funding Partnership for People with Disabilities is being created to award grants totalling about $1 million. These grants will be awarded to local coalitions, which will facilitate the integration and participation of persons with disabilities in all aspects of American life. Many nonprofit disability and human-services organizations are assessing their skills and organizing themselves to provide ADA-related services and technical assistance. This volume is intended as a resource for those efforts.

We also seek researchers as an audience: in academia, state and federal agencies, private think tanks, and consulting firms. We would like to harness the interest of researchers by presenting a case for the necessity of data collection and evaluation and policy-relevant analysis. There is simply too much at stake to proceed with implementation in the absence of impact evaluation.

Generalists constitute another audience as they search for a resource to orient them about the ADA and its origins. In this category would be journalists, students of public policy, and interested parties in the public at large.

Persons with disabilities and disability rights organizations are another audience. The book is intended to provide them an understanding of the rights they are guaranteed under the Act and a sense of the history and experience that serve as building blocks for those rights.

Finally, we intend to contribute to the ADA industry forming in Washington and nationwide. Composed of consultants, researchers, attorneys, and academics who earn their living by assisting nonprofit organizations to provide services and technical assistance, and aiding businesses in their steps toward compliance, this industry is developing rapidly in conjunction with the large implementation effort.

HOW TO USE THIS BOOK

Some will want to read this book from cover to cover; others will select topics of particular interest. The book will be useful both in orienting those who need a general sense of the law and its mandates and in supplying a reference for specific areas of inquiry, such as how technology can be used to provide reasonable accommodations. We encourage everyone to read this introduction, which provides a summary and overview of the knowledge detailed in the book. For readers who seek specific information about a particular topic, a short index is provided.

Two appendices are included as references: Appendix A is a chart, entitled ADA: Implementation Dates, indicating which federal agencies monitor the implementation of the different titles of the law, the effective dates of the provisions of the law, and the dates for issuance of regulations by the various federal agencies. Appendix B, Resource Organizations, is a list of organizations with a national scope which could be used as resources for additional information or assistance.

TOWARD IMPLEMENTATION

Like religion, policies have their greatest impact when they are translated into daily behavior. This translation, referred to as implementation in the world of public policy, is already underway. At the time we go to press, all five sets of regulations required by the law have been issued in proposed form. Proposed guidelines for barrier-free environments have been published as well as a federal government-wide technical-assistance plan. Over $13 million have been appropriated by the U.S. Congress for specific technical-assistance efforts. Workshops and conferences are underway throughout the country. Compliance manuals are being drafted.

All of these activities might be considered the first level of implementation—organizations and agencies reviewing and preparing information about the law as we approach effective dates. The next level of implementation will come when the rubber meets the road—when the effective dates of the law arrive and entities are legally responsible for complying with the Act.

WHAT WE KNOW

The book addresses itself to a range of questions. First, what exactly does the ADA require? What is the basis of those requirements? What do we know about creating a world that supports, promotes, and enables persons with disabilities to live independent, productive lives? What does the research tell us? What do the experts tell us? What is the best thinking in the emerging field of disability research? Furthermore, how can we use the knowledge we have to implement the ADA?

One of the clear conclusions of this book is that we do not know enough. Rare are the circumstances, however, when we have sufficient knowledge. Although our research-based information is limited, it is certainly adequate to support effective implementation efforts. Ignoring the knowledge we already have about creating an accessible world would not be in the spirit of the ADA. Finally, it is important that we publicly determine what we know and what we do not so that our future research efforts will be meaningful.

The fact that our knowledge base is limited should not be disheartening nor should it provide a rationale for doing anything other than proceeding full speed ahead. After all, the Americans with Disabilities Act and most of its predecessor legislation is about rights—and rights are based on values, not on knowledge. Knowledge plays a critical role in policy fine tuning and in effective implementation by assisting us to discover what works under what conditions; however, knowledge alone is never the sole determinant of public-policy choices. Now that the key public-policy choices have been made, the task before us is to use the knowledge we have to implement the law effectively and to generate more knowledge in order to improve the results of our efforts.

The following points of knowledge relevant to the implementation of the ADA are distilled from the articles presented in this book:

• We have the knowledge and skills to make jobs, places, and services accessible for people with disabilities.

• The cost of making places of employment and public accommodations accessible is generally reasonable and manageable.

• Negative attitudes toward persons with disabilities and discrimination have contributed to the status of persons with disabilities as the poorest, least educated, and least employed minority.

• The precise number of persons with disabilities varies widely depending upon the definition used, the situation of the particular individual, the nature of the impairment and the concomitant degree of limitation, and the particular aspect of society in which participation is being sought.

• Most persons with disabilities are not working and want to work.

• Employers find persons with disabilities to be good employees; however, the labor-force participation rate for persons with disabilities has declined in the last two decades.

• In terms of programs intended to gain and maintain employment for persons with disabilities, effectiveness is more a function of the management of the programs and the severity of the disability of the individuals served than of the type of program providing the service.

• Full implementation of the ADA will require a re-examination of public and private programs intended to serve persons with disabilities to ensure that their goals are in harmony with the goals of the ADA.

• When people with disabilities work and are consumers of goods and services it is good for the economy.

• With almost two decades of experience in implementing civil-rights laws for people with disabilities, we are well equipped to implement the ADA.

ONWARD

At this point, when the promise of a new mandate has captured our attention, yet the daily toil of transforming the policy into practice has not fully arrived, a range of anticipatory thoughts about the impact of the law is surfacing in the American consciousness. In a recent letter to a U.S. senator, a businessman requested that the legislation be amended or abolished. He said that the law is so vague it is a "horror story for American employers." The reasonable accommodation provisions are so general that employers will be required to make expenditures until they reach the brink of bankruptcy. In his view, "The law constitutes a hunting license for lawyers and for unscrupulous persons with fictitious or questionable 'disabilities.'"

A well-known disability-rights activist expressed a view at the opposite end of the spectrum. She holds that people with disabilities are not organized enough to insist on a level of enforcement that would result in the ADA being anything more than a "public-spirited gesture." She feels that the administration's support of the ADA was a "low-risk commitment to a relatively unorganized group." In fact, enactment of the legislation represents a token gesture intended to remove disability rights from the public agenda. In her words, "One of the best ways to kill a civil rights concept is to pass a law and not enforce it" (Johnson 1989).

In this book, we stand in the water between these two shores. Perhaps these two very different perspectives articulate the challenge of implementation. The law is not intended to bankrupt businesses, nor to be a one-time raising of the flag. It is not crafted to be a hunting license for attorneys; neither is it crafted to be ignored. It is in the implementation of this law— the movement from policy to practice— that we have the opportunity to prove both commentators wrong. It is our belief that a reasoned and steady approach using the considerable knowledge and experience we have gained in the last few decades will yield the result intended by the law: increased independence and inclusion of persons with disabilities. This is the end toward which this book is dedicated.

The next few pages, along with the editor's notes preceding each article, provide a guide to the requirements of the law and the knowledge and distilled experience that can guide us as we implement it.

SECTION I: GETTING ORIENTED

Section I orients us by considering the social and policy context that generated the ADA. It considers the American experience of disability, the growth of the disability-rights movement, and the identity of persons with disabilities as a minority group; attitudes toward persons with disabilities; the nature of discrimination and civil rights in terms of persons with disabilities; the legislative and programmatic building blocks on which ADA is based; a history and overview of the requirements of the legislation; definitions of disability and the demographics they have generated.

In the first article, "The Social and Policy Context of the ADA," I consider the ADA as a policy that sends a message about what society's attitudes should be toward persons with disabilities: respect, inclusion, and support. I scrutinize the status of persons with disabilities: the largest, poorest, and least educated minority in America. They are a minority of second-class citizens: socially, economically, vocationally, and educationally. Their history is largely one of isolation and segregation. They are a group of people who have been defined by what they are not, rather than by what they are. They have been described in terms of "diseases, deformities, and abnormalities," identified by labels and diagnoses, and have frustrated the medical profession because it could not cure them. They have been considered lifelong children who need to be taken care of and shielded from life's vicissitudes.

People with disabilities share the experience of discrimination with women and other minorities, repeatedly confronting obstacles of prejudice and stereotypes. In addition, physical and communication barriers have kept them outside of the mainstream. They have encountered policies that exclude them by implication. In virtually every aspect of society—housing, employment, education, recreation, transportation, public accommodations, communication, health services, and even voting—persons with disabilities have been shunned.

Efforts to change this state of affairs have been underway for at least 15 years—in terms of shifts in attitudes, the growth of the disability-rights movement and the identity of persons with disabilities as a minority group, the changing language of disability, and the gradual evolution of disability-rights laws.

A wide range of programs, services, and organizations is in place throughout the nation to provide support for persons with disabilities. The Americans with Disabilities Act is the new framework that comprehensively articulates the goals toward which all these programs and services must now reorient themselves.

In the second article, "Essential Requirements of the Act: A Short History and Overview," Nancy Lee Jones describes the legislative history of the ADA and provides an overview of the requirements of the Act. Drawing on the substantive requirements and history of the application of section 504 of the Rehabilitation Act and the procedural requirements of title VII of the Civil Rights Act of 1964, the ADA is more noteworthy for its breadth of application than its novelty of concept and procedure.

Intended to provide civil-rights protections to persons with disabilities that are comparable to the rights afforded to women and other minorities, the ADA extends the existing prohibition against discrimination (which applies only when federal funds are involved) to a prohibition in virtually every segment of society. Discrimination is prohibited in employment, state and local services, transportation, public accommodations, and telecommunications. For the first time, the private sector must comply with a comprehensive disability antidiscrimination mandate.

The law requires that "reasonable accommodations" be made in the employment setting for persons with disabilities who are qualified to perform the "essential functions" of the job. If the accommodation creates an "undue hardship" on the business, it is not required. All state and local services are prohibited from excluding participation or denying benefits of services, programs, or activities to persons with disabilities. (This prohibition is currently in force under section 504 of the Rehabilitation Act, which obligates states and localities that receive federal funds to comply. Therefore, considerable experience with compliance already exists in this arena.)

Transportation must be accessible to people with disabilities, in time. All newly purchased or leased public buses must be equipped so that they are accessible for persons with disabilities. (Retrofitting of existing buses is not required.) All new rail vehicles and stations must be accessible. At least one car on each train must be accessible within five years of enactment and key rail-transit stations must be accessible within three years. In addition, paratransit or alternative transportation services (most frequently minivan service) must be available to those who cannot use accessible mainline bus services because of a mental or physical impairment. If the provision of paratransit and other special transportation services would impose an undue financial burden on the entity, it is only required to the extent that providing the service would not impose such a burden.

Places of public accommodation must be accessible to persons with disabilities — motels, restaurants, bars, movie theaters, convention centers, grocery stores, clothing stores, museums, libraries, amusement parks, schools, day-care centers, gyms, bowling alleys . . . Alterations that are "readily achievable" must be made to existing buildings and new construction must be barrier free. Reasonable modifications must be made to policies and auxiliary aids provided they do not create an undue burden on the business or fundamentally alter the nature of the goods or services provided.

Title IV of the Act requires the establishment of interstate and intrastate telecommunication relay services. These services will enable persons with hearing or speech impairments to have equal access to the telephone system.

The last title of the Act contains a range of provisions, including an application of the Act to the U.S. Congress, and a list of categories of individuals excluded from coverage by ADA, such as drug users, transvestites, and homosexuals.

Jones notes, "The challenge facing disability policy makers will be to integrate financial support for rights at a time of increasing budgetary concerns." She proposes an examination of the Individuals with Disabilities Education Act (formerly the Education for All Handicapped Children's Act, P.L. 94–142) as a model for such an effort.

In the final article in this section, "The Demographics of Disability," Mitchell P. LaPlante explores various definitions of disability and the numbers they have generated. Persons who consider themselves to have a disability, disability-rights advocates, professionals who study disability, and the general public disagree about the meaning of disability. Researchers tend to think of disability as involving a degree of limitation in some aspect of functioning. Differences exist in defining the degree of the limitation and types of functioning included in the meaning of disability. Some disability-rights advocates hold that persons with health conditions who may not experience any limitation in functioning may be stigmatized and discriminated against simply because of their condition. They believe these individuals should be included in the definition of disability. Finally, some persons who have activity limitations do not perceive themselves as having a disability.

The ADA defines disability as a physical or mental impairment that substantially limits one or more major life activities, a record of such an impairment, or being regarded as having such an impairment. Although the definition denotes the perimeters of who will be covered by the ADA, the final determination will be made on a case-by-case basis according to the particulars of the individual situation.

The ADA estimates the number of persons with one or more physical or mental disabilities as 43 million, noting that this number is increasing as the population ages. Data from various surveys described by LaPlante provide estimates of people with disabilities ranging from 34- to 120 million depending on the definition of disability being utilized.

Disability prevalence varies considerably in different regions of the country. One study reported a range of work-disability rate (defined as activity limitation) from 5.7 percent (in Denver) to 19.8 percent (in San Bernadino/Riverside). Another study indicated that differences in characteristics such as income, employment levels, educational levels, and health explained 90 percent of the variation. With such geographic variation, the impact and implications of the ADA are likely to vary in different parts of the country.

Although estimates of the numbers of persons with disabilities are useful in providing rough guides, their application in determining the numbers of persons ADA will cover must be approached with caution. Disabilities are not necessarily immutable characteristics, like sex and race. A particular disability may limit functioning in one situation (e.g., riding a bus), while having no impact in another situation (e.g., using a word processor). All persons with a particular disability will not be limited in the same manner, mainly because of other intervening characteristics, such as educational level and availability of family and community support. Beyond the obvious accommodations, such as ramps for persons using wheelchairs and braille for persons who are blind, the determination of appropriate accommodations demands an individualized approach.

SECTION II: EMPLOYMENT—THE HEART OF INDEPENDENCE

Our jobs are inextricably woven into the fabric of our identities. Competence, self-esteem, financial independence, and security are all fruits of working. As Chai R. Feldblum writes in the opening article, "Employment Protections," "Having a stable and fulfilling job is a basic component of the American dream."

Persons with disabilities have frequently been denied the opportunity to pursue employment according to their choice and abilities. The 1986 Harris Poll estimated that there are approximately 8 million working-aged persons with disabilities who are not working, but would like to work. In the marketplace, stereotypes and prejudice have kept some doors firmly closed to them. The closed doors have been reinforced by many of our public policies, which have sent the message that dependence is what we expect from persons with disabilities.

Feldblum reviews the antidiscrimination requirements of the ADA as they relate to employment. She writes: "The basic principle . . . is that qualified persons with disabilities must be judged on their merits and abilities for particular jobs and must not have employment opportunities unjustly foreclosed to them because of myths or stereotypes regarding their disabilities." The discrimination prohibition extends to all aspects of employment: the application and recruitment processes, working at the job, job promotions, firings, and participation in benefits and privileges of the job that are offered to employees without disabilities.

The ADA prohibits employment discrimination against persons who are "otherwise qualified." A person who is "otherwise qualified" is a person who can perform the "essential functions" of the job with or without "reasonable accommodation." The "otherwise qualified" individual must satisfy the skill, experience, education, and other job-related criteria. The employment requirements take effect for employers with 25 employees or more on July 26, 1992, and for employers with 15 employees or more on July 26, 1994.

In the second article in this section, "Employment Strategies for People With Disabilities: A Prescription for Change," Paul G. Hearne reviews what we know about increasing the employment and employ-ability of people with disabilities. A substantial majority of persons with disabilities of working age are not working (66 percent), and the overwhelming majority of them want to work (78 percent). Most man-agers give employees with disabilities high ratings for performance and note that the cost of accommodating an employee with a disability is quite manageable; one study indicates that 50 percent of accommoda-tions cost $50 or less. Persons with disabilities are not frequently hired, except by companies that make concerted efforts.

In terms of the economy, changes in demography, manufacturing processes, and the rise of the service sector are creating opportunities for persons with disabilities. However, the recession and pressures of inter-national competition are reducing overall demand for labor, particu-larly in terms of employees who may require expenditures.

There are numerous programs and services intended to result in employment and increased employability for persons with disabilities. These include an infrastructure of services provided by the state vocational-rehabilitation programs, sheltered workshops, and rehabili-tation facilities. Collaborative and relatively recent models include job-matching programs, supported employment, Projects with Industry, and Independent Living Centers. Differences in the success of these programs are primarily a function of the severity of the disabilities of the program participants and the management of the program.

The ADA mandate serves as a prescription for change in the future design and delivery of programs and services intended to result in increased employment for persons with disabilities. Tax incentives, changes in the Rehabilitation Act, and more private and public–private partnerships are in order.

In "The Recent History and Immediate Future of Employment among Persons with Disabilities," Edward H.Yelin challenges the widely held optimism about future employment prospects for persons with disabilities. He notes that in the last two decades the labor-force participation rate for persons with disabilities fell 4 percent while it increased 12 percent for persons without disabilities. Despite the anti-discrimination mandate in the public sector (section 504 of the Reha-bilitation Act) and a huge expansion of the labor force in the 1980s, persons with disabilities are worse off than they were 20 years ago in terms of employment.

"Persons with disabilities, like those from minority races, appear to constitute a contingent labor force, suffering displacement first and disproportionately from declining industries and occupations, and experiencing gains in ascending ones only after those without disabilities are no longer available for hire," writes Yelin. In terms of the impact of section 504 on the employment of people with disabilities in the public sector, Yelin notes that its contribution may have been one of "things getting worse more slowly." The implication is for proactive and highly visible monitoring of the impact of the ADA.

Monitoring is particularly critical for industries and occupations undergoing rapid expansion and contraction. In these industries, history indicates that people with disabilities have not shared commensurately with other workers during periods of the growth, and have suffered disproportionately during retrenchment. Yelin recommends modifications to the National Health Interview Survey and the Current Population Survey as a means of monitoring the employment of persons with disabilities. The Equal Employment Opportunity Commission (EEOC) should establish a statistical database on the employment of persons with disabilities as part of the monitoring effort. More data on the interaction among impairments, job demands, and work status would provide an objective basis for determining whether employment status is related to discrimination or to actual functional capacity.

Finally, Thomas N. Chirikos considers "The Economics of Employment." In one calculation, the EEOC recently concluded that the total annual benefit of this title of the law could be $402,663,000 (Equal Employment Opportunity Commission 1991). This calculation includes a consideration of the overall macroeconomic impact of the provisions: productivity gains brought to the marketplace by persons with disabilities and decreased support payments to persons with disabilities as well as increases in taxes generated by these employees. In a separate calculation, Chirikos (Personal communication: memo to Milbank Memorial Fund, October 1, 1990) postulated that if the ADA were to eliminate totally job-related discrimination, about $10 billion in earnings of persons with disabilities already at work could be added to the national income in a year. Clearly, it is to the economic interest of the nation for people to be employed rather than unemployed or receiving public support.

Chirikos concludes that a rise in accommodation costs could be used as an indicator of the ADA's success in increasing employment for persons with disabilities. He notes that although available evidence indicates little or no expense for the cost of reasonable accommodations in the past, that may change in the future. "Evidence of negligible accommodation costs would be more compelling if a very large fraction of the population of persons with disabilities was already employed," he observes. In addition, as more persons with disabilities join the labor force, they are likely to have more severe impairments than people with disabilities who are currently in the labor force. Accommodation costs are likely to rise for persons with more severe impairments. If costs are more than is currently anticipated, we may have to explore the expanded use of subsidies and alternative means of cost sharing between the employer and the employee.

SECTION III: AN INCLUSIVE INFRASTRUCTURE

In concluding her article, Feldblum notes that the ADA is a law deliberately designed to be comprehensive because of the interdependent nature of the various aspects of society that must be accessible. "In order for people with disabilities to enter the mainstream of America, they must have meaningful opportunities to obtain employment; they must have access to public services and to goods and services offered by private businesses; they must have accessible transportation in order to get to these jobs, goods and services; and they must have a means of communicating with employers, businesses and others. " An inclusive infrastructure supports persons with disabilities in exercising their rights in the marketplace.

In "Equal Access to Public Accommodations," Robert L. Burgdorf Jr. notes that persons with disabilities are an isolated segment of the population. They go to the movies, attend the theater and other live performances, attend sporting events, and eat in restaurants far less frequently than persons without disabilities because they feel unwelcome and fearful, and also because of physical barriers and explicit exclusion.

Intended to increase the participation of persons with disabilities, the ADA prohibits discrimination in a broad range of places of public accommodation including motels, restaurants, theaters, movie houses, stadiums, concert halls, auditoriums, stores, doctors' offices, gas stations, museums, parks, zoos, schools, day-care centers, banks, gyms, and golf courses. Persons with disabilities are entitled to the full and equal enjoyment of the goods, services, facilities, privileges, advantages, and accommodations of all covered entities.

The Architectural and Transportation Barriers Compliance Board (ATBCB) has issued proposed accessibility guidelines for ADA, which build on the ones they issued for the Architectural Barriers Act of 1968 and section 504 of the Rehabilitation Act of 1973. Experience in using accessibility guidelines is considerable. Already two-thirds of the states currently incorporate or reference the standards that ATBCB used to develop their guidelines. Particularly noteworthy is the National Park Service, which has a number of guides available for making parks and fishing accessible to person with physical, hearing, and speech impairments.

The cost of making new construction accessible is generally considered to be between one-tenth and one-half of one percent of the total construction costs. The cost of remodeling existing inaccessible buildings is generally estimated to be between one-half and three percent of construction costs of an overall renovation or of a building's underlying value.

Concluding that we all stand to benefit from a more accessible world, Burgdorf writes: "Given that a significant portion of the populace has a disability or will experience one at some point, such requirements do not represent a fiscal sacrifice for a select few, but a basic insurance policy provided by our entire society on behalf of the entire society."

Robert A. Katzmann addresses another critical component of an accessible infrastructure: transportation. In "Transportation Policy," Katzmann notes that the best estimates of persons with disabilities who are limited in the use of public transportation date from 1977, when a total of 7.4 million persons over five years old who lived in urban areas were identified as being constrained to some extent from using public transportation. Of that total, 1.4 million were unable to use public transit at all. These estimates are generally considered low, particularly in light of demographic shifts from cities to suburbs.

Persons with disabilities have long been concerned about inadequate transportation. One survey reflected that 28 percent of nonworking people with disabilities cited a dearth of accessible or affordable transportation as a reason why they were not employed. Manufacturers have developed accessible vehicles and usually do so when it is required by law or government rules. The absence of standards for devices to secure wheelchairs and similar mobility units, however, has complicated the task for manufacturers.

Localities vary in the nature and level of accessible and paratransit services. One study indicated that a substantial number of systems have a policy in place whereby they will only purchase accessible buses. Over the last decade, many subway systems have improved accessibility, in some cases fully (notably San Francisco and Washington, D.C.). Improvements have been made in bus-lift maintenance. Over time, costs have gone down and operators have learned to anticipate and prevent problems. Some states have innovative training programs for transit personnel.

The cost of attaining accessible transportation also varies, with most estimates being criticized by different parties as too high or too low. In 1990, 35 percent of the national transit fleet was equipped with accessible features. The Department of Transportation (DOT) estimates that the cost of lift-equipped buses nationwide will range from $675 to $735 million over 30 years on a present-value basis. They estimate that the provision of paratransit services on a 24-hour response-time basis will be $1.1 billion. Estimates of rail transit accessibility range from $21,334,057 to $72,669,809 annualized for 10 years.

Karen Peltz Strauss examines the telecommunications requirements of the ADA in her paper, "Implementing the Telecommunications Requirements." These provisions are an extension of the 1934 "universal service" mandate, which requires that communication by wire or radio be made available to all Americans wherever possible. The ADA requires that telephone relay services be available for all local and long-distance telephone calls by July 26, 1993. Relay services enable persons who are hearing or speech impaired who use TDDs (telecommunication devices for the deaf) to communicate, through a third party, with users of conventional telephones.

The relay services are required to operate 24 hours per day, seven days a week with no restrictions on the content of the messages. Calls are to be confidential and messages must be relayed without being altered. Users of the relay services are to pay rates no greater than the rates paid for functionally equivalent voice communication services.

In July 1990 approximately 40 states either had statewide systems in place or planned to have them begin operation shortly. Although many states have some system in place, almost all will need to make some changes in order to comply with the ADA—for example, provide 24-hour service or add interstate service. Costs of providing relay services range from four to seven dollars per minute, with costs distributed among all telephone subscribers at a rate of 5 cents to 13 cents per month. Three million dollars was the figure provided by the FCC as the potential start-up cost figure for a relay service.

The demand for relay services has been remarkable. For example, the California system originally anticipated 50,000 calls per month, but received 87,511 in the first month alone. By July 1988 they were handling nearly 250,000 calls per month.

The considerable experience to date yields numerous recommendations for providing relay services: they should be fully integrated into the existing telecommunications network; adequate funds should be available to avoid temporary limitations in services; consumers should be involved in designing and monitoring services.

The availability of relay services will result in increased freedom, independence, and privacy for persons who are deaf, hearing impaired, and speech impaired. "These individuals will be able to use the telephone to easily access businesses, colleagues, friends, and relatives, something that hearing individuals have taken for granted for approximately half a century," Strauss concludes.

In the final article of Section III, "Public Health Powers: The Imminence of Radical Change," Lawrence O. Gostin examines the convergence of public-health policy and disability-rights mandates. He suggests that the ADA will be the impetus for reestablishing the boundaries on the exercise of public health powers. "Seen through the lens of the ADA," he writes, "public health regulation may be regarded as discrimination against persons with disabilities."

Persons with communicable diseases are clearly covered by the ADA. However, if they pose a "direct threat to the health or safety of others" and such a direct threat cannot be eliminated by reasonable accommodations or reasonable modifications, they may not be protected by the ADA. Although the ADA clearly allows for taking action to protect the health and safety of all persons in employment and public accommodations, it also provides antidiscrimination protection for persons with communicable diseases. Yet the essence of public-health regulation is that persons may be treated differently based upon a scientific assessment of the risk of transmission of a disease or condition.

The convergence of the rights of individuals with communicable diseases and the responsibility of the public health authorities to regulate in the public interest hinges on the application of scientific evidence in determining what constitutes a "direct threat." Congress resolved one of the most controversial issues raised during consideration of the ADA (the question of whether an employee with an infectious or communicable disease could be transferred from a food-handling job) by turning to the application of science. If the infectious condition is determined by the Secretary of Health and Human Services to be transmitted through the food supply, an employer may refuse to assign an individual with that condition to a food-handling job. Gostin argues that this same application of scientific and medical analysis should be used in determining whether an individual poses a "direct threat."

The ADA is particularly significant for public-health law and for individuals who others believe may constitute a danger, but who in fact do not. Gostin concludes that the ADA will engender a new way of thinking about public-health law, a way in which "courts must search for scientifically convincing evidence of harm to the public to justify depriving persons with disabilities of equal opportunities."

SECTION IV: REINFORCEMENTS FOR THE MANDATE

This last section examines two areas of resources available for implementing the ADA. Certain provisions in the tax code and assistive technology for people with disabilities can both be used in the creation of a more inclusive world. At least three provisions in the tax code could alleviate some of the financial burden of implementing the ADA. The application of technology to solve accommodation challenges can provide remarkable and effective solutions.

In "Tax Incentives," Daniel C. Schaffer reminds us that Congress often uses the tax code to promote social and economic goals. Since 1976 a deduction has been available to businesses for removing barriers in facilities or public transportation vehicles. The current limit on that deduction is $15,000.

Shortly after the enactment of the ADA, Congress added an "access credit" to the tax code, which enables small businesses to claim credit against taxes for one-half of eligible expenditures exceeding $250, but not greater than $10,250. The credit can be claimed for a broader range of expenses than the deduction, including the provision of auxiliary aids and services.

Virtually no information is available about the usage of the deduction over the past 15 years. It appears likely that its use has been minimal based on estimates of annual revenue loss to the federal treasury ($7 million in 1986). An analysis of the use of the deduction and the credit could provide a revealing picture of the types of expenditures and accommodations taking place in a range of settings. Such an analysis would be an important contribution to assessing the implementation of ADA.

A third provision of the tax code, the Targeted Jobs Tax Credit (TJTC), has been available to employers since 1978. The credit is available for hiring members of particular groups whose rate of unemployment is high or who have special employment needs. The credit allowed is 40 percent of the wages paid to an employee (up to $6,000) during the first year of employment. Persons with disabilities constitute a small group of those targeted by TJTC. (In 1987 only 6.9 percent of the total number of TJTC-certified persons were members of the target-group "vocational rehabilitation referrals.") The TJTC needs to be examined in light of ADA, both in terms of how it might be further strengthened to support the goals of the ADA and in its application to preemployment inquiry.

In "The Role of Technology in Removing Barriers," John C. DeWitt examines the use of technology in removing communication and other barriers encountered by persons with disabilities. Known as "assistive technology," these devices and interventions have exploded in the marketplace; however, they are not yet widely deployed or available for persons with disabilities. Capable of making dramatic changes in the lives of persons with disabilities, DeWitt notes that "assistive technology has extended horizons in education and employment, for personal independence and social integration."

Assistive technology can enhance limited functions, such as seeing, or it can enable one function to be substituted for another (e.g., hearing for seeing). Limitations in hearing, seeing, speaking, interpreting, and moving can be addressed by a range of assistive-technology applications, most of which have proven track records in a variety of settings. Many assistive-technology features, such as curb cuts and volume amplification on telephones, provide benefits for virtually everyone, not just persons with disabilities. DeWitt reviews basic design features that incorporate accessibility standards for a broad range of disabilities.

Using assistive technology is an accommodation best understood as a process of removing barriers to opportunities. It requires a problem-solving approach that must incorporate training, maintenance, upgrading, and replacement if necessary.

The benefits of technology include enhanced functioning and productivity for the individual as well as increased participation (and therefore financial contribution) in the marketplace. Having an accessible workplace and marketplace is good business. The costs of assistive technology are often minimal, particularly as demand for them increases. Assistive technology is frequently limited to the cost of an "add-on" for existing equipment, such as a personal computer.

Many tasks become possible for persons with disabilities by the use of assistive technology. DeWitt holds that the success of the ADA will depend on the creative use of technology as much as upon the good will of the American public.

REFERENCES

Architectural and Transportation Barriers Compliance Board. 1991. Americans with Disabilities Act Accessibility Guidelines for Buildings and Facilities: Proposed Rule, 36 CFR, part 1191, January 22. Washington.

Equal Employment Opportunity Commission. 1991. Equal Employment Opportunity for Individuals with Disabilities Notice of Proposed Rulemaking, billing code 6750–06. *Federal Register* (February 28). Washington.

Johnson, M. 1989. Enabling Act. *Nation* (October 23): 446.

I. Getting Oriented

Discrimination occurs in every facet of disabled people's lives. There is not one disabled American alive today who has not experienced some form of discrimination. Of course, this has very serious consequences. It destroys healthy self-concepts, and it slowly erodes the human spirit. Discrimination does not belong in the lives of disabled people.

I. King Jordan, president of Gallaudet
University, testifying before Congress on
May 9, 1989

The Social and Policy Context of the Act

Jane West

EDITOR'S NOTE

Persons with disabilities are often perceived as second-class citizens and are offered second-class opportunities. Many disability policies reflect these perceptions by promoting segregation and dependence. The disability-rights movement, with the independent-living movement at its center, has made some progress in changing societal attitudes about persons with disabilities. This progress is reflected in the legislative building blocks that preceded the Americans with Disabilities Act and in the ADA itself.

Focusing disability policy on the promotion of independence and integraton is no small task. The ADA requires us to understand that civil rights for persons with disabilities involves an accommodation imperative *and necessitates an individualized assessment for each situation. West sets the stage for this challenge as she explores the social and policy environment that generated the ADA.*

Jane West served as staff director for the U.S. Senate Subcommittee on Disability Policy under the chairmanship of Senator (now Governor) Lowell Weicker and as senior policy analyst on the Presidential Commission on the HIV Epidemic chaired by Admiral James Watkins, Ret. She directed the National Council on Disability's study and report to the President and Congress, The Education of Students with Disabilities: Where Do We Stand? *Her research includes two studies on the formation of disability policy:* The Handicapped Children's Protection

Act of 1986: A Case Study of Policy Formation *and* The Formation of
National Disability Rights Policy in the 100th Congress (1986–88). *She
received her doctorate from the University of Maryland and is currently
an independent consultant in Washington, D.C.*

As a declaration of equality for persons with disabilities, the
Americans with Disabilities Act (ADA) sends a clear directive
to society regarding what its attitudes toward persons with disabilities should be: respect, inclusion, and support. The ADA is the
result of two decades of effort, mainly by the disability-rights movement and its allies, to change policies based on quite different attitudes: pity, patronization, and exclusion. In establishing equality of
opportunity, full participation, independent living, and economic self-
sufficiency as the nation's proper goals for persons with disabilities,[1] the
ADA reflects a commitment to its own prescription.

   In this article, I will examine the social and policy context of the
ADA in terms of the evolution of attitudes toward persons with disabilities. I will consider both societal attitudes toward persons with disabilities and the attitudes persons with disabilities hold toward themselves.
I will examine these attitudes through three lenses: the experience of
disability in America, the changing language of disability, and federal
disability-rights legislation over the past 20 years. I will analyze how our
public policies and our language, both the results of negotiation, have
defined and reflected the changing relationships between persons with
disabilities and the society at large. This article documents a gradual
change in attitudes, of which ADA is the latest outcome.

CURRENT STATUS OF PERSONS WITH DISABILITIES

Only in the last decade have we begun to consider persons with disabilities as a distinct minority group that can be described in terms of
demographic characteristics and in relation to other minority groups.
(See the articles by LaPlante and Yelin in this volume.) Although the
limited data that we have for this purpose often raise more questions
than they answer, we can make significant descriptive statements.

   When compared with other minority groups, persons with disabilities are distinguished in virtually every category by their disadvantaged
status. The ADA notes:

Census data, national polls, and other studies have documented that people with disabilities, as a group, occupy an inferior status in our society, and are severely disadvantaged socially, vocationally, economically, and educationally.[2]

A few specific examples illustrate the status of persons with disabilities in the late 1980s:

- Fifty percent of adults with disabilities had household incomes of $15,000 or less. Only 25 percent of persons without disabilities had household incomes in this bracket.[3]
- Two-thirds of all Americans with disabilities between the ages of 16 and 64 were not working at all. Sixty-six percent of these would have liked to work. (Louis Harris and Associates 1986)
- Where only 15 percent of all adults aged 18 and over had less than a high-school education, 40 percent of all persons with disabilities aged 16 and over had not finished high school. (Louis Harris and Associates 1986)
- Whereas 56 percent of all students participated in post-secondary education programs, only 15 percent of students with disabilities did. (Wagner 1989)
- Persons with disabilities participated in social events (e.g., dining out, movies, attending sporting events) far less frequently than persons without disabilities. (Louis Harris and Associates 1986)

Furthermore, the situation for persons with disabilities has grown worse in the last two decades — at least in terms of economic well-being. A recent study concluded that in the mid-1960s the income levels of persons with disabilities were close to those without disabilities. Their relative well-being declined in the next decade, reaching a low in the recession of the early 1980s. Since then, people with disabilities have regained most of the ground they lost; however, those gains are very unevenly distributed and increases in household incomes have come mainly from increased wage earnings by household members who do not have disabilities. Nonwhite persons with disabilities who are not well educated are the worst off (Burkhauser, Haveman, and Wolfe 1990).

DISCRIMINATION AGAINST PERSONS WITH DISABILITIES

It is generally accepted that discrimination plays a significant role in the outcomes described above. Congress believes that the elimination of discrimination will facilitate the achievement of the goals of equal opportunity, full participation, independent living, and economic self-sufficiency. The establishment of "a clear and comprehensive national mandate for the elimination of discrimination against individuals with disabilities"[4] is the ADA's contribution toward meeting these goals.

Discrimination against the estimated 43 million persons with mental and physical disabilities has been documented repeatedly (Arangio 1979; English 1971; Livneh 1982; Presidential Commission on the Human Immunodeficiency Virus 1988; U.S. Commission on Civil Rights 1983; U.S. Senate Committee on Labor and Human Resources 1989). Findings in the ADA hold that society has tended to isolate and segregate persons with disabilities[5] and that discrimination continues to be pervasive in virtually all aspects of life.[6] The ADA finds that persons with disabilities have been "subjected to a history of purposeful unequal treatment, and relegated to a position of political powerlessness" primarily because of social stereotypes.[7] Persons with disabilities who are members of other groups that frequently encounter discrimination, like African Americans and women, may encounter dual discrimination (Brown 1981; Burkhauser, Haveman, and Wolfe 1990), leaving them to wonder on which basis they are rejected.

Discrimination against persons with disabilities might be considered to have two aspects: (1) *prejudice* and (2) *barriers*. Persons with disabilities share with other groups the experience of being the target of prejudiced, or "pre-judged" attitudes. However, many of the barriers confronted by persons with disabilities are unique to them.

PREJUDICE

Prejudice is an attitude that distorts social relationships by overemphasizing some characteristic, such as race, gender, age or disability (U.S. Commission on Civil Rights 1983). Although a range of prejudicial attitudes is examined later in this article, let it suffice now to note that prejudice often gives birth to myths, stereotypes, and stigma, which are associated with a negative exaggeration of the individual's impairment to the exclusion of other attributes. Persons with disabilities have long encountered a generic stereotype, which holds that "you are less of a person if an aspect of your functioning is impaired." Impaired functioning translates to the assumption of impaired personhood.

This prejudicial outlook about the capabilities of persons with disabilities has foreclosed certain opportunities to them. An employer may not consider hiring a receptionist who is blind, assuming that he would be incapable of performing the tasks of the job. A training program for dentists may refuse to admit a candidate who cannot hear, assuming she would be unable to understand the instructors or communicate with patients.

Women and other minority groups share the experience of being the recipient of prejudiced attitudes and concomitant discriminatory policies and practices. One of the damaging effects is that many come to believe what they hear and internalize the experiences of discrimination they confront, resulting in beliefs of inadequacy and low self-esteem.

BARRIERS AND THE ACCOMMODATION IMPERATIVE

The other aspect of discrimination against persons with disabilities is *barriers*, defined as *any aspects of the social or physical environment that prohibit meaningful involvement by persons with disabilities*: stairs for a person in a wheelchair; lack of a TDD for a person who cannot hear seeking to use the phone; a health service for a person who cannot hear and is not provided an alternative way to communicate.

This second aspect of discrimination against persons with disabilities—barriers—generates an *accommodation imperative* when the exercise of their civil rights is at issue. The accommodation imperative requires that efforts be undertaken to render the experience in the environment available in a meaningful way to the person with a disability. Without the accommodation imperative, the notion of equal opportunity for persons with disabilities may be inviable. An opportunity may not be equal if there is neither accommodation nor accessibility. A job on the third floor of a building with no elevator is not an equal opportunity for a person in a wheelchair. An educational program for a student who is blind that provides no alternative reading method, such as braille or a reader, is not an equal opportunity.

In order to achieve nondiscrimination, society enters into a contract with a person who has a disability. Society agrees to structure or manipulate the social and physical environment in every reasonable way with the goal of creating an experience that is a meaningful equal opportunity for the individual with the disability. This obligation may involve an allocation of resources or an expenditure of funds. The person with a disability agrees to make the same effort at citizenship that we expect from everyone else.

The ADA affirms that it is not enough to hang up a sign and say, "We do not discriminate on the basis of disability." In order for an opportunity to be truly equitable, more is required from society than a passive commitment to equal opportunity. Whereas simply eliminating exclusionary policies may at times be sufficient for people with disabilities and members of other special classes (e.g., racial and ethnic minorities and women), there are times when more may be required.

Often a stated goal of nondiscrimination policy for persons in other stigmatized groups is to be treated in a neutral fashion, or just like everyone else; this may not be the case for persons with disabilities. The goal may be to "forget" that the individual is a woman, or an African-American, as standards are applied. It is often said that the law should be administered in a "color blind" fashion. While this may be the case in some situations for persons with disabilities, in other situations the goal, in fact, may be the opposite: a recognition of the functional impairment and an effort to adapt an environment or situation to enhance functioning and/or discover alternatives that will yield meaningful involvement. Rather than viewing the environment as a series of obstacles that exacerbate an impairment, the ADA requires it to be seen as a medium that can provide opportunities to ameliorate the results of functional impairments or to develop alternatives that enable accomplishment of a particular task.

One of the most significant aspects of the accommodation imperative is that it must be individualized. Although persons with disabilities are a group—and may be considered a "protected class" for purposes of civil rights, or a set of people defined by particular characteristics in terms of eligibility for certain services and programs—people with disabilities are, more than any other descriptor, individuals. The uniqueness of each person with a disability in terms of how that disability may or may not affect his or her functioning and in what circumstances is an essential aspect of considering discrimination against persons with disabilities.

Unlike race and gender, moreover, disability is often a dynamic and changing characteristic. A disability that may require no accommodation in one situation may demand complex technological intervention in another. Furthermore, some disabilities change in their intensity from day to day or week to week and may require different accommodations at various times. The same impairment often affects individuals differently. A critical aspect of accommodations is flexibility.

While ordinary citizens and national leaders may have a definitive sense of what it means not to discriminate against a racial minority, this is not the case for persons with disabilities. Until recently, persons with disabilities have been a notably silent and nonvisible minority in society. The addition of the accommodation imperative to the concept of civil rights requires a change in our thinking.

ATTITUDES TOWARD PERSONS WITH DISABILITIES

Being the target of discrimination and negative attitudes may be the one common experience shared by the diverse group of persons with disabilities. Research documents that persons without disabilities perceive persons with disabilities with a range of negative attitudes (English 1971), although the percentage holding these biases is unknown. Studies about attitudes toward persons with disabilities have been ongoing since the 1950s.

Several studies have indicated that males have more negative attitudes toward persons with disabilities than females (English 1971). Favorable attitudes are more likely to occur among persons with higher incomes and educational levels (Livneh 1982). Mental disabilities are the most negatively perceived (Arangio 1979). The sources of these negative attitudes include sociocultural conditioning and childhood influences (Livneh 1982). The terms "handicappism," "physicalism," and "normalism" have been offered as disability correlates to "racism" and "sexism" when referring to prejudices toward persons with disabilities (Longmore 1985).

Persons with disabilities have documented and described a number of second-class relationships with society. They have articulated the experience of being invisible or ignored; of engendering discomfort; of being objects of pity; of being adulated as inspirational for overcoming seemingly insurmountable obstacles; of negotiating a bargain with society.

The experience of being repeatedly ignored or unnoticed has been described as one of "disconfirmation," whereby one is denied recognition as a person (Golfus 1989). Disconfirmation comes in many forms: being deserted by former friends after sustaining an impairment or being dismissed by a receptionist who is too busy with "real work" and "important people." Disconfirmation comes frequently from the very individuals and programs designed to support people with disabilities. Persons with disabilities experience rejection from both services and individuals (e.g., counselors, educators, therapists) because they do not fit into a prescribed mold of behavior or symptoms. The message is, "There's nothing wrong with the program, there's something wrong with you."

Persons without disabilities frequently experience discomfort and embarrassment when interacting with persons with disabilities (U.S. Commission on Civil Rights 1983). They may feel unsure of how to act around a person with a disability. (Should they offer help? Should they ignore the disability? Should they comment on the disability?) The discomfort could reflect an awareness that persons without disabilities are vulnerable to death, injury, and disease—a vulnerability most of us are eager to forget. Anyone can become a person with a disability virtually in a matter of seconds. Finally, discomfort may come from a concern about what other people will think if you associate with a person with a disability: will you be considered second rate by association? Feelings of discomfort have caused proprietors to reject persons with disabilities from restaurants, movie houses, zoos, and other public places. Proprietors may believe they will drive other customers away because they engender discomfort and even revulsion.

Persons with disabilities are frequently looked upon with pity (U.S. Commission on Civil Rights 1983). This is most clearly seen in fund-raising efforts by nonprofit organizations, which may depict individuals with disabilities in a pity-invoking manner in hopes of appealing to charitable instincts. When a charitable attitude goes overboard, it may turn into pity or patronization. Attitudes of pity are rarely accompanied by attitudes of respect for the dignity of persons with disabilities, but are grounded in the belief that "I am better than you are." Pity and patronization rarely engender independence and empowerment, but rather dependence and low self-esteem.

Persons with disabilities have often been looked upon with horror. Portraying having a disability as a "fate worse than death" sends a clear message to persons with disabilities. This attitude is often utilized to sell insurance policies or "scare" people with certain conditions into getting treatment so they don't regress and reach this state "worse than death." For example, a recent memo from the general manager of an insurance agency to agents included a photo of a body next to a wrecked car, with the caption: "Do you think he's dead? He's not, but he might have been better off if he were. He is dead from the waist down. He'll never walk again." The memo was intended to inspire agents to sell disability insurance (*Disability Rag* 1990).

Many persons with disabilities resent being viewed as heroes or hero-ines, as remarkable achievers, as inspiration for the average person with everyday problems. The person with the disability may be described as "courageous" or "inspirational" because he or she accomplishes things while having a disability, or in spite of it. Commenting on being repeatedly described as "courageous," Stephen Hawking, the brilliant Cambridge University scientist who has Lou Gehrig's disease, noted his aversion to being repeatedly labeled a superhero because he has a disability. Readers of the *Disability Rag*, a voice of the disability-rights movement, noted that being described as "courageous" was the one aspect they hated the most about how people with disabilities are portrayed in the media (*Disability Rag* 1990). They see it not as a view of respect and equality, but as one where a person with a disability is not considered to be like every one else.

Many of these attitudes are reflections of a widely held conviction in our society that youth, beauty, and success are to be striven for at virtually any cost. This conviction leaves scant space for tolerance of persons with disabilities, much less for any affirmation of their equal-ity. Furthermore, these attitudes define persons with disabilities from the perspective of society at large, not from the perspective of persons with disabilities themselves. Persons with disabilities have been defined negatively by society; their identity has been shaped by society and given to them.

To negotiate this imposed identity, persons with disabilities have struck a bargain with society, according to one disability-rights activist (Johnson 1989). The society agrees to marginal acceptance of the person with the disability as long as that person cheerfully strives to be normal. The more normal he or she becomes, the more acceptance the person gains. Many persons with disabilities are uneasy with this bargain. Their discomfort has in part spurred the disability-rights movement, which strives to place self-definition in the hands of persons with disabilities.

Changing attitudes toward persons with disabilities is a long, slow process. Attitudes are learned and conditioned over many years. Changing attitudes will take time. In recent years, the disability-rights movement has begun that process.

THE DISABILITY-RIGHTS MOVEMENT

It has been suggested that the ultimate test of a minority group is self-identification (Hahn 1985). Persons with disabilities, like other oppressed groups, move to claim the power to define themselves, to develop their own identity, culture, and pride. This movement toward self-identification can be seen in the growth of the disability-rights movement, the independent-living movement, the evolving political sophistication and power of the disability interest groups in Washington, the changes in language we use to talk about people with disabilities, and shifts in public policy.

Seventy-four percent of people with disabilities surveyed by Louis Harris and Associates (1986) said they feel at least some sense of common identity with other people with disabilities. Forty-five per cent said they feel that people with disabilities are a minority group in the same sense as African Americans and Hispanics. Those who were younger and who had disabilities beginning at earlier periods in their lives were more likely to see people with disabilities as a minority group.

Persons with disabilities, however, face unique challenges in solidifying as a minority group. Although the negative experience of encountering discrimination and demeaning attitudes is common to other minority groups, many of the positive minority-group experiences are lacking for persons with disabilities (Johnson 1987; Kriegel 1969). Unlike other minority groups, persons with disabilities have generally grown up in isolation from each other and there is no sense of a subculture or of positive shared experiences with which they can identify (Johnson 1987; Zola 1988). Emphasis on functional limitation has encouraged persons with disabilities to "overcome" their disabilities, not to identify with them (Hahn 1985). Some have noted that there is a case to be made for segregated schools for youngsters with disabilities, in order to foster disability identity and culture (Johnson 1987; Thomas 1989).

The trademarks of minority pride, such as slogans, rituals, clothing, hairstyles, and songs, are in their infancy in the disability community. The equivalent of "Black is Beautiful" or "Sisterhood is Powerful" has yet to emerge from the disability community (Zola 1988). The challenge of turning stigma into pride is at the heart of solidifying persons with disabilities as a minority. One disability-rights commentator noted, "If we neglect the cultural aspects of our movement, we will fail" (Johnson 1987, 9).

Although the emergence of persons with disabilities as a cultural minority is just beginning, the disability-rights movement has grown considerably in the last decade. Leadership of disability organizations and interest groups is increasingly in the hands of persons with disabilities themselves and federal programs affecting persons with disabilities are more often administered by persons with disabilities.

At the heart of the emergence of the disability-rights movement is the philosophy of independent living. The independent-living philosophy emerged in the 1960s bolstered by the civil-rights movements for African Americans, the women's rights movement, and the tenor of the times, which challenged the status quo. Persons with severe disabilities were seeking alternatives to institutionalization, segregated programs, and service delivery systems that offered limited alternatives and little support for self-determination. Independent living, at its core, is a set of values dedicated to self-determination and personal control over one's own life. Equal opportunity to participate in all aspects of society, including freedom of choice and risk taking, are tenets of the independent living philosophy (DeJong 1979; Lachat 1988).

The independent-living movement has rejected the role of patient for persons with disabilities and has embraced consumer-controlled decision making instead. The fact that many disabilities are conditions that may be lifelong has led to a rejection of the medical model, which sets the goals of palliation or cure, embracing instead a management approach that seeks maximum independence. Living in the community as other members of society do, and not in institutions and segregated settings, is another trademark of independent living.

This evolving consciousness of independent living has been a significant contributor to a growing a sense of a disability community and a call for civil-rights reforms. Independent living has also emerged as an important service-delivery model with hundreds of centers currently providing services throughout the country. The independent-living consciousness has shepherded in a gradual shift in policy focus from custody to cure to care to rights.

THE LANGUAGE OF DISABILITY

A recent article in the *Wall Street Journal* about the Americans with Disabilities Act was entitled "Disabilities Act Cripples through Ambiguity" (Weaver 1991). In a recent effort to raise money for persons with disabilities, Jerry Lewis described a wheelchair as "that steel imprisonment that long has been deemed the dystrophic child's plight" (*Disability Rag* 1990, 30)

Contrast these with some current posters recently issued by the National Easter Seal Society. A person in a wheelchair sits at the bottom of a flight of stairs and the caption reads: "For some people the search for an apartment is all uphill." Another poster pictures a person's hand meeting a person's hook (prosthetic device) for a handshake. The caption reads, "Sometimes the worst thing about having a disability is that people meet it before they meet you" (*Disability Rag* 1991, 36).

The difference in the language of these statements indicates efforts to move away from patronizing and stigmatizing descriptors to empowering and respectful terminology. The language also reflects the thinking that the individual's particular impairment is less of a difficulty than the person's reception by society at large. In testifying before Congress in support of the passage of the ADA, Governor (formerly Senator) Lowell Weicker of Connecticut (1989) noted that the biggest obstacle for people with disabilities was not so much what God hath wrought, but rather what man has imposed by custom and law.

The language used in the ADA, and throughout this book, is what is often called the "people first" language: for example, "individuals with disabilities" or "persons with disabilities." This terminology evolved as a rejection of descriptors that focus on the impairment, not the person: for example, the deaf, the blind, the disabled, cripples.

The terminology "disabled" and "disability" is generally preferred to "handicapped" and "handicap." In proposing a change in the name of the U.S. Senate Subcommittee on the Handicapped to the U.S. Senate Subcommittee on Disability Policy, Senator Tom Harkin (D-Iowa) noted that the term "handicapped" has a negative connotation and it was the responsibility of the subcommittee to do the opposite of what the name implied: "It is our responsibility to develop public policy which removes the barriers in this society for people with disabilities and enables them to pursue their independence in an environment of respect and support . . ." (Harkin 1989).

The names of other important national organizations have changed in recent years also. The National Council on the Handicapped is now the National Council on Disability. The President's Committee on Employment of the Handicapped has become the President's Committee for the Employment of People with Disabilities.

This year a New York foundation—the National Cristina Foundation—sponsored a contest, offering a $50,000 reward to whoever could come up with a word or phrase for the abilities of people with disabilities. This phrase was intended to convey a positive empowering message about persons with disabilities, rather than the negative demeaning messages so much of the terminology implies. The winning phrase was "people with differing abilities."

There are differences of opinion about the proper language of disability in the disability community and elsewhere. Some feel that the energy spent on determining the proper language is better spent on "real" issues, like accessing attendant services *(Disability Rag* 1990). Other people see their disability as a central feature of their identity and choose to call themselves "deaf people" or "cripples" (Zola 1988). In their view, to consider the disability as a secondary feature is not being true to their identity. Another view is that preoccupation with particular language and terminology is evasive, euphemistic, and contains the seeds of backlash. In fact, one entry to the contest sponsored by the National Cristina Foundation was "severely euphemized" *(Disability Rag* 1990, 14)

LEGISLATIVE BUILDING BLOCKS FOR THE ADA

The ADA is the culmination of years of legislative action. Legislation for people with disabilities can be thought of in at least three categories: programs and services, income maintenance, and civil rights. Numerous pieces of civil-rights legislation promoting the full participation and independence of persons with disabilities predate the adoption of ADA. In addition, many programs and service-delivery systems that provide education, training, and support services for persons with disabilities have been established by the federal government. Although some of these programs have been criticized for promoting dependence rather than independence (Berkowitz 1987), a good number are intended to support the goals of the ADA.

In the last two decades, federal laws have made incremental changes that created the possibility of enacting the ADA. These laws are grounded in the core concepts pervading the ADA: full participation and independence. Although bills were repeatedly introduced since the mid 1960s to amend generic civil-rights laws to include persons with disabilities (Burgdorf 1990), none received serious legislative consideration. In 1977 the White House Conference on Handicapped Individuals recommended amending all titles of the Civil Rights Act of 1964 to include discrimination on the basis of disability. Nor did legislation introduced in the mid 1980s to provide antidiscrimination protection for persons with HIV and AIDS gain serious consideration.

In 1986, the National Council on Disability, a presidentially appointed disability-policy agency, issued a report to the President entitled *Toward Independence*, recommending the enactment of comprehensive antidiscrimination legislation for people with disabilities. This report was followed up by another one, *On the Threshold of Independence*, in 1988, which included a draft of the legislation. At that same time the Presidential Commission on the Human Immunodeficiency Virus issued its final report calling for similar legislation. The National Council asked then Senator Weicker, the historical legislative champion of disability rights, to introduce the legislation. Senator Weicker agreed. When the Senate changed from a Republican to a Democratic majority in 1987, Senator Tom Harkin became chairman of the Subcommittee on Disability Policy. He joined Senator Weicker, then the ranking minority member of the subcommittee, to champion the ADA, and eventually to become its chief sponsor in Congress.

With the unique opportunity of a civil-rights initiative emanating from a Republican administration agency, the well-organized disability-interest groups, joined by the newly emerging AIDS interest groups, seized the opportunity for action. It was at this point that Congress seriously began to consider comprehensive antidiscrimination protection for persons with disabilities.

The following federal laws could be considered legislative building blocks for the ADA:

• *The Architectural Barriers Act of 1968*[8] mandated that all buildings constructed, altered, or financed by the federal government after 1969 be accessible and usable by persons with physical disabilities. In 1973, the Architectural and Transportation Barriers Compliance Board (ATBCB) was established to develop guidelines and accessibility standards and to enforce these standards. The guidelines took effect in September 1982.

• In 1973, *sections 501, 503 and 504*[9] were enacted as part of the Rehabilitation Act. Section 504 prohibits discrimination against otherwise qualified persons with disabilities in any program or activity receiving federal funds and in executive agencies and the Postal Service.

Sections 501 and 503 require affirmative-action plans for the hiring and advancement of persons with disabilities in the federal government and any contractors receiving federal contracts over $2,500.

Section 504 is the most significant building block for the ADA. Its 17-year history of implementation has delineated many core concepts of the ADA, such as "reasonable accommodation" and "undue burden." Numerous court decisions have examined questions raised by section 504, such as how to determine when a person with a disability is "otherwise qualified," when a "reasonable accommodation" crosses the line and becomes an "undue burden," and when a person with a disability presents a threat to the health and/or safety of others. The implementing regulations for section 504, which emanate from numerous federal agencies and are voluminous, have offered definitions of key terms, such as who is and is not considered a person with a disability. The article in this volume by Nancy Lee Jones provides an analysis of section 504.

In 1988 section 504, as well as other civil-rights statutes, was amended by the Civil Rights Restoration Act.[10] This legislation overturned the Supreme Court's *Grove City College v. Bell*[11] decision and defined coverage of section 504 as broad (e.g., extending to an entire university) rather than narrow (e.g., extending just to one department of the university) when federal funds were involved. The Civil Rights Restoration Act was particularly significant as an ADA building block because of the Humphrey–Harkin provision, which amended the Rehabilitation Act's definition of an individual with a disability. This provision incorporated the standards and approach outlined by the Supreme Court in deciding *School Board of Nassau County, Florida v. Arline*,[12] and clarified that an individual with a contagious disease or infection who posed a "direct threat" to the health or safety of others was not covered by section 504. The amendment was in response to concerns that employers might be required to hire a person with a contagious disease or infection, especially AIDS or HIV infection, when that individual posed a direct threat to others. Lawrence O. Gostin discusses the "direct threat" language, as incorporated in the ADA in his article.

• In 1975, *The Education for All Handicapped Children Act*[13] was enacted. Now called the *Individuals with Disabilities Education Act*,[14] this law mandates a free, appropriate public education for all children with disabilities. It requires that they be educated in the "least restrictive environment" or with their nondisabled peers to the maximum extent appropriate. Integration of students with disabilities is often called "mainstreaming." Over four million students with disabilities are currently in programs receiving federal support.

• *The Developmental Disabilities Assistance and Bill of Rights Act*,[15] also enacted in 1975, includes a small federal grant program administered by state Developmental Disabilities Councils and is intended to coordinate and fund services for persons with developmental or severe long-term disabilities whose onset occurred prior to age 22 and usually require lifelong services. Largely in response to substandard and abusive situations in institutions for persons with mental retardation, the bill of rights declared that persons with developmental disabilities have a right to appropriate treatment, services, and habilitation that maximize the developmental potential of the person and take place in a setting least restrictive to personal liberty. Although not enforceable, the bill of rights is a statement of congressional intent.

The Developmental Disabilities Act also established in every state a system of protection and advocacy organizations that are independent of any service-providing organization. They advocate for and represent the rights of persons with developmental disabilities, in addition to providing information and referral services.

• In 1980 Congress passed the *Civil Rights of Institutionalized Persons Act*[16] authorizing the U.S. Department of Justice to sue states for alleged violations of the rights of institutionalized persons, including persons in mental hospitals or facilities for persons with mental retardation.

• In 1984, Congress enacted the *Voting Accessibility for the Elderly and Handicapped Act*.[17] The law requires that registration and polling places for federal elections be accessible to persons with disabilities.

• In 1986 Congress acted to overturn a Supreme Court decision which held that air carriers operating at federally funded airports were not subject to Section 504. *The Air Carriers Access Act of 1986*[18] prohibits discrimination against persons with disabilities by all air carriers and provides for enforcement under the Department of Transportation.

• Although housing was originally included as a part of the first version of the Americans with Disabilities Act, it was dropped when the opportunity materialized to include persons with disabilities in the *Fair Housing Act Amendments of 1988*.[19] The Fair Housing Act added persons with disabilities as a group protected from discrimination in housing. This was the first time the antidiscrimination mandate for persons with disabilities was extended into the private sector. The law mandates accessibility standards for all new housing construction for multifamily dwellings and ensures that persons with disabilities are able to adapt their dwelling place to meet their needs. Many of the features that appear in the ADA come directly from Fair Housing.

In addition to civil-rights laws, there are a number of programs, services, and organizations that support the independence of persons with disabilities. The breadth and depth of support systems and services for persons with disabilities extends to every state in the Union. There are publicly sponsored programs and services at the federal, state, and local levels of government; private programs exist at these three levels as well. A number of public\private partnerships provide services and programs for persons with disabilities. Many of these are described elsewhere in the book (notably by Paul G. Hearne), and others are listed under Resource Organizations in Appendix B.

Programs and services for persons with disabilities have considerable range. Some are targeted to specific disabilities (such as the state Rehabilitation Agencies for the Blind) and others serve all disabilities. Some provide strictly information and referral services, whereas others provide direct services, such as rehabilitation counseling or legal representation. Still others provide funds for persons with disabilities to pursue higher education or purchase adaptive devices. Some are run by persons with disabilities and provide peer-support services.

Programs and services for persons with disabilities are frequently described as a patchwork—difficult to access, unwieldy, excessively bureaucratic, and of a labyrinthine nature (Berkowitz 1987). Various initiatives have been considered over the years to promote the goals of consolidation and coordination (National Council on Disability 1986, 1988). While the degree of coordination of programs and services varies considerably by state, there is a core of programs in every state that forms a support system for persons with disabilities (U.S. Department of Education 1988).

THE IMPACT OF FEDERAL DISABILITY RIGHTS
LAWS TO DATE

The impact of federal disability-rights laws can be assessed in many ways. In fact, much of this volume describes that impact. Three studies attempt to look directly at what that impact has been: The survey by

Louis Harris and Associates (1986) reports how people with disabilities view the impact of federal laws. The others examine the impact of section 504 of the Rehabilitation Act after ten years of implementation.

The 1986 Louis Harris poll, *Disabled Americans' Self Perceptions: Bringing Disabled Americans Into the Mainstream*, asked 1,000 Americans with disabilities if they believed that life had improved for persons with disabilities in the past decade. Seven out of ten believed that life had improved somewhat or a lot. Two-thirds of those polled believed that federal laws passed since the late 1960s to provide better opportunities for persons with disabilities have helped a great deal, or somewhat. The survey noted that this remarkable endorsement for federal programs and laws is unsurpassed in the firm's history of measuring public support for federal laws. Seventy-five percent of respondents to the survey also believed that federal antidiscrimination laws should be strengthened.

An analysis of ten years of enforcement of section 504 of the Rehabilitation Act concluded: "While section 504 has unlocked the door for handicapped persons to enter the mainstream of society, it has failed in its goal of opening that door wide" (Tucker 1990, 915). Three reasons are cited for this limited impact: (1) inadequate enforcement of the law; (2) conflicting interpretations of the "reasonable accommodation" requirement; and (3) the limited scope of the law. Tucker described the federal government's enforcement of section 504 as "at best lethargic and at worst ineffectual" (877).

Percy undertook a comparative analysis of the impact of antidiscrimination laws on employment of people with disabilities at the federal and state levels. He concluded that the federal government has made some progress in employing people with disabilities, "although it falls short of employing persons with targeted disabilities in proportion to their numbers in the general population" (1990,16). Federal agencies vary considerably in their employment of people with disabilities, with some of the largest agencies falling below the government-wide average.

Overall, state agency representatives and state advocacy-group representatives described their states' efforts to employ people with disabilities as slightly less effective than the performance of the federal government in their state. Both federal and state officials noted that negative attitudes and misconceptions about people with disabilities were obstacles to compliance. They also noted the importance of agency leadership in successful compliance. State officials and advocacy groups saw competition from other policy issues in the state as an obstacle to compliance with employment mandates. The level of federal funding available for complying with employment mandates was a concern of state officials. Percy concluded that although many of the obstacles to complying with employment mandates encountered by state and federal government are similar, there is virtually no evidence of joint commitment or cooperation.

Edward H. Yelin, in his article, suggests that the impact of section 504 of the Rehabilitation Act on employment was one of slowing the pace of worsening conditions. The studies I have cited indicate that life has improved somewhat for persons with disabilities. All agree that there is more to be done.

CONCLUSIONS

The enactment of the ADA is the culmination of two decades of evolution of attitudes toward persons with disabilities. The enactment of the Americans with Disabilities Act is a landmark more for its comprehensiveness than its conceptual novelty. What the Americans with Disabilities Act does, in essence, is (1) to codify many regulatory concepts and guidelines from section 504 and other predecessor laws and (2) to extend the section 504 prohibition against discrimination to the private sector. The net result is that persons with disabilities now enjoy a degree of antidiscrimination protection comparable to that of women and members of other minority groups.

Just four years ago, in 1987, Edward Berkowitz began his book, *Disabled Policy*, with the statement, "America has no disability policy." He went on to describe the many contradictory, uncoordinated, and disparate programs and policies intended to serve persons with disabilities: some promoting dependence and segregation and others supporting independence and integration. With the enactment of the ADA, we can say that America at last has chosen the goals and some of the methods of its disability policy. We have chosen independence over dependence and integration over segregation. The goals for the nation articulated by the ADA will serve as standards against which we can measure and modify other disability policies, programs, and services for persons with disabilities.

The ADA is not intended to be a panacea. The ADA is a law that sends a clear message about what our society's attitudes should be toward persons with disabilities. The ADA is an orienting framework that can be used to construct a comprehensive service-delivery system. It has been said, "The ADA will not get you out of bed in the morning." The ADA is intended to open the doors of society and keep them open, but its effect will be limited unless we are as equally committed to providing adequate education, training, and support services as we are to eradicating discrimination.

NOTES

1. P.L. 101–336, 104 Stat. 327, 42 U.S.C. 12101 §2(a)(8).
2. P.L. 101–336 §2(a)(6)
3. U.S. Senate, August 30, 1989. *The Americans with Disabilities Act of 1989: Report from the Committee on Labor and Human Resources*, 101–116 (to accompany S. 933) at 9.
4. P.L. 101–336 §2(b)(1).
5. P.L. 101–336 §2(a)(2).
6. P.L. 101–336 §2(a)(3) and (5).
7. P.L. 101–336 §2(a)(7).
8. 42 U.S.C. 4151–57.
9. 29 U.S.C 791–94.
10. P.L. 100–259.
11. 465 U.S. 555 (1984).
12. 107 S. Ct. 1123 (1987).
13. P.L. 94–142; 20 U.S.C 1232, 1401, 1405–20, 1453.
14. 20 U.S.C. §1400 et seq.
15. 42 U.S.C 6000–81.
16. P.L. 96–247.
17. 42 U.S.C 1973 (1984).
18. P.L. 99–435.
19. P.L. 100–430.

REFERENCES

Arangio, A.J. 1979. *Behind the Stigma of Epilepsy: An Inquiry into the Centuries-Old Discrimination against Persons with Epilepsy*. Lanham, Md.: Epilepsy Foundation of America.
Berkowitz, E.D. 1987. *Disabled Policy America's Programs for the Handicapped*. New York: Cambridge University Press.

Brown, D. 1981. Jobs and Disabled Women: Double Discrimination and Little Help from the Women's Movement. *Disabled USA* 4(8).

Burgdorf, R.L. 1990. History. In *The Americans with Disabilities Act: A Practical and Legal Guide to Impact, Enforcement and Compliance*. Washington: Bureau of National Affairs.

Burkhauser, R.V., R.H. Haveman, and B.L. Wolfe. 1990. *The Changing Economic Condition of the Disabled: A Two Decade Review of Economic Well-being*. Washington: National Council on Disability.

DeJong, G. 1979. *The Movement for Independent Living: Origins, Ideology, and Implications for Disability Research*. East Lansing, Mich.: Michigan State University.

Disability Rag. 1990. Special Issue We Wish We Wouldn't See . . . (Winter.)

———. 1991. Kudos. 36 (March/April).

English, R.W. 1971. Correlates of Stigma towards Physically Disabled Persons. *Rehabilitation Research and Practice Review* 2 (4): 1–17.

Golfus, B. 1989. Disconfirmation. *Disability Rag* (November/December).

Hahn, H. 1985. Disability Policy and the Problem of Discrimination. *American Behavioural Scientist* 28: 293–318.

Harkin, T. 1989. Resolution introduced to change Senate subcommittee name, November 11. *National Association of Rehabilitation Facilities Rehabilitation Review*.

Harris, L., and Associates. 1986. *Disabled Americans' Self Perceptions: Bringing Disabled Americans into the Mainstream*. New York.

Johnson, M. 1987. Emotion and Pride: The Search for a Disability Culture. *Disability Rag* (January/February).

———. 1989. The Bargain. *Disability Rag* (September/October).

Kriegel, L., 1969. Uncle Tom and Tiny Tim: Some Reflections on the Cripple as Negro. *American Scholar* 38: 412–30.

Lachat, M.A. 1988. *The Independent Living Service Model: Historical Roots, Core Elements and Current Practice*. Hampton, N.H.: Center for Resource Management.

Livneh, H. 1982. On the Origins of Negative Attitudes toward People with Disabilities. *Rehabilitation Literature* 13 (11/12): 338–47.

Longmore, P. 1985. A Note on Language and the Social Identity of Disabled People. *American Behavioral Scientist*. 28 (3): 419–23.

National Council on Disability. 1986. *Toward Independence*. Washington.

———. 1988. *On the Threshold of Independence*. Washington.

Percy, S.L. 1990. *Implementing Civil Rights Policies: The Case of Disability Rights*. Paper presented at the Annual Meeting of the American Political Science Association, San Francisco, Calif., August 28 to September.

Presidential Commission on the Human Immunodeficiency Virus Epidemic. 1988. *Report of the Presidential Commission on the Human Immunodeficiency Virus Epidemic*. Washington.

Thomas, R. 1989. Testimony before the National Council on Disability, June 8. *The Education of Students with Disabilities: Where Do We Stand?* Washington: National Council on Disability.

Tucker, B.P. 1990. Section 504 of the Rehabilitation Act after Ten Years of Enforcement: The Past and the Future. *University of Illinois Law Review* 1989 (4): 845–921.

U.S. Commission on Civil Rights. 1983. *Accommodating the Spectrum of Individual Abilities*. Washington.

U.S. Department of Education. 1988. *Summary of Existing Legislation Affecting Persons with Disabilities*. Washington: Office of Special Education and Rehabilitative Services Clearinghouse on the Handicapped.

U.S. Senate Committee on Labor and Human Resources. 1989. *Hearings on S. 933, The Americans with Disabilities Act of 1989*, Senate Hearing 101–156, May 9, 10, 16 and June 22. Washington.

Wagner, M. 1989. *The Transition Experience of Youths with Disabilities: A Report from the National Longitudinal Transition Study*. Menlo Park, Calif.: SRI International.

Weaver, C. L. 1991. Disabilities Act Cripples through Ambiguity. *Wall Street Journal* (January 31).

Weicker, L.W. 1989. Testimony on the Americans with Disabilities Act. *Hearings before the Committee on Labor and Human Resources and the Subcommittee on the Handicapped on S. 933*, Senate Hearing 101–156. Washington.

White House Conference on Handicapped Individuals. 1977. *Final Report*, vols. 1–3. Washington.

Zola, I.K. 1988. The Language of Disability: Problems of Politics and Practice. *Journal of the Disability Advisory Council of Australia* 1 (3): 13–21.

Essential Requirements of the Act: A Short History and Overview*

Nancy Lee Jones

EDITOR'S NOTE

Remarkable for both its comprehensive content and its bold mandate, the Americans with Disabilities Act (ADA) is one of few laws that legitimately belongs under the rubric of "landmark legislation." Nancy Lee Jones holds that the ADA highlights a trend of moving from the judicial to the legislative arena in the development of civil-rights policy. Jones walks us through the development of key concepts of the ADA, including "reasonable accommodation" and "undue hardship," as she examines the rich 17-year history of articulating antidiscrimination requirements under section 504 of the Rehabilitation Act. She reviews the legislative history and describes the requirements of the law, as well as offering a glimpse of the next generation of ADA-related issues: the provision of health insurance and the parameters of the definition of disability. Concluding that rights and funding must go hand in hand, Jones calls for an examination of the Individuals with Disabilities Education Act as a potential model for post-ADA disability legislation.

As a legislative attorney for the American Law Division of the Congressional Research Service of the U.S. Library of Congress, Jones advised Congress throughout its consideration of the ADA. She provides impartial counsel and legal analysis to members of Congress, their

---

*The views expressed in this article are the views of the author, not necessarily those of the Library of Congress.

staffs, and congressional committees on a range of issues. With a J.D. from Georgetown University, Jones has published a number of articles on disability law, including "The Education for All Handicapped Children Act: Coverage of Children with AIDS" in the Journal of Law and Education, *and "Educational Rights of the Handicapped" in* The Harvard Journal on Legislation.

The Americans with Disabilities Act (ADA) is a landmark piece of legislation guaranteeing the civil rights of 43 million Americans with disabilities. As the most significant piece of civil-rights legislation since the Civil Rights Act of 1964, the ADA's enactment will profoundly change the legal rights of individuals with disabilities. The ADA points toward a future where its promise of civil rights combines with existing programs of financial support to create meaningful equality of opportunity for individuals with disabilities.

This legislation has not occurred in a vacuum; in order to understand its concepts and possible effect, it is necessary to look to the broad societal forces that have shaped its history and to examine predecessor statutes. It is sufficient to note here that the legal and social trends relating to persons with disabilities are a part of even larger societal tensions involving basic questions about the functions of government and the responsibilities of society to its citizens. Ultimately, the tension that runs through much of this century's jurisprudence arises over conflicts between individual liberty and the interests of society. The civil-rights movement is an example of this theme, especially as it is expressed in equal-protection analysis under the fourteenth amendment. Equal-protection theory has evolved into a tripart test, with differing weights given to certain kinds of individual rights, which are balanced against state interests. For example, statutes that involve distinctions based on race are deemed to be "suspect," and the balance is shifted in favor of the individual. Statutes that involve less critical interests, on the other hand, must only be rationally related to a legitimate state interest to pass constitutional muster. The Americans with Disabilities Act is one of the most recent expressions of this balancing of interests.

Historically, the ADA marks the first pure civil-rights statute for persons with disabilities that has broad application. Unlike section 504, which prohibits discrimination against individuals with disabilities solely in programs or activities receiving federal financial assistance, the ADA prohibits discrimination even when federal funds are not involved.[1] The ADA is a detailed and complicated statute that enacts many of the concepts expressed in regulations under section 504 into law. Two recent acts — the Civil Rights Restoration Act of 1987[2] and the Fair Housing Act Amendments of 1988[3] — included other minority groups and were limited in application; however, the disability component of each act served as an important precedent during ADA enactment (West 1991). The form of the ADA owes much to politics: both the careful negotiations within congressional committees and the felt necessity to be explicit to the future writers of regulations. Enactment of statutes like the ADA may also indicate that the cutting edge of civil-rights application is moving to the legislative arena as the judicial atmosphere becomes less conducive to expansive interpretation of individual rights (Marshall 1989).

ENACTMENT OF THE ADA

Prior to examining the specific requirements of the ADA, it is helpful to chronicle briefly its legislative journey. Although legislative attempts to implement various concepts in the ADA have been long-standing (Burgdorf and Bell 1984),[4] the original proposal for the ADA was offered by the National Council on Disability, an independent federal agency whose statutory functions include providing recommendations to the Congress regarding individuals with disabilities.[5] The National Council initially proposed antidiscrimination legislation in its 1986 report to Congress and the President, *Toward Independence*. A draft of the legislation was included in their 1988 report, *On the Threshold of Independence*. Legislation of this type was also recommended in the 1988 report of the Presidential Commission on the Human Immunodeficiency Virus [HIV] Epidemic.

Legislation was introduced in the 100th Congress,[6] and a joint House and Senate hearing was held, but no further action was taken. A substantially revised version of the ADA[7] was introduced in both the House and Senate on May 9, 1989. The revised bill included changes in the definition of disability, and the requirement for reasonable accommodation (Jones 1989). The amended bill passed the Senate on September 7, 1989.

In the House, the legislative process was complicated by the bill's referral to four committees: Education and Labor, Energy and Commerce, Transportation and Public Works, and Judiciary. Education and Labor is the committee that has had traditional jurisdiction over disability issues in the House. Whereas many in the other committees were familiar with certain aspects of the legislation, they lacked detailed expertise in disability issues. This created long, and occasionally frustrating, days and nights for disability advocates, who often served as educators for the committee members.

Due to the joint referral to four committees, House consideration would have been complicated in any event, but the resignation of the chief Democratic House sponsor, Representative Coelho, added to the difficulties. Mr. Coelho, an individual with epilepsy who had personally experienced discrimination as a result of his condition had been an impassioned advocate of the legislation (U.S. Congress 1988). Representative Hoyer assumed House leadership of the ADA and, as described in a recent article in the *Congressional Quarterly*, "shepherded the bill through a procedural and jurisdictional labyrinth . . . called 'complex enough to kill any bill' " (Rovner 1990b). ADA passage through the Senate was smoother because it was referred to only one committee, Labor and Human Resources, and was guided by the strong leadership of Democratic Senators Harkin and Kennedy.

Critical to passage of the ADA was the strong bipartisan support it received in both the House and the Senate. In the Senate, Republican Senators Dole and Hatch were key proponents of the legislative concepts; Representative Bartlett played a similar role in the House.

After numerous Committee hearings and votes, the ADA passed the House on May 22, 1990. During the course of the lively debate, numerous amendments were offered; the most controversial one, added by Representative Chapman and passed by the House, concerned food handlers with contagious diseases. This amendment, actively supported by the National Restaurant Association, would have permitted workers with communicable diseases to be transferred out of food-handling jobs—even if the disease could not be transmitted by food handling. The supporters of the amendment did not argue that HIV infection, the condition that prompted the amendment, could be spread by handling food, but rather that public perceptions were such that to provide protections to HIV-infected persons would create severe hardships for businesses.[8]

Opponents strongly criticized this argument as bowing to public misperceptions and perpetuating discrimination. As Representative McDermott stated: "The amendment is not about the reality of contagious disease. Let us be honest: it is about the fear of AIDS . . . As long as anyone in our country remains ignorant, this amendment says, as long as anyone is still afraid, the food industry may cater to that ignorance and fear."[9]

Another major difference before the conference committee was the ADA coverage of Congress. The version passed by the Senate during its debate[10] contained a very brief statement that the provisions of the act shall apply in their entirety to the Senate, House, and all the instrumentalities of Congress or either House. Opponents strenuously objected to this amendment, not because of its substance, but because it was seen as possibly creating constitutional separation-of-powers questions. In the House, the language was changed to provide for internal House remedies to eliminate the problems inherent in executive-branch enforcement of legislation binding on Congress.

The conferees agreed to a conference report, but the Senate, on July 11, 1990, voted to recommit the legislation to conference, where a compromise was reached (Rovner 1990a). On July 12, the House voted to pass the ADA[11] and on July 13 the Senate followed suit.[12] President Bush signed the legislation on July 26.

SECTION 504 OF THE REHABILITATION ACT OF 1973

One of the key rationales used to support the ADA was that it was essentially an extension into the private sector of section 504, an already existing federal statute.[13] Many of the concepts used in the ADA originated in section 504 jurisprudence, although section 504 differs from the ADA in several respects, the most significant departure being ADA's coverage of entities not receiving federal funds. The ADA contains a specific provision stating that, except as otherwise provided in the act, nothing in the act shall be construed to apply a lesser standard than the standards applied under title V of the Rehabilitation Act of 1973[14] or the regulations issued by federal agencies pursuant to such title.[15] A basic understanding of the legal theories underlying section 504 is thus critical to any analysis of the ADA.

Section 504 was enacted with little debate and most likely little understanding of its critical role in the development of civil-rights policy. Its original language was about a paragraph; even with subsequent amendments the provision is only several pages long. In contrast, the ADA is more than 50 pages in length. Yet, in many significant ways, the two statutes contain similar requirements. Much of the difference in length can be explained by the insertion of the language of the section 504 regulations in the statutory text of the ADA. (For an indepth analysis of disability rights prior to the ADA, see Percy 1989.)

It is important to note the basic difference between civil-rights statutes for persons with disabilities and civil-rights statutes prohibiting discrimination on the basis of race, sex, or national origin, such as title VII of the Civil Rights Act of 1964.[16]

Seldom do race, sex, or national origin present any obstacle to an individual when performing a job or participating in a program. Disabilities by their very nature, however, may make certain jobs or types of participation impossible. Compounding this difficulty is the fact that both disabilities and jobs vary widely. Although an individual with a particular type of disability may not be able to perform one type of job, he or she may be eminently qualified for another. In addition, unlike discrimination on the basis of race, sex, or national origin, discrimination against persons with disabilities is more often motivated, not by ill will, but rather by thoughtlessness or by ignorance of an individual's abilities. The Supreme Court clearly indicated this[17] when it stated that the purpose of section 504 was "to ensure that handicapped individuals are not denied jobs or other benefits because of the prejudiced attitudes or the ignorance of others [and] that society's accumulated myths and fears about disability and disease are as handicapping as the physical limitations that flow from actual impairment."[18]

The requirements of section 504 can be broken down into several component parts: an individual must be handicapped, otherwise qualified, subjected to discrimination solely on the basis of handicap, and such discrimination must be in a program or activity that receives federal financial assistance, an executive agency, or the U.S. Postal Service. The definitional section applicable to section 504 defines the term individual with handicaps as "any individual who (i) has a physical or mental impairment which substantially limits one or more of such person's major life activities, (ii) has a record of such an impairment, or (iii) is regarded as having such an impairment."[19] The regulations provide further guidance and specifically list certain covered impairments.[20] In addition, the Supreme Court dealt with the definitional issue in section 504 in the context of contagious diseases. The Court, in an opinion written by Justice Brennan, found that a person with the contagious disease of tuberculosis may be a handicapped individual under section 504.[21] Thus, the definition of handicapped individual, as defined by statute and regulation and interpreted by the Supreme Court, is a broad one. However, the broad definition is limited by the requirement that an individual be "otherwise qualified."

The term "qualified handicapped person" is defined in the regulations as meaning "[w]ith respect to employment, a handicapped person who, with reasonable accommodation, can perform the essential functions of the job in question and (b) with respect to services, a handicapped person who meets the essential eligibility requirements for the receipt of such services."[22] The first Supreme Court decision concerning section 504 involved this very issue: whether a hearing-impaired applicant for a college nursing program could be denied admission to the program. The Court found, in *Southeastern Community College v. Davis*, that an otherwise qualified handicapped individual "is one who is able to meet all of a program's requirements in spite of his handicap."[23]

However, this holding does not negate the requirement for reasonable accommodation. The Supreme Court, in *Alexander v. Choate*, further elaborated on the Davis decision:

> We held that the college was not required to admit Davis because it appeared unlikely that she could benefit from any modifications that the relevant HEW regulations required . . . and because the further modifications Davis sought—full-time, personal supervision whenever she attended patients and elimination of all clinical courses—would have compromised the essential nature of the college's nursing program . . . Such a "fundamental alteration in the nature of a program" was far more than the reasonable modifications the statute or regulations required.[24]

The Court in *Choate* went on to conclude that section 504 required a balancing approach between the rights of persons with disabilities to be integrated into society and the legitimate interests of grantees in preserving the integrity of their programs.[25]

Finally, there must be discrimination in order for there to be a violation of section 504. The regulations promulgated pursuant to section 504 provide detailed guidelines for determining discriminatory practices. First, there are general prohibitions against discrimination which include, among others, exclusion of a qualified handicapped person from participation in the benefits of a program that receives federal financial assistance.[26] There are also guidelines relating to employment discrimination that require reasonable accommodation "unless the recipient can demonstrate that the accommodation would impose an undue hardship on the operation of its program."[27] In addition, the regulations discuss program accessibility and when inaccessibility may be considered discrimination.[28]

Despite these guidelines, determining when discrimination has occurred is not always an easy task. The Supreme Court held that a Tennessee state proposal to reduce from 20 to 14 the number of annual inpatient hospital days that state Medicaid would pay hospitals was not a violation of section 504.[29] The Court, in a unanimous opinion by Justice Marshall, found that the 14-day limitation was neutral on its face, did not rest on a discriminatory motive, and did not deny persons with disabilities meaningful access to or exclusion from the package of Medicaid benefits. In arriving at this holding, the Court found that section 504 does not require proof of discriminatory intent; a disparate impact may be sufficient. However, not all actions that have a disparate impact on persons with disabilities are discrimination under section 504. Again, the Court emphasized that section 504 requires a balancing approach, so that rights are given to persons with disabilities and to covered entities.

In summary, section 504 contains a broad definition of individuals with disabilities and requires reasonable accommodation. However, such individuals must be otherwise qualified and their rights are balanced against the rights of recipients of federal financial assistance to preserve the integrity of their programs. Section 504 does not provide bright lines or absolute rules; rather, in light of the myriad of different disabilities and job and program requirements, it provides for a very individualized approach. This same approach was essentially adopted in the ADA.[30]

OVERVIEW OF THE ADA

SHORT TITLE AND DEFINITIONS

Section 1 contains the short title and the table of contents of the act.[31] Section 2 contains statements concerning congressional findings and purpose. Congress found that 43 million Americans have one or more physical or mental disabilities and that they are a discrete and insular minority faced with unfair and unnecessary discrimination.[32] The purpose of the ADA is described as providing a "clear and comprehensive national mandate for the elimination of discrimination against individuals with disabilities." Section 3 contains definitions of auxiliary aids and services, disability, and state.[33] The term *disability* is defined as meaning with respect to an individual "(A) a physical or mental impairment that substantially limits one or more of the major life activities of such individual; (B) a record of such an impairment; or (C) being regarded as having such an impairment." This definition is drawn from the definitional section applicable to section 504 of the Rehabilitation Act.[34]

Because the definition of disability is a key concept in the ADA, it is important to examine its parameters. Like section 504, its approach is functional rather than itemized. A purely illustrative list that appeared in the House and Senate Reports included the following: orthopedic, visual, speech and hearing impairments, cerebral palsy, epilepsy, muscular dystrophy, multiple sclerosis, HIV infection, cancer, heart disease, diabetes, mental retardation, emotional illness, specific learning disabilities, drug addiction, and alcoholism.[35] In the three-part definition quoted above, a physical or mental impairment (A), is defined in the same manner as under section 504: "any physiological disorder or condition, cosmetic disfigurements, or anatomical loss affecting one or more of the following body systems: neurological; musculoskeletal; special sense organs; respiratory, including speech organs; cardiovascular; reproductive; digestive; genito-urinary; hemic and lymphatic; skin; and endocrine." A mental impairment is defined as "any mental or psychological disorder, such as mental retardation, organic brain syndrome, emotional or mental illness, and specific learning disabilities."[36] Not encompassed by the definition are physical characteristics such as eye color, or left-handedness, environmental, cultural or economic disadvantages, or minor physical impairments.[37] To be covered, an impairment must limit a *major* life activity. The ADA also adopted the Supreme Court's interpretation in *School Board of Nassau County v. Arline*[38] of the definition of handicapped person as including a person with a contagious disease.

The second aspect (B) of the definition of disability is having a record of a disability. Like the interpretation accorded section 504 under its regulations,[39] having a record of an impairment is interpreted to include a history of an impairment and being misclassified as having an impairment.[40] This component of the definition, then, would cover individuals who have a history of cancer, or a mental or emotional illness.

The third component of the definition of disability is being regarded as having a disability. The ADA uses the same definition of this phrase as is used in section 504: it means an individual "(A) has a physical or mental impairment that does not substantially limit major life activities but that is treated . . . as constituting such a limitation; (B) has a physical or mental impairment that substantially limits major life activities only as a result of the attitudes of others toward such impairment; or (C) has none of the impairments defined but is treated . . . as having such an impairment."[41] The phrase "regarded as having such an impairment" was added to the definition of individual with handicaps in the Rehabilitation Act in 1974 as part of a revision of the definition to reflect more appropriately the coverage of discriminatory practices. The Senate report on the amendment indicated that it reflected congressional concern with prohibiting discrimination based not only on simple prejudice, but also on stereotypical attitudes and ignorance about individuals with disabilities.[42] This component would cover children who are not mentally retarded but who are erroneously placed in class for mentally retarded children,[43] as well as individuals who are denied employment because they are inaccurately perceived as having a disability that might limit the ability to perform the job.[44] As the ADA report of the House Judiciary Committee stated, this part of the definition "is intended to cover persons who are treated by a covered entity as having a physical or mental impairment that substantially limits a major life activity. It applies whether or not a person has an impairment, if that person was treated as if he or she had an impairment that substantially limits a major life activity."[45]

TITLE I — EMPLOYMENT

Title I provides that no covered entity shall discriminate against a qualified individual with a disability because of the disability in regard to job-application procedures, the hiring, advancement, or discharge of employees, employee compensation, job training, and other terms, conditions, and privileges of employment.[46] The term *employer* is defined as a person engaged in an industry affecting commerce who has 15 or more employees; however, for the two years following the effective date of the title, an employer means a person engaged in an industry affecting commerce who has 25 or more employees.[47] The term *qualified individual with a disability* is defined as "an individual with a disability who, with or without reasonable accommodation, can perform the essential functions of the employment position that such person holds or desires."[48]

Title I incorporates many of the concepts set forth in the regulations promulgated pursuant to section 504, including the requirement to provide reasonable accommodation unless such accommodation would pose an undue hardship on the operation of the business.[49] Undue hardship is defined as meaning an action requiring significant difficulty or expense when considered in light of various factors, including (1) the nature and cost of the accommodation needed, (2) the overall financial resources of the facility, (3) the overall financial resources of the covered entity and the number, type, and location of its facilities, and (4) the type of operation or operations of the covered entity, including the composition, structure, and functions of the work force, the geographic separateness, administrative, or fiscal relationship of the facility or facilities in question to the covered entity.

Section 103 specifically lists some defenses to a charge of discrimination:

1. The alleged application of qualification standards has been shown to be job related and consistent with business necessity and such performance cannot be accomplished by reasonable accommodation.
2. The term *qualification standards* can include a requirement that an individual shall not pose a direct threat to the health or safety of other individuals in the workplace.
3. Religious entities may give a preference in employment to individuals of a particular religion to perform work connected with carrying on the entities' activities. In addition, religious entities may require that all applicants and employees conform to the religious tenets of the organization.

The Secretary of Health and Human Services is required to list infectious and communicable diseases transmitted through the handling of food and if the risk cannot be eliminated by reasonable accommodation, a covered entity may refuse to assign or continue to assign an individual with such a disease to a job involving food handling.[50]

Another controversial issue concerned the application of the ADA to drug addicts and alcoholics. The act provides that an employee or applicant for employment who is currently engaging in the illegal use of drugs is not considered to be a qualified individual with a disability.[51] This section also provides that a covered entity may prohibit the illegal use of drugs and the use of alcohol at the work place.

As with section 504, the ADA broadly defines an individual with disabilities, but limits the application of the nondiscrimination requirement by requiring that an individual be "qualified." This balancing approach[52] means that with regard to employment an individual must be able to perform the "essential functions" of the job with "reasonable accommodation" and without creating an "undue burden" on the employer.

The Senate report on the ADA describes essential functions as meaning job tasks that are "fundamental and not marginal."[53] An example of a nonessential function would be a requirement for a driver's license where driving is not a major function or for which driving functions can be reassigned.[54] The essential-functions language aroused considerable concern in the business community, which argued that the employer's views should determine what constitutes essential functions. Their argument was not accepted; however, the ADA requires consideration of the employer's judgment as to what is essential and accepts a job description written prior to advertising or interviewing applicants as evidence of the essential functions of the job.

One of the critical concepts in the ADA is that of "reasonable accommodation."[55] The ADA has defined reasonable accommodation as including making existing facilities used by employees readily accessible to and usable by individuals with disabilities; job restructuring; part-time or modified work schedules; reassignment to a vacant position; acquisition or modification of equipment or devices; appropriate adjustment or modifications of examinations, training materials, or policies; and provision of qualified readers or interpreters; and other similar accommodations. As in interpretation of section 504, the application of the concept of reasonable accommodation is fact specific and varies depending on the particular situation presented.[56]

Although an employer may be obligated to provide reasonable accommodation, this requirement is not unlimited. Such accommodation is not required under the ADA if it can be shown that it would impose an "undue hardship on the operation of the business of such covered entity." The term "undue hardship" is defined in the ADA as an action requiring significant difficulty or expense; certain factors are listed for consideration in making this determination. The ADA, like section 504, embodies a flexible, case-by-case approach to the determination of undue hardship and specifically rejects the notion of a cost cap. An amendment was offered on the House floor that would have created a presumption of undue hardship if a proposed accommodation would have cost more than 10 percent of the annual salary of the position involved. The opponents of this proposal argued that this would work to the disadvantage of workers in lower-level jobs and did not focus on the resources of the employer.[57]

The remedies and procedures in sections 705, 706, 707, 709, and 710 of the Civil Rights Act of 1964[58] are incorporated by reference.[59] This would provide for certain administrative enforcement as well as allowing for individual suits. Presently, these remedies would include injunctive relief and back pay, but not compensatory and punitive damages.[60] The Equal Employment Opportunity Commission is to promulgate regulations no later than one year after the date of enactment. The agencies with enforcement authority for employment discrimination in the ADA and under the Rehabilitation Act of 1973 are to develop, within 18 months, coordination procedures to avoid a duplication of effort or varying enforcement standards. Title I will become effective on July 26, 1992, 24 months after enactment.[61]

TITLE II – PUBLIC SERVICES

Title II provides that no qualified individual with a disability shall be excluded from participation in or be denied the benefits of the services, programs, or activities of a public entity or subjected to discrimination by any such entity.[62] *Public entity* is defined as state and local governments, any department or other instrumentality of a state or local government, and the National Railroad Passenger Corporation.[63] This title also provides specific requirements for public transportation by intercity and commuter rail and for public transportation other than by aircraft or certain rail operations.[64] All new vehicles purchased or leased by a public entity that operates a fixed-route system are to be accessible and good-faith efforts must be demonstrated in the purchase or lease of accessible used vehicles. Retrofitting of existing buses is not required. Paratransit services would be required in most circumstances other than those involving commuter bus service. Generally, within five years, rail systems are to have at least one car per train that is accessible to individuals with disabilities.

The enforcement remedies of section 505 of the Rehabilitation Act of

1973[65] are incorporated by reference.[66] These remedies would be similar
to those of title VI of the Civil Rights Act of 1964 and would include
damages and injunctive relief. The Attorney General is to promulgate
regulations relating to subpart A of the title (Prohibition against Discrimination and other Generally Applicable Provisions), although such
regulations are not to include matters within the scope of the authority
of the Secretary of Transportation.[67] Subpart B provides that the Secretary of Transportation shall issue regulations.[68] Generally, the effective
date for title II is 18 months, but the date varies for some sections such
as that relating to public entities operating fixed route systems.[69]

TITLE III – PUBLIC ACCOMMODATIONS AND SERVICES OPERATED
BY PRIVATE ENTITIES

Title III provides that no individual shall be discriminated against on
the basis of disability in the full and equal enjoyment of the goods,
services, facilities, privileges, advantages, or accommodations of any
place of public accommodation by any person who owns, leases (or
leases to), or operates a place of public accommodation.[70] Entities to be
covered by the term *public accommodation* are listed and include,
among others, hotels, restaurants, theaters, auditoriums, laundromats,
museums, parks, zoos, private schools, day-care centers, professional
offices of health care providers, and gymnasiums.[71] Religious institutions or entities controlled by religious institutions are not included on
the list. There are some limitations on the nondiscrimination requirement and a failure to remove architectural barriers is not a violation
unless such a removal is "readily achievable."[72]

Readily achievable is defined as "easily accomplishable and able to
be carried out without much difficulty or expense."[73] It is interesting to
contrast this requirement with the undue hardship requirement for
employment. The legislative history of the ADA indicates that Congress intended the undue hardship standard to be a "much higher
standard."[74] The examples given of readily achievable accommodations
in the committee reports further emphasize this distinction. The kind
of barrier removal required was described as including the addition of
grab bars, ramping a few steps, and lowering telephones.[75] The nondiscrimination mandate also does not require that an entity permit an
individual to participate in or benefit from the services of a public
accommodation where such an individual poses a direct threat to the
health or safety of others.[76]

Title III also contains provisions relating to the prohibition of discrimination in certain public-transportation services provided by private entities.[77] Purchases of over-the-road buses are to be made in accordance with regulations issued by the Secretary of Transportation.[78] In issuing these regulations, the Secretary must take into account the recommendations of a study on the subject to be done by the Office of Technology Assessment.[79]

The remedies and procedures of title II of the Civil Rights Act shall be the powers, remedies, and procedures title III of the ADA provides to any person who is being subjected to discrimination or any person who has reasonable grounds for believing that he or she is about to be subjected to discrimination with respect to the construction of new or the alteration of existing facilities in an inaccessible manner.[80] Title II of the Civil Rights Act has generally been interpreted to include injunctive relief, not damages. In addition, state and local governments can apply to the Attorney General to certify that state or local building codes meet or exceed the accessibility requirements of the ADA.[81] The Attorney General may bring pattern or practice suits with a maximum civil penalty of $50,000 for the first violation and $100,000 for a violation in a subsequent case. The monetary damages sought by the Attorney General do not include punitive damages. Courts may also consider an entity's "good faith" efforts in considering the amount of the civil penalty. Factors to be considered in determining good faith include whether an entity could have reasonably anticipated the need for an appropriate type of auxiliary aid to accommodate the unique needs of a particular individual with a disability.[82] With some exceptions, the effective date of title III is 18 months after enactment.[83]

TITLE IV—TELECOMMUNICATIONS

Title IV amends title II of the Communications Act of 1934[84] by adding a section providing that the Federal Communications Commission shall ensure that interstate and intrastate telecommunications relay services are available, to the extent possible and in the most efficient manner, to hearing-impaired and speech-impaired individuals.[85] Any television public-service announcement that is produced or funded in whole or part by any agency or instrumentality of the federal government shall include closed captioning of the verbal content of the announcement.[86] The FCC is given enforcement authority with certain exceptions and the services shall be provided not later than three years after the date of enactment.[87]

Title V contains an amalgam of provisions, several of which generated considerable controversy during the ADA debate. Section 501 concerns the relationship of the ADA to other statutes and bodies of law. Subpart (a) states that "except as otherwise provided in this act, nothing in this Act shall be construed to apply a lesser standard than the standards applied under title V of the Rehabilitation Act . . . or the regulations issued by Federal agencies pursuant to such title." Subpart (b) provides that nothing in the Act shall be construed to invalidate or limit the remedies, rights, and procedures of any federal, state, or local law that provides greater or equal protection. Nothing in the act is to be construed to preclude the prohibition or restrictions on smoking. Subpart (c) limits the application of the act with respect to the coverage of insurance; however, this subsection is not to be used as a subterfuge to evade the purposes of titles I and III. Finally, subsection (d) provides that the act does not require an individual with a disability to accept an accommodation which that individual chooses not to accept.[88]

Section 502[89] abrogates the eleventh amendment state immunity from suit. Section 503[90] prohibits retaliation and coercion against an individual who has opposed an act or practice made unlawful by the ADA. Section 504[91] requires the Architectural and Transportation Barriers Compliance Board to issue guidelines regarding accessibility. These guidelines are to include procedures and requirements for alterations of historic buildings or facilities. Section 505[92] provides for attorneys' fees in "any action or administrative proceeding" under the act. Section 506[93] provides for technical assistance to assist entities covered by the act in understanding their responsibilities. Section 507[94] provides for a study by the National Council on Disability regarding wilderness designations and wilderness land-management practices and "reaffirms" that nothing in the wilderness act is to be construed as prohibiting the use of a wheelchair in a wilderness area by an individual whose disability requires the use of a wheelchair. Section 513[95] provides that "where appropriate and to the extent authorized by law, the use of alternative means of dispute resolution . . . is encouraged . . ." Section 514[96] provides for severability of any provision of the act that is found to be unconstitutional.

The coverage of Congress was a source major controversy during the House-Senate conference on the ADA. The Senate-passed version had provided that the ADA's requirements shalll apply in their entirety to the Senate, the House, and all the instrumentalities of the Congress. This language incorporated the provisions in various titles providing for administrative enforcement of the ADA, thus raising constitutional issues regarding separation of powers and speech and debate clause immunity. The House took a different approach and applied the rights and protections of the ADA to the Congress but provided for the official of each instrumentality of Congress to establish remedies and procedures for these rights. After considerable debate, existing Senate and House procedures concerning discrimination were codified and the concept of a private rights of action was dropped.[97]

Two other controversial areas were covered in title V—sex and drugs. Section 510[98] provides that the term "individual with a disability" in the ADA does not include an individual who is currently engaging in the illegal use of drugs when the covered entity acts on the basis of such use. An individual who has been rehabilitated would be covered. However, the conference-report language clarifies that the provision does not permit individuals to invoke coverage simply by showing they are participating in a drug-rehabilitation program; they must refrain from using drugs. The conference report also indicates that the limitation in coverage is not intended to be narrowly construed only to persons who use drugs "on the day of, or within a matter of weeks before, the action in question." The definitional section of the Rehabilitation Act that would be applicable to section 504 is also amended to create uniformity with this definition and to add some provisions relating to alcohol use.

Section 508[99] provides that an individual shall not be considered to have a disability solely because that individual is a transvestite. Section 511[100] similarly provides that homosexuality and bisexuality are not disabilities under the act and that the term disability does not include transvestism, transsexualism, pedophilia, exhibitionism, voyeurism, gender-identity disorders not resulting from physical impairments, or other sexual behavior disorders, compulsive gambling, kleptomania, or pyromania, or psychoactive substance use disorders resulting from current illegal use of drugs.

Because title V of the ADA contains no effective-date section, there has been some confusion about the deadline for its substantive provisions, such as the amendments to the definition of handicapped individual in the Rehabilitation Act and the congressional coverage section.

This was most likely an oversight because the original version of the ADA contained one effective-date clause for the entire act and the various titles were later amended to provide separate dates for the differing titles. It could be argued that, in the absence of a specific provision, title V is effective immediately upon enactment. However, when the act is read as a whole, it would appear more logical that the effective date should be gleaned from the dates in the corresponding titles. For example, where the definition of individual with handicaps for the Rehabilitation Act is used with regard to employment, the effective date of the employment title of the ADA would arguably be the applicable date. Because the rationale for the change in the Rehabilitation Act was to create similar coverage to the ADA, a change at the time title I of the ADA becomes effective would appear the most logical. With regard to the Rehabilitation Act, this issue may be clarified during congressional debate on its reauthorization.

BEYOND THE ENACTMENT

The Americans with Disabilities Act was carefully crafted and based upon years of regulatory and judicial experience with section 504. However, section 504 itself still has some ambiguities and the ADA will undoubtedly be further clarified by regulations, possible amendment, and eventually judicial interpretation (see Samborn 1990). A few of the more troublesome ambiguities will be briefly examined here.

THE DEFINITION OF DISABILITY

Despite extensive regulatory and judicial discussion, the exact line between what is a disability and what is not blurs at the outer edges. Clearly, environmental, cultural, and economic disadvantages would not be covered.[101] Similarly, simple physical characteristics such as blue eyes or black hair would not be covered and neither age nor homosexuality would be included in the definition.[102] Not even all physical or mental impairments would be covered. The physical or mental impairment must be severe enough to result in a substantial limitation of one or more major life activities. Thus, a person with an infected finger would not be covered.

The definition of disability would also include individuals who have a record of an impairment, such as a person with a history of cancer, and individuals who are "regarded as" having an impairment.[103] A severe burn victim would be an example of an individual who is regarded as having an impairment. But what about discrimination based on smoking, obesity, unattractiveness, or a genetic trait causing an individual to be more susceptible to certain illnesses?

The smoking-related issue was raised during the ADA debate but is not as clear-cut as it might appear. The ADA states that nothing in the act is to be construed "to preclude the prohibition of, or the imposition of restriction on, smoking in places of employment covered by title I, in transportation covered by title II or III, or in places of public accommodation covered by title III."[104] This provision appears to be aimed at the protection of nonsmokers from passive smoking. The unresolved issue is to what extent a smoker may be covered by the definition of an individual with disability and thus protected from discrimination in other contexts, such as employment.

Only one federal court has dealt with the question of the coverage of obesity under section 504 and it did not reach the merits of the issue.[105] However, a fourth-circuit case, Forrisi v. Bowen,[106] rejected an acrophobic plaintiff's claim under section 504 where the plaintiff had testified that his fear of heights had never limited a major life activity. This case, however, did not analyze the issue of whether the plaintiff was "regarded as having a disability" and thus may be decided differently today in light of the Supreme Court's decision in *School Board of Nassau County v. Arline*. As noted above, discrimination arising from disfiguring scars in a burn victim would give rise to an actionable complaint. What then about discrimination based on obesity or physical appearance? One commentator has noted that "[i]t thus seems an arbitrary distinction to say that an employer cannot refuse to hire a person who has a disfiguring scar on his chin, for example, but can refuse to hire someone whose chin is jutting or unusually shaped" (*Harvard Law Review* 1987). Another commentator has noted that courts may interpret the ADA to include persons who are physically unattractive (Lindsay 1989/1990).

The issue of whether refusal to hire an individual because of possible genetic traits that may make them more susceptible to injury is a complex one. Several members of Congress, however, noted during passage of the ADA that individuals with such genetic traits would be protected under the act.[107] In *UAW v. Johnson Controls, Inc.*,[108] the Supreme Court will have the opportunity to examine a related issue: whether fertile women can be excluded from workplaces that expose employees to substances potentially hazardous to fetuses without violating title VII of the Civil Rights Act of 1964 (*Harvard Law Review* 1990; OuYang 1990; Williams 1981).

A conceptual distinction could be made to eliminate from coverage conditions that are self-imposed or volitional. To some extent, this has been done in the ADA by the limitations on drug addicts, alcoholics, and certain sexual conditions. This distinction has a certain appeal because there is no other protected class in civil-rights law that an individual can "will" him- or herself to join. There is some support for this position in section 504 case law; specifically in *Tudyman v. United Airlines,* where the weight of muscle mass gained from a self-initiated body-building program kept the plaintiff from employment as an airline steward. However, the attractiveness of this distinction pales when the difficulty of determining what is volitional is examined. For example, some recent research has indicated that a tendency toward obesity is genetic. Is smoking by an individual who is addicted to nicotine truly volitional? Would it be valid to deny protection to an individual who became paraplegic due to "volitional" motorcycle racing?

The definition of "individual with disability" under both section 504 and the ADA is a broad one and goes beyond "traditional" disabilities. However, despite its breadth, there are limitations and the line between what is a disability and what is not is often blurred, particularly with the part of the definition that covers individuals who are "regarded as" having an impairment.

THE SITE-SPECIFIC ISSUE

One of the major controversies during consideration of the ADA in the House Education and Labor Committee revolved around the issue of whether ADA coverage was "site specific." An entity cannot discriminate under the ADA, but there is an exception for this requirement if the accommodation required would impose an undue burden on the business. The question arose, when considering the definition of an undue burden, whether only the resources of a specific store or those of an entire national corporation would be considered. In other words, would the nondiscrimination provisions cover all of the stores in a national chain equally? The committee heard an argument stating that because the factors constituting an undue burden on a business may vary depending on which store of a national chain is involved, each store therefore should be considered independently. Another argument put forward was that the location of a particular branch should not be determinative because the resources of the parent corporation could be used for any reasonable accommodation requirements.

This debate was resolved with a compromise: the definitions of undue hardship and readily achievable were amended to include considerations of "the type of operation or operations of the covered entity, including the composition, structure, and functions of the workforce of such entity; the geographic separateness, administrative, or fiscal relationship of the facility or facilities in question to the covered entity."[109] The House Education and Labor Committee report further elaborated on this compromise.

> The addition of these factors reflects the Committee's intent that, in determining whether a reasonable accommodation would constitute an undue hardship, courts should look at and may weigh the financial resources and operations of those local facilities that are being asked to provide an accommodation, because the financial resources of local facilities may vary significantly. The factors further reflect the Committee's intent that, in determining whether a reasonable accommodation would constitute an undue hardship, the financial resources of the larger covered entity, and any of those financial resources available to the local covered entity, should be looked at and may be weighed by the court as well.[110]

The report went on to observe that a court would be expected to look at the "practical realities" of the situation.[111]

Exactly how a court would take these various factors into consideration and the weight each would be given is uncertain. Regulatory guidance on this issue would greatly aid interpretation although the complexities of corporate organization may make this task a difficult one.

CUSTOMER PREFERENCE

Another difficult issue presented by the undue burden language revolves around the question of to what extent, if any, customer preference can be used as a factor to limit the requirements of the ADA. This issue was raised during House debate on the Chapman amendment where the main argument made in support of the amendment was that customers would refuse to patronize food establishments if an employee was known to have a communicable disease and that this could cause the business to close with a resulting loss of jobs.[112] Strong objections were raised to this argument as catering to "fear and prejudice"[113] and the resolution of the issue in conference was to deny coverage only in those situations where there was a risk to the public health.

Generally, the resolution of this issue comports with case law on customer preference under title VII. There, for example, the mere fact that customers may prefer that flight attendants be female has not been found to be sufficient to allow discrimination based on sex. However, under title VII there have been certain situations where customer preference may be sufficient for there not to be a finding of discrimination; for example, a female resident of a nursing home may have such a strong preference for a personal bathing attendant of the same sex that it would not be discrimination to hire on that basis. The unresolved issue under the Americans with Disabilities Act is whether there would be any situations so extreme as to allow customer preference. Given the rejection of this concept in the compromise on the Chapman amendment, it would appear likely that there would be few, if any, of these situations.

INSURANCE

The next generation of issues relating to individuals with disabilities will probably arise in the context of health care insurance. The Americans with Disabilities Act contains a specific exception relating to insurance:

> Title I through IV of this Act shall not be construed to prohibit or restrict — (1) an insurer, hospital or medical service company, health maintenance organization, or any agent, or entity that administers benefit plans, or similar organizations from underwriting risks, classifying risks, or administering such risks that are based on or not inconsistent with State law; or (2) a person or organization covered by this Act from establishing, sponsoring, observing or administering the terms of a bona fide benefit plan that are based on underwriting risks, classifying risks, or administering such risks that are based on or not inconsistent with State law; or (3) a person or organization covered by this Act from

establishing, sponsoring, observing or administering the terms of
a bona fide benefit plan that is not subject to State laws that
regulate insurance. Paragraphs (1), (2), and (3) shall not be used
as a subterfuge to evade the purposes of title I and III.[114]

The legislative history of this provision indicates that it was added so
that the ADA would not "affect the way the insurance industry does
business in accordance with the State laws and regulations under which
it regulates."[115] The last sentence of the section was added to insure that
the provision was not used to evade the requirements of the Act. Thus,
an employer could not deny a qualified individual with disabilities a
job because the employer's current insurance plan does not cover the
person's disability or because the employer's insurance costs would
increase. Similarly, employee benefit plans are not violative of the
ADA because they do not address the specific needs of every individual
with disabilities.[116] However, there is some uncertainty about what
would be considered to be a subterfuge. This may not need to be an
intentional act and the mere fact that the benefit plan is already in
effect at the time of the ADA's enactment may not be determinative.
The result of this may encourage employers not to offer insurance
benefit plans. The exact parameters of what is a subterfuge would
benefit from regulatory guidance.

IMPLICATIONS FOR TECHNOLOGY

The ADA's requirements for reasonable accommodation implicate
technology in several ways. First, what is reasonable accommodation
may well depend upon the technologies that are available and so the
specific requirements may vary as technological advances are made. The
definition of reasonable accommodation itself includes an "acquisition
or modification of equipment or devices."[117] Second, the ADA requires
certain technologies; for example, the requirements for telecommunications relay services. The main issue this raises is to what degree technological adaptations are required. For example, is electronic equipment access required by the ADA? The answer to this is most likely
affirmative although, like other kinds of reasonable accommodations,
it would be subject to a balancing and the requirement may depend on
whether such access would pose an undue burden.[118]

Interestingly, there may be an issue of balancing to be accomplished
in the area of expected technological advances. In a case arising under

section 504, *Nelson v. Thornburgh*,[119] the court balanced the cost of providing readers or electronic devices for visually impaired income maintenance workers and found that the accommodation sought was a small fraction of the organization's budget. The court concluded that the cost of accommodation was "quite small" and was likely to diminish as technology advances.

THE FUTURE OF DISABILITY LAW AND POLICY

The ADA is undoubtedly a landmark in the development of disability law and policy. It will have a profound effect on American life and, as President Bush stated in his comments on signing the legislation, it places the United States in the forefront of the world community regarding disability rights. And it does so at a time when the aging of the population portends an increase in the number of individuals with disabilities. What then does the future hold for disability law and policy?

First, there will be continuing refinements and interpretations of the ADA and existing statutes with regard to ambiguous areas. The trend away from paternalism and toward civil rights will continue. However, this does not mean that financial aid and benefits for persons with disabilities should or will end.[120] The concept of reasonable accommodation inherent in the nondiscrimination mandates of section 504 and the ADA implies some type of assistance. Increasingly, as issues of insurance and technology are explored, it will become clear that in order to have rights, there must also be financial support for those rights.

The challenge facing disability policy makers will be to integrate financial support for rights at a time of increasing budgetary concerns (see Cohn 1990; Fox 1990). At first blush, this would seem an impossibility, but the benefits in terms of increasing tax revenues and additions to the work force would argue against a simplistic rejection of the idea. This blending of civil rights and benefits is not entirely without precedent in existing law: Individuals with Disabilities Education Act (formerly called the Education for All Handicapped Children Act)[121] provides valuable guidance on the melding of these concepts. It provides grants but also very specific rights and there are years of experience working with its requirements. EHA is limited, however, by the fact that its civil-rights provisions are contingent upon the receipt of the grant funds. Although for EHA this has been a marginal limitation because presently all states have chosen to receive funding under the statute, it might well be a major limitation if the funding levels were to decrease. Thus, although EHA is a glimpse of a future melding of funding and rights, it is not a complete model. The future of disability law and policy lies in a creative merger of the benefits gained from provisions relating to financial support and those relating to civil rights. This merger is most likely to occur in the congressional arena because judicial activism regarding civil rights appears to be on the wane. The ADA is a crucial step on the road to this future blending of rights and funding.

NOTES

1. 29 U.S.C.§794.
2. P.L. 100–259.
3. P.L. 100–430.
4. For example, see S. 446, 96th Cong.; H.R. 5510, 96th Cong.; H.R. 255, 97th Cong.; H.R. 1919, 97th Cong.; H.R. 3187, 97th Cong.; H.R. 3187, 97th Cong.; H.R. 1200, 98th Cong.; H.R. 1294, 99th Cong.; H.R. 370, 99th Cong.; H.R. 3071, 100th Cong. All of these bills would have amended title VII of the Civil Rights Act, 42 U.S.C. § 2000e-2(a), by including persons with disabilities generally or by including a specific type of disability such as cancer.
5. 29 U.S.C. §781.
6. S. 2345 and H.R. 4498.
7. S. 933 and H.R. 2273.
8. This amendment would have also provided for alternative employment for the employee. For supporting comments, see 136 Cong. Rec. H 2479 (daily ed. May 17, 1990) (Comments of Representative Bartlett).
9. 136 Cong. Rec. H 2489 (daily ed. May 17, 1990).
10. S. 933. See 135 Cong. Rec. S 10780 (daily ed. Sept. 7, 1989).
11. 136 Cong. Rec. H 4629 (daily ed. July 12, 1990).
12. 136 Cong. Rec. S 9695 (daily ed. July 13, 1990).
13. §504 of the Rehabilitation Act of 1973, 29 U.S.C. §794.
14. 29 U.S.C. 790 et seq.
15. ADA, §501, 42 U.S.C. §12201.
16. 42 U.S.C. § 2000e et seq.
17. *School Board of Nassau County v. Arline*, 480 U.S. 273 (1987).
18. See also *Alexander v. Choate*, 469 U.S. 287, 295 (1985).
19. 29 U.S.C. §706(8).
20. 28 C.F.R. §41.31.

21. See supra, note 17.

22. 28 C.F.R. §41.32.

23. 442 U.S. 397 (1979) at 406.

24. 469 U.S. 287 (1985) at 300.

25. Id. at 300. The section 504 statutory requirement that discrimination be "solely by reason of his or her handicap" has been little used. See *Pushkin v. Regents of University of Colorado*, 658 F.2d 1372 (1981).

26. 28 C.F.R. §41.51.

27. 28 C.F.R. §41.53.

28. 28 C.F.R. §§41.56–41.58.

29. *Alexander v. Choate*, supra note 24.

30. This flexibility in the ADA has been strongly criticized as creating subjectivity and vagueness (Lindsay 1989/1990).

31. 42 U.S.C. §12101 note.

32. 42 U.S.C. §12101.

33. 42 U.S.C. §12102.

34. 29 U.S.C. §706 (8).

35. S. Rep. No. 116, 101st Cong., 1st Sess. 22 (1989); H. Rep. No. 485, 101st Cong. 2d Sess. Part 2 at 51 (1990). Section 504 uses the term "individual with handicaps" whereas the ADA refers to "disability," reflecting congressional use of "up-to-date, currently accepted terminology." S. Rep. No. 116, 101st Cong., 1st Sess. 21 (1989); H.Rep. No 485, 101st Cong. 2d Sess., Part 2 at 50–51 and Part 3 at 26–27 (1990).

36. S. Rep. No 1165, 101st Cong., 1st Sess. 21 (1989); H. Rep. No 485, 101st Cong., 2d Sess. Part 2 at 51; Part 3 at 28 (1990).

37. S. Rep. No.116, 101st Cong. 1st Sess. 22 (1989).

38. See supra, note 17.

39. 45 C.F.R. §84.3.

40. S. Rep. No. 116, 101st Cong. 1st Sess. 23 (1989); H. Rep. No. 485. 101st Cong., 2d Sess. Part 2 at 52–53 (1990).

41. H.Rep. No. 485, 101st Cong., 2d Sess. Part 3 at 29 (1990), quoting 45 C.F.R. 84.3.

42. S.Rep. No. 1297, 93d Cong., 2d Sess., reprinted in [1974] *U.S. Code Cong. & Ad. News* 6373, 6389.

43. *Carter v. Orleans Parish Public Schools*, 725 F.2d 261 (5th Cir. 1984).

44. See, e.g., *Duran v. City of Tampa*, 430 F.Supp. 75 (M.D. Fla. 1977).

45. H. Rep. No. 485, 101st Cong., 2d Sess. Part 3 at 29 (1990). It should be noted that the report language emphasizes the *substantial* nature of the limitation, whether such limitation is genuine or perceived. This parallels section 504 case law. See, e.g., *Forrisi v Bowen*, 794 F.2d 931 (4th Cir. 1986).

46. 42 U.S.C. §12112.

47. 42 U.S.C. §12111.

48. Id.

49. See 45 C.F.R. Part 84.

50. 42 U.S.C. §12113.

51. 42 U.S.C. §12114.

52. See *Alexander v. Choate*, note 18 supra.

53. S. Rep. No. 116, 101St Cong. 1st Sess. 26 (1989).
54. Id.
55. Indeed, the House Judiciary Committee has stated that the reasonable accommodation requirement is central to the nondiscrimination mandate of the ADA. H.Rep. No. 485, 101st Cong. 2d Sess. Part 3 at 39.
56. See e.g., *Southeastern Community College v. Davis*, 442 U.S. 397 (1979); *Alexander v. Choate*, 469 U.S. 287 (1985). For an excellent discussion of reasonable accommodation under the ADA, see Bureau of National Affairs 1990: *The Americans with Disabilities Act*, 114–19.
57. 136 Cong. Rec. H 2470 (May 17, 1990).
58. 42 U.S.C. §§2000e-4, 2000e-5, 2000e-6, 2000e-8.
59. 42 U.S.C. §12117.
60. If legislation similar to the Civil Rights Act of 1990, S. 2104, 101st Cong., is enacted, the remedies referred to may change.
61. 42 U.S.C. §12111.
62. 42 U.S.C. §12132.
63. 42 U.S.C. §12131.
64. 42 U.S.C. §§12141–12150, 12161–12165.
65. 29 U.S.C. §794a.
66. 42 U.S.C. §12133.
67. 42 U.S.C. §12134.
68. 42 U.S.C. §12149.
69. 42 U.S.C. §§12131, 12141, 12161.
70. 42 U.S.C. §12182.
71. 42 U.S.C. §12181.
72. 42 U.S.C. §12182.
73. 42 U.S.C. §12181.
74. H.Rep. No. 485, 101st Cong. 2d Sess. Part 3, at 40 (1990).
75. S. Rep. No. 116, 101st Cong., 1st Sess. 66 (1989).
76. 42 U.S.C. §12182.
77. 42 U.S.C. §12184.
78. 42 U.S.C. §12186.
79. 42 U.S.C. §12185.
80. 42 U.S.C. §12188.
81. Id.
82. Id.
83. 42 U.S.C. 12181.
84. 47 U.S.C. 201 et seq.
85. 47 U.S.C. §225.
86. 47 U.S.C. §611.
87. 47 U.S.C. §225.
88. 42 U.S.C. §12201.
89. 42 U.S.C. §12202.
90. 42 U.S.C. §12203.
91. 42 U.S.C. §12204.
92. 42 U.S.C.§12205.
93. 42 U.S.C. §12206.

94. 42 U.S.C. §12207.
95. 42 U.S.C. §12212.
96. 42 U.S.C. §12213.
97. 42 U.S.C. §12209.
98. 42 U.S.C. §12210.
99. 42 U.S.C. §12208.
100. 42 U.S.C. §12211.
101. S. Rep. No. 116, 101st Cong. 1st Sess. 22 (1989).
102. Id.
103. Id.
104. 42 U.S.C. §12201.
105. *Russell v. Salve Regina College,* 649 F.Supp. 391 (D.R.I. 1986). See also *Tudyman v. United Airlines,* 608 F. Supp. 739 (C.D.Calif. 1984). A recently reported Maryland decision found that four overweight women had suffered unfair discrimination because of their perceived disability of obesity under a Maryland state statute (Valentine 1990 a,b).
106. 794 F.2d 931 (4th Cir. 1986).
107. See 136 Cong. Rec. H 4623. There is a record of genetic discrimination against individuals identified through genetic tests as being carriers of a disease-associated gene, most recently during sickle-cell screening programs during the 1970s. Under the ADA, such individuals may not be discriminated against simply because they may not be qualified for a job sometime in the future.
108. 886 F.2d 871 (7th Cir. 1989), cert. granted 58 U.S.L.W. (March 26, 1990).
109. 42 U.S.C. §12111 (10) (B) (iv) and §12181 (9) (D).
110. H.Rep.No.485, part 2, 101st Cong., 2d Sess. 68 (1990).
111. Id.
112. 136 Cong. Rec. H 2479 (daily ed. May 17, 1990)(Comments of Representative Bartlett).
113. Id. (Comments of Rep. Waxman).
114. 42 U.S.C. §12201 (c).
115. S.Rep. No. 116, 101st Cong. 1st Sess. 84 (1989).
116. Id. at 85. The Senate Report also notes that this view is in keeping with the Supreme Court's interpretation of section 504 in *Alexander v. Choate,* 469 U.S. 287 (1985).
117. 42 U.S.C. §12111(9)(B). The term "auxiliary aids and services" is also defined as including the "acquisition or modification of equipment or devices." 42 U.S.C. §12102.
118. One of the interesting ramifications of the ADA may be the spur it provides to the development of technologies to aid persons with disabilities. Congress has already recognized the importance of technological developments to persons with disabilities in the Technology-Related Assistance for Individuals with Disabilities Act, P.L. 100–407, 29 U.S.C. §§2201 et seq. and the Education for All Handicapped Children Act, 20 U.S.C. §§ 1461–62.
119. 567 F.Supp. 369 (E.D.Pa. 1983), aff'd 732 F.2d 146 (3d Cir. 1983), cert.denied, 469 U.S. 1189 (1984).
120. The question of financial support to individuals with disabilities is a complex

one. One recent commentator has argued that the ADA takes the wrong approach by attempting to mandate new social legislation without providing funding (Burkhauser 1990).

121. 20 U.S.C. §1400 et seq.

REFERENCES

Burgdorf, R., and C. Bell. 1984. Eliminating Discrimination against Physically and Mentally Handicapped Persons: A Statutory Blueprint. *Mental and Physical Disability Law Reporter*: 64–71.

Burkhauser, R. 1990. Morality on the Cheap: The Americans with Disabilities Act. *Regulation* (August).

Cohn V. 1990. Rationing Medical Care. *Washington Post* (July 31): 11.

Fox D. 1990. Financing Health Care for Persons with HIV Infection: Guidelines for State Action. *American Journal of Law and Medicine* (16): 223.

Harvard Law Review. 1987. Facial Discrimination: Extending Handicap Law to Employment Discrimination on the Basis of Physical Appearance. 100: 2035, 2044–2045.

———. 1990. Title VII—Equal Employment Opportunity—Seventh Circuit Upholds Employer's Fetal Protection Plan (*UAW v. Johnson Controls, Inc.*, 886 F.2d 871 [7th Cir. 1989]). 103: 977.

Jones, N. 1989. The Americans with Disabilities ACT (ADA): An Overview of Selected Major Legal Issues. *Congressional Research Service Report No. 89–433A* (July 25).

———. 1990. The Americans with Disabilities Act: Major Distinctions between the Senate and House Versions as Passed. *CRS General Distribution Memorandum* (June 5).

Lindsay, R. 1989/1990. Discrimination against the Disabled: The Impact of the New Federal Legislation. *Employee Relations Law Journal* 15: 333–45.

Marshall, L. 1989. Let Congress Do It: The Case of an Absolute Rule of Statutory Stare Decisis. *Michigan Law Review* 88:177.

Merritt, O. 1988. The Constitutional Balance between Health and Liberty. *Hastings Center Report* 2 (December):2–17

OuYang, E. 1990. Women with Disabilities in the Work Force: Outlook for the 1990s. *Harvard Women's Law Journal* 13:13-33.

Percy. 1989. *Disability, Civil Rights and Public Policy.* Tuscaloosa: University of Alabama Press.

Rovner, J. 1990a. Congress Clears Sweeping Bill to Guard Rights of Disabled. *Congressional Quarterly* (July 14):2227.

———. 1990b. Steny Hoyer: A Tireless Shepherd. *Congressional Quarterly* (May 26):1657.

Samborn R. 1990. Will Disabilities Law Produce Litigation? *National Law Journal* 3:12.

U.S. Congress. 1988. 100th Congress, 2nd Session. Joint Hearing on the Americans with Disabilities Act of 1988 by the Subcommittee on the Handicapped of the Senate Committee on Labor and Human Resources and the Subcommittee on Select Education of the House Committee on Education and Labor. Washington.

Valentine, D. 1990a. 4 Overweight Women Win Suit on Job Bias. *Washington Post* (August 4): D7.

———. 1990b. 367-Pound Woman Realizes Driving Ambition. *Washington Post* (August 18): B1.

West, J. 1991. *The Formation of National Disability Rights Policy in the 100th Congress.* Washington: National Institute on Disability and Rehabilitation Research.

Williams, J. 1981. Firing Women to Protect the Fetus: The Reconciliation of Fetal Protection with Employment Opportunity Goals under Title VII. *Georgetown Law Journal* 69:641.

The Demographics of Disability

Mitchell P. LaPlante

EDITOR'S NOTE

Underlying the consideration of who is covered by the Americans with Disabilities Act (ADA) is the question of who counts as having a disability. The estimate of 43 million Americans with disabilities cited in the legislation appears to be a reasonable working number, although it is likely to prove modest under the definition of disability used in the ADA. Although a definition of disability that would yield a precise count (either you're in or you're out) would appease our desire for precision and quantification, we would in the process lose an important component of this public policy: the understanding that disability itself is not always precise and perfectly quantifiable. As we massage working definitions while implementing the ADA, let us remember that the world of disability is dynamic: it can differ from one day to the next and varies according to the person and the situation.

Mitchell P. LaPlante is assistant research sociologist at the Institute for Health and Aging, School of Nursing, University of California at San Francisco. LaPlante is also director of the Disability Statistics Program funded by the National Institute on Disability and Rehabilitation Research of the Department of Education and the Office of the Assistant Secretary for Planning and Evaluation of the Department of Health and Human Services. LaPlante received his doctorate in sociology from Stanford University. His publications include Data on Disability from the National Health Interview Survey 1983–85 *and* Disability in Basic Life Activities across the Life Span, *both published by the National Institute on Disability and Rehabilitation Research.*

In this article, I will examine the various definitions of disability, how to organize existing data in order to estimate who might benefit from the Americans with Disabilities Act (ADA), and how the data might be used by those responsible for implementing the Act. After analyzing and considering the ADA definition of persons with disabilities from the perspective of researchers, disability advocates, and people with disabilities, I will compare and discuss estimates of the size of the population with disabilities according to these perspectives. I will present information on the types of impairments and geographic variation in disability rates and will then discuss how existing data can inform us about the extent of discrimination. In conclusion, I will suggest how to improve our ability to estimate the impact of the ADA and evaluate its progress.

WHO COUNTS AS A PERSON WITH A DISABILITY? CONCEPTUAL DISTINCTIONS

By any reckoning, persons with disabilities comprise the single largest minority group ever defined, eclipsing the elderly and black populations (about 26 million and 28 million, respectively). Furthermore, the population is extremely heterogeneous. The definition and estimation of its size has been based on demographic research by census and survey that shows variation both in severity of disability and in identification of persons as having a disability, whether by self-assessment or assessment by others. For convenience, let us adopt a working definition of disability as a limitation in the performance of actions and/or activities resulting from some physical and/or mental difference. Let us call such physical and mental differences *impairments.*

Seemingly little disagreement exists over the concept of impairment, in large part because the assessment of impairment often takes place at the clinical level and most persons are content to leave conceptual arbitration to health and other clinical professionals. This is not the case for the concept of disability, as persons who consider themselves to have a disability, professionals who study disability, and the general public disagree about its meaning. It is no surprise that if disability is perceived to mean different things to different people, demographic counts and estimates of the number of persons with a disability will also differ. Resolving differences in estimates is extremely important if we are to determine accurately the magnitude of disability and the discrimination associated with it.

ANALYSIS OF THE ADA DEFINITION

I will briefly review the ADA definition of a person with a disability as meeting one or more of the following criteria:

a. A physical or mental impairment that substantially limits one or more of the major life activities of such individual
b. A record of such an impairment
c. Being regarded as having such an impairment

This definition was used in section 504 of the Rehabilitation Act of 1973. Clearly, our working definition is incorporated under part a. The ADA goes further, however, by including individuals defined under parts b and c. Note that persons who consider themselves disabled but are not considered by others to be so are implicitly included in the ADA definition.

The ADA definition restricts disability to impairments that substantially limit one or more of the major life activities. The Senate and House reports accompanying the Act provide guidance as to what constitutes major life activities and substantial limitations:

A physical or mental impairment does not constitute a disability under the first prong (part [a]) of the definition for purposes of the ADA unless its severity is such that it results in a "substantial limitation in one or more major life activities." A "major life activity" means functions such as caring for one's self, performing manual tasks, walking, seeing, hearing, speaking, breathing, learning, working, and participating in community activities. (U.S. House of Representatives 1990, 51)

Because the concept of major life activity is defined by examples, the precise range of activities covered by the definition is not clearly circumscribed. A further clarification relating to "substantial limitation" is given:

> A person is considered an individual with a disability for purposes of the first prong (part (a)) of the definition when the individual's important life activities are restricted as to the conditions, manner, or duration under which they can be performed in comparison to most people. (U.S. House of Representatives 1990, 52)

Although the term "substantial limitation" is well defined, precisely who is covered by the Act remains subject to interpretation because of the manner in which life activities are defined as noted above.

In comparing the ADA definition of disability with other perspectives, I will highlight the relationship of different definitions to estimates of the prevalence of disability in the population. In particular, I will compare the estimate of 43 million persons with a disability as referenced in the ADA with estimates derived from other perspectives.

THREE PERSPECTIVES

There are several ways of looking at the definitional issue: the perspective of researchers, the perspective of advocates for persons with disabilities, and individual self-perception. I address the perspective of researchers first.

THE PERSPECTIVE OF RESEARCHERS

Disability is often equated by researchers with limitations in performing socially expected roles and activities — working, parenting, voting, and so forth — because of a health condition. This perspective has been elaborated by, among others, Saad Nagi (Nagi 1965; 1969; 1991). In the United States, disability policy often focuses on major roles and activities, particularly work and ability to live independently in the community.

At the most basic level, disability refers to limitations in performing actions or activities because of an impairment. An impairment is a loss of mental, anatomical, or physiological structure or function that may be caused by active disease, residual losses from formerly active disease, and congenital losses or injury not associated with active disease (Nagi

1991; World Health Organization 1980). Impairments refer to body structure and the functioning of its various subsystems indicated by signs and symptoms such as reduced pulmonary function, restricted range of joint motion, particular categories of impairments like paraplegia, and particular diagnoses of health conditions—for example, AIDS. It is important to note that impairments encompass not only physical and sensory losses, but chronic diseases as well. This definition of impairment is consistent with that of the ADA (U.S. House of Representatives 1990, 51).

Disability involves limitations in actions or activities that are due to such impairments. Limitations may include individual difficulty as well as incapacity in doing things. By focusing attention on incapacity, disability is confined to the "tip of the iceberg" (Verbrugge 1990). In the ADA, limitation is broadly defined as restrictions in the conditions, manner, or duration under which activities are performed compared with other persons.

Although there is not much disagreement over the terms *impairment* and *limitation,* many disagree about what constitutes disability. Largely, this debate concerns the extent to which disability refers to actions versus activities. Actions are the basic units of human performance (Homans 1974). That disability involves action distinguishes it from a purely biological and medical phenomenon (i.e., impairment), which disability clearly is not. But to what actions does disability refer? There is a seemingly infinite range of actions to consider. Physical and mental actions are the ways through which individuals interact with the physical and social world. Talking, thinking, remembering, walking, seeing are examples of actions. Activities very often are the components of occupying roles like student or teacher. Playing, working, reading a newspaper are examples of activities.

The utility of this conception is its recognition that a specific activity can be accomplished by different sets of actions. Individuals can sometimes modify how an activity is performed by changing the actions that are required. A person with paraplegia may not be limited in the activity of driving if he or she has a car fitted with hand and arm controls, for example. Certain actions can sometimes compensate for others that a person is limited in performing without changing the essential nature of the activity.

Given these observations, it follows that a specific impairment will not necessarily have the same impact on activities that different people can do. The impact depends on the nature of the activities, the human and physical capital of the individual (e.g., intelligence, education), and characteristics of the individual's environment (e.g., family and community support). Due to differences in their nature and the degree to which they are valued, there is often considerable flexibility in the extent to which various activities can be modified.

Nagi refers to problems in performing actions that are caused by impairments as *functional limitations* and problems in performing activities as *disability*. The WHO definition of disability is "any restriction or lack (resulting from an impairment) of ability to perform an activity in the manner or within the range considered normal for a human being" (World Health Organization 1980). In the WHO framework, disability refers to problems due to impairments in performing actions (functional limitations) and activity (World Health Organization 1980, 14), but problems in performing highly valued roles are defined separately as *handicap*.

In the ADA, the examples of major life activities include some actions, such as seeing or hearing, that are often referred to as functional limitations, and some activities, such as working, that are well within what is generally considered the traditional province of disability. Underlying the concept of actions and activities is a basic typology of human function that suggests a breakdown of human activity into different levels of action systems. Another possibly more useful typology may be one that ranks activities in terms of their life importance. Granger suggests that activities can be ordered by their importance in fulfilling human drives (Granger 1984). At the more basic level are survival activities such as personal care and activities to maintain the individual's household. At a higher level are activities related to economic survival and recreation. Higher-order drives include recreation and satisfaction of creative urges. Verbrugge (1990) argues that disability is defined by limitations in all valued domains of human activity or function.

It is clear that the field of disability research has not reached a consensus on the definition of disability. I do not attempt to resolve these conceptual differences here but only to illustrate the implications of these differences in definitions for who counts as having a disability.

DEMOGRAPHIC ESTIMATES OF IMPAIRMENT AND DISABILITY

Impairment. The National Health Interview Survey (NHIS) provides estimates of the numbers of persons at all ages who have impairments as well as those with limitations in activities due to a health condition or impairment, whether physical or mental. The most prevalent disease reported in the United States is chronic sinusitis, which affects about 34 million persons (Adams and Benson 1990). Some 31 million persons have arthritis, followed by 28 million with hypertension and 28 million with a deformity or orthopedic impairment. Based on a different survey, almost 50 percent of the working-aged population has one or more chronic health conditions or impairments (Ferron 1981). Some 79 percent of persons aged 60 years and older had at least one of nine common diseases (Guralnik et al. 1989).

Functional Limitation. As I have categorized the situation above, functional limitations are more fundamental measures of limitations in human action (as opposed to activity). The Survey of Income and Program Participation (SIPP) provides an estimate of 37 million persons, or 21 percent of the U.S. population aged 15 and older, with functional limitations in 1984 (U.S. Bureau of the Census 1986). These include persons who are limited in getting around inside and outside of the home, speaking, hearing, seeing, ascending stairs, lifting, and walking. This list includes four of the major life activities referenced in the ADA. The most prevalent limitation was in walking (19 million). About 13.5 million persons, or 7.5 percent of the population aged 15 and older, cannot perform one or more of these actions.

This is hardly a complete list of functional limitations. Omitted are bodily disposition limitations such as crouching, kneeling, stooping, sitting, reaching, dexterity, endurance, and tolerance, to name a few. In 1978, about half of the population aged 18 to 64 had one or more limitations in walking, using stairs, standing, sitting, stooping, crouching, kneeling, lifting weights over 10 pounds, reaching, handling, or fingering (Lando, Cutler, and Gamber 1982). About 31 percent of such persons were limited in work. Limitations in any of these actions could place an individual at risk of being unemployed. It should be noted, however, that the largest category was for limitations in lifting weights over 10 pounds (50 million) and that the prevalence would be considerably lower if that category were omitted. Nevertheless, the number of persons with functional limitations would far exceed 37 million if all the functional limitations mentioned above were considered.

Canada and Great Britain have recently conducted surveys of disability. The Canadian Health and Activity Limitation Survey employed questions on functional limitations and an open-ended activity-limitation question. It is estimated that, in 1987, around 14 percent of the entire Canadian population (including persons residing in institutions) had a functional or activity limitation (Statistics Canada 1988), while about 15 percent of adults aged 15 years or more fell into these two limitation categories. This survey used a more extensive list of functional limitations than the SIPP, but a smaller percentage of Canadians than Americans were found to be limited in function. In the British survey, a more extensive list of functional limitations than in the SIPP was also used (Martin, Meltzer, and Elliot 1988). About 14 percent of all adults (aged 16 years or more) were estimated to have a functional limitation in 1986. This percentage is also less than the prevalence of functional limitations in adult Americans as measured by the SIPP.

Thus, although I argue that a more extensive list of functional limitations would yield a higher prevalence than does the SIPP, more extensive lists do not yield a higher prevalence of functional limitations in other countries. Survey error, differences in health status, or variations in the environment may account for the observed differences. A more careful comparison and consideration of these survey results is warranted.

Activity Limitation. According to the NHIS, in 1989 there were close to 34 million persons, or 14 percent of the U.S. population, at all ages living outside of institutions who were limited in activities considered normal for their age group (Adams and Benson 1990). About 9 percent of adults aged 18 to 44 years were limited in activity and 22 percent of those aged 45 to 64 years. The NHIS estimate includes persons limited in major life activities such as work and housework, as well as 11 million persons, or 4.5 percent of the U.S. population, who are limited "in any way in any activity" other than the major activities appropriate to their age group. The nature of these limitations has not been documented, but NCHS indicates that it includes community and other social and recreational activities. It is likely that the measure does not include all major life activities as intended by the ADA.

In summary, current data indicate that there are at least 120 million persons with impairments in the United States. Of those, well over 37 million experience selected functional limitations, and at least 34 million persons experience limitations in some major life activities.

THE PERSPECTIVE OF DISABILITY-RIGHTS ADVOCATES

Some disability-rights advocates object that the activity-limitation perspective promoted by researchers does not go far enough: persons with health conditions may not consider themselves to be limited in activity. Some may be stigmatized and discriminated against just as people are who have an activity limitation. Thus, it is not necessary for a person to be limited in action; what matters is that they have an impairment to which others respond negatively. As with persons with disabilities, adverse treatment may occur directly, as in outright stigmatization or avoidance, diminished earnings, and lack of adequate health insurance, or indirectly, in terms of obstacles in the built environment (Pfeiffer 1987). In short, this perspective argues that the rights of all persons with impairments should be protected.

The definition of disability used in the ADA restricts disability only to those impairments that cause limitations in major life activities. An exception is provided in that persons with impairments who are not limited in major life activities, but are perceived by others to be limited, are included in the ADA. However, it is clear that the ADA definition does not include all persons with impairments. How exclusive the Act will be depends on how the definition of the term "major life activities" evolves as the law is implemented.

INDIVIDUAL SELF-PERCEPTION

Here I evaluate whether people consider themselves as having a disability if they are not limited in activity. A telephone survey conducted by the International Center for the Disabled (ICD) in 1986 measured disability both in terms of activity limitation and whether a person considered him- or herself to have a "disability" (self-defined) or felt they would be so considered by others. This survey defined disability in a manner similar to the definition of disability used in the ADA. Of Americans aged 16 years or more, 15 percent were found to have a disability. This estimate is close to the NHIS estimate for the same age range (Rice and LaPlante 1988). About 97 percent of the sample had some level of activity limitation. This survey also asked questions to screen in persons with learning, emotional, mental, or physical disabilities or talking, hearing, or seeing disabilities. The ICD survey attempted to cover all the bases for counting people with disabilities that the NHIS measure of activity limitation could conceivably miss. Because the two surveys yield similar estimates, it would appear that the question on activity limitation, which has been a part of the NHIS protocol since 1957, is a comprehensive measure of the concept of disability as perceived by researchers and individuals. The ICD survey excluded persons with chronic illnesses and impairments that do not limit activity unless they considered themselves, or felt they would be considered by others, as having a disability.

Many persons with activity limitation do not consider themselves as having a disability. In fact, only half actually considered themselves as having a disability in the ICD survey. Some 47 percent of individuals with limitations stated that others consider them to have a disability after they get to know them well (this percentage drops to 32 percent for first encounters, suggesting that the more that is known about a person with a disability, the more likely they will be perceived by others as having a disability).

Self-identification as a person with a disability was highest (68 percent) for persons unable to perform major activities (i.e., major roles). Only 20 percent of persons limited in other than major activities considered themselves disabled or felt that others would consider them disabled. Of persons who did not consider themselves to be disabled, 20 percent stated that others would consider them disabled. Thus, there are in fact a small number of people who do not consider themselves as having a disability who are considered by others to have a disability. In general, persons are more likely to consider themselves as having a disability or to be so considered by others the more severely limited in activity they are. Thus, arguments of some researchers and advocates to broaden the definition of disability by including less severe functional limitations and impairments appear to expand disability beyond individual perceptions.

RECONSIDERING THE SIZE OF THE POPULATION COVERED BY THE ADA

As Burgdorf (1990) has also observed, the ADA figure of 43 million persons with disabilities is derived from a table providing an estimate of the number of persons with impairments based on the 1980 NHIS (Institute of Mathematica Policy Research 1984). The number is an inappropriate measure of the ADA definition for two reasons. First, impairments are defined in the NHIS to be functional or structural musculoskeletal and neuromuscular abnormalities and other abnormalities of visual and auditory senses, speech, and intelligence (National Center for Health Statistics 1986). The number does not include impairments of internal organs and tissue due to disease, such as HIV or emphysema. If the definition of impairment as including chronic disease were taken into account, the number of persons with impairments would constitute more than half of the population. Second, the estimate is not restricted to limitation in major life activities.

It is estimated from the 1990 NHIS that 34 million persons living outside of institutions are limited in some activity because of an impairment. An additional two million persons reside in nursing homes, facilities for persons with mental retardation, and mental hospitals for persons with mental illness (LaPlante 1989). The activity-limitation measure is a more valid indicator of disability than counts of impairments because it is related to performance of activities. However, it probably undercounts persons with disabilities because, as operationalized in the NHIS, it may not cover all major life activities. Persons identified as having a major activity limitation are most likely to consider themselves as having a disability, but we must be careful not to neglect how public programs, in particular income-security programs, which focus on inability to work, may influence the identities of persons with disabilities.

In response to the question of who counts as having a disability, there is a range of answers depending on whether disability is considered to include basic human actions, like seeing, or walking, or lifting, or whether disability is restricted to more complex activities. Policy must decide at what level the problem of health-related discrimination should be addressed — impairment, basic human actions, or limitations in more complex activities. The stakes in terms of the potential numbers of persons covered are high.

TYPES OF DISABLING IMPAIRMENTS

Different impairments have varying effects on functioning. With the demographic transition from acute to chronic diseases and increasing life expectancy and aging of the population that has occurred during this century, impairments due to chronic disease have become increasingly significant as causes of disability. The emergence of chronic diseases as causes of disability has broadened the conceptualization of disability and how society responds to disability. As shown in figure 1, about 29 percent of these persons limited in activity owe their limitations to physical and sensory impairments. The majority of persons with activity limitations have chronic diseases. Fifteen conditions with the highest prevalence of causing activity limitation are shown in table 1.

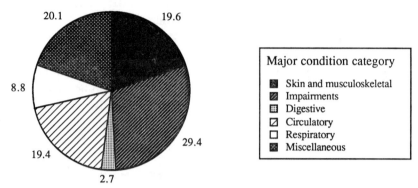

FIGURE 1. Distribution of conditions reported as main cause of activity limitation by major condition category, United States, 1983–1985 (in percent). (*Note*: Miscellaneous category includes conditions of the genitourinary, nervous, endocrine, metabolic, and blood-forming systems; cancer affecting sites other than these five categories; and mental illness.)
Source: LaPlante (1988).

People with activity limitations have on average 1.6 conditions that cause them to be limited. All conditions identified as causes of a person's limitation and those considered to be the main cause are listed separately. Arthritis is now the leading disease that causes activity limitation in the United States and is second in prevalence to orthopedic impairments (LaPlante 1988). It is important to recognize that chronic disease is often not as highly visible as physical impairment, which may present difficult decisions for disclosure of such information.

Health conditions and impairments vary in the likelihood of causing activity limitation. In table 2, conditions are ranked in terms of the percent of persons with a specific condition who are limited by the condition. Many of the most disabling conditions are childhood diseases, such as mental retardation and cerebral palsy. In general, highly disabling conditions tend to be low in prevalence, whereas those that occur frequently tend not to be highly disabling. The prevalence of disabling conditions, as shown in table 1, is thus a function of the prevalence of the condition and the chance that the condition causes disability. Arthritis is a major cause of disability, not because it often causes disability when it occurs, but because arthritis is highly prevalent in the population.

TABLE 1
Conditions with Highest Prevalence of Activity Limitation, All Ages: United States, 1983–1985

Main cause	Prevalence[a]	%	All causes	Prevalence[a]	%
All conditions[b]	32,540	100.0	All conditions[b]	52,718	100.0
Orthopedic impairments	5,220	16.0	Orthopedic impairments	6,987	13.3
Arthritis	4,000	12.3	Arthritis	6,130	11.6
Heart disease	3,736	11.5	Heart disease	5,575	10.6
Visual impairments	1,438	4.4	Hypertension	3,506	6.6
Intervertebral disk disorders	1,424	4.4	Visual impairments	2,900	5.6
Asthma	1,411	4.3	Diabetes	2,111	4.0
Nervous disorders[c]	1,289	4.0	Mental disorders[d]	1,837	3.5
Mental disorders[d]	1,284	3.9	Asthma	1,783	3.4
Hypertension	1,239	3.8	Intervertebral disk disorders	1,699	3.2
Mental retardation	947	2.9	Nervous disorders[c]	1,601	3.0
Diabetes	885	2.7	Hearing impairments	1,405	2.6
Hearing impairments	813	2.5	Mental retardation	1,047	2.0
Emphysema	649	2.0	Emphysema	994	1.9
Cerebrovascular disease	610	1.9	Cerebrovascular disease	939	1.8
Osteomyelitis/bone disorders	360	1.1	Abdominal hernia	595	1.1

Source: LaPlante (1988).
[a] In thousands.
[b] See LaPlante (1988) for content of condition categories.
[c] Nervous disorders include epilepsy, multiple sclerosis, Parkinson's disease, and other selected nervous disorders.
[d] Mental disorders include schizophrenia and other psychoses, neuroses, personality disorders, other mental illness, alcohol and drug dependency, senility, and special learning disorders (mental deficiency is not included).

TABLE 2
Conditions with Highest Risk of Disability, by Type of Disability, All Ages: United States, 1983–1986

Chronic condition	Number of conditions[a]	Percent causing activity limitation	Rank	Percent causing major activity limitation	Rank	Percent causing need for help in basic life activities	Rank
Mental retardation	1,202	84.1	1	80.0	1	19.9	9
Absence of leg(s)	289	83.3	2	73.1	2	39.0	2
Lung or bronchial cancer	200	74.8	3	63.5	3	34.5	4
Multiple sclerosis	171	70.6	4	63.3	4	40.7	1
Cerebral palsy	274	69.7	5	62.2	5	22.8	8
Blind in both eyes	396	64.5	6	58.8	6	38.1	3
Partial paralysis in extremity	578	59.6	7	47.2	7	27.5	5
Other orthopedic impairments	316	58.7	8	46.2	8	14.3[b]	12
Complete paralysis in extremity	617	52.7	9	45.5	9	26.1	6
Rheumatoid arthritis	1,223	51.0	10	39.4	12	14.9	11
Intervertebral disk disorders	3,987	48.7	11	38.2	14	5.3	—
Paralysis in other sites (complete/partial)	247	47.8	12	43.7	10	14.1[b]	13
Other heart disease/disorders[c]	4,708	46.9	13	35.1	15	13.6	14
Cancer of digestive sites	228	45.3	14	40.3	11	15.9[b]	9
Emphysema	2,074	43.6	15	29.8	—	9.6	15
Absence of arm(s) hand(s)	84	43.1	—	39.0	13	4.1[b]	—
Cerebrovascular disease	2,599	38.2	—	33.3	—	22.9	7

Source: LaPlante (1990). Data are from the National Health Interview Survey, 1983–1986, and estimates (annual averages) based on household interviews of the civilian noninstitutionalized population.
[a] In thousands.
[b] Figure has low statistical reliability or precision (relative standard error exceeds 30%).

GEOGRAPHIC VARIATION IN DISABILITY PREVALENCE

Disability prevalence varies considerably across the country and the impact of the ADA may also vary by geographic area. As shown in figure 2, rates of work disability are generally highest in the southern states. The states of Arkansas and West Virginia have the highest rates while Alaska and Hawaii have the lowest. The state populations with highest prevalence also have low educational attainment and income. Haber (Haber 1987) found that much of the variation in disability prevalence at the state level was attributable to socioeconomic differences of the states. He found that six variables explained 90 percent of the variation. These variables included income, employment and unemployment levels, low educational achievement, health, and region. Work in progress by Haber (1990) on 330 metropolitan statistical areas (MSAs) shows a similarly strong effect of socioeconomic variables on work disability prevalence.

The 1980 Census is the only source that provides direct estimates of disability by state or metropolitan area. The Census only included work disability, so measures of activity limitation due to impairment are not available. Until 1982, the NHIS provided estimates of disability for 30

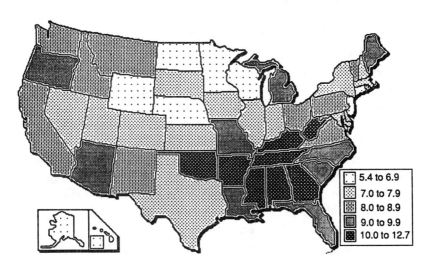

FIGURE 2.   Persons aged 16 to 64 with a work disability by state, United States, 1980 (in percent).
Source: United States Census 1980. Reprinted with permission from Kraus and Stoddard (1989).

standard metropolitan statistical areas (SMSAs). In 1980–1981, Denver had the lowest rate of activity limitation (around 6 percent) whereas San Bernadino/Riverside had the highest rate (20 percent) (National Center for Health Statistics 1984). Some of these differences can be traced to the age distribution of these populations, but nevertheless they are large and the communities must deal with them. The ADA applies to nonelderly and elderly persons with disabilities alike, and while employment expectations differ by age, expectations in many other areas of social activity are similar.

DISABILITY AND DISCRIMINATION

Another axis in the evaluation of the impact of the ADA concerns the extent of discrimination toward people with disabilities. Not everyone with a disability experiences discrimination. Disability should not be equated with discrimination; some fraction, perhaps even the majority of persons with disabilities, do not feel they are discriminated against. It may be assumed that an even smaller fraction of persons with impairments that do not limit actions or activity feel they are discriminated against. Let us explore how persons with disabilities view their situation, which offers a baseline measure for considering the potential impact of the ADA.

The ICD survey asked a wide range of questions about the perceived impact of disability on quality of life, including work, social life, daily activities, education, and perceived barriers. No other survey has sought to elicit from persons with disabilities what they think can be done to increase their participation in society.

It is clear from the ICD survey that social participation of persons with disabilities is low. They attend cultural events, shop for groceries, and eat out less frequently than persons who do not have disabilities. The survey did not elicit information about specific barriers in social activity, such as the role of attitudes.

Persons with disabilities are less satisfied with life. As we know from Census and the NHIS surveys, the ICD survey found persons with disabilities to be less educated and to have less income. The ICD survey is one of the few surveys to elicit opinions about barriers to work. People with disabilities stated that they were affected by many different kinds of barriers, reflecting the nature of their impairments as well as the variety of activities in which they are limited.

Of persons who had work experience while they had a disability, 35 percent stated that their employers had made some accommodation at work. Workplace accommodations have been shown to increase the job opportunities of persons with disabilities. Nagi (1976) found that for persons with similar levels of functional limitations, job adjustments by employers or respondents increased their chances of working. In the ICD study of working-aged persons with disabilities, however, 25 percent also said they had encountered job discrimination (ICD table 34). Thus, the world of work has both supported and hindered significant numbers of persons with disabilities. Of persons with disabilities who work less than full time or were not working, 47 percent stated that employers would not recognize that they were capable of working a full-time job (ICD table 32). Lack of available jobs in the individual's line of work or inability to find any jobs were also mentioned by 40 percent of this group. Other reasons cited for lack of full employment included poor education, lack of transportation, and lack of assistive equipment. However, most persons with activity limitation felt it was the limitation rather than employer's attitudes that prevented them from getting the type of job they desired.

Of those either unemployed and looking for work or unable to work, 77 percent felt that their limitation was more of a barrier than employers' reactions. This compares with 56 percent of those working full or part time (ICD table 37). These data reinforce the notion that many persons with severe disabilities may not be able to work in traditional jobs. If we generalize to data from the NHIS during 1983–1985 (with some trepidation because the data sources are substantially different), of the 9.9 million persons aged 18 to 69 who say that they are unable to work, we might expect that some 23 percent would be able to work if the working environment were made more hospitable. Perhaps up to 44 percent of the 7.6 million persons who are limited in the kind or amount of work they can do would be able to have better jobs if the working environment were made more hospitable. Johnson and Lambrinos (1987) found that negative attitudes toward people with impairments had a negative effect on wages even when social and educational characteristics were taken into account.

One of the most cited findings of the ICD survey is that 66 percent of persons with disabilities who are not working would like a job. Those who are not working include the unemployed, all of whom are by definition looking for work, those who are retired, keeping house, or going to school. It would be interesting to know specifically what fraction of the population who say they are unable to work want a job. Is it 23 percent or 66 percent of the 9.9 million who are now unable to work who could be employed? This is an important target population that represents a large increase in the American work force. By many counts, however, the reality is that the population of persons with disabilities has been treated as a reserve work force and is more likely to be unemployed when economic times are rough.

Outside the world of work, about 57 percent of persons limited in activity believe that their limitation has prevented them from reaching their full abilities as a person. Conversely, 43 percent feel that their limitation has not prevented them from reaching their full abilities. Of those who cannot perform their major activity, 69 percent feel they are so prevented. The more severe the limitation, the more likely that it prevents fulfillment in work or other activities.

There is no doubt that discrimination toward people with disabilities exists. However, discrimination is not homogeneous for all persons with disabilities. The evidence is that people with disabilities are not equally likely to be discriminated against. Thus, not all of the 36 million persons with activity limitations are discriminated against, and those who are do not experience discrimination to the same degree.

THOUGHTS TOWARD EVALUATION

With the passage of the Americans with Disabilities Act, a new level of demand for data on persons with disabilities has emerged. Because of changes expected to be wrought by the ADA, a variety of information must be collected to assess and monitor opportunities in employment, transportation, public accommodations and public services, and telecommunications. There is a need to assess and monitor the social status and opportunities of persons with disabilities in the United States. Many gaps can be enumerated where important information is lacking. The field of disability statistics lags well behind many areas of health and social statistics. Data collection is often episodic and incomplete. Different agencies collect information for different purposes with little integration. Some of the momentum behind the ADA could be directed profitably toward data development and coordination (Levine, Zitter, and Ingram 1990).

Ultimately, the impact of the ADA should be to increase the economic and social opportunities of persons with impairments that cause limitations in major life activities. In order to demonstrate such an impact, baseline information is needed on the current economic and social activity of such persons. The ICD survey provides some baseline information. A repeat of that survey after the ADA has had an opportunity to make a difference would provide some data to assess changes from the time of the original study. It is imperative for the evaluation of the ADA that existing data-collection efforts such as SIPP and NHIS continue to field questions on impairments, functional limitations, and limitations in employment and other activities.

Two centrally important axes in evaluating the impact of the ADA concern the definitional issue and the quantification of discrimination. To better address both axes, there is a need to develop data sources that include measures of impairment, functional limitation, activity limitation, and measures of social and economic activity, including individual perceptions of what persons with impairments can do and desire to do. A shortcoming of the ICD survey, for example, is that no data are available on the functional characteristics of the 66 percent of persons who would like a job. These data would help to clarify their employability prospects. National surveys like SIPP and NHIS need to be strengthened in terms of measuring limitations of function and in the broader spectrum of life actvities.

Assessing which individuals will benefit from the ADA is not easily done. National data provide estimates of persons with disabilities and/ or persons prevented from performing certain activities because of health problems. These data are individual attributions and do not provide information about whether the reason a person says he or she has a disability or is prevented from carrying out certain activities is due to barriers that could be overcome. In that sense, the ADA is a social experiment that could provide such data. To the extent that the ADA is successful in removing barriers, persons with specific impairments and equal levels of functioning should become more active socially and economically.

Another issue concerns the diversity of the population of persons with disabilities. Assessment is more straightforward for mobility problems and physical impairments than for chronic illness. For example, it is straightforward to estimate who benefits from refitting doors in offices to accommodate a wheelchair: the roughly 1 million people who use a wheelchair. Other examples can be provided of the numbers of persons benefitting from removal of specific architectural barriers (LaPlante and Grant 1988). However, to assess the employability of persons with multiple sclerosis, AIDS, or emphysema requires an understanding of the nature of the impairment and its relationship to functional losses, which may also be dynamic.

There is also a clear requirement for direct estimates of disability prevalence by state and local areas that can be used to determine local needs.

SUMMARY AND CONCLUSIONS

In this article, I have attempted to clarify some of the disparate estimates and ways of measuring disability that have been used in different surveys. The definitional issue has implications for the size of the population that will be covered by the ADA. I have reviewed several perspectives, including that of researchers, disability advocates, and individual self-perceptions, which need to be considered in understanding the meaning of disability. Disability involves limitations in actions and activities because of mental and physical impairments. Comparison of these different perspectives reveals that the differences lie in the range of activities that are considered. At least 36 million persons, over 14 percent of the U.S. population, are limited in selected activities. Depending on what are considered to be major life activities, the population covered by the ADA could vastly exceed that figure.

Little information is available about the extent to which persons with disabilities, however defined, are affected by discrimination and unequal treatment. Limited data are available from one survey conducted by the International Center for the Disabled, which indicate that as many as 66 percent of persons with activity limitations who are not working would like a job. On the other hand, many persons with activity limitations indicate that their limitations are an important cause of their unemployment. About a quarter of persons with activity limitations due to impairments have experienced discrimination in some form.

The impact of the ADA will likely vary by impairment. Because the prevalence of chronic diseases is far greater than the prevalence of physical and sensory impairments, chronic diseases are more frequently the cause of disability. The risk of disability is highest for impairments with low prevalence. Because states and local areas differ in the prevalence of disability, the impact of the ADA will also be likely to vary by geographic area. For some states, the rate of work disability is more than twice the rate of other states. Yet, research indicates that much of the variation is due to socioeconomic characteristics of areas. This reflects, at the macroeconomic level, that persons with disabilities are more likely to be poor and less educated than persons without disabilities.

Because of differences in understanding what disability is and insufficient knowledge about the extent of the problem of discrimination toward persons with disabilities, assessment of the potential impact of the ADA is challenging. Improvements in data are necessary to better understand the abilities of persons with activity limitations to participate in the work environment and in social and recreational opportunities in the larger physical and social environment. We can hope that the momentum behind the ADA can be directed to provide a data-collection system for an ongoing assessment of the effectiveness of the ADA in increasing the participation of persons with disabilities in society.

REFERENCES

Adams, P. F., and V. Benson. 1990. Current Estimates from the National Health Interview Survey, 1989. *Vital and Health Statistics* 10(176).

Burgdorf, R. L. 1990. Changes in the Workforce, Changes in the Workplace: Employment Policy and People with Disabilities. Washington: District of Columbia School of Law. (Unpublished paper.)

Ferron, D. T. 1981. *Disability Survey 72: Disabled with Nondisabled Adults*, research report no. 56. Washington: Social Security Administration, U.S. Department of Health and Human Services.

Granger, C. V. 1984. A Conceptual Model for Functional Assessment. In *Functional Assessment in Rehabilitation Medicine*, eds. C. V. Granger and G. E. Gresham, 14–25. Baltimore: Williams & Wilkins.

Guralnik, J. M., A. Z. LaCroix, D. F. Everett, and M. G. Kovar. 1989. Aging in the Eighties: The Prevalence of Comorbidity and Its Association with Disability. *Advance Data from Vital and Health Statistics* (170).

Haber, L. D. 1987. *State Disability Prevalence Rates: An Ecological Analysis of Social and Economic Influences on Disability*. Washington: National Institute on Disability and Rehabilitation Research.

_____. 1990. Disability Prevalence and Labor Market Opportunity: An Analysis of Metropolitan Area Environmental Effects. (Unpublished paper.)

Homans, G. C. 1974. *Social Behavior: Its Elementary Forms.* San Francisco: Harcourt Brace Jovanovich. Institute of Mathematica Policy Research. 1984. *Digest of Data on Persons with Disabilities.* Washington: National Institute of Disability and Rehabilitation Research.

Johnson, W. G., and J. Lambrinos. 1987. The Effect of Prejudice on the Wages of Disabled Workers. *Policy Studies Journal* 15(3):571–90.

Kraus, L. E., and S. Stoddard. 1989. *Chartbook on Disability in the United States.* Washington: National Institute on Disability and Rehabilitation Research.

Lando, M. E., R. R. Cutler, and E. Gamber 1982. *1978 Survey of Disability and Work,* SSA pub. no. 13-11745. Washington: Social Security Administration, U.S. Department of Health and Human Services.

LaPlante, M. P. 1988. *Data on Disability from the National Health Interview Survey, 1983–85.* Washington: National Institute on Disability and Rehabilitation Research.

_____. 1989. *Disability in Basic Life Activities across the Life Span.* Disability statistics report no. 1. Washington: National Institute for Disability and Rehabilitation Research.

_____. 1990. *Disability Risks of Chronic Illnesses and Impairments.* Disability statistics report no. 2. Washington: National Institute on Disability and Rehabilitation Research.

LaPlante, M. P., and L. Grant. 1988. *Persons Who Need or Benefit from Accessibility Features in the Built Environment.* Report prepared for the Architectural and Transportation Barriers Compliance Board.

Levine, D. B., M. Zitter, and L. Ingram. Eds. 1990. *Disability Statistics: An Assessment.* Washington: National Academy Press.

Martin, J., H. Meltzer, and D. Elliot. 1988. *The Prevalence of Disability among Adults,* OPCS Surveys of Disability in Great Britain, report no. 1. London: Office of Population and Surveys, Social Survey Division, Great Britain.

Nagi, S. Z. 1965. Some Conceptual Issues in Disability and Rehabilitation. In *Sociology and Rehabilitation,* ed. M. B. Sussman. Washington: American Sociological Association.

_____. 1969. Congruency in Medical and Self-Assessment of Disability. *Industrial Medicine* 38(3):27–83.

_____. 1976. An Epidemiology of Disability among Adults in the United States. *Milbank Quarterly* (54):439–67.

_____. 1991. Disability Concepts Revisited: Implications to Prevention. In *Disability in America: Toward A National Agenda for Prevention,* eds. A. M. Pope and A. R. Tarlov, Appendix A. Washington: National Academy Press.

National Center for Health Statistics. 1984. Health Characteristics by Geographic Region, Large Metropolitan Areas, and Other Places of Residence: United States, 1980–81. *Vital and Health Statistics* 10(146).

_____. 1986. *Public Use Data Tape Documentation, Part 3: Medical Coding Manual and Short Index, National Health Interview Survey, 1985.* Hyattsville, Md: U.S. Department of Health and Human Services, Public Health Service.

Pfeiffer, D. 1987. Policy, Percentages, and Disability. Boston, Mass: Suffolk University. (Unpublished paper.)

Rice, D. P., and M. P. LaPlante. 1988. Chronic Illness, Disability, and Increasing Longevity. In *The Economics and Ethics of Long-Term Care and Disability*, eds. S. Sullivan and M. E. Lewin, 9-55. Washington: American Enterprise Institute.

Statistics Canada. 1988. Addendum to the Daily: Disabled Canadians. *Statistics Canada Daily* (May 31): 1–12.

U.S. Bureau of the Census. 1986. Disability, Functional Limitation, and Health Insurance Coverage: 1984/85. *Current Population Reports*, series P-70, no. 8. Washington.

U.S. House of Representatives. 1990. *Americans with Disabilities Act of 1990: Report Together with Minority Views*, report no. 101–485, part 2. Washington.

Verbrugge, L. M. 1990. The Iceberg of Disability. In *The Legacy of Longevity*, ed. S. M. Stahl, 55–75. Newbury Park, Calif.: Sage.

World Health Organization. 1980. *International Classification of Impairments, Disabilities, and Handicaps*. Geneva.

II. Employment: The Heart of Independence

I also want to say a special word to our friends in the business community. You have in your hands the key to the success of this Act. For you can unlock a splendid resource of untapped human potential that, when freed, will enrich us all.

President George Bush at the signing ceremony for the ADA on July 26, 1989

Employment Protections

Chai R. Feldblum

EDITOR'S NOTE

The orientation of many disability policies requires people with disabilities to spend their energy proving that they cannot work (or learn, or care for themselves . . .) so they can qualify for the support of public dollars. One of the great contributions of the Americans with Disabilities Act (ADA) to disability policy is its mandated change of focus — from asking people what they cannot do to asking them what they can do, and then providing them with the necessary supports to use their skills and proceed.

At the heart of this disability-policy orientation is the equal-employment-opportunity mandate in ADA. The employment provisions are remarkably precise and at the same time flexible, reflecting an understanding of the wide range and complex nature of disabilities and the necessity of individualization. Building on the 17-year history of section 504 of the Rehabilitation Act, the ADA equal-employment-opportunity mandate is not so much new as it is refined and revisited. Chai R. Feldblum examines the requirements of the law, paying particular attention to how employers can use the flexibility of the law to maximize opportunities for employees with disabilities and business effectiveness.

Feldblum is legislative counsel with the American Civil Liberties Union. She helped draft the original ADA introduced in the 101st Congress and was principal legal advisor to the disability and civil-

rights communities during the two-year legislative consideration of the
ADA. Feldblum clerked for Justice Harry A. Blackmun during the
Supreme Court term in which the landmark School Board of Nassau
County v. Arline *case was decided and served as director of legislative*
research at AIDS Action Council. She was a participant in shaping two
pieces of legislation that served as building blocks for the ADA: the
Civil Rights Restoration Act and the Fair Housing Amendments Act.

A graduate of Harvard Law School, Feldblum has spoken and written
widely on disability issues. Her articles include "The Americans with
Disabilities Act: Definition of Disability," published in the American
Bar Association Labor Lawyer, *and "Workplace Issues: HIV and Dis-*
crimination," which appeared in AIDS Policy for the 1990's. *She is*
working with Robert L. Burgdorf Jr. on a legal treatise, Disability Discrimination Law, *to be published by the Bureau of National Affairs in*
1992.

Having a stable and fulfilling job is a basic component of the
American dream. Every one of us would like to have a job that
is enjoyable and stimulating and that provides us with sufficient income to meet our needs. People with disabilities are no different. People with disabilities would like to obtain jobs that meet their
needs and are suited to their talents, and, like everyone else, they
would like to secure promotions and advance in their careers.

The difficulty faced by many people with disabilities, however, is
that they are often not given the opportunity to demonstrate their
talents and abilities to perform certain jobs. Instead, myths and stereotypes regarding the person's inability to perform a job, or simply fears
about hiring a person with a disability for a particular job, preclude the
individual from receiving offers of employment or promotion.

Title I of the Americans with Disabilities Act (ADA) addresses the
employment of people with disabilities. It establishes a general prohibition against discrimination in employment on the basis of disability
and sets forth, in some detail, what constitutes "discrimination" in the
context of employment.

The employment title of the ADA can be best understood as deriv-
ing from two distinct laws. The substantive provisions of the title stem
from the Rehabilitation Act of 1973, which is examined by Nancy Jones
in her article in this volume. The Rehabilitation Act prohibits discrimination, including employment discrimination, on the basis of handicap
by the federal government, federal contractors, and entities that receive

federal funds.[1] Thus, decisions such as who is a person with a "disability," what constitutes "discrimination" on the basis of disability, or what is required as a "reasonable accommodation," are derived from similar substantive requirements established under the Rehabilitation Act. The goal of the drafters of the ADA was to draw as much as possible from 15 years of experience under the Rehabilitation Act in order to create a workable and understandable law.

The procedural requirements of the ADA's employment title, by contrast, are drawn from title VII of the Civil Rights Act of 1964. Title VII prohibits discrimination on the basis of race, sex, religion, or national origin by employers with 15 or more employees.[2] One of the purposes of the ADA was to establish long-awaited parity in federal civil-rights laws between people with disabilities and other minorities and women. Thus, the procedural requirements of the ADA—which employers are covered under the ADA and which remedies are provided by the law—are drawn from and are essentially equal to those in title VII.

PERSON WITH A DISABILITY[3]

A "person with a disability" under the ADA, as derived substantially from the Rehabilitation Act, is defined as someone who

1. Has a physical or mental impairment that substantially limits that person in one or more major life activities, or
2. Has a record of such a physical or mental impairment, or
3. Is regarded as having such a physical or mental impairment.[4]

This three-prong definition of disability in the ADA dates back to 1974. In 1973, when Congress passed the Rehabilitation Act and included within it the affirmative action and anti-discrimination protections of sections 501, 503, and 504, a person with a handicap was defined as someone whose disability limited his or her employability and who could therefore be expected to benefit from vocational rehabilitation.[5]

One year later, after reviewing attempts by the Department of Health, Education and Welfare (DHEW) to devise regulations to implement the Act, Congress concluded that this definition—although appropriate for the vocational rehabilitation sections of the Rehabilitation Act—was too narrow to deal with the range of discriminatory practices in housing, education, and health care programs covered by section 504. Congress, therefore, amended the definition in 1974, broadening it to include the three prongs that have remained the basis of the section 504 definition ever since.[6]

The first prong of the definition of a person with a disability is someone who has a "physical or mental impairment that substantially limits one or more of the major life activities of such individual."[7] The various committee reports to the ADA, as well as the regulations issued by DHEW in 1977 to implement section 504 of the Rehabilitation Act, explain that a "physical or mental impairment" is

> any physiological disorder or condition, cosmetic disfigurement, or anatomical loss affecting one or more of the following body systems: neurological; musculoskeletal; special sense organs; respiratory, including speech organs; cardiovascular; reproductive, digestive; genito-urinary; hemic and lymphatic; skin; and endocrine; [or] any mental or psychological disorder . . .[8]

Neither the regulations issued to implement the Rehabilitation Act nor the ADA legislative reports attempt to set forth a list of specific diseases or conditions that would make up physical or mental impairments. The reason is straightforward: it would be impossible to ensure the comprehensiveness of such a list given the variety of possible physical and mental impairments that may exist.[9] The ADA legislative reports, however, give examples of some of the diseases and conditions that would be covered:

> orthopedic, visual, speech, and hearing impairments, cerebral palsy, epilepsy, muscular dystrophy, multiple sclerosis, infection with the Human Immunodeficiency Virus, cancer, heart disease, diabetes, mental retardation, emotional illness, specific learning disabilities, drug addiction and alcoholism.[10]

An impairment, therefore, is some physiological or mental disorder. It does not include simple physical characteristics, such as eye or hair color.

Having a physical or mental impairment, however, is only the first part of the definition. The impairment must also be one that "substantially limits" the person in a "major life activity." The legislative reports to the ADA set forth an illustrative list of major life activities: "caring for one's self, performing manual tasks, walking, seeing, hearing, speaking, breathing, learning, and working."[11]

Most serious medical conditions do have a substantial impact on basic life activities. For example, someone with emphysema will have substantial difficulty in breathing; someone who is a paraplegic will have substantial difficulty in walking; and someone with dyslexia will have substantial difficulty in learning.[12]

The term "people with disabilities," therefore, is not limited to what has sometimes been termed "traditional disabilities." The ADA covers a wide range of individuals—from people who use wheelchairs, to people who have vision or hearing impairments, to people with epilepsy or cerebral palsy or HIV disease or lung cancer or manic depression.

The second prong of the definition of disability covers a person with a "record" of an impairment. This prong is designed to extend protection to an individual who had a physical or mental impairment at some point in the past, who has recovered from that impairment, but who nevertheless experiences discrimination based on the *record* of having the impairment. Examples of such discrimination would include individuals who have recovered from cancer or from a mental illness, but who experience discrimination because of the stigma or the fear associated with such disabilities.[13]

The third prong of the definition covers people who are "regarded as" having an impairment. This prong is designed to extend protection to a person who may not have any impairment at all, or to a person who has some relatively minor impairment, but who is regarded by others as having a physical or mental disorder serious enough to limit him or her in some major life activity. For example, a person may have a significant physiological cosmetic disorder, such as a large birthmark on a cheek, that does not, in fact, substantially limit the person in any way. An employer, however, may view that disorder as substantially limiting that person's ability to work and to interact with others, and may discriminate against the person on that basis. Similarly, a person may not have any disorder at all, but may be erroneously perceived by an employer as having a mental or physical illness and may be discriminated against on that basis.[14]

As can be seen, the definition of disability under the ADA—as under the Rehabilitation Act—is a broad and comprehensive one.

However, it is important to keep in mind that it is the responsibility of the person alleging discrimination to prove that he or she is covered under the law. In other words, the individual who alleges that discrimination has occurred must prove either that he or she has a physical or mental impairment that substantially limits him or her in a major life activity, or that he or she has a record of such an impairment, or that he or she was regarded by the person who engaged in the discriminatory act as having such an impairment. This burden of proof always rests with the individual who alleges the discrimination.[15]

Specific categories of people with various disabilities received special attention during the passage of the ADA—either to emphasize their inclusion or to establish their exclusion:

PEOPLE WITH AIDS

People with HIV disease (which includes individuals who have any form of Human Immunodeficiency Virus [HIV] illness, from asymptomatic HIV infection to full-blown AIDS) are included within the first prong of the definition of "disability."[16] People with HIV disease have been covered under the Rehabilitation Act for years.[17] In order to receive protection under the law, such individuals, just like people with any other disability, may not pose a "direct threat" to the health or safety of others.[18]

PEOPLE WITH ALCOHOL DEPENDENCY

A person who is dependent on alcohol is covered under the ADA as a person with a disability.[19] Such individuals are covered under title V of the Rehabilitation Act as well.[20] By contrast, a person who simply uses alcohol on a casual basis, and is not dependent on alcohol, would not be considered to have an "impairment" and therefore would not be covered under the first prong of the definition of disability.[21]

PEOPLE WHO ILLEGALLY USE DRUGS

Individuals who are current illegal users of drugs are not covered under the ADA.[22] Although such individuals had previously been covered under the Rehabilitation Act, the ADA amends that Act as well to provide for the same exclusion of current illegal drug users.[23] Under this exclusion, an employer may take adverse actions against an individual who currently illegally uses drugs, because of the use of such drugs, regardless of whether the drug use has any adverse impact on the person's job performance.

Although individuals who currently illegally use drugs are not protected under the ADA, individuals who have overcome drug problems are protected. For example, individuals who have successfully completed (or are successfully enrolled in) a supervised rehabilitation program and are no longer using drugs, or individuals who have been successfully rehabilitated through other means and are no longer using drugs, are considered as individuals with a "record" of a disability and are protected from discrimination. In addition, individuals who are erroneously perceived as being illegal drug users are covered as well.[24]

PEOPLE WITH SELECTED MENTAL AND SEXUAL DISORDERS

Most individuals with mental impairments are covered under the ADA. Such individuals have been covered under the Rehabilitation Act for years.[25] There is a long history of discrimination against people with mental disabilities in this country, often based on ungrounded myths and fears regarding such disabilities. Of course, such individuals, just like people with any other disability, must be qualified for the jobs they desire in order to seek redress for discrimination under the ADA.[26]

Despite the fact that the qualification requirements of the ADA protect employers against individuals with mental disabilities who would not be able to perform a job, or would pose a threat to others, the ADA also removes, as a blanket matter, a select group of mental and sexual disorders from the list of impairments covered under the Act. The excluded impairments are: pedophilia, exhibitionism, voyeurism, gender identity disorders that are not the result of physical impairments, other sexual behavior disorders, compulsive gambling, kleptomania, pyromania, and psychoactive substance use disorders resulting from the current illegal use of drugs. Transvestism and transsexualism, which are officially defined as mental impairments by the American Psychiatric Association, are also listed among the exclusions.[27]

PEOPLE WHO ARE GAY

A person who is gay or bisexual is not considered, under current medical or psychological diagnoses, to have either a mental or physical impairment.[28] Thus, such individuals were never covered, solely by

virtue of their sexual orientation, under the Rehabilitation Act, and are
not covered under the ADA. Section 511(a) of the ADA explicitly
states that "homosexuality and bisexuality are not impairments and as
such are not disabilities under this Act."

PEOPLE WHO ASSOCIATE WITH PEOPLE WITH DISABILITIES

The ADA also extends antidiscrimination protection to a class of individuals not covered under the Rehabilitation Act. The ADA prohibits
an employer from discriminating against a qualified applicant or
employee who does not have a disability because the employer knows
that the applicant or employee associates with a person who has a
disability.[29] For example, an employer could not refuse to hire an applicant simply because the applicant's wife or husband uses a wheelchair.
Similarly, an employer could not fire an employee simply because the
employee lives with a person who has AIDS.[30]

The ADA does not limit the forms in which the association with the
person with a disability must take place. Thus, individuals who associate with persons with disabilities through a range of activities—being
their friend, spouse, domestic partner, relative, business associate,
advocate or caregiver—are covered under the association provision. The
individual alleging discrimination, however, bears the burden of proving that the discrimination occurred because of his or her known association with a person with a known disability.[31]

QUALIFIED PERSON WITH A DISABILITY

The fact that an individual has a disability establishes the initial coverage for that person under the ADA. The law also requires, however,
that the person be a "qualified person with a disability."[32] The requirement that a person with a disability be "qualified" was placed in the
ADA, as Congress had previously placed it in the Rehabilitation Act,
essentially to address (often misplaced) fears that the laws' antidiscrimination provisions would mandate the hiring or retention of people
with disabilities, even when those disabilities made the individuals
unable to perform particular jobs.

A qualified person with a disability is defined, in the ADA, as a
person who, "with or without reasonable accommodation, can perform

the essential functions of the employment position that such individual holds or desires."[33]

This requirement consists of two basic components. The first component deals with "essential functions." It is not the purpose of the ADA, just as it is not the purpose of other civil-rights laws, to force employers to hire individuals who cannot actually perform the particular jobs under consideration. Often, however, employers may list among a job's functions certain activities that are not necessary for the performance of the job. For example, an employer might require—perhaps for ease of identification—that all employees have a driver's license, even though driving is not a basic requirement for the job. Or an employer may require that a clerical person be able to answer the telephone, even though the basic job is one of filing.

Many times these additional nonbasic job requirements have no impact on people with disabilities. However, sometimes a person with a disability is perfectly qualified to perform all the essential functions of a job, but is unable to perform one marginal or nonbasic job requirement. If the person with a disability is denied the job because of inability to perform that requirement, the person's employment opportunities have been unjustifiably limited because of his or her disability.

To address this concern, the ADA establishes that employers may refuse to hire or to retain individuals who cannot perform the "essential functions" of a job. "Essential functions" mean basically what they sound like: functions that are not marginal or tangential to the job in question. Thus, an employer is allowed to refuse to hire or retain a person with a disability who, because of the disability, truly cannot perform an essential function of the job. It is not legitimate, however, for the employer to refuse to hire or to retain a person with a disability who cannot perform some job task that is marginal to the job."[34]

The second component of a "qualified person with a disability" is that of reasonable accommodation. A person with a disability is often qualified to perform a job—if some adjustment is first made in the structure, schedule, physical layout, or equipment. For example, a person who uses a wheelchair may need a table adjusted for height or may need a ramp built to allow access. Persons with varying degrees of hearing impairments may need a telephone amplifier or an interpreter. Someone with a chronic physical condition may need some time off each week for medical treatments. If these adjustments or modifications—which are called "reasonable accommodations"—are made, a person with a disability might then be qualified for the particular job he or she seeks.[35]

As described in greater detail below, the ADA requires that employers provide such reasonable accommodations to their applicants and employees. Moreover, in assessing whether an individual is qualified to perform the essential functions of a job, an employer must first take into account whether there are any reasonable accommodations that will enable the individual to perform those functions.[36]

FORMS OF DISCRIMINATION PROHIBITED

Like most other civil-rights laws, the ADA sets forth a general prohibition against employment discrimination. Unlike most other civil-rights laws, however, the ADA also sets forth specific examples of what constitutes such discrimination.

As a general rule, the ADA provides that no "covered entity"[37] shall discriminate against a qualified person with a disability because of the disability of such individual in a range of employment decisions: in job-application procedures, the hiring, advancement, or discharge of employees, employee compensation, job training, and other terms and conditions of employment.[38] Essentially, every type of employment decision is covered. The basic requirement is that a qualified person with a disability may not be discriminated against — simply on the basis of his or her disability — in terms of hiring, firing, promotions, recruitment, conditions of the employment position, or any other aspect of employment.

The ADA then lists specific examples of what discrimination "on the basis of disability" includes. First, an employer may not limit, segregate, or classify applicants or employees on the basis of disability in a way that adversely affects the opportunities or status of such individuals.[39] This is a relatively straightforward application of the antidiscrimination provision. An employer could not, for example, have all employees with disabilities work in a separate, segregated section of the workplace, or pay employees with disabilities on a lower pay scale for work equivalent to that performed by other employees.

Second, an employer may not enter into a contractual arrangement that has the effect of subjecting the employer's employees to discrimination.[40] In other words, an employer may not do indirectly, through a contract or a license, what he or she may not do directly under the ADA. Although this is a logical requirement, employers will need to reflect on its ramifications. For example, this provision means that if an employer contracts with another entity to provide training for employees of the business, the training must be given in a place and manner that is accessible to any employees with disabilities. Similarly, if the employer holds an annual retreat or convention for its employees, the employer must pick a site that is accessible to its employees with disabilities.[41] These would be the types of reasonable accommodation requirements the employer would have if it were acting directly. Just as there is an "undue hardship" limitation on reasonable accommodations that must be offered by the employer, however, there is also an identical "undue hardship" limitation that applies when the employer contracts with other entities.[42]

Third, an employer must provide reasonable accommodations to the known physical or mental limitations of a person with a disability who is otherwise qualified to perform a particular job, unless providing such accommodations would impose an "undue hardship" on the employer. In addition, an employer may not refuse to hire a person with a disability simply because the person will require a reasonable accommodation.[43] This area is discussed in greater detail below.

Fourth, an employer may not have a qualification standard, employment test, or other job-selection criterion that "screens out" people with disabilities.[44] For example, an employer may not have, as a qualification standard for a job, that applicants may not depend on physical devices in order to walk. Such qualification standards would directly "screen out" people with certain disabilities — for example, people who use wheelchairs or crutches.

An employer may also not have a qualification standard, employment test, or other job-selection criterion that "tends to screen out" people with disabilities.[45] For example, an employer may not have, as a qualification standard for a job, that applicants possess a driver's license. Although this standard appears neutral on its face, because it does not refer directly to any disability, in application this standard will "tend to screen out" people with disabilities — for example, some people with epilepsy and some people who use wheelchairs who cannot drive.

There is also a necessary and logical limitation to this prohibition. An employer *may* have a qualification standard, test, or criterion that directly screens out, or that tends to screen out, people with disabilities, if that standard or criterion is in fact *necessary* for the individual to meet in order to perform a particular job. In the words of the ADA, the standard or criterion must be "job-related and consistent with business necessity."[46]

Fifth, there are a series of requirements regarding medical exams and inquiries, as well as requirements regarding general testing, that fall within the antidiscrimination prohibition. These are discussed separately in a later section, "Medical Exams and Inquiries."

In setting forth these specified forms of prohibited action, the ADA is different from most other civil-rights laws. The majority of civil-rights laws simply set forth a general prohibition on discrimination. The regulations issued to implement such laws, and the subsequent cases brought under such laws, then fill out the types of action that are considered to be "discrimination."[47]

The detailed form of the ADA is primarily the result of three factors. First, it took significant time and effort for the first section 504 regulations to be issued by the relevant federal agencies. Supporters of the ADA were therefore interested in having the ADA be as explicit and detailed as possible so as to ensure that implementation of the ADA would not be excessively dependent on the issuance and content of regulations.

Second, existing section 504 regulations and case law acted as a guiding principle for the extensive negotiations that took place on the ADA. As a result, many detailed section 504 regulations were transported, almost verbatim, into the ADA.[48]

Third, and perhaps of key importance, there are aspects of discrimination against people with disabilities that often are not readily apparent to many individuals. By having the ADA address these issues explicitly in the statute, Congress ensured that it would review those areas directly—and would provide direction and/or limitations in these areas if it chose to do so. The following three sections, which explain the reasonable accommodation requirements, the prohibitions on medical exams and inquiries, and the available defenses for employers, form a good example of areas that benefited from explication in the statute and in the accompanying legislative reports.

REASONABLE ACCOMMODATION

Reasonable accommodation is a key aspect of antidiscrimination protection for people with disabilities. As explained above, a person with a disability may often be perfectly qualified to perform a job—if some modification or adjustment is first made in the job structure or environment. The ADA mandates that employers provide these modifications and adjustments, called "reasonable accommodations," to applicants and employees with disabilities.[49]

The ADA lists a number of modifications that fall within the framework of reasonable accommodations:

1. Modifying the physical layout of a job facility so as to make it accessible to individuals who use wheelchairs or who have other impairments that make access difficult
2. Restructuring a job to enable the person with a disability to perform the essential functions of the job[50]
3. Establishing a part-time or modified work schedule (for example, to accommodate people with disabilities who have treatment needs or fatigue problems)[51]
4. Reassigning a person with a disability to a vacant job[52]
5. Acquiring or modifying equipment or devices (such as buying a hearing telephone amplifier for a person with a hearing impairment)
6. Adjusting or modifying exams, training materials, or policies (for example, giving an application examination orally to a person with dyslexia or modifying a policy against dogs in the workplace for a person with a service dog)
7. Providing qualified readers or interpreters for people with vision or hearing impairments[53]

These are simply examples of types of accommodations that could be required. The basic characteristic of a reasonable accommodation is that it is designed to address the unique needs of a person with a particular disability. Thus, an accommodation for one person might be one that falls within one of the above categories, or it might be a different type of accommodation personally identified by the person with a disability or by the employer. The underlying goal is to identify aspects of the disability that make it difficult or impossible for the person with a disability to perform certain aspects of a job, and then to determine if there are any modifications or adjustments to the job environment or structure that will enable the person to perform the job.

As can be imagined, some accommodations are inexpensive and easy to institute, whereas others are costly and difficult to implement. In light of that fact, the ADA sets a limitation on the employer's obligation to provide a reasonable accommodation. Under the law, an employer need not provide an accommodation if doing so would impose an "undue hardship" on the employer. An accommodation is considered to rise to the level of an undue hardship if providing it would result in a "significant difficulty or expense" for the employer.[54]

Whether an accommodation is considered to be a significant difficulty or expense for the employer depends on a series of factors about the particular business. The ADA sets forth the following factors to be weighed:

1. What is the nature of the needed accommodation and how much will it cost?
2. What are the financial resources available to the employer, how big is the employer (i.e., how many individuals are employed), and what effect will the accommodation have on the employer's expenses, resources, or other areas?
3. What type of operation does the employer run, and what impact will the accommodation have on it and on the work force?[55]

The ADA's approach to undue hardship, therefore, is to require an assessment of the nature and cost of the accommodation in light of the employer's financial resources, workplace, and operations. As the legislative reports to the ADA emphasize, the undue-hardship standard is thus a *relative* standard. An accommodation that would constitute an undue hardship for one employer would not necessarily be so for another.[56]

This flexible approach in determining undue hardship is well illustrated in the section 504 case of *Nelson v. Thornburgh*.[57] In that case, a court ordered the Pennsylvania Department of Public Welfare to provide several accommodations, including the use of readers, computers, and braille forms, for a number of workers who were blind. Although the costs of the accommodations were substantial, the court concluded that they did not rise to the level of an undue hardship because they were only a small fraction of the state agency's personnel budget.[58]

The fact that the ADA's undue-hardship standard is a flexible one caused some concern to representatives of the business community during passage of the ADA. Understandably, businesses want certainty; it is hard for an employer to imagine providing reasonable accommodations if the employer can never be sure whether a particular accommodation would ultimately be required under the law or not.

Although this desire for certainty is understandable, the various alternatives to the flexible approach would in all likelihood restrict the opportunities available to people with disabilities and would restrict needed flexibility for employers as well. For example, a requirement that employers spend up to 10 percent of their gross income on reasonable accommodations would not take into account the employer's other expenses or whether those expenses have been particularly heavy in a specific year. A requirement that employers spend up to 10 percent of their net income on accommodations would allow employers to allocate all of their income to other expenses (including discretionary expenses) before any resources would be considered for accommodations. An approach that tied the accommodation limit to a certain percentage of an employee's salary would mean that a wide range of accommodations, which would be perfectly reasonable to expect large employers to provide, would not be required simply because the person with a disability was in a low-paying job.

In the final analysis, therefore, Congress chose to continue the flexible undue-hardship approach that had been used successfully under the Rehabilitation Act for over 15 years. This approach ensures that the different resources and needs of small companies, compared with large ones, are appropriately taken into account in each individual case, while still providing the essential protection of reasonable accommodations for people with disabilities.

Although the undue-hardship standard is a flexible one, there is a specific process for determining whether a reasonable accommodation is necessary and what is the best reasonable accommodation to adopt. This process is spelled out in the legislative reports to the ADA and may provide useful guidance to employers.

First, an employer's duty to provide a reasonable accommodation is triggered by a request from an employee or applicant.[59] Employers do not have to speculate about what particular disability a person might have or about what particular accommodation might be useful for that person. Rather, if a person with a disability needs some accommodation in order to perform the essential functions of a job, it is the responsibil-

ity of that person to identify for the employer the general nature of his
or her disability and the type of accommodation needed.

Second, the employer—through consultation with the individual
with a disability—should identify what the barriers are to the individual's performance of particular job functions. There are two components to this analysis. The employer and the individual should first
identify the abilities and limitations of the individual and should then
identify those job tasks or work-environment factors that limit the
individual's effectiveness or performance in light of the disability.[60]

Third, the employer should identify possible accommodations that
will address the problematic work-environment factors or job tasks and
will allow the individual to perform the job. The first source of information should be the person with the disability. As the legislative
reports to the ADA recognize, people with disabilities often have significant life experience in ways to accomplish tasks differently and may
have suggestions for accommodations that are substantially cheaper or
easier to implement than an employer might devise independently.[61]
Other resources to consult include state vocational rehabilitation agencies, the Job Accommodation Network of the President's Committee on
the Employment of People with Disabilities, private rehabilitation centers, private disability organizations, and employer networks.[62] See
Appendix B in this book for a list of resources.

Fourth, having identified various possible accommodations, the
employer should assess the potential effectiveness of each
accommodation—that is, the employer should assess which accommodation will best achieve the goal of giving the employee the maximum
opportunity to perform the job functions.[63]

Finally, the employer should implement the most appropriate
accommodation that does not impose a significant difficulty or expense
for the employer. As the legislative reports make clear, if there are two
equally effective accommodations, which cost essentially the same and
are equally easy to implement, the expressed choice of the person with
a disability should be given primary consideration.[64] Nevertheless, as a
bottom line, the employer can decide which accommodation to
choose—as long as the chosen accommodation meets the requirement
of giving the individual a meaningful opportunity to perform the
job.[65]

The provision of reasonable accommodations is a key component for
ensuring real and effective employment opportunity for people with
disabilities. Although some people with disabilities do not need any

reasonable accommodations at all, others do require reasonable accommodations as an integral aspect for ensuring their effective performance of job functions.

MEDICAL EXAMS AND INQUIRIES

The ADA includes detailed requirements for medical examinations and inquiries. These requirements are designed to accommodate two necessary and legitimate concerns—one on the part of people with disabilities and the other on the part of employers. The concern of people with disabilities is to get a fair chance to demonstrate their abilities for a particular job before an employer is informed about a disability that is irrelevant to a job. The concern of employers is to be allowed to assess whether an applicant or employee is qualified for, or remains qualified for a particular job.

JOB APPLICANTS

In order to understand the ADA's requirements for medical exams and inquiries of job applicants, it is useful to first contemplate the following common scenario. A person with a disability, such as epilepsy, or diabetes, or Hodgkin's cancer in remission, applies for a job. One of the first steps in the application process is to fill out a medical questionnaire, which asks, "What medical conditions do you have or have you ever had?" The person with the disability truthfully fills out the questionnaire. The person then completes various other steps in the application process, including an interview, submission of a writing sample, and listing of references. At the end of the process, the applicant is denied the job.

At this point, the applicant has no firm knowledge of why he or she was denied the job. It could be that the prospective employer, seeing that the person had a disability, such as diabetes, epilepsy, or a slight hearing impairment, decided not to offer the person the job. In that case, the other steps in the process were basically irrelevant. On the other hand, it could be that the employer was not affected at all by the applicant's disability, but that the applicant's references or writing sample did not meet the employer's standards. The problem for the person with a disability, however, is that although the discrimination *may* have occurred because of his or her disability, that person can never definitively know the truth. In fact, many people with disabilities are often denied jobs because their disability is identified early in the application process and that fact taints the remainder of the application process.[66]

To address this problem, the ADA, following the precedent of section 504 of the Rehabilitation Act,[67] establishes a two-step process for medical examinations and inquiries of job applicants.

The first step is the initial application stage. At that point, an employer may not require an applicant to submit to any medical examination, or to respond to any medical inquiries, such as filling out medical history questionnaires.[68] The employer may, however, ask the applicant whether the applicant can perform job-related functions.[69] Thus, for example, an employer may ask, in the initial application stage, whether the person has the educational and professional qualifications necessary for the job. The employer may also ask whether the applicant can do specific job functions, such as drive a car, lift 50 pounds, or answer the telephone, if these are essential functions of the job. The employer may not, however, ask generally whether the applicant has a disability that would prevent the person from doing the essential functions of the job.

After an employer has determined that the applicant possesses the necessary qualifications for a particular job, and decides (for whatever other reasons) to hire this person, the employer must extend to that applicant a conditional job offer, which then triggers the second step of the process. At this point, the employer may require the applicant to undergo a medical examination or respond to medical inquiries, and may condition the final offer of employment on the results of those medical tests or inquiries.[70]

Certain conditions, however, are placed on the use of such examinations or inquiries. First, if an employer wishes to require a medical examination, the examination must be required of *all* applicants for a particular job category, not simply of selected applicants. For example, an employer may not require that only applicants who "look weak" must fill out a medical questionnaire. Rather, the requirement of filling out a medical questionnaire must be a routine one requested of all applicants for a particular job category.[71]

Second, the information obtained as a result of the medical examinations must be kept strictly confidential. This information must be maintained on forms separated from the general application forms, in separate medical files that are treated as confidential medical records.

Only a limited number of individuals may gain access to these records.[72]

This confidentiality requirement represents an important protection for applicants with disabilities. Although there is no general federal confidentiality law for medical records, the ADA creates a cause of action for breaches of confidentiality of medical records obtained by the employer through testing of job applicants. This protection supplements whatever other causes of action an individual may have under state laws for breaches of confidentiality (e.g., through medical records or privacy laws).

Third, and of key importance, the results of the medical examination may not be used to withdraw the conditional job offer from an applicant unless the results indicate that the applicant is no longer qualified to perform the job.[73] Thus, assume for example, that a necessary qualification for a job was to lift 50 pounds on a regular basis. If the examination or inquiry revealed that the applicant, even with reasonable accommodation, could not fulfill this necessary requirement of the job, then the results of the exam could legitimately be used to withdraw the conditional job offer. By contrast, if the exam revealed that the person had Hodgkin's cancer in remission, or some other disability that did not affect the person's lifting ability, the conditional job offer could not legitimately be withdrawn.

This two-step process addresses the two concerns outlined above. On the one hand, it protects applicants with disabilities by allowing them to isolate the occurrence of a discriminatory hiring practice. On the other hand, it protects employers by allowing them to discover possible disabilities that will, in fact, limit an applicant's ability to perform a job prior to the applicant's receiving a final job offer.

ON-THE-JOB EMPLOYEES

The ADA's restrictions on medical exams and inquiries of employees are different from those for applicants. As the legislative reports to the ADA explain, once an employee is on the job, the person's *actual* performance is the best measure of that person's ability to do the job. Thus, under the ADA, the only medical exams or inquiries that an employer may require of employees are those that are "job-related and consistent with business necessity."[74]

The reasoning for this requirement is straightforward. Under the ADA, an employer does not have the right to pry into an employee's medical condition simply for the sake of curiosity. As the legislative reports explain, "An inquiry or examination that is not job-related serves no legitimate employer purpose, but simply serves to stigmatize the person with a disability."[75]

By contrast, an examination or inquiry that is necessary to ascertain the person's actual ability to continue to perform an essential function of the job would be valid under the ADA as "job-related and consistent with business necessity."[76] The employer could demand that an employee undergo such a valid examination. Moreover, unlike medical examinations for job applicants, such examinations can be required of a specific employee if the need arises to question his or her continued ability to do the job.

The ADA makes clear that employers may continue to offer voluntary medical examinations to their employees—for example, as part of "corporate wellness" programs. Results of such examinations, however, are subject to the same confidentiality requirements that govern pre-employment tests and similarly may not be used to discriminate against an individual who remains qualified for a job.[77]

HEALTH INSURANCE BENEFITS

The ADA provides some protection to people with disabilities in the area of health insurance benefits, although final resolution in this area will probably come only in court decisions.

The ADA provides that a covered entity may not discriminate against an employee in the "terms or conditions of employment."[78] The legislative reports note that these terms and conditions include "fringe benefits available by virtue of employment, whether or not administered by the covered entity."[79] A covered entity may also not participate in a contractual relationship that has the effect of subjecting the employees of the covered entity to discrimination, including a contractual relationship with "an organization providing fringe benefits to an employee of the covered entity."[80]

The ADA, therefore, does seem to contemplate that certain practices in the provision of fringe benefits, including presumably health insurance, would be illegal under the Act. The ADA, however, does include a general provision for insurance: An insurer cannot be prohibited or restricted from underwriting or classifying risks in a way that complies with or is not inconsistent with state law; nor can a covered entity, such as an employer, be restricted in establishing a benefit plan that underwrites or classifies risks in a manner that is based on, or not inconsistent with, state law.[81]

This provision, however, also has its own exception built into it. According to the provision, these insurance exceptions may not be used as a "subterfuge" to evade the purposes of the ADA.[82]

The various legislative reports, and some members of Congress, attempted to provide guidance in this area.[83] Various principles may be derived from this legislative guidance:

1. Employers may not refuse to hire an individual because the individual will cost the employer more in terms of insurance premiums (or, in the case of self-insured plans, in terms of health-care costs). Thus, an employer could not refuse to hire a person with diabetes because such an individual might cost more in terms of health insurance coverage.[84]

2. Employers and insurance companies may continue to include preexisting-condition clauses in their health plans, even though such clauses eliminate benefits for a specified time period for people with disabilities. Thus, an employer could have a health plan that does not cover treatment for diabetes for a specified time period, if the employee had diabetes upon entering the health plan.[85]

3. Employers and insurance companies may limit coverage for certain *procedures* or *treatments*. For example, a health plan presumably may place a limit on the amount of kidney dialysis it will cover or the number of blood tranfusions it will reimburse.[86]

4. An employer may not, however, have a health plan that denies coverage "completely" to an individual based on diagnosis. For example, although a plan may include certain limitations for people with kidney disease (e.g., a limit on the amount of kidney dialysis), the plan cannot deny coverage to that person with kidney disease for conditions not connected to the permissible procedure limitations—for example, coverage for treatment of a broken leg.[87] Moreover, the plan could also not deny coverage to that individual for *other* procedures or treatments connected with the kidney disease itself.[88]

The overall thrust of the ADA's legislative history appears to be that insurance companies, and employers buying insurance plans, should be allowed to continue offering such plans as long as exclusions or limitations in the plan are based on sound actuarial principles. Obviously, however, it may make some sense, as an actuarial matter, to try to deny coverage completely for people with kidney or heart disease. Such an attempt, however, may well be seen as a subterfuge for evading the purposes of the law, if in practice it will prevent people with such diseases from being employed. Thus, it is quite possible that it would not be permissible to deny coverage completely, as a blanket matter, for one disability—such as kidney or heart disease.

DEFENSES

There are a number of defenses to a charge of discrimination under the ADA. Some of these defenses are similar to those existing under general civil-rights law; other defenses are specific to the ADA.

First, the ADA prohibits discrimination on the basis of *disability*, not on any other ground. Thus, a general defense for the refusal to hire a person with a disability might be that there was no longer money to fund the desired position or that the company was moving into a different area of emphasis than that offered by the person with a disability. These reasons may result in refusal to hire a particular person (including a person with a disability) that has nothing to do with disability per se. Even reasons that may appear completely irrational— for example, a policy of hiring only graduates of Northwestern University for particular jobs—are not invalid as long as they are not based on disability and do not result in a disparate impact on people with disabilities.

Second, the framework for proving intentional discrimination is essentially the same under the ADA as it is for other employment antidiscrimination laws. The person alleging discrimination bears the initial burden of proving the facts of discrimination: (1) the person is a member of the protected class (i.e., the person has a disability or associates with someone with a disability); (2) the person possesses the necessary qualifications, apart from the disability, to do the desired job; and (3) the person was rejected for (or fired from) the job under circumstances that give rise to an inference that the decision was based on the person's disability.[89]

Once the person alleging discrimination establishes this prima facie case of discrimination, the burden shifts to the employer. At that point, the employer could prove that the employment decision was made for reasons *other* than the applicant's or employee's disability. Or the employer could admit that the employment decision *was* based on the person's disability, but could prove that the plaintiff's disability made him or her *not* "qualified" for the job. For example, the employer could prove that the person's disability prevented him or her from doing the job, that there was no reasonable accommodation that would allow the person to do the job, or that the only possible reasonable accommodation would impose an undue hardship on the employer.

At that stage, the burden shifts back to the person alleging discrimination. If the employer has produced evidence to prove that the employment decision was made for reasons other than disability, the applicant or employee could produce evidence to prove that this was a pretext and that, in fact, the decision *was* based on disability. Conversely, if the employer has produced evidence to prove that the person was not qualified for the job, the applicant or employee could produce evidence to show that he or she was qualified for the job, that there was an available reasonable accommodation, and/or that the available reasonable accommodation was not an undue hardship.[90]

The ADA also sets forth some specific defenses of qualification standards. For example, an employer may have, as a qualification standard, that a person with a disability not pose a "direct threat to the health or safety of other individuals in the workplace."[91] "Direct threat" is defined in the ADA as posing "a significant risk to the health or safety of others which cannot be eliminated by reasonable accommodation."[92]

This direct-threat qualification standard is a long-standing requirement under the Rehabilitation Act. It is a logical requirement: in order for a person with a disability to be qualified for a particular job, that person cannot pose a direct threat to the health or safety of others in the workplace. The definition of direct threat in the ADA is taken directly from a case decided under section 504 of the Rehabilitation Act—the Supreme Court decision in *School Board of Nassau County v. Arline*.[93] The essential requirement for this defense is that the perceived health or safety threat posed by the person with a disability must be based on solid facts and not on speculation or generalizations.[94]

The ADA also provides that religious entities may require that all applicants and employees "conform to the religious tenets" of the religious entity.[95] In other words, a valid qualification standard for a religious entity may be that all individuals conform with that entity's religious tenets and requirements. Even if it is an individual's disability that makes him or her incapable of fulfilling those tenets, the ADA allows religious entities to apply those requirements and to refuse to hire or retain such an individual.

In general, the defenses allowed under the ADA comport with the basic principles underlying the law: to ensure that people with disabilities are given full and meaningful opportunities for employment, while protecting the right of employers to hire individuals who can appropriately perform the essential functions of particular jobs.

COVERAGE AND ENFORCEMENT

The employment title of the ADA adopts the same scope of coverage of employers, and the same administrative and judicial remedies, that are provided under title VII of the Civil Rights Act of 1964 for individuals who are discriminated against on the basis of race, sex, religion, or national origin.[96] This parity was specifically adopted by the sponsors of the ADA in order to ensure that people with disabilities were granted the same rights and remedies that are available to other minorities and to women.

Like title VII, therefore, the employment title of the ADA will ultimately cover all businesses that employ 15 or more employees. However, the ADA also includes a significant phase-in period. In July 1992, the employment title becomes effective for employers with 25 or more employees. Two years later, in July 1994, the employment title becomes effective for employers with 15 or more employees.[97]

The employment title of the ADA also adopts the same enforcement mechanism and remedies provided under title VII of the Civil Rights Act of 1964. As under title VII, a person charging discrimination must first go through the administrative process established under the Equal Employment Opportunity Commission (EEOC). The EEOC has well-established procedures that individuals who allege discrimination on the basis of race, sex, religion, or national origin have used for years under title VII and these same procedures will apply to people with disabilities.[98]

Apart from the administrative procedures available through the EEOC, a person charging discrimination also has the right to bring a private lawsuit in court.[99] The rules that apply to title VII lawsuits will apply to the ADA as well. Thus, for example, if a person alleging discrimination wins his or her case, the relief available will be "injunctive relief." This may include a judicial order reinstating the person in a job, an order requiring the person to be granted a specific job, and/or an order requiring that money be paid to compensate the person for lost wages (known as "backpay" and, at times, "frontpay").[100] The relief currently available under title VII does not, however, include the right to receive compensatory or punitive damages.[101]

Finally, the ADA explicitly provides that the law should not be construed to invalidate or limit the remedies or rights of any federal law or state law that provides greater or equal protection to people with disabilities.[102] This "antipreemption" provision is designed to ensure explicitly that other federal laws (such as the Rehabilitation Act of 1973) and other state laws will continue to provide protection to people with disabilities. This also includes the remedies, such as compensatory and punitive damages, that may be available under state laws.[103]

CONCLUSION

The ADA is a remarkably comprehensive law, addressing the broad-ranging areas of employment, public services, transportation, public accommodations, and communications. The decision to pursue a comprehensive law was a very deliberate one on the part of its sponsors. Each of these areas is interdependent. In order for people with disabilities to enter the mainstream of America, they must have meaningful opportunities to obtain employment; access to public services and to goods and services offered by private businesses; accessible transportation to reach these jobs, goods, and services; and a means of communicating with employers, businesses, and others.

The employment section of the ADA addresses the employment piece of this interdependent picture. The basic principle underlying this section is that qualified persons with disabilities must be judged on their merits and abilities for particular jobs and must not have employment opportunities unjustly foreclosed to them because of myths or stereotypes regarding their disabilities. At the same time, the employment section is designed to be workable for the thousands of employers who will be required to abide by its requirements.

The two- to four-year phase-in period before the ADA fully applies to private employers will be most effective if it is used for comprehensive education. With such education and understanding, the ADA can be a source of support for both employers and for people with disabilities.

NOTES

1. See 29 U.S.C. §791, 793, 794 (1985 & Supp.).
2. 42 U.S.C. §2000e et seq. (1981 & Supp.).
3. Parts of this section are based on C.R. Feldblum (1991): The Americans with Disabilities Act: The Definition of Disability, 7 ABA *Labor Lawyer* 1:11–27.
4. ADA §3(2). This is the same definition of a "person with a handicap" that Congress adopted for purposes of title V of the Rehabilitation Act of 1973. People with disabilities, and their advocates, prefer to use the term "disability" rather than "handicap." In recognition of that preference, the term "disability" is used throughout the ADA.
5. 29 U.S.C. §706(8)(A) (1985 & Supp.).
6. See S. Rep. No. 1297, 93rd Cong., 2d. Sess., 16, 37–38, 50 (1974).
7. ADA §3(2)(A).
8. See Report of the Senate Committee on Labor and Human Resources, 101st Cong., 1st Sess., S. Rep. No. 101–116 at 22 (henceforth Senate Report); Report of the House Committee on Education and Labor, 101st Cong., 2d. Sess., H. Rep. No. 101–485, Part 2 at 51 (henceforth Education and Labor Report); Report of the House Committee on the Judiciary, 101st Cong., 2d. Sess., H. Rep. No. 101–485, Part 3 at 28 (henceforth Judiciary Report). See also 45 C.F.R. §84.3(j) and Appendix A, No. 3 (1985).
9. Another reason it is difficult to develop a comprehensive list is that there is no way of knowing what specific physiological disorders may develop in the future. See Senate Report at 22; Education and Labor Report at 51; Judiciary Report at 28 (noting the advent of new disabilities, such as AIDS).
10. Education and Labor Report at 51; see also Senate Report at 22; Judiciary Report at 28. Although drug addiction is a recognized physical disorder, the current illegal use of drugs is not protected under the ADA. See Judiciary Report at 28, note 17.
11. See Senate Report at 22; Education and Labor Report at 52; Judiciary Report at 28.
12. These are all examples of major life activities. As the Department of Justice

has pointed out, another significant life activity is that of procreation and intimate personal relations, in which people infected with the human immunodeficiency virus are substantially limited. See Memorandum of Douglas W. Kmiec, Acting Assistant Attorney General, Office of Legal Counsel, Department of Justice, September 27, 1988 at 9.

13. See Senate Report at 23; Education and Labor Report at 52–53; Judiciary Report at 29.

14. See Senate Report at 23; Education and Labor Report at 53; and Judiciary Report at 29.

15. See, e.g., *Prewitt v. United States Postal Service*, 662 F.2d 292, 309 (5th Cir. 1981); *Pushkin v. Regents of the University of Colorado*, 658 F.2d 1372, 1385 (10th Cir. 1981).

16. See Education and Labor Report at 52; Judiciary Report at 28, note 18; Senate Report at 22; statement of Rep. Edwards, 136 Cong. Rec. H 4624 (July 12, 1990).

17. See, e.g., *Ray v. School District of DeSoto County*, 666 F.Supp. 1524 (M.D.Fla. 1987); *Thomas v. Atascadero Unified School District*, 662 F.Supp. 376 (C.D.Cal. 1986); *Chalk v. United States District Court*, 840 F.2d 701 (9th Cir. 1988).

18. See discussion under section on defenses for explication of the "direct threat" qualification standard.

19. See, e.g., Education and Labor Report at 78.

20. See, e.g., 45 C.F.R. Part 84, Appendix A, No.3 (1985); *Simpson v. Reynolds Metals Co.*, 629 F.2d 1226 (7th Cir. 1980); *Crew v. OPM*, 834 F.2d 140 (8th Cir. 1987).

21. The person, however, could be covered under the third prong of the definition if he or she were regarded as being an alcoholic.

22. ADA §104(a), §510.

23. ADA §512.

24. ADA §104(b)

25. See, e.g., *Gardner v. Morris*, 752 F.2d 1271 (8th Cir. 1985); *Doe v. New York University*, 666 F.2d 761 (2nd Cir. 1981).

26. See discussion of qualification requirements under the ADA in the section entitled "Qualified Person with a Disability."

27. ADA §511(b).

28. Homosexuality was removed in 1973 by the American Psychiatric Association from the list of mental disorders set forth in the *Diagnostic and Statistical Manual III*.

29. ADA §102(b)(4).

30. Although protection for people who associate with people with disabilities does not appear in the Rehabilitation Act, it is not a new concept. Such protection was also included in the Fair Housing Act when Congress passed a series of amendments to that law in 1988. See 42 U.S.C. §3604(f)(1)–(2) (1977 & Supp.).

31. See Judiciary Report at 38.

32. ADA §102(a).

33. ADA §101(8).

34. This concept of "essential functions" comes directly from the 1977 DHEW regulations issued to implement Section 504. See 45 C.F.R. §84.3(k) (1985).
35. See Senate Report at 34–35; Education and Labor Report at 33–34; Judiciary Report at 31–32.
36. ADA §102(b)(5)(A)–(B). See also Education and Labor Report, at 62–67.
37. The term "covered entity" includes employers, employment agencies, labor organizations, and joint labor-management committees. ADA §101(2).
38. ADA §102(a).
39. ADA §102(b)(1).
40. ADA §102(b)(2).
41. See Education and Labor Report at 60; Judiciary Report at 37.
42. See Education and Labor Report at 60–61; Judiciary Report at 37–38.
43. ADA §102(b)(5)(A)–(B).
44. ADA §102(b)(6).
45. Id.
46. ADA §102(b)(6).
47. See, e.g., title II, title VII, and title VIII of the Civil Rights Act of 1964, 42 U.S.C. §§ 2000a, 2000e, 2000f. See also section 504 of the Rehabilitation Act, 29 U.S.C. §794(a) (1985 & Supp.).
48. See C.R. Feldblum: Medical Exams and Inquiries under the Americans with Disabilities Act: A View from the Inside—Symposium on the Americans with Disabilities Law, *Temple Law Review* (summer 1991).
49. ADA §102(b)(5)(A).
50. Job restructuring may include eliminating nonessential elements of the job, exchanging assignments with other employees, or redesigning procedures for task performance. See Education and Labor Report at 62.
51. See Education and Labor Report, at 62. See also statement of Rep. Edwards, 136 Cong. Rec. H 4624 (July 12, 1990); statement of Rep. Owens, 136 Cong. Rec. H 4623 (July 12, 1990).
52. An employer is not required to create a new job for an employee with a disability who is no longer able to perform his or her present job. However, if a vacant job exists that the person is qualified to perform, reassignment to that job would be a required reasonable accommodation. See Education and Labor Report at 63.
53. ADA §101(9). A reasonable accommodation could also include providing an attendant. See Education and Labor Report at 64.
54. ADA §101(10) (definition of undue hardship); §102(b)(5)(A) (requirement to provide a reasonable accommodation unless it imposes an undue hardship).
55. ADA §101(10). The factors regarding the type of operation and work force of the employer (category three) are probably best understood as simply a subset, or an application, of the factors in category two.
56. See Judiciary Report at 41; Senate Report at 35–36; Education and Labor Report at 67.
57. 567 F.Supp. 369 (E.D.Pa. 1983)
58. Id., at 380. As one legislative report noted, after summarizing the *Nelson v. Thornburgh* case: "[T]he same accommodations may be an undue hardship

for a small employer because they would require expending significant proportions of available resources." Judiciary Report at 41.

59. See Senate Report at 34; Education and Labor Report at 64.
60. Senate Report at 35; Education and Labor Report at 66.
61. Senate Report at 34; Education and Labor Report at 65.
62. The Education and Labor Report included the "800 number" for the Job
    Accommodation Network in its report. Education and Labor Report at 64
    (1-800-526-7234). Some private rehabilitation agencies, such as Allied Ser-
    vices in Scranton, Pennsylvania, are taking a strong role in offering technical
    assistance to employers. As employers recognize the usefulness of having
    trained consultants to turn to in the reasonable accommodation area, one
    hopes that more companies trained in the latest technology and sensitive to
    disability issues will be available for use by employers.
63. Senate Report at 35; Education and Labor Report at 66.
64. Senate Report at 35; Education and Labor Report at 66–67. In fact, if the
    accommodations are equal to that extent, most employers would probably
    take into account the preference of the individual with the disability.
65. Senate Report at 35; Education and Labor Report at 66–67; Judiciary Report
    at 40.
66. See Senate Report at 39; Education and Labor Report at 72.
67. See 45 C.F.R. §84.11 (1985).
68. ADA §102(c)(2)(A).
69. ADA §102(c)(2)(B).
70. ADA §102(c)(2)(B). There is no requirement for the employer to "job vali-
    date" these medical exams or inquiries.
71. ADA §102(c)(3)(A). The requirement of a "particular job category" is an
    important one for employers. In other words, an employer can give a test to
    check lifting strength to all its construction employees, without having to
    require that the same test be given to all its management and clerical employ-
    ees. See Education and Labor Report at 73.
72. ADA §102(c)(3)(B).
73. ADA §102(c)(3)(C).
74. ADA §102(c)(4)(A). See Education and Labor Report at 75; Senate Report at
    39.
75. Education and Labor Report at 75; see also Senate Report at 39.
76. ADA §102(c)(4)(A).
77. ADA §102(c)(4)(B)–(C).
78. ADA §102(a)
79. See Judiciary Report at 35; Education and Labor Report at 55.
80. ADA §102(b)(2).
81. ADA §501(c). The provision also provides that a covered entity may establish
    or administer a bona fide benefit plan that is not subject to state laws that
    regulate insurance.
82. ADA §501 (c).
83. See Senate Report at 29 and 84–86; Education and Labor Report at 59 and
    136–138; Judiciary Report at 37–38 and 70–71. See also statement of Rep.
    Owens, 136 Cong. Rec. H4623 (July 12, 1990); statement of Rep. Edwards,

136 Cong. Rec. H4624 (July 12, 1990); statement of Rep. Waxman, 136 Cong. Rec. H4626 (July 12, 1990); statement of Sen. Kennedy, 136 Cong. Rec. S9697 (July 13, 1990).

84. See, e.g., Education and Labor Report at 136; statement of Rep. Owens, supra note 83 at 4623; statement of Rep. Edwards, supra note 83 at 4624.
85. See, e.g., Education & Labor Report at 59; Judiciary Report at 38.
86. See, e.g., Education and Labor Report at 59; Judiciary Report at 38.
87. See Education and Labor Report at 59; Judiciary Report at 38.
88. See Judiciary Report at 38. See also statement of Rep. Waxman, supra note 83 at 4626; statement of Rep. Edwards, supra note 83 at 4624. This last example seems to indicate that it would not be legitimate to have a blanket exclusion of a particular disability.
89. See *Pushkin v. Board of Regents of the U. of Colorado*, 658 F.2d 1372, 1385–1387 (10th Cir. 1981); see also *Prewitt v. United States Postal Service*, 662 F.2d 292, 309–310 (5th Cir. 1981).
90. See, e.g., *Prewitt*, 662 F.2d, at 307–310.
91. ADA §103(b).
92. ADA §101(3).
93. 480 U.S. 273 (1987).
94. See, e.g., Judiciary Report at 45.
95. ADA §103(c).
96. ADA §101(5) and §102(a) (coverage); §107(a) (enforcement).
97. ADA §101(5)(A).
98. ADA §107(a) (incorporating by reference the administrative procedures of title VII, 42 U.S.C. §2000e-5).
99. ADA §107(a) (incorporating by reference the private right of action available under title VII, 42 U.S.C. §2000e-5[f]).
100. See 42 U.S.C. §2000e-5(g) (incorporated in ADA §107[a]).
101. See, e.g., *Shah v. Mt. Zion Hospital & Medical Center*, 642 F.2d 268, 272 (9th Cir. 1981).
102. ADA §501(b).
103. See Education and Labor Report at 135; Judiciary Report at 69–70; statement of Rep. Hoyer, 136 Cong. Rec. E1920–21 (June 13, 1990).

Employment Strategies for People with Disabilities: A Prescription for Change

Paul G. Hearne

EDITOR'S NOTE

If an antidiscrimination mandate is to yield a higher employment rate among persons with disabilities, it must be complemented by training, support, and placement services for persons with disabilities as well as technical assistance for employers. With over a decade of experience in facilitating job placements for persons with disabilities, Paul G. Hearne authoritatively reviews the major programs and service systems in place that will support persons with disabilities as they pursue employment in the private sector. He considers the provision of "reasonable accommodations" in the workplace under section 504 and recalls employers' fears about the potential cost of accommodations when section 504 was enacted. Concluding that costs never proved to be an obstacle, he notes that "their [employers']determination to comply with both the law and with contemporary best practice in addressing the needs of their employees made the costs of accommodation a trivial problem." He reviews sources of technical assistance.

Hearne is president of the Dole Foundation for Employment of People with Disabilities in Washington, D.C. When he joined the Dole Foundation, Hearne became the first individual with a disability to direct a foundation for persons with disabilities. A graduate of Hofstra Law School, Hearne has been an advocate of people with disabilities for over two decades. He currently serves as chairman of the AT&T Consumer Advisory Group for the AT&T Special Needs Center. He

111

*served as executive director of the National Council on Disability dur-
ing congressional consideration of the ADA and as executive director of
Just One Break, Inc. in New York from 1979 to 1989. Just One Break
was the first job-placement agency in the United States for persons with
disabilities, placing over 300 individuals annually in full-time competitive jobs. Hearne's awards include the Howard A. Rusk Award for
significant contributions to the field of vocational rehabilitation and
the Barbara M. Paley Memorial Award for Service to the Disabled.*

The purpose of the Americans with Disabilities Act (ADA) is to
enable persons with disabilities to participate fully in American
life by prohibiting practices that systematically discriminate
against them. Full participation in American life means many things,
but the most important may be paid employment for persons able and
willing to engage in it. I will describe current knowledge about increasing the employment and employability of persons with disabilities. (In
the preceding chapter, Chai R. Feldblum discusses the obligations of
employers under the ADA.) This article is directed to an audience of
persons with disabilities, employers in the private and public sectors,
and government officials, at all levels.

The enactment of the ADA signaled a change in America's public
policy toward employing people with disabilities. This change has
occurred in less than two decades. When President Richard M. Nixon
vetoed the Rehabilitation Act of 1973, he complained that it "would
cruelly raise the hopes of the handicapped [for gainful employment] in
a way that we could *never* responsibly hope to fulfill" (Nixon 1973).
When President George Bush signed the ADA, in July 1990, he pro-
claimed, in striking contrast, the "end to the unjustified segregation
and exclusion of people with disabilities from the mainstream of American life" (Bush 1990).

What had changed in 17 years? Change had occurred among persons
with disabilities, in the United States economy and its labor market, in
attitudes of employers toward employing persons with disabilities, and
in the policies and professional practices of the public and private
agencies that assist persons with disabilities to enter the work force.

Many people, myself included, believe that these changes are incomplete. Much more must be done to enable persons with disabilities to
retain, restore, or claim their independence. However, the progress of
the past two decades makes it conceivable that more gains will continue
to take place in the future.

Such progress depends on learning well the lessons of the past, which is my principal subject. I will begin with a brief summary of what has been learned during the past two decades about employing persons with disabilities. Senior corporate managers and officials of general government should read the summary closely, as it contains information that their human resources staff and consulting rehabilitation professionals should have told them already.

The rest of the article expands on and qualifies this summary. First, a section on the labor market describes current knowledge about employees, employers, and the economic environment. The next section, on programs for employing persons with disabilities, reviews the recent history of major intervention, public and private. The final section looks to the future.

WHAT WE KNOW: A SUMMARY

Persons with Disabilities. The majority (66 percent) of working-aged persons with disabilities are not working, although the overwhelming majority (78 percent) want to work (Harris 1986).

Employers. A large percentage of managers give employees with disabilities high ratings for performance. Moreover, three-quarters of all managers say that the average cost of employing a person with a disability is not excessive. Nevertheless, the hiring of persons with disabilities is not widespread except by companies that make special efforts (Harris 1987).

The Economy. There is good news and bad. On the one hand, changes in demography and in manufacturing processes and the rise of the service sector are creating new opportunities for productive work by persons with disabilities. On the other hand, the current recession and the pressures of international competition are reducing overall demand for labor, especially for workers who are likely to require new expenditures for accommodations and fringe benefits (Burkhauser, Haveman, and Wolfe 1990; Johnston and Packer 1987).

Programs to Increase the Employment and Employability of Persons with Disabilities. There are a bewildering variety of these programs, each with supporters and detractors. However, there is solid evidence for two generalizations:

1. When persons with disabilities receive opportunities for paid employment, as well as services, they are more likely to enter and remain in the labor market (Kiernan and Stark 1989).
2. Differences in the success of programs (of both the same and different types) are mainly the result of (a) the severity of the disabilities of the persons served; and (b) the management (personnel, planning, and execution) of each program (J.M. Foundation 1986).

THE LABOR MARKET

The labor market for persons with disabilities is too often described in a disaggregated fashion. Persons with disabilities are polled, counted, and assessed separately from employers, whose attitudes, in turn, are investigated as if the structure of the economy and the strength of demand for goods and services did not matter. I will call attention in this section to the results of research and analysis about these aspects of labor markets.

THE ECONOMY

Almost everyone who writes about employing persons with disabilities cites the recent book *Workforce 2000: Work and Workers for the 21st Century*. Most people, however, read it selectively, in order to justify their prior optimism or pessimism about the future. A careful reading of the book, in conjunction with other studies and with breaking news about the economy, suggests a different message.

That message is as follows. Economic forecasters tell us that there will be opportunities for increasing the employment of persons with disabilities, but only if we seize them. Thus the low birth rate in the United States since the 1970s, relative to the prior two decades, means that labor markets will be tighter: more jobs will be available for fewer workers. At the same time, however, competition from firms in countries that pay lower wages for comparable work, combined with cost-cutting pressures at home, are giving employers in the United States incentives to lay off older workers, who are more expensive in both pay and benefits.

Barriers to employing persons with disabilities were rising in the years before the enactment of ADA. The percentage of men with a work disability who were working full time fell by 7 percent between 1981 and 1988. Moreover, in 1980, men with disabilities earned 23 percent and women 30 percent less than men and women without disabilities. By 1988 these numbers had fallen to 36 percent for men and 38 percent for women. Similarly, the number of workers who became disabled on the job increased by 33 percent between 1985 and 1988, while the number who returned to work fell from 48 to 44 percent (Rochlin 1989). Elsewhere in this book, Edward Yelin describes the effects of these layoffs in the recent past and suggests ways to track them more precisely in the future.

Similarly, the transformation of the U.S. economy from manufacturing to services creates both opportunities for and impediments to employing people with disabilities. Opportunities for employing people in new or expanding occupations have been created alongside more part-time work with lower wages and poor or nonexistent fringe benefits.

Finally, the health of the economy is as important as its structure for assessing enhancement of employment opportunities for persons with disabilities. The ADA is being launched during wide predictions of the worst economic downturn in more than a decade. Even before this downturn began, moreover, the well-being of persons with disabilities was declining and persons with multiple disabilities were losing economic ground at an especially rapid rate.

The current recession will make employers more cautious about the potential costs of the ADA. Many employers who cheerfully and voluntarily paid the costs of workplace accommodations for people with disabilities during the recent boom are likely to resist making accommodations that are mandated by the ADA. They will certainly oppose proposals to raise state and federal taxes in order to increase the employability of persons with disabilities. Moreover, it will be difficult for the federal government to authorize additional tax expenditures (for tax credits or mandated fringe benefits, for example) that would provide incentives to employers to hire and retain persons with disabilities.

Persons with disabilities have sought and gained the right of access to the mainstream of American life. As a result, they will be subjected to the burdens as well as sharing in the successes of our economy.

PERSONS WITH DISABILITIES

Pessimists about the state of the economy, and therefore of its labor markets, should not underestimate the will to work of persons with disabilities. The history of the introduction and passage of the ADA and of the important post-1973 legislation that paved its way is evidence of how successfully persons with disabilities have translated aspiration into political action. The famous 1986 survey, *Disabled Americans' Self-Perception*, conducted by Louis Harris and Associates (1986), documented the strength of this group's desire to work—and their frustration about barriers to employment.

EMPLOYERS

Similarly, many employers, especially larger ones, have concluded that increasing the employment and the employability of persons with disabilities is good business. Another Harris survey documented this point. So did an earlier survey by Berkeley Planning Associates (1982) under contract with the U.S. Department of Labor and a more recent one conducted by the Bureau of National Affairs (1990). A number of studies have concluded that the costs of most workplace accommodations are not onerous (Job Accommodation Network 1987). These costs are often no more expensive than the costs of supporting other workers. Many accommodations benefit the entire work force (improved lighting and ramps, for example). A number of individual firms have documented their positive experience with increasing employment opportunities for persons with disabilities. These firms include AT&T, Du Pont, and IBM (Du Pont 1990).

PROGRAMS

However, only a relative handful of persons with disabilities and employers will, unaided, find each other in the labor market. A labor market, without any subsidized training, placement, support, or accommodations, works reasonably efficiently for highly educated and skilled persons with the least severe disabilities and for employers with uncommon profitability, intense social conscience, and, often, a strong desire to improve or maintain their corporate image.

For the remaining persons with disabilities and employers, however, a variety of programs have proven to be necessary. Each program has constituencies: clients, professionals, voluntary associations, employers, philanthropists, and government officials. Sometimes these constituencies overlap. Most often they compete. Each constituency, in the American way, has competitors who would rather see funding go to their constituency. With only a few exceptions, the programs to assist persons with disabilities in obtaining and retaining employment rely on a mix of public and private funds, public and voluntary auspices, public regulation, and voluntary oversight.

Moreover, precisely what programs do to, for, or with whom is strongly influenced by local circumstances. A national public program, like Vocational Rehabilitation, or a national voluntary program, like Goodwill Industries, will not operate in precisely the same way in each state and city. Goods and services produced by local economies vary, as do the conditions of local labor markets. So will the incidence, prevalence, and severity of disability in the population. More important, there are vast local differences in the management and results of similar programs.

Employers as well as persons with disabilities must come to practical terms with this diversity of program type and quality. The most effective strategies for coping with diversity will involve local planning by leaders in the private, public, and voluntary sectors, and the creation of networks that serve both employers and persons with disabilities. Each firm, as well as each organization representing and serving persons with disabilities, will need to be aware of program capacities and performance in their own geographical area.

These firms and organizations, moreover, will require access to data that service agencies are sometimes reluctant to provide. The data include the benefits provided by the service agency to present and former clients, the results of providing those benefits (in the context of the severity of disability in the population served), and information about the agency's productivity. In other words, employers should require that organizations serving persons with disabilities be as businesslike as they are.

A diverse population requires diverse services. Elsewhere in this book, Mitchell LaPlante describes the diversity of persons with disability in the United States. Moreover, the number of people with disabilities who want to work but cannot—in technical terms, the rate of work disability—varies widely among the states (Kraus and Stoddard 1989). Thus, there is a need for good programs of every type described below.

Readers should be wary of misplaced enthusiasm for programs that seem to have the lowest unit costs and the greatest success in placing clients in paid employment. Their laudable characteristics often result from their clients being the least severely disabled. Moreover, measures of success have limited meaning if there is no appropriate follow-up for the period of time that the person with a disability maintains employment. In addition, cost effectiveness in not the full measure of a successful job placement.

Readers should also be wary of programs in which professionals have full responsibility for deciding when clients are ready for vocational experience or job placement. More persons with disabilities have voices than have spoken to date.

I will describe three types of programs. The first, and largest, are the traditional programs for persons with disabilities, mainly the most severe disabling conditions. The second are promising recent approaches that involve active collaboration among employers, persons with disabilities, and service agencies. The third are programs that assist employers in making workplace accommodations that enable persons with disabilities to be productive employees.

TRADITIONAL PROGRAMS

This section defines and describes the results of research and analysis about the three most familiar, and by far the largest, programs to assist persons with disabilities in attaining and retaining employment that is consistent with their abilities. These programs are Vocational Rehabilitation, sheltered employment, and rehabilitation facilities. The distinctions among these programs are often blurred. For example, Vocational Rehabilitation may fund or maintain rehabilitation facilities and sheltered workshops. These workshops are often managed by rehabilitation facilities. Moreover, all three programs participate in the relatively new supported employment initiatives.

Vocational Rehabilitation. The federal–state Vocational Rehabilitation program has long been the major service program in the field. It now receives more than 90 percent of the funds appropriated under the omnibus Rehabilitation Act. The program allots funds to the states to provide rehabilitation services to persons with "physical and mental handicaps" in order to prepare them to "engage in gainful employment to the extent of their abilities." Services provided in each state, either directly or by contract, include "evaluation of employment potential, physical or mental restoration, vocational training, special devices required for employment, job placement, and follow-up services" (Smith 1987a).

The Vocational Rehabilitation program accords priority to persons with severe handicaps. Emphasis on this priority since 1975 has been one factor contributing to a decline in the number of persons served from 1.2 million to 930,000, while the number of persons rehabilitated (that is, gainfully employed) has declined from 325,000 to 220,408 (National Association of Rehabilitation Facilities 1990).

Like any large public program with a broad and difficult mandate, Vocational Rehabilitation has both supporters and very vocal critics. Its supporters claim that its benefits exceed its costs. A recent study found $5.55 in lifetime earnings for each dollar spent on Vocational Rehabilitation programs (Smith 1990). In 1989 the U.S. Department of Education reported that for every dollar spent on Vocational Rehabilitation, $11 is contributed to the tax base.

Critics of Vocational Rehabilitation, and especially critics, like myself, who have had personal experience with the program, have charged repeatedly that the program is isolated and has overly complicated standards of eligibility for client services, long waiting lists, and uneven administration. The charge of isolation is supported by evidence of insufficient linkages to programs and services that promote employment skills and goals for youths with disabilities, inadequate linkages between Vocational Rehabilitation offices and the business community, and poor coordination with voluntary and private agencies providing rehabilitation services. For example, in many communities, one job applicant is "marketed" to the same local employer by both public and private agencies (Center for Independent Living 1978).

Many critics also claim that federal and state eligibility standards for Vocational Rehabilitation services are too complex. Because of the difficulties of understanding and complying with these requirements, rehabilitation professionals often avoid making referrals to services to which their clients may be entitled.

Like all federal–state programs, Vocational Rehabilitation leaves considerable discretion to state officials. Vocational Rehabilitation services are in education departments in some states, and in labor departments in others. Standards for services and the quality of program administration vary widely among the states.

Sheltered Employment. This is one of the oldest and most problematic of programs to employ persons with disabilities. A sheltered workshop is a public or nonprofit organization that is certified by the U.S. Department of Labor to pay subminimum wages to "persons with diminished earning capacity" (Smith 1987b). Approximately a quarter of a million persons are now served in more than 5,000 of these workshops (Kiernan and Stark 1986). These persons have a variety of disabilities that include, mental retardation, alcoholism, blindness, and mental illness. Many have reduced earning capacity due to advancing age. An increasing number are homeless.

Sheltered workshops are problematic for two reasons: (1) controversy about what they achieve and (2) dispute about whether they will have sufficient markets in the future. Many critics have claimed that very few persons advance from sheltered workshops into gainful employment at market wages. They urge that only persons with the most severe disabilities be placed in these programs, with more people being shifted to programs of supported employment. Other informed observers dispute this pessimistic view. Goodwill Industries, for example, claims that a significant number of its clients move from sheltered employment to the labor market.

The second reason that sheltered employment is problematic involves the shift to a service economy. The workshops may not provide useful experience for persons whose only chance for gainful employment is to be providers of services. Moreover, it is not clear how many workshops can remain viable, even at subminimum wages, in the face of competition from other countries in packaging and light manufacturing.

Rehabilitation Facilities. The important generalization about the thousands of nonprofit medical, vocational, and residential rehabilitation facilities is that they are essential to the effective implementation of the ADA. The facilities are currently financed through a mix of grants, contracts, corporate and foundation contributions, and individual donations. The activities of these facilities that are most important to the success of the ADA are community-based supported work, work-adjustment programs, work services, and occupational skill-training programs. Supported employment will be addressed below, along with other emerging strategies.

A great deal is known about the scope and effectiveness of rehabilitation facilities. The National Association of Rehabilitation Facilities issues publications describing and assessing the activities of its members (Morrison 1991). Since 1986, the annual publications of J.M. Foundation, its National Awards for Excellence in Vocational Programs, have been perhaps the best source for information about the effectiveness of rehabilitation programs (J.M. Foundation 1986). For the first several years of the awards these publications emphasized the wide range of effectiveness of programs within each type. Effectiveness, the J.M. Foundation staff and their advisers concluded, is independent of the resources available to a facility, its size, or the economic conditions of its community (J.M. Foundation 1987). More recently, the foundation's publications have presented evidence that aggressive planning and management improve the effectiveness of all programs, regardless of type or location (J.M. Foundation 1989).

PROMISING COLLABORATIVE PROGRAMS

In what follows, four types of programs are described:

1. Programs to make local labor markets work more effectively both for employers and persons with disabilities
2. Projects with Industry
3. Supported employment
4. Centers for independent living

All four types of program rely for effectiveness on vigorous cooperation among persons in the public and private sectors and persons with disabilities as individuals and in groups. Advocates for these programs want them to receive additional financial support from Vocational Rehabilitation, from other titles of the Rehabilitation Act, from state agencies for mental health and mental retardation/development disabilities, and from the private sector.

Job-Matching Programs. These programs develop rapport between a local business community and persons with disabilities who are eager and able to enter the work force. The job fair is a prototypical example of a matching program. In one widely replicated model, a company invites other employers in its region to participate in a day-long "fair" during which they interview persons with disabilities. The companies that agree to participate identify specific jobs that are vacant. A job-placement agency for people with disabilities recruits, prescreens, and matches candidates with these jobs. Where appropriate, the agency suggests accommodations in the job specifications or the workplace and assists the new employee in arranging transportation. In my experience as a program director of Just One Break Job Fair in New York City, I saw

50 to 75 companies while attending the fair in 1990, conducted three or four interviews for each position, and hired approximately 12 of each 100 candidates at the end of the fair.

Projects with Industry (PWI) is a well-known, federally sponsored program authorized by the Vocational Rehabilitation Act. It provides competitive employment for persons with disabilities on the basis of agreements between rehabilitation organizations and private employers. Several studies have documented that success in PWI projects requires strong linkages between rehabilitation providers and employers, especially where employers provide specific job skills. In 1986, 13,000 job placements under PWI occurred across the country at a cost of $1,164 per placement (Morrison 1991).

Supported Employment. Originally developed as an alternative to sheltered workshops, supported employment is targeted to those individuals with severe disabilities who require special support services in order to maintain employment. These support services may be needed on a long-term basis or a time-limited one until the employment stabilizes. This program model holds considerable promise for persons with severe disabilities who have not competed successfully for employment or whose competitive employment has been interrupted or intermittent. Since 1987, supported work programs have been eligible for modest federal support under the Rehabilitation Act.

Most rehabilitation professionals agree that supported work programs for persons with disabilities who were previously regarded as unemployable should meet reasonably precise criteria for employment status, integration, and the provision of support. The employment criteria in general use are that participants should be paid for an average of 20 hours per week for work in a job site in their community. The accepted criteria for integration are that there be eight or fewer workers with disabilities per site who work in close proximity to other workers, and that job descriptions be personalized to each individual. The criteria for support are that it be ongoing, and include public or private funds to facilitate and maintain employment, provide reemployment assistance, and coordinate resources necessary to sustain an employee in a job (National Association of Rehabilitation Facilities 1989a).

Four supported work models have been devised, implemented, and evaluated. In the most frequently used model, individual placement with a "job coach," individuals with severe disabilities are placed in employment and given ongoing support by a trained specialist. An "enclave" model consists of small groups of persons with severe disabilities working together under supervision in an integrated setting. "Mobile work crews" is a model in which small groups of persons with disabilities travel to various sites with a supervisor and provide contractual services. Opportunities for interaction with persons without work disabilities are planned to occur regularly at these sites. The least frequently used model is "entrepreneurial" (or "small business" or "benchwork"). In this model, a new small enterprise, employing persons with and without disabilities, produces goods or services.

Evidence about the performance of these program is sketchy but encouraging. In a 1989 study of more than 500 organizations, 81 percent reported that an average of 73 percent of their supported employees received salaries "within the normal range for nonhandicapped employees engaged in the same type of work." The individual placement (job coach) model was "reported to be the most cost effective as well as the most difficult to administer." Referrals to these programs came mainly from sheltered workshops, but also in significant numbers from work-activity programs and school systems. This study predicts a huge growth in demand for supported work programs in the next several years. Almost half of the rehabilitation clients currently in programs could be served by supported work by 1992 (National Association of Rehabilitation Facilities 1989a).

A study of exemplary supported employment practices published later in 1989 found that effective programs deviated from federal guidelines in significant ways. Practice in the field seems to be outrunning theory and regulation. For example, enclaves are used effectively as transition sites; there is excellent social integration in some programs with more than eight supported employees per site; off-site supervision is frequently provided to individuals with chronic mental illness; and programs sometimes provided training prior to placement in supported employment (National Association of Rehabilitation Facilities 1989b). These findings reinforce the conclusions of the J.M. Foundation's reports about the enormous variation in effectiveness within programs of any particular type.

Independent Living. Although originally not an employment initiative, the independent living movement has become increasingly important in this field. The fundamental principle of independent living is that people with disabilities *themselves*—not their counselors or other professionals—should have the primary influence on their own lives. People with disabilities should assert that influence in order to gain their maximum potential and make their own choices.

The concept of community has been the basis of the movement since the first of what are now some 200 independent living centers was established in Berkeley, California in the early 1970s. The centers are run by boards of directors that are composed primarily of people with disabilities. Services provided by the centers pertinent to employment include self-management, acquisition of daily living skills, and peer and benefit counseling.

Beginning in 1987, the Rehabilitation Act authorized discretionary grants to independent living centers to "help provide a range of services including advocacy with respect to legal and economic rights" (Smith 1987b). As the centers gain competence, constituents, and funds, they will be increasingly important in the implementation of the ADA and other national and local policies.

WORKPLACE ACCOMMODATIONS

Considerable experience is available to assist employers in making the workplace accommodations mandated by the ADA. In this section I will define accommodations from the point of view of employees and employers, assess what is known about their cost, and identify sources of technical assistance to employers and to persons with disabilities.

What Accommodations Are. A workplace accommodation is any intervention that facilitates a person's ability to perform a job. Such interventions include changes in the physical environment (e.g., ramps, restrooms, menus in braille), changes in the tools of work (for instance, devices that assist persons with visual impairments to read, or assisted listening devices), and changes in how jobs are structured (for example, task descriptions or modified work schedules). The required type of accommodation will obviously vary with the individual employee, the requirements—and the purposes—of a particular job, and the environment of each workplace.

What Accommodations Cost. Although there is strong evidence that most workplace accommodations are not prohibitively expensive (Berkeley Planning Associates 1982), some members of the business community continue to be apprehensive and others are agitated about their potential costs. A well-known economist has fantasized that the ADA will create "open-ended litigation" in which federal agencies try to force employers to "share their wealth with the disabled regardless of the actual relation between the productivity of the disabled worker and the costs of accommodation" (Burkhauser 1990).

What is the source of this concern? In part it is the normal and understandable nervousness among employers about any increase in the cost of doing business, and especially an increase that cannot easily be quantified precisely because accommodations must be tailored to each employee. Moreover, most employers have both practical and ideological objections to costs that are mandated by government. These objections are amplified because employers' obligations are measured by a legal criterion, the absence of "undue hardship," which will require ongoing clarification. The economist quoted above has his own agenda. He raised the specter of excessive cost in order to argue that federal mandates should be accompanied by federal subsidies.

The pertinent history of the costs of workplace accommodations is what happened in response to section 504 of the Rehabilitation Act of 1973. This legislation required that accommodations be made by employers who received federal funds. Initially, section 504 aroused the same apprehension and agitation that surfaced with the ADA. However, many senior managers now recall that their fears about the cost of accommodations under section 504 were stimulated by human-resources and budget officers who were professionally eager to call attention to yet another claim on scarce resources. Many of these managers also recall that their determination to comply with both the law and with contemporary best practice in addressing the needs of their employees made the costs of accommodation a trivial problem. In several studies, managers told surveyors that the costs of most accommodations could easily be met within existing budget allocations. In a 1982 study, for example, half of the accommodations had no or a trivial cost; another third cost less than $500 (at 1982 prices); fewer than 10 percent cost more than $2,000 (again in 1982 prices) (Berkeley Planning Associates 1982). A 1987 study found that 50 percent of accommodations cost less than $50, 69 percent less than $500, and less than 1 percent more than $5,000 (Job Accommodation Network 1987).

Sources of Technical Assistance. Employers have many sources of technical assistance available to them in making accommodations. The most efficient technical assistance can often be provided by employees or prospective employees with disabilities themselves: just ask them what they need in order to perform their jobs. Many employees have access to other experts on their own staffs or in their communities. When implementing section 504, for example, many hospital managers discovered that their employees with disabilities and staff physical therapists already knew precisely what needed to be done in every department. In many communities, moreover, Independent Living Centers and other organizations of and for people with disabilities are eager to suggest ways to make cost-effective accommodations.

A significant source of technical assistance for employers and persons with disabilities is the Job Accommodation Network (JAN), established in 1984 by the President's Committee on Employment of Persons with Disabilities. The JAN has a national data bank of more than 20,000 successful accommodations. In response to calls to toll-free numbers, JAN determines the limitations of an individual based on her or his disability and the requirements of the job. The JAN staff recommends an appropriate accommodation. JAN staff estimate that for every 100 calls they receive, 72 facilitate the job placement of a person with a disability. In response to the ADA, JAN is acquiring more incoming toll-free lines and adding staff.

In sum, fear that the ADA requirements for workplace accommodations will add enormous costs and stimulate nightmarish litigation are unjustified. More likely, the ADA will provide opportunities for employers, employees, and public officials to work together to create a more productive and decent American workplace.

TOWARD THE FUTURE

If the ADA is to contribute to more productive employment for more people, a great deal must be done in a very short time in a discouraging economic environment. Employers, persons with disabilities, and medical and vocational professionals require a great deal of education. Federal, state, and local benefit programs for people with disabilities must be reexamined critically and, in many instances, modified. Funding for implementing the ADA needs to be found, even in these hard times, from both direct and tax appropriations. Technical assistance should be timely, trusted, and effective. Congress needs to exercise continuous oversight over both its own agencies' and the nation's implementation of ADA. Perhaps most important, the private sector must become increasingly comfortable about entering into partnerships with both the disability community and government leaders in implementing the Act—and in achieving its profound implications for Americans' lives.

Many individuals and organizations are suggesting improvements in each of these areas. My personal list of suggestions is long and detailed. Among other important matters, this list includes:

- proposals for additional tax incentives to employers to hire persons with disabilities and make appropriate accommodations
- many changes in the Rehabilitation Act in order to make services and training more effective
- proposals for private and public–private partnerships to implement the ADA and facilitate employing persons with disabilities

The implementation of the ADA should result in profound changes in the lives of persons with disabilities. These persons are indeed "equal to the task," as we know from both systematic research and from a mass of anecdotal evidence. Implementing the specific provisions of the ADA will enable persons with disabilities to have better access to transportation, public accommodations, employment, communications systems, and other aspects of daily living that persons without disabilities take for granted. For disability policy in the United States, and especially for that policy as it applies to employment, the ADA is a new beginning that builds on years of effort by many concerned citizens. It is a prescription for change.

REFERENCES

Berkeley Planning Associates. 1982. *A Study of Accommodations Provided to Handicapped Employees by Federal Contractors*. Oakland, Calif: Berkeley Planning Associates.

Bureau of National Affairs. 1990. *The Americans with Disabilities Act: A Practice and Legal Guide to Impact, Enforcement and Compliance*. Washington: Author.

Burkhauser, R.V. 1990. Morality on the Cheap. The Americans with Disabilities Act. *Regulation* 3: 47–56.

Burkhauser, R.V., R.H. Haveman, and B.L. Wolfe. November 1990. The Changing Economic Conditions of the Disabled: A Two Decade Review of Economic Well-Being. (Unpublished paper.)

Bush, G. 1990. Statement by the President of the United States at the Signing of the Americans with Disabilities Act, July 26.

Center for Independent Living/Disability Rights Education Defense Fund. 1978. *Consumer Guide to 504*. Berkeley, Calif: Disability Rights Education Defense Fund.

Du Pont, E.I. de Nemours and Company. 1990. *Equal to the Task*, 2nd. ed. Wilmington, Del.

Harris, L., and Associates. 1986. *Disabled Americans' Self-Perceptions: Bringing Disabled Americans into the Mainstream.* A Survey Conducted for the International Center for the Disabled. New York.

———. 1987. *The ICD Survey II: Employing Disabled Americans.* New York.

J.M. Foundation. 1986. *National Awards for Excellence in Vocational Programs.* New York.

———. 1987. *Learning from the Best: A Profile of America's Finest Vocational Programs Serving People with Disabilities.* New York.

———. 1989. *An Agenda for Excellence.* New York.

Job Accommodation Network. 1987. *Evaluation Survey, April 1987.* Washington: President's Commission on Employment of People with Disabilities.

Johnston, W.B., and A.E. Packer. 1987. *Workforce 2000: Work and Workers for the Twenty-First Century.* Indianapolis: Hudson Institute.

Kiernan, W.E., and J.A. Stark. 1989. *Pathways to Employment for Adults with Developmental Disabilities.* Baltimore: Paul H. Brookes Company.

Kraus, L.E., and S. Stoddard. 1989. *Chartbook on Disability in the United States.* Washington: U.S. National Institute on Disability and Rehabilitation Research.

Morrison, M.H. 1991. Rehabilitation Facilities and Employment of People with Disabilities: What We Have Learned. Washington: National Association of Rehabilitation Facilities. (Unpublished memorandum.)

National Association of Rehabilitation Facilities. 1989a. *Supported Employment in Context.* Washington.

———. 1989b. *Exemplary Supported Employment Practices.* Washington.

———. 1990. Tables from Report on State Vocational Rehabilitation Agencies for Fiscal Years 1921 to 1989. Washington. (Unpublished.)

Nixon, R.M. 1973. Statement vetoing the Rehabilitation Act of 1973. *The Congressional Record*, 93rd Congress, 2nd Session, March 27: 2087–90.

Rochlin, J. 1989. Testimony regarding Comprehensive Civil Rights Protection for Persons with Disabilities, September 13, 1989. U.S. Congress, House, 101st Congress, 1st Session. Washington: Subcommittee on Selection Education, Committee on Education and Labor.

Smith, M.F. 1987a. *Vocational Rehabilitation and Related Programs for Persons with Handicaps.* Washington: Congressional Research Service, Library of Congress.

———. 1987b. *Sheltered Workshops for Persons with Handicaps: Background Information and Recent Legislative Changes.* Washington: Congressional Research Service, Library of Congress.

———. 1990. *Vocational Rehabilitation and Related Programs for Persons with Handicaps: FY 1991 Budget Request.* Washington: Congressional Research Service, Library of Congress.

U.S. Department of Education. 1989. *Annual Report of the Rehabilitation Services Administration on Federal Activities Related to the Administration of the Rehabilitation Act of 1973, as Amended.* Washington: Author.

The Recent History and Immediate Future of Employment among Persons with Disabilities

Edward H. Yelin

EDITOR'S NOTE

Edward H. Yelin challenges the conventional wisdom that the combination of the boom in the service industry and the need for workers yields a rosy outlook for employment of persons with disabilities. Even with the 17-year-old antidiscrimination mandate of section 504 of the Rehabilitation Act, he points out that persons with disabilities continue to experience disproportionate rates of unemployment and layoffs: "The employment picture for persons with disabilities has worsened dramatically over the last two decades, despite the presence of section 504 of the Rehabilitation Act and a huge expansion of the labor force during the 1980s."

With section 504 protections contributing to the employment of persons with disabilities by helping to prevent a bad trend from becoming worse, what are the prospects for the ADA in terms of improving employment of persons with disabilities? Yelin argues for regular monitoring of employment trends through a highly visible reporting mechanism, paying particular attention to businesses and industry undergoing rapid expansion and contraction.

Yelin is associate professor of medicine and health policy at the University of California, San Francisco. He is the author of numerous articles on work disability, including "Displaced Concern: The Social Context of the Work Disability Problem" published in the Milbank Quarterly *and "The Impact of HIV-Related Illness on Employment" in the* American Journal of Public Health. *Yelin is also the author of a forthcoming book on the politics of work disability.*

The Americans with Disabilities Act (ADA) is the latest in what is now the 26-year history of civil-rights legislation beginning with the Civil Rights Act of 1964 and designed to reduce discrimination against racial and ethnic minorities, women, and, more recently, persons with disabilities.[1] ADA succeeds, by close to two decades, the passage of the Rehabilitation Act of 1973 (with its landmark section 504 barring discrimination against persons with disabilities by any program or activity receiving federal funds or conducted by executive agencies) (see Scotch [1984] for a description of the regulations underlying section 504). Although civil-rights legislation generally has had a salutary effect on access to public and private facilities and transportation, the record with respect to employment is, at best, a mixed one. Although laws bar discrimination against minorities in employment, they cannot provide the skills to compete in the contemporary economy or reduce the physical distance between where minorities live and where the jobs are. Laws bar discrimination against women in employment, but they cannot ensure women the same kind of work or pay as men. The ADA bars discrimination against persons with disabilities in employment, but it may not convince employers that such persons will be productive or purchase the equipment to help them do their jobs. In short, the law cannot guarantee work.

My purpose here is to speculate about the employment prospects of persons with disabilities in the wake of the ADA, to describe some of the mechanisms by which we might monitor the impact of the ADA on work, and to suggest a few strategies both to improve the employment situation of persons with disabilities and our ability to measure it.

Most analysts are sanguine about the employment prospects of persons with disabilities, citing as evidence for this optimism the expansion of the service sector of the economy over the last decade and the small size of the cohorts now entering the labor force (Interstate Conference of Employment Security Agencies 1990; Kutscher 1989; Silvestri and Lukasiewicz 1989). Based on the research that I and others have done on the labor-force participation of persons with disabilities, however, I do not share this optimism (U.S. Bureau of the Census 1989; Yelin 1986; 1989). The employment picture for persons with disabilities has worsened dramatically over the last two decades, despite the presence of section 504 of the Rehabilitation Act and a huge expansion

of the labor force during the 1980s. Whereas it is true that the recent
expansion of the service sector redounded to persons with disabilities,
this trend did not offset declines in other sectors of the economy. More
important, in the years to come, the service sector apparently will not
expand at the same rate as in the 1980s.

Thus, despite passage of the ADA, persons with disabilities may face
a difficult time sustaining employment. With the apparent onset of a
recession, we will have to be extremely vigilant to ensure that persons
with disabilities do not bear a disproportionate share of the costs of
retrenchment. I am not sure we have the tools to assess the impact of
ADA on employment, let alone to do something about it.

LABOR-FORCE DYNAMICS IN THE 1970s AND 1980s

Table 1 summarizes the dramatic changes that have been taking place
in the U.S. labor market over the past two decades. The labor-force
participation rate of working-aged adults increased by 10 percent during this time. However, this overall increase masks a slight 3 percent
decline in the labor-force participation rate of men, and a phenomenal
36 percent growth in the labor-force participation rate of women.
Women with disabilities did not share fully in the growth in labor-force
participation among women generally, and men with disabilities experienced a disproportionate share of the decline among men. Thus, the
labor-force participation rate of women with disabilities increased 30
percent, but this was only 83 percent as fast as the growth among
women without disabilities. In contrast, the labor-force participation
rate of men with disabilities declined by 15 percent, five times the
decline among men without disabilities.[2]

The entrance of women into the labor market has been well chroni-
cled, as has the overall growth in the percentage of working-aged adults
in the labor force. The declining labor-force participation of men has
not received as much attention. In addition, most of the public is
unaware of the extent to which the gains among women are concen-
trated among young women and the losses among men are concen-
trated among older men, in effect transforming the labor market from
one dominated by men of long job tenure to one dominated by women
who only began to work recently. Table 2 highlights these changes.
Between the early 1970s and late 1980s, the proportion of women aged

132   Edward H. Yelin

Table 1
Secular Changes in Labor Force Participation Rates of U.S. Adults, Aged 18–64,
1970–1972 vs. 1985–1987, by Gender and Disability Status

Gender	Disability status	1970–1972	1985–1987	Change (%)
Both	All statuses	63%	69%	+ 10
	With disability	46	44	– 4
	No disability	65	73	+ 12
Men	All statuses	85	82	– 3
	With disability	64	54	– 15
	No disability	88	85	– 3
Women	All statuses	43	58	+ 36
	With disability	27	35	+ 30
	No disability	45	62	+ 38

Source: Author's analysis of 1979 through 1987 National Health Interview Survey. This survey defines disability in terms of activity limitation due to chronic disease, impairment, or injury. Labor force participation rates are defined as the percentage of a group employed or actively looking for work. Preliminary analysis of the 1988 NHIS data, just made available, confirms the continuation of trends displayed here. Some of the estimates in tables 1 and 2 may differ by 1% to 2% from the true percentages in the population due to a combination of sampling variability and rounding errors.

18 to 44 in the labor force grew by 45 percent and the absolute number more than doubled. The proportion of women aged 45 to 54 in the labor force also grew dramatically (rising by 30 percent), but the proportion of women aged 55 to 64 in the labor force increased by only 3 percent. During this time, the proportion of men aged 55 to 64 in the labor force decreased by 17 percent (to 68 percent), and the absolute number actually declined slightly. The proportion of men aged 45 to 54 in the labor force declined much more slowly, reaching 89 percent by the late 1980s. Because the magnitude of the increase among young women exceeded the decline among older men, the proportion of all adults in the labor force increased by 10 percent, as shown in table 1. Thus, more of us are in the labor force, but overall the labor force has been feminized, primarily by the influx of younger women and the withdrawal of older men.

Race and disability status (separately and in combination) have

TABLE 2

Secular Changes in Labor Force Participation Rates of U.S. Adults, Aged 18–64, 1970–1972 vs. 1985–1987, by Gender, Race, Age, and Disability Status

Gender	Age	Disability status	All races 1970–1972	All races 1985–1987	All races Change (%)	Whites 1970–1972	Whites 1985–1987	Whites Change (%)	Nonwhites 1970–1972	Nonwhites 1985–1987	Nonwhites Change (%)
Men	18–44	All statuses	83%	83%	−0	83%	84%	+1	80%	73%	−9
		With disability	69	63	−9	71	67	−6	52	40	−23
		No disability	84	84	0	85	86	+1	82	76	−7
	45–54	All statuses	93	89	−4	94	91	−3	86	81	−6
		With disability	69	60	−13	73	64	−12	45	37	−18
		No disability	98	95	−3	98	96	−2	97	91	−6
	55–64	All statuses	82	68	−17	82	69	−16	77	62	−19
		With disability	53	38	−28	54	40	−26	40	25	−38
		No disability	93	79	−15	92	79	−14	93	78	−16
Women	18–44	All statuses	42	61	+45	41	62	+51	50	58	+16
		With disability	32	44	+38	32	46	+44	30	34	+13
		No disability	43	62	+44	41	63	+54	52	60	+15
	45–54	All statuses	46	60	+30	46	64	+39	56	65	+16
		With disability	24	30	+25	29	40	+38	31	28	−10
		No disability	51	70	+37	50	68	+38	63	75	+19
	55–64	All statuses	40	41	+3	39	41	+5	42	43	+2
		With disability	21	21	0	21	22	+5	22	20	−9
		No disability	45	50	+11	44	49	+11	51	58	+14

Source: See footnote to table 1.

133

accentuated both trends (table 2). That is, the withdrawal of older
nonwhite men from the labor force has been occurring faster than the
withdrawal of older white men, and the entrance of younger nonwhite
women has been occurring slower than among younger white women.
Meanwhile, the labor-force participation rate of older men with disabilities is falling faster than among those without disabilities, while the
labor-force participation rate of younger women with disabilities has
been rising more slowly than among those without. Finally, as might be
expected, nonwhites with disabilities fare the poorest: older nonwhite
men with disabilities have sustained the largest fall in labor-force participation rates, and younger nonwhite women with disabilities are
entering the labor market more slowly than white women—regardless
of disability status—and more slowly than nonwhite women without a
disability. Indeed, nonwhite women aged 45 to 54 and 55 to 64 with
disabilities, alone among all women, actually have experienced a reduction in labor-force participation rates.

Whereas labor-force participation rates among white men aged 55 to
64 without disabilities declined 14 percent over the past two decades, in
this age group the rates fell 16 percent among nonwhite men without
disabilities, 26 percent among white men with disabilities, and 38
percent among nonwhite men with disabilities. Similarly, whereas
labor-force participation rates increased 54 percent among white
women aged 18 to 44 without disabilities, in this age group the rates
rose 44 percent among women with disabilities (a substantial, albeit
smaller, increase), but only 15 percent among nonwhite women without disabilities and by 13 percent among women with disabilities.
Note, too, that nonwhite women aged 45 to 54 and 55 to 64 with
disabilities experienced 10 and 9 percent declines, respectively, in
labor-force participation rates at a time of increasing participation
among this age group of white and nonwhite women without disabilities and even among white women with them.

To summarize, the overall labor-force participation rate—regardless
of gender, age, or disability status—increased 10 percent over the last
two decades because the increases among young women overshadowed
the decreases experienced by older men. Likewise, this overall increase
masks substantial increases among persons without a disability (12 percent) and a worsening employment picture for those with disabilities
(the labor-force participation rate fell by 4 percent among all working-
aged persons with a disability, dropping even more, as noted above,
among some subgroups). Thus, on balance, the person with a disability

fared worse in the labor market at the end of the period than at the beginning, even though the labor force expanded both absolutely and relatively during this time. The only groups with disabilities that fared better—white women of all ages and young nonwhite women—experienced much smaller gains in their labor-force participation than comparable women without disabilities.

THE ECONOMIC CONTEXT OF EMPLOYMENT TRENDS

The downward trend in employment among persons with disabilities did not affect those in all occupations and industries evenly. Instead, the trend was part of the more general transformation of the economy. At a time when the words "downsizing," "displacement," and "outsourcing" became part of the everyday lexicon, persons with disabilities experienced these phenomena first hand. The occupations and industries that they left were those in decline: principally manual labor and craft occupations in the manufacturing, construction, agriculture, and mining industries in the first part of the period (a trend that continues) and then professional and managerial occupations in the financial and wholesale/retail industries in the last few years.

In contrast, the booming service industry absorbed hundreds of thousands of persons with disabilities to fuel its expansion, a fact not lost on anyone visiting a fast-food salad bar recently. The proportion of persons with disabilities in the service industry increased 18 percent over the last two decades; the increase since the 1982 recession alone was 28 percent. As one might expect, older men with disabilities left the declining industries and younger women with disabilities entered ascending ones. For example, the proportion of white men aged 55 to 64 with disabilities in laboring occupations declined by 29 percent since 1970 and the proportion of black men aged 55 to 64 with disabilities in laboring occupations declined 43 percent during this time. Overall, this occupation contracted 20 percent in relative terms. Meanwhile, the proportion of women aged 18 to 44 with disabilities in the service industry grew 27 percent after 1970.

Although not all occupations and industries fit the pattern perfectly, enough do that I can state this general rule: persons with disabilities, like those from minority races, constitute a contingent labor force, suffering displacement first and disproportionately from declining

industries and occupations, and experiencing gains in ascending ones
only after those without disabilities are no longer available for hire.
Because the prevalence of disability is much higher among persons in
the immediate preretirement years and because the number of occupations and industries descending has been greater than the number
ascending, the decreases in the labor-force participation of older workers with disabilities overshadow the gains among younger ones, and so,
overall, labor-force participation rates among persons with disabilities
have declined.

THE IMPACT OF SECTION 504

Section 504 of the Rehabilitation Act of 1973 bars discrimination in
employment among persons with disabilities in programs or activities
receiving federal funds or conducted by federal agencies. Because section 504 served as a model for the Americans with Disabilities Act, its
impact on employment in the intervening years may prove a bellwether
for the ADA. The publicly available data are insufficient to evaluate
the impact of section 504 on employment by recipients of federal funds
in the private sector. The legislation appears to have had mixed results
on the employment of persons with disabilities in government.[3]
Between 1970 and 1982, the number of government workers grew
absolutely (from about 4.5 to over 6 million workers) and as a proportion of the entire labor force (from 5.7 to 5.8 percent). This represents a
growth of 2 percent in relative terms. During this time, the number of
government workers with disabilities increased from .45 to .62 million
and the proportion of all government workers with disabilities rose
from 9.9 to 10.2 percent of the governmental work force, or by 3
percent in relative terms.

   In the intervening years, government employment contracted quite
severely, shrinking 11 percent in absolute terms and 19 percent in
relative terms between 1982 and 1987. The absolute number of government workers with disabilities declined by 18 percent during this time
and the proportion of government workers with disabilities declined
from 10.2 to 9.4 percent, or by 8 percent in relative terms. Meanwhile,
the absolute number of government workers without disabilities
declined by 10 percent (far smaller than the 18 percent decline among
government workers with disabilities) and, by definition, the propor-

tion of all government workers without disabilities rose from 89.2 to 90.6, an increase of 2 percent in relative terms. Thus, section 504 was not successful in ensuring that persons with disabilities shared in the employment gains occurring during the earlier period when government employment was expanding. Later, the legislation did not prevent workers with disabilities from bearing a disproportionate share of the retrenchment in government employment that was occurring throughout the 1980s. Nevertheless, persons with disabilities working in government fared much better than those in other sectors of the economy undergoing retrenchment.

These data on the impact of section 504 suggest that the ADA may not be successful either in preventing disproportionate displacement among persons with disabilities from industries undergoing retrenchment or in assisting such persons in finding work in the expanding sectors of the economy. Morever, we must remember that even though government workers with disabilities fared better than those in other declining industries in recent years, the proportion of persons with disabilities in government continued to fall during this time, suggesting that the old saw about things getting worse more slowly may apply here.

IN THE IMMEDIATE WAKE OF ADA

The employment "boom" of the 1980s was, in fact, a service and financial-industry boom, coupled with a manufacturing and extractive-industry bust.[4] Because the magnitude of the service boom exceeded that of the manufacturing bust, overall the labor force expanded 14 percent in absolute terms and 3 percent in relative terms during the decade, in the process absorbing the young, especially women, minorities, and some persons with disabilities.

Unfortunately, the service boom appears to be ending and its demise may signal tough times ahead for persons with disabilities. Service-industry employment expanded 4.5 percent a year in the 1980s, but the rate of increase fell substantially in the last two years (to 3.5 percent a year) and, ominously, the Bureau of Labor Statistics projects increases of about 2.5 percent a year in the 1990s (U.S. Bureau of the Census 1990). Although still large, this growth may not be sufficient to offset projected continuing declines in employment in goods-producing industry. More important, the projections of increases within services and slight declines in manufacturing preceded the onset of the crisis in the Middle East and so may very well be too optimistic. The rising price of oil may cause a severe slump in the automotive and steel industries, hastening the decline in manufacturing, and the service and retail industries may be reluctant to hire new employees if fears of rapid inflation prove well founded, dampening the growth in these sectors.

The decline in manufacturing, whether accelerated by the situation in the Middle East or not, will hasten the withdrawal of older men from the labor force, and older men with disabilities will be particularly hard hit. In contrast, the end of the service boom will slow the entrance of younger women into the labor force, perhaps decreasing the rate of labor-force participation among younger women with disabilities for the first time in the last two decades.

MONITORING THE EMPLOYMENT PICTURE AMONG PERSONS WITH DISABILITIES

WHAT AND HOW TO MONITOR

These data suggest that the employment picture of the approximately 19.1 million working-aged adults with disabilities has worsened over the past two decades.[5] The analysis derives from the National Health Interview Survey (NHIS), an annual cross-sectional sample of the non-institutionalized population designed primarily to monitor the health status of the population and its access to health care. The NHIS collects no information on past employment history or current hours of work, and so it provides only a partial snapshot of current employment trends, ignoring the route the individual took to his or her current situation and precluding an analysis of a partial reduction of work time due to disability. In addition to these structural limitations, the public-use tapes of the survey become available at least a year after data collection, so the trends being incompletely monitored are old ones. The National Center for Health Statistics (NCHS — the agency administering the NHIS) does not publish the labor-force data from the survey regularly; instead, their publication depends on the analyses done by individual investigators.

The primary survey designed to monitor labor-force trends is the Current Population Survey (CPS), administered by the Census Bureau for the Department of Labor's Bureau of Labor Statistics. The CPS collects information on the work status of approximately 60,000 individuals each month. However, the CPS asks its respondents to report their disability status only once annually in its March supplement and these data do not include information on the conditions causing the disability or the duration of the impairment. Moreover, the data from the CPS, when publicly available on computer tapes, may be a year and a half old; the Bureau of Labor Statistics has published the results of the CPS March supplement only twice: in 1983 and 1989 (U.S. Bureau of the Census 1983; 1989).

Thus, any data we have on the labor-force participation of persons with disabilities will be more than a year old (and is likely to be several years old), and will be incomplete insofar as the Health Interview Survey provides poor information on labor-force history and current work status, and the March CPS makes only a cursory attempt to measure health status.

The structural limitations of the NHIS and CPS notwithstanding, these two surveys could provide useful information to monitor the impact of ADA on employment among persons with disability at very little additional cost. The National Center for Health Statistics should be encouraged to publish the results of the NHIS labor-force participation questions in a timely fashion, certainly within a year of the completion of each year's data collection. They should also be encouraged to ask respondents currently working the length of their average work week and the number of weeks worked in the past year, and to ask those no longer in the labor force when and why they left work, as well as the occupation and industry for the time prior to illness of those claiming to be out of the labor force for health reasons. These are all standardized items in labor-force questionnaires, the addition of which would increase the one-hour interview time of NHIS respondents by no more than one or two minutes. However, with these additions and the health-status data already included in the survey, the NHIS would provide a much more systematic view of the impact of disability on the labor force.[6]

Because the CPS is the primary source of labor-market data—one to which the media and other analysts of labor-force trends turn to keep tabs on employment—it should be augmented for use in monitoring the impact of ADA on employment. The employment picture among persons with disabilities would then garner the same attention as that of women and minorities, making the front page of most newspapers and the network newscasts when released each month. The March supplement to the CPS includes five items that can be used to infer work loss resulting from disability: a basic disability screen, a question about retirement due to disability, one ascribing last year's work status to disability, one ascribing this year's work status to disability, and questions about Medicare and Supplemental Security Income (SSI) coverage if the respondent is under the age of 65. Including these items in the monthly questionnaire in the CPS would add less than two minutes to the basic interview. However, a health screen analogous to the one included in the NHIS could be completed in as little as 30 seconds, and would provide enough information to monitor employment trends among those with and without disabilities on an ongoing basis. Monthly monitoring of employment among persons with disabilities seems warranted, if only because the data from the NHIS and March supplement to the CPS have not received sufficient attention to make the public aware of the worsening labor-force situation of persons with disabilities, whereas the public is aware of the CPS data released monthly by the Bureau of Labor Statistics.[7]

However the employment situation ultimately is monitored, particular attention must be paid to the industries and occupations undergoing rapid expansion and contraction because persons with disabilities have not shared proportionately in the employment gains in expanding sectors of the economy, while bearing a disproportionate share of the retrenchment in contracting ones. The CPS may not be sufficiently large to monitor the employment status of persons with disabilities within individual industries and occupations, perhaps necessitating periodic enlargement of the sample or, at the very least, merging several months worth of data.

The Equal Employment Opportunity Commission collects information periodically from large employers on the hiring of women and minorities within different occupations and industries (U.S. General Accounting Office 1989). This database, although not reflective of the entire labor force, might be expanded to include questions about employment of persons with disabilities.

PAYING FOR THE COSTS OF MONITORING

The ADA places significant responsibility for enforcement of the employment provisions of the law in the hands of the Equal Employment Opportunity Commission (EEOC), a role the EEOC performs for other civil-rights legislation. Typically, the EEOC carries out its mandate by investigating individual claims of discrimination. The Congressional Budget Office estimates that the EEOC will need about $15 million a year for these activities as they relate to the ADA (Senate Committee on Labor and Human Resources 1989). However, it is well within EEOC's purview to pursue the goal of enforcement by supporting research on the entire class of persons with disabilities, many of whom may have experienced discrimination without filing a formal claim; the database described above is one way EEOC carries out this mandate. The EEOC thus would appear to be the most appropriate agency to fund the incremental data-collection activities described here. The funds themselves could come from the monies appropriated to the EEOC to investigate individual claims of discrimination, or, to ensure adequate oversight in enforcement, from an additional appropriation.

ASSESSING EMPLOYABILITY IN THE SERVICE ECONOMY

One of the apparent paradoxes surrounding the ADA is that the labor-force participation of persons with disabilities is declining just as the physical basis of work erodes. Manufacturing employment is down, and in more of the manufacturing that remains workers neither supply physical power themselves (production typical of early industrial enterprises) nor run machines that do (production typical of mass-production industry in the post-War period). Instead, manufacturing workers increasingly monitor computer-run production by analyzing digitized versions of the analog production process at some remove from the actual factory floor (Hirschhorn 1984; Zuboff 1988). In this postindustrial manufacturing, and in much of the remainder of the service economy, physical impairment should not preclude work.

The erosion of the physical basis of employment has led many analysts to suggest that declining labor-force participation rates are now due either to the aging of the population, which results in severe disabilities among a greater proportion of the potential work force, or to the Social Security Disability Insurance (SSDI) program, whose generous benefits allow workers to withdraw from work when they have the physical capacity to persevere on the job (see Yelin [1986, 1989] for a review of both literatures). However, both theories have proven easy to refute. The aging hypothesis holds that more workers are being pushed into the age brackets with the highest risk for disability. But the labor-force participation rate has decreased *among men of all ages with disabilities*, refuting the notion that age creep accounts for the rise in work-disability rates. The hypothesis that SSDI (or other disability-entitlement programs) were responsible for the rise in work-disability rates seemed valid a decade ago when the rates were rising in tandem with increases in the real value of disability benefits. However, in the interim the real value of benefits has been reduced, but work-disability rates continue to climb.[8]

The analysts who believed that the declining significance of brute-force work in the service economy would reduce work-disability rates overlooked the fact that the demand for the labor of older men, the group most heavily represented in the manufacturing sector, would decline with these changes. They also overlooked other impediments to keeping persons with disabilities employed. The increasing physical distances separating work and home are especially taxing to persons with disabilities, many of whom cannot drive. More important, the rhythms of the workaday world are often at odds with the medical conditions causing physical impairment. When many of us envision persons with disabilities, we think about congenital conditions or injuries, both of which are of unvarying intensity. Most persons with disabilities, however, have chronic conditions characterized by periods of flare and remission lasting weeks and months, and with symptoms that vary throughout the day. This variance makes planning work activities difficult. Arthritis is the most common cause of work loss. The person with this condition typically is prone to morning stiffness, which makes getting up and out very difficult. During a flare, the person with arthritis may have to reduce work activities both to garner rest and to visit the doctor. There is now accumulating evidence that individuals with chronic diseases as diverse as cancer, arthritis, and AIDS who can control the pace and scheduling of work activities are less liable to stop working, precisely because they have the capacity to meld their conditions with their jobs (Greenwald et al. 1989; Yelin, Henke, and Epstein 1987; Yelin et al. 1991). In contrast, workers with inflexible working conditions are more likely to drop out of the labor force because they cannot meet the stringent time requirements of work, not because they lack the physical capacity to work.[9]

The ADA places a responsibility on employers to make reasonable accommodations so that persons with disabilities can continue to work.

The research showing that the time dimension of work may be more critical than the actual physical demands of the job in determining the work outcomes of chronic disease has important implications for the enforcement of these reasonable accommodation provisions because it implies that slight changes in work rules may redound to the person with a disability far more than expensive modification of the physical plant or retooling of industrial processes.

The preliminary findings relating discretion over the pace and scheduling of work activities to work-disability rates also suggest several research and enforcement strategies in the wake of the passage of ADA. The research would be designed to help both persons with disabilities and industry assess work capacity in more realistic terms and to provide information to policy makers on the extent to which work disability is due to factors within work, for example, the physical and time requirements of jobs, and to those outside of work, for example, transportation to and from work. The enforcement strategies would use the data from the research to delimit industry's ability to make persons with disabilities bear a disproportionate share of retrenchment in employment. I shall deal with each in turn.

RESEARCH TO ASSIST IN THE IMPLEMENTATION OF THE ADA

Work loss arises from disability when there is a discordance between the demands of a job and the impairment an individual experiences. A job requires lifting, the individual cannot lift; a job requires punctuality, the individual experiences morning stiffness lasting past the scheduled beginning of work. The Department of Labor collects data on the physical demands of work as part of its mandate to update the Dictionary of Occupational Titles. However, no ongoing surveys collect information relating physical impairments to the physical demands of work. (The last survey to do this in a systematic fashion was the 1978 Social Security Administration Survey of Disability and Work.) During the 1970s, the Department of Labor collected information on the time demands of jobs and employees' discretion over work activities through its Quality of Employment Surveys. These data have not been collected since. Moreover, no survey has ever collected information relating impairments to workers' discretion over pace and scheduling of activities. The extant information relating impairments to the physical demands of work is outdated due to the subsequent changes within manufacturing and growth of the service industry, and the growing recognition that time and pace are more important than physical demands in determining work status suggests that data concerning these parameters be collected for the first time.[10] Likewise, there is no contemporary information on the mode and duration of the commute to work among persons with and without disabilities and, thus, no way we can estimate the extent to which transportation is an impediment to continued employment.

The passage of the ADA may provide a window of opportunity to conduct the kind of systematic research needed to monitor employment among persons with disabilities. In addition to the permanent revisions for the NHIS and CPS that I suggested earlier, we need a one-time special survey to estimate the interactions between impairments and working conditions in the contemporary economy. Although the primary purpose of such a survey would be informational, it could be used by the Equal Opportunity Employment Commission to refine policy guidelines for employment based on the ADA.

Persons with disabilities would use the information from a systematic disability survey to estimate their work prognosis in much the same way they ask their physicians to estimate the probability of adverse medical outcomes, such as death. Working with vocational counselors, they would be able to focus job searches on industries and occupations that accommodate others with impairments much like their own.

Industry could use the results of the survey to provide more accurate information on how their production processes interact with their employees' impairments, with the hope of forestalling the premature withdrawal from jobs in which the fit between job demands and impairments remains a good one. This information could also alert employers to those situations in which minor modifications of the physical environment would allow workers to continue on the job, especially those in which the impairment does not affect the actual work. A flight of stairs is as much an impediment to the word processor with osteoarthritis of the knee as heavy lifting and bending are to the steel worker with the same condition, even though the word processing is unaffected by the arthritis and steel manufacturing is.

In a similar vein, systematic data on the fit between the time demands of jobs and impairments might assist employers in redesigning jobs to suit the needs of their employees with disabilities for flexibility. Let me amplify with two examples. Clerical work within the insurance industry was one of the fastest-growing jobs in the 1980s. Traditionally, clerical workers within insurance companies have had to maintain very strict schedules even though the work they do (processing claims) could be done any time and, in this day and age, almost anywhere. Because of these strict time requirements, this job has had very high work-disability rates. In contrast, the computer industry — also undergoing rapid expansion — frequently allows very flexible scheduling and, not surprisingly, the work disability rate among their clerical workers has been relatively low.

Sometimes work rules are an integral part of production processes. The automotive assembly line could not operate without a punch clock or the cars would not be made (whether this is the best way to assemble cars is another matter); the retail outlet needs its sales force during its posted hours of operation. All too frequently, however, the work rules bear little relation to what is actually being done and, where this is so, relaxing them might very well lower work disability rates. Systematic data from a special survey could prove useful in pinpointing the obvious discordancies. The President's Committee on Employment of People with Disabilities would appear to be the appropriate agency to distribute such information given its mission to advocate for the employment-related interests of persons with disabilities.

ENFORCEMENT OF THE EQUAL EMPLOYMENT OPPORTUNITY
MANDATE OF THE ADA

The labor-force participation data presented above provide ample evidence that persons with disabilities have suffered employment discrimination over the last two decades, with older male workers with disabilities bearing a disproportionate share of the retrenchment in declining industries and occupations and female workers with disabilities not sharing proportionately in the growth sectors.

The ADA vests the Equal Employment Opportunity Commission with the responsibility to write and then to enforce regulations against discrimination in employment. The experience with previous civil-rights legislation suggests that a two-pronged approach is necessary. First, the EEOC can pursue individual claims of discrimination that come before it. However, only a fraction of the hundreds of thousands — perhaps millions — of individuals who will suffer discrimination subsequent to the passage of the ADA will ever file such a claim. Therefore, a second monitoring effort is necessary. The EEOC should seek to establish a statistical basis for discrimination. Augmented NHIS, CPS, and special disability surveys can assist in this activity, demonstrating, on the one hand, that persons with disabilities suffered a disproportionate amount of displacement from the labor force and, on the other, that individuals with specific impairments do continue to function in jobs with a certain level of physical demand. The passive strategy of waiting for aggrieved individuals to file claims will not suffice. Individuals with disabilities can never know whether their layoffs represent a disproportionate share of the retrenchment in a contracting industry. They cannot amass the statistical evidence to support this sort of claim of discrimination, nor are they likely to be able to prove on a case-by-case basis that they can function at work. Although the adjudication of applications for Social Security Disability benefits proves that defining work capacity is inherently a subjective process, having information on the statistical relations among job demands, physical impairments, and labor-force participation will at the very least suggest those situations in which the discrimination is most egregious.[11] Old survey data, based on the manufacturing economy and ignoring the time dimension of work, will not serve this function. The EEOC must have a more contemporary model of work upon which to base its enforcement of ADA's employment provisions.

CONCLUSION

While the evidence for discrimination in employment against persons with disabilities is compelling, it emanates primarily from the testimony of individuals or from data that are old, irregularly collected, and analyzed on an ad hoc basis by researchers outside of government. Our ability to monitor the impact of the ADA on employment requires the collection and timely dissemination of data on the labor-force participation of persons with disabilities. I advocate including disability-screening items in the monthly Current Population Surveys to accomplish this goal. Our ability to improve the job prospects of persons with disabilities, however, requires current data on the interactions among impairments, job demands, and work status, both to indicate how well such persons function at work and to assist efforts to provide an objective basis for determining whether employment status is related to discrimination or actual functional capacity. This kind of data can only be obtained from a special disability survey like those administered on behalf of the Social Security Administration in the 1960s and 1970s.

NOTES

1. P.L. 88–352.
2. Unless specifically noted, the data concerning the labor-force participation of persons with and without disability cited here derive from my analysis of the National Health Interview Surveys (NHIS), 1970 through 1987. A more extensive review of these data appears in Yelin (1989).
3. The data on government workers that I discuss here include *all* government workers—federal, state, and local. It was not possible to separate out federal workers from these data. A caveat, therefore, is in order. While section 504 prohibits discrimination in "programs or activities" receiving federal funds, the question of how broadly to interpret the term "program or activity" has been the subject of extensive consideration. Prior to the Supreme Court's decision in *Grove City College v. Bell*, 465 U.S. 555 (1984), the term "program or activity" was interpreted broadly. Thus, from 1973 to 1984, if some section of a state or local department received federal funds, the entire department (and all of its workers) were covered under the section 504 requirements. In the 1984 case of *Grove City College*, the Supreme Court ruled that "program or activity" was to be interpreted narrowly. Under that ruling, if a particular section of a department received federal funds, *only* that section was covered by section 504. This ruling was ultimately overturned by Congress in 1988 by enactment of the Civil Rights Restoration Act, P.L. 100–259. Thus, after 1988, a broad range of state and local employees were once again covered by section 504.

   Although it is possible that *some* state and local government employees are not covered by section 504 (because no federal funds are received by the "program or activity" and there is no comparable state of law), it is improbable that this number would be significant. In addition, for purposes of these data, it is unlikely that state and local governments dramatically changed their policies or practices during the period the *Grove City College v. Bell* decision stood (1984–1988).
4. I use the terms "boom" and "bust" to mean a rise and decline in the proportion of the population employed in the different sectors of the economy. Of course these quantitative changes in the shares of employment have implications for the quality of work and the overall health of the economy. Rather than enter the debate comparing the jobs gained with those lost in such parameters as pay, tenure, and potential for growth or continuing the endless discussion about what the transformation from a manufacturing to a services economy portends in the long term, I am limiting the analysis here to the less contentious issue of the sheer numbers of workers.
5. Because the figure of 43 million persons with disabilities in the United States has been bandied about so much (the ADA itself quotes this figure), I should point out here that the 19.1 million figure I use is from the NHIS and includes only working-aged adults, 18 to 64, with disability defined in terms of activity limitation due to chronic disease, impairment, or injury.
6. The changes noted above represent additions to the recurrent questions in the NHIS. However, the NHIS frequently includes supplemental studies in addition to the questions asked of respondents each year. The NHIS sample could

also be used for a supplemental study in which respondents with and without disabilities were followed longitudinally to study patterns of retrenchment from work and risk factors for work loss following onset of disability. Currently, all we know about the process of withdrawal from work in the presence of illness comes from studies using cross-sectional data to make longitudinal inferences.

7. Likewise, special surveys conducted by the Social Security Administration and Census Bureau, while providing useful information to program administrators and the research community, have not gotten the public's attention. Thus, my emphasis on the monthly CPS.

8. The early econometric studies of the role of entitlement programs in labor-force participation rates attributed almost all of the reduction in older male labor-force participation to the SSDI program. The later studies find only small effect (or none). Interestingly, the later studies use more sophisticated models of the impact of health on work, suggesting that the earlier results were due to improper control for health status. For reviews of these studies, see Wolfe (1984) and Yelin (1986).

9. This discussion is not meant to imply that physical capacity is never an impediment to work. Clearly, there are thousands of individuals whose medical conditions preclude employment. However, the situation in which there is poor concordance between the time requirements of work and chronic illness occurs more often than that in which the brute-force demands of a job are too great.

10. The studies relating discretion over the pace and scheduling of work activities to work disability used small, clinically derived samples or inferred the time characteristics of jobs by matching data from the Quality of Employment Surveys to surveys such as the 1978 Social Security Administration Survey of Disability and Work.

11. Stone (1984) demonstrates how disability determinations are inherently subjective, frustrating attempts to treat them as medically unambiguous decisions.

REFERENCES

Greenwald, H., S. Dirks, E. Borgatta, R. McCorkle, M. Nevitt, and E. Yelin. 1989. Work Disability among Cancer Patients. *Social Science and Medicine* 29:11.

Hirschhorn, L. 1984. *Beyond Mechanization: Work and Technology in a Postindustrial Age.* Cambridge, Mass.: MIT Press.

Interstate Conference of Employment Security Agencies. 1990. Workforce Trends: An Assessment of the Future for Employment.

Kutscher, R. 1989. Projections Summary and Emerging Issues. *Monthly Labor Review* 112 (11):66–74.

Scotch, R. 1984. *From Good Will to Civil Rights: Transforming Federal Disability Policy.* Philadelphia: Temple University Press.

Senate Committee on Labor and Human Resources, 1989. Letter from Mr. Robert D. Reischauer, Director, Congressional Budget Office, to Hon. Edward F.

Kennedy, Chairman, Committee on Labor and Human Resources. In *Report on S. 993, The Americans with Disabilities Act (no. 101–116)*, 90–91.

Silvestri, G., and J. Lukasiewicz. 1989. Projections of Occupational Employment, 1988–2000. *Monthly Labor Review* 112 (11): 42–65.

Stone, D. 1984. *The Disabled State*. Philadelphia: Temple University Press.

U.S. Bureau of the Census. 1983. Labor Force Status and Other Characteristics of Persons with a Work Disability. *Current Population Reports*, series P-23, no. 127, July. Washington.

———. 1989. Labor Force Status and Other Characteristics of Persons with a Work Disability. *Current Population Reports*, series P-23, no. 160, July. Washington.

———. 1990. Statistical Abstract of the United States, 1990, 394–95. Washington.

U.S. General Accounting Office. 1989. *Equal Employment Opportunity: Women and Minority Aerospace Managers and Professionals, 1979–1986*. GAO/HRD-90–16, October. Washington.

Wolfe, B. 1984. Measuring Disability and Health. *Journal of Health Economics* 3:187–93.

Yelin, E. 1986. The Myth of Malingering: Why Individuals Withdraw from Work in the Presence of Illness. *Milbank Quarterly* 64(4): 622–49.

———. 1989. Displaced Concern: The Social Context of the Work Disability Problem. *Milbank Quarterly* 67 (suppl. 2, part 1): 114–66.

Yelin, E., R. Greenblatt, H. Hollander, and J. McMaster. 1991. The Impact of HIV-Related Illness on Employment. *American Journal of Public Health* 81 (1):79–84.

Yelin, E., C. Henke, and W. Epstein. 1987. The Work Dynamics of the Person with Rheumatoid Arthritis. *Arthritis and Rheumatism* 30:5.

Zuboff, Shoshana. 1988. *In the Age of the Smart Machine: The Future of Work and Power*. New York: Basic Books.

ACKNOWLEDGMENTS

Supported by Grant AM-20684 from the National Institute of Arthritis, Musculoskeletal, and Skin Diseases and Research Career Development Award AG-00273 from the National Institute on Aging (to Dr. Yelin). The author gratefully acknowledges the advice of his colleagues, Drs. Patricia P. Katz, Curtis Henke, and Wallace Epstein.

The Economics of Employment

Thomas N. Chirikos

EDITOR'S NOTE

Thomas N. Chirikos provides an economic analysis of the supply and demand of workers with disabilities and concludes that "low levels of accommodation costs observed at present may be attributable to the low employment levels of persons with disabilities. These variables should be expected to move together in the future." Positing that persons with disabilities who enter the labor force post ADA are likely to be more severely impaired than those currently employed, therefore requiring more expensive accommodations, Chirikos argues that an increase in employment will result in higher accommodation costs.

If we accept Chirikos' conclusions, the critical question for accommodation costs becomes the question of who pays. When people with disabilities are working, it clearly benefits the economy; however, the cost to individual businesses may be prohibitive in certain circumstances. Chirikos concludes that "redistributive issues in generating employment for persons with disabilities will have to be faced more squarely. Policy tools beyond the scope of the ADA may have to be used to ensure that persons with disabilities are fully integrated into the American economy, including the expanded use of subsidies and alternative means of sharing the burden between the employer and employee." Clearly Congress recognized this redistributive issue when enacting the small-business tax credit for ADA-related expenditures. The Chirikos logic leads to the conclusion that the more successful the

ADA, the more cost-sharing strategies are needed. Monitoring and collecting data about the costs and benefits of accommodation and their distribution are essential as the ADA undergoes implementation.

Chirikos is professor of health economics in the department of health policy and management, College of Public Health, University of South Florida at Tampa. He has published numerous articles related to the economics of health and medical care in such journals as Journal of Chronic Diseases, Journal of Health Economics, Journal of Human Resources, Medical Care, Milbank Quarterly, *and* Review of Economics and Statistics.

When it is completely phased in, title I of the Americans with Disabilities Act of 1990 (ADA) will extend the prohibition of job-related discrimination against persons with disabilities to all firms in the private sector employing 15 or more workers. The title complements sections 501, 503, and 504 of the 1973 Rehabilitation Act prohibiting discrimination and mandating affirmative action in the employment of individuals with disabilities by agencies of the federal government or private firms with federal contracts over $2,500. Consistent with the provisions of this earlier legislation, title I requires that reasonable accommodations be provided for persons with disabilities (either already qualified persons, or as a means of enabling them to be qualified) unless the employer can demonstrate that the accommodation will impose an undue hardship in terms of difficulty or expense. Within this framework, title I clearly intends to improve the economic prospects of persons with disabilities by equalizing their opportunities for employment and thereby integrating them more fully into the American economy.

The need for this integration is not only long overdue but is also of special urgency in view of recent data indicating that the economic gap between Americans with disabilities and Americans without disabilities has grown even wider over the decade of the 1980s.[1] Census Bureau data, for example, show that between 1980 and 1988 the proportions of "work-disabled men" aged 16 to 64 years who were in the labor force or working full time fell steadily, while the proportion of these men who were unemployed rose by several percentage points; as a result, the ratio of average earnings between men with disabilities and men without disabilities of working age also fell steadily over this period, from 77 to 64 percent for all workers and from 91 to 81 percent for year-round, full-time workers (Bennefield and McNeil 1989). Similar changes are observed for working women. Moreover, Haveman and Wolfe (1989) estimate that the real level of income transfers to persons with disabilities who qualified for them also fell over much of this period. Although the reduction in transfer income varied across subgroups of the population of persons with disabilities, it clearly compounded the economic hardship of low labor-market earnings of these persons. After recording substantial relative gains in the 1960s and 1970s, individuals with disabilities find themselves at the end of the 1980s again losing economic ground to those without disabilities.

The extent to which title I may be expected to reverse these trends in the earnings and economic well-being of the population with disabilities is open to question. On the one hand, the long-standing differential between persons with disabilities and persons without disabilities in the factors that correlate highly with labor-market success, especially the amount of job training and formal schooling completed, will not necessarily be affected by the Act, at least in the short run. On the other hand, there is evidence (reviewed later in this article) that the economic disadvantage of persons with disabilities stems in large measure from discriminatory employment practices that title I is designed to eliminate. Yet, even in this latter case, otherwise qualified persons with a disability may still find some jobs inaccessible because reasonable accommodation may be too costly; that is, it may be judged as imposing an undue hardship on the employer. Title I, in other words, may be expected to improve the employment prospects of these individuals only within the limits established by the costs of reasonable accommodation. If these costs are on average low, title I should be expected to augment the relative economic status of persons with disabilities. If, however, the costs are high, the ADA legislation will not necessarily achieve its employment goal and other strategies will have to be implemented to reverse the widening economic gap between persons with disabilities and the rest of the American population.

Despite their pivotal role in the potential success of title I, and despite their equally significant role in the historical impact of related sections of the 1973 Rehabilitation Act, remarkably little is known about the costs of reasonable accommodation. Few data on these costs in terms either of level distribution across sectors of the economy, or variations across the population of persons with disabilities are presently available (cf. Applied Management Sciences 1985; U.S. Commission on Civil Rights 1983; U.S. Government Accounting Office 1989). Furthermore, little empirical or theoretical research has been conducted on the topic, particularly by professional economists (cf. Collignon 1986). As a result, a review of published findings about the costs associated with the employment of workers with disabilities yields limited information. Economists, however, have an established framework for thinking about such issues, and some useful insights may be obtained by applying this framework to questions about accommodation costs. Economists have also investigated in indirect fashion some relationships suggested by the application of this framework to disability policy issues. Because specialists in the disability field appear at times to be unaware of the relevant economic literature, a review of some of this research may provide useful insight.

The primary objective of this article is to examine the extent to which the costs of reasonable accommodation may be expected to influence the employment opportunities of persons with disabilities. The conventional assumption is that these costs are negligible and in virtually all cases outweighed by the benefits of employing such persons. Fragmentary empirical evidence tends to confirm this assumption. However, there is little reason to suppose that these conditions will necessarily prevail over time as the ADA is implemented. For one thing, the costs of accommodating greater numbers of persons with disabilities may rise because the severity level of disabling impairments or health conditions will increase at the margin as supply grows. For another, wage discrimination against workers with disabilities has afforded the opportunity for some employers to shift the incidence of the costs of accommodation to these workers themselves. If this cost shifting is reduced or eliminated, the demand for workers with disabilities may fall. The costs of reasonable accommodation, in other words, should be expected to vary with the supply of, and demand for, persons with disabilities. In this article, I will review what economists have learned in investigating some of the supply-and-demand characteristics of the labor market for these workers.

A secondary objective of this article is to sketch some data and research needs for appraising the extent to which the employment opportunities and economic status of persons with disabilities change over time — in other words, the degree to which title I may be judged successful. The discussion is designed not only to identify major deficiencies in the present knowledge base about the costs and benefits of employing such workers, but also to lay some groundwork now for appraising the impact of the legislation. The delays encountered in writing the regulations for various sections of the Rehabilitation Act of

1973 are probably responsible for the absence of any early evaluation scheme for that legislation (Percy 1989); this should be avoided under the ADA. The need to think at this time about the manner in which the social impact of title I will be investigated assumes even greater importance in view of (a) the division of responsibilities across different agencies of the federal government for ensuring compliance and (b) the large number of methodological difficulties that confound any evaluation of public policy in the disability arena.

The article is organized as follows: In the next section, I will consider the definition of the costs of reasonable accommodation from an economic perspective and apply the concepts of supply and demand to account for possible variations in the level and distribution of these costs. This economic framework is then used to explore some of the provisions of title I. I will then go on to summarize what is known empirically about costs, the supply of persons with disabilities to the labor market, and the corresponding dimensions of the demand for these workers. Following this summary, I describe a framework for evaluating the employment effects of title I and propose a longitudinal data-collection effort that would assist in measuring progress toward employment goals. In closing, I draw the main conclusions of the analysis.

THINKING ECONOMICALLY ABOUT TITLE I

COSTS OF ACCOMMODATION

Title I prohibits job discrimination against otherwise qualified persons with disabilities and mandates that reasonable accommodation be provided. Reasonable accommodation is not required if it causes the employer (covered entity) "undue hardship" in terms either of difficulty or expense. Undue hardship is to be judged in the light of such factors as the nature and cost of the accommodation, the overall financial resources of the facility or covered entity, and/or the type of operations of that entity. Title I of the ADA legislation, like section 504 of the 1973 Rehabilitation Act before it, clearly intends to avoid circumstances in which reasonable accommodation imposes "high" costs on employers, although what will be viewed as unacceptably high costs remains to be worked out legally on a case-by-case basis.

In the context of the legislation, the case-by-case determination of undue hardship implies that the costs of reasonable accommodation cannot be estimated or even defined with any degree of certainty. From an economic viewpoint, however, these costs must refer to the opportunity cost of employing a person with a disability rather than a person without a disability in a given job. This opportunity cost is gauged as the difference, if any, in the total (present) value of the resources used to hire, place, and maintain either kind of worker in a specific job assignment. Three aspects of this definition are noteworthy:

1. There are, in effect, costs of accommodation for all workers. The presumption in the legislation is that these costs are greater at the margin for the person with a disability, but theoretically that need not be the case. In principle, a full accounting of the costs of developing and maintaining a labor force, especially the costs of firm-specific training, turnover, leaves for medical and personal reasons, and the shirking of job responsibilities is required in order to judge correctly the extra costs, if any, of accommodating workers with disabilities.

2. These costs encompass the value of all resources, including the opportunity costs of the employer's and employee's time, and the value of any capital goods, irrespective of whether they are provided by the employer, employee, or some third party. Although some accommodations are no doubt essential to the performance of a given job function, most may vary by the burden of time and effort that is placed on persons with disabilities themselves. Conceptually, the value of this time should be taken into account when accommodation costs are computed. Some sharing of this burden, either through substitution of capital equipment for the time of the employee with a disability or the time of the employer for that of the employee, should force the costs of accommodation to some minimum level. That level should be calculated, irrespective of its incidence or distribution across the parties involved.

3. Costs of accommodations may be incurred continuously over time, rather than simply at a single point in time such as the day the person is hired. The continuing costs incurred in providing interpreters for persons with hearing impairments is a case in point. These cost streams should account for any changes over time in expected annual cost levels and then should be present valued by standard techniques.[2] At the firm level, accommodation costs should also be prorated over the number of persons with identical disabilities; for example, one-half of the present value of the cost of the services of the interpreter would be assigned to each of two workers with hearing impairments hired at the

same time and having the same expected work life. Some past expenses should also be accounted for in computing accommodation costs from a social perspective. Employment programs that prepare individuals with disabilities for competitive employment should be included in cost calculations, particularly when these programs relieve the employer's burden in ensuring job readiness; cf. Bellamy, Rhodes, and Albin (1986); Poole (1987); and Wehman (1981).

COST DETERMINANTS

Accommodation costs are expected to vary across firms and industries, the population of persons with disabilities, and time. Policy makers must understand the determinants of these variations in order to judge either claims of undue hardship or the aggregate employment effects of title I. In conceptual terms, accommodation costs will be established by the interplay of the demand for, and supply of, workers with disabilities.

Demand. Conventional economic theory suggests that the demand for workers with disabilities, like that of other workers, will be derived from the demand for the employer's product and depends fundamentally on the ratio between the benefits they provide to, and the costs they impose on, the employer. In the standard textbook case, benefits to the employer are gauged by the added output (marginal productivity) of the last worker hired, whereas costs reflect the wages paid that worker together with the other costs associated with recruiting and maintaining a labor force, including in this case the costs of accommodation. Because benefits in this sense are expected to decline as more workers are added to the production process, and because profit-maximizing firms are always expected to equalize the benefit/cost ratio in deciding whether to hire an additional worker, the demand for persons with disabilities is expected to vary inversely with both wages and these other costs.[3]

Put simply, more of these workers will be hired at low accommodation costs than at high costs, all things being equal. If accommodation costs are a fixed proportion of the wage rate, proportionately fewer workers with disabilities will be hired than workers without such limitations, even though the productivity or economic benefits to the firm of the two groups may be equal at the margin. If accommodation costs are not simply a fixed percentage of the wage rate, fewer workers with disabilities may be hired than their counterparts without disabilities, even if their productivity is higher than workers without disabilities. Clearly, the relative demand for workers with disabilities at any wage rate hinges critically on the extent to which their productivity balances or otherwise compensates for the costs of their accommodation.

Supply. In contrast to demand, average accommodation costs are expected to rise as the supply of persons with disabilities increases, with a corresponding rise in the extra or marginal cost of hiring an individual with a disability as more such individuals are added to the firm's labor force. It is possible, of course, that a single employer hiring additional persons with identical disabilities may actually be able to lower the average cost of accommodation. For instance, if ramps are built and doorways enlarged at a given cost for the first worker who uses a wheelchair, then the costs of accommodating all additional workers who use wheelchairs should be zero. The cost of this accommodation averaged over all wheelchair-using workers would then decline continuously as more of these employees are hired. However, it seems highly unlikely that the mix of disabilities will remain unchanged as the number of persons with disabilities entering the labor market increases.

As the supply of such workers grows and the mix or composition of their impairments changes, the average cost of accommodation may be expected to rise for at least two reasons. First, the average severity level of specific physical or mental limitations will rise as more persons with those disabilities enter the labor market. Generally speaking, individuals with less severe impairments are more apt to seek work first, in part because of a higher degree of functional capacity, and in part because they are less likely to qualify for disability-related income transfers. As supply grows, however, individuals with increasingly severe levels of impairment are likely to look for work, and average accommodation costs will tend to rise. Second, as more persons with disabilities enter the labor market, it is more likely that the average worker will have more than one impairment. This will also cause average accommodation costs to rise. This reasoning implies, in turn, that the marginal or extra cost of hiring a worker with a disability will increase as the number of such workers increases.

Cost and Employment. The foregoing suggests that the employment of workers with disabilities and the level of accommodation costs are jointly determined. In economic terminology, these outcomes are simultaneously determined by the interaction of the demand and supply relationships described above.[4] At the point at which demand and supply are equated, the marginal benefit (the value of added output)

of hiring a person with a disability and the marginal cost of accommodating that person are equal. A major implication is that observed
accommodation costs and employment levels will be highly correlated
both at various points in time and over time. From this perspective, low
levels of accommodation costs observed at present may be attributable
to the low employment levels of persons with disabilities. These variables should be expected to move together in the future. Although
various patterns are possible, an underlying assumption in the following discussion is that accommodation costs will probably rise as the
supply and demand for workers with disabilities increases in response to
ADA implementation.

Economic Aspects of Title I. The framework sketched above may now
be used to clarify further several key provisions of title I from an economic perspective. Consider initially the undue-hardship clause. Any
employment level of persons with disabilities that exceeds the level
expected by equating the firm's demand and supply for such workers
may be interpreted economically as a case for undue hardship.[5] The
reason is that the marginal contribution of these additional workers to
the value of the firm's output is less than the extra costs of their
accommodation. Similarly, note that any actual employment level that
falls short of the level expected on the basis of supply-and-demand
characteristics represents a corresponding hardship of, or discrimination
against, persons with disabilities. In both cases, the operational implication is that claims of undue hardship or discrimination should force
comparisons between observed employment levels and those predicted
on the basis of the demand-and-supply conditions facing the firm.

Consider next the concept of reasonable accommodation, which
many disability specialists believe is best viewed as a process of removing barriers to a particular individual's equal employment opportunity
(U.S. Senate 1989). From the economic viewpoint sketched above,
reasonable accommodation may be interpreted as efforts to change the
responsiveness of the demand and supply of workers with disabilities to
accommodation costs.[6] Even though employment demand is expected
in principle always to vary inversely with costs, the degree to which it
does may be changed by policy means. To illustrate, a 10 percent
decrease in accommodation costs (all other things being equal) may
result in an increase in employment of less than, more than, or just 10
percent. Clearly, the employment goals of the ADA will be facilitated
in this case by any effort that makes the response in demand more than
the proportional drop in costs.

Operationally, the responsiveness of the demand relationship for workers with disabilities depends on the nature of production technology and job requirements, the character of the impairments that impede the functional capacities of workers with disabilities, and the human capital and other job skills that these individuals bring to the job. The responsiveness of supply depends crucially on the distribution of impairments across the population of persons with disabilities, and the extent to which these impairments are acquired on the job or prior to any firm-specific work experience. It is worth pointing out that the responsiveness of both demand and supply can be improved by better preparation of workers with disabilities for the world of work through vocational rehabilitation, transitional employment services, and completion of formal schooling.

Finally, the provisions of title I generally may be interpreted from an economic perspective as intending to raise the level of demand for, and supply of, workers with disabilities in the labor market.[7] Put simply, title I should be evaluated by its ultimate impact on the employment of persons with disabilities. If, as suggested above, title I reduces discriminatory practices and changes attitudes of employers, the demand for workers with disabilities should shift up. Eliminating discriminatory practices may also encourage more persons with disabilities to seek work, thus shifting supply up as well. Progress under title I should ultimately be manifest in higher employment rates for a growing supply of workers with disabilities and, because they are jointly determined, in the observation of higher average accommodation costs. Paradoxically, the observation that costs of accommodation are low and stable over time may reflect only that little meaningful progress has been made recently in putting individuals with disabilities to work. Despite the undue-hardship clause, this should change if the ADA legislation is successful.

RESEARCH ON THE ECONOMICS OF DISABILITY

The preceding discussion suggests several key focal points for applied economic research on workers with disabilities, including cost and employment trends, the responsiveness of supply and demand relationships to accommodation costs, and the factors that contribute to historical changes in employment and cost levels over time. Although past research on these topics is not extensive, some findings are available in the published literature. This section reviews some of this literature, beginning with available work that has attempted directly to calculate the costs of accommodating persons with disabilities.

COSTS OF ACCOMMODATION

Only a few items were found in a search of the literature that included quantitative estimates of the costs of accommodation. One was the consultant's report prepared under a mandate of the Office of Management and Budget for the Secretary of (HEW) Health and Human Services prior to the implementation of section 504 of the 1973 Rehabilitation Act (O'Neill 1976). This report surveyed several unpublished studies dealing with the restructuring of jobs occasioned by the placement of persons with disabilities and the extent to which insurance costs rose as a result of such placements. As anticipated, these studies showed that most job placements of persons with various kinds of disabilities, including limitations such as complete loss of sight, required no modification or special arrangements at all. Similarly, insurance costs did not rise as a result of hiring additional workers with disabilities. In the aggregate, O'Neill estimated that accommodating workers with disabilities under section 504 would cost in the mid-1970s about $50 million annually (or the equivalent of roughly $115 million in 1990 dollars), mostly for building modifications to enhance physical accessibility; he also estimated roughly that the costs of economic discrimination at the time ran annually about ten times that amount (i.e., $1.2 billion), concluding that the accommodation costs could easily be absorbed by the national economy.[8] These estimates, however, are in the nature of "back-of-the-envelope" computations and therefore are too rough to be credible.

Employer attitude surveys also indicate that the costs of reasonable accommodation are typically inexpensive. However, these results are anecdotal and rarely based on extensive data collection or analysis. The Harris poll conducted for the International Center for the Disabled (Harris 1987), for example, asked a sample of managers simply whether any accommodation had been made for a worker with a disability and, if so, whether the costs of such accommodation were "very, somewhat, not too, or not expensive at all." Because dollar figures were not used and the opinions expressed were not necessarily based on the review of any records of the firm, the finding that a majority of the respondents felt these costs were "not too expensive" is difficult to interpret. That the group of respondents is self-selected in terms of whether workers with disabilities were actually accommodated further confuses the interpretation because firms that might have refused to make very expensive accommodations are unrepresented in the sample.

Anecdotal evidence is also available in a recently completed evaluation of the Jobs Accommodation Network (JAN) of the President's Committee on Employment of the Handicapped (JAN 1987). Information on accommodation costs in this case was obtained principally from employers who called JAN to facilitate the accommodation of one of their employees with a disability. The results show that about 30 percent of all accommodations are costless and another 47 percent are about $1,000 or less. These findings, however, are subject to considerable selection bias, particularly because the decision to hire a worker with a disability in most cases preceded the call to the network.

The most extensive study of accommodation costs thus far conducted is the Berkeley Planning Associates (BPA) *Study of Accommodations Provided to Handicapped Employees by Federal Contractors* (Berkeley Planning Associates 1982) prepared for the Employment Standards Administration of the U.S. Labor Department (see Collignon 1986). The salient features of this analysis may be summarized as follows. A national sample of 2,000 private-sector firms with federal contracts stratified by size and industry was sent a questionnaire requesting detailed information on the employment of workers with disabilities, the nature and costs of accommodating these workers, and the impact of such accommodation on the firms and their employees. There were follow-up questionnaires sent to the large fraction of the sample that did not respond to the survey; follow-up telephone interviews with a select subset of firms to obtain more detailed data, including case studies of ten firms that were judged by the investigators to have an exemplary record of hiring persons with disabilities; and a survey of workers in a selected number of these firms to provide an employee perspective of the accommodation issue.

The BPA researchers also found that accommodation of persons with disabilities in the firms providing survey responses was neither difficult nor costly, with more than one-half of all accommodations reckoned at "zero" cost, and an additional 30 percent at less than the equivalent of $675 in 1990 dollars. The median outlay for more costly accommodations over this level was less than $2,700, with only 2 percent spending over $27,000, again in inflation-adjusted 1990 dollars. The researchers found, however, that the likelihood of such accommodation and its cost level were systematically related to the skill level of the workers, with highly skilled individuals receiving more, and more expensive, accommodations than less skilled workers. Accommodation costs were also likely to occur in large firms rather than small ones. Finally, the cost of accommodations varied by type of impaired function, as the earlier discussion of the rising supply costs of accommodation suggests. Accommodations were most extensive and expensive for workers with blindness and those using wheelchairs, and least expensive generally for individuals with mental limitations. Nonetheless, a sizable proportion of the work force with disabilities had more than one type of impairment and frequently received more than one type of accommodation. The primary finding that the costs of accommodation were generally negligible is even more remarkable in light of these facts.

However, some doubt may be expressed about the validity of the accommodation cost data yielded by the BPA study. One reason is that employers responding to the survey tended to count only the capital costs of changes in the physical environment as the relevant costs of accommodation, choosing either to ignore or minimize the time costs of other personnel, such as managerial workers, in setting up jobs for persons with a disabilities. Furthermore, only the costs covered by the firm were counted: the cost of equipment or work aids purchased either by the person with a disability or from a public-sector program such as vocational rehabilitation was excluded from the computations. The study results would have been more convincing had the opportunity costs of all resources deployed for the accommodation been added up, distributed among the employer, the employee, and other parties, and then compared with the costs of accommodating workers without disabilities.

Another concern is the selection bias in the results attributable both to the low response rate of returned questionnaires and to the restricted focus only on workers with disabilities who were already employed. Although the BPA study's 18 percent response rate compares favorably with other sample surveys of private-sector firms, it nonetheless casts uncertainty about the extent to which the results reflect self-selected responses of firms with the best records for hiring persons with disabilities. The investigators, of course, were clearly concerned about the low response rate, and they examined the pattern of nonresponses in some detail. They found no significant differences in the nonresponse pattern by firm size or industry, but there were differentials in respect both to the amount of government-contract business and the extent to which the industry was regulated. What could not be compared, however was the degree to which respondents and nonrespondents differed in the number or proportion of persons with disabilities in the total work force. The gaps are understandable: a sizable number of respondents refused to participate in the study because they had no data on the disability status of their employees. Yet, it is easy to imagine that many of the firms without recorded data employed fewer workers with disabilities than firms that kept them, and that the results were accordingly biased by differential response patterns of firms in each category.

Although the potential problem of nonresponse bias was recognized by the BPA investigators, less concern was expressed for the possible confounding influence of restricting the analysis only to employed persons with disabilities. This is an especially serious problem in view of the likelihood that those persons who can be accommodated at negligible cost will be the first to be accommodated. Indeed, given the low levels of employment of persons with disabilities and the discrimination practiced against them, finding that those who acquired jobs had essentially costless accommodations may paradoxically confirm the proposition that accommodation costs rise with the size of the labor force with disabilities. It is, of course, impossible to reject this hypothesis with the BPA data because persons with disabilities who did not acquire jobs were excluded from the survey and the costs of their accommodations are unknown. Clearly, we need to learn more about the costs of accommodating persons who are presently out of the labor force.

LABOR SUPPLY OF PERSONS WITH DISABILITIES

The ADA's definition of disability is three pronged: physical or mental impairments that substantially limit one or more major life activities; a record of such an impairment(s); or being regarded as having such an impairment. The latter two elements are crucial, of course, in combatting discrimination, but they complicate any appraisal of the labor-market behavior of individuals with disabilities and, correspondingly, recent economic research examining that behavior. The difficulty is that persons with a record of an impairment or regarded as having one who are nonetheless gainfully employed are typically not enumerated as disabled nor are they necessarily eligible for the major social-insurance programs designed to cushion the adverse economic consequences of disability. Most disability programs, indeed, restrict eligibility only to those individuals with impairments that actually limit major role responsibilities—the ability to hold any job at all. Yet, similar impairments do not always produce similar degrees of limitation in role functioning. In fact, the probability that a given impairment will disable is mediated by a complex set of demographic, socioeconomic, and medical factors. These mediating factors are central to understanding the labor-market behavior of persons with disabilities, and have thus been the primary focal point of much research by economists working in the disability field. In reviewing some of this work here, the narrower definition of disability as inability to fulfill role functioning (work) is taken as a given.

In this context, considerable interest in econometric studies has centered on the relative importance of health-impairment factors and transfer payments from public and private pension programs in explaining the dramatic decline over the past 25 years in the labor-force participation rates of American men; see, for example, Chirikos and Nestel (1981; 1985), Leonard (1986), Sammartino (1987), and Yelin (1986). Generally speaking, the literature since the late 1970s has highlighted the inducements or disincentive effects of social-insurance programs, particularly the Social Security Disability Insurance (SSDI) program, in the reduced participation rates of men. However, some of these studies have probably underestimated the impact of health conditions relative to economic variables, according to more recent analyses. Haveman and Wolfe (1984) show that Parsons' (1982; 1984) earlier estimates of the effects of the replacement rate on the labor-force participation of men were too high and, by implication, that his estimates of the impact of poor health were too low (see also Bound 1989). Nevertheless, virtually all economists who have studied the issue take as given the likelihood that disability transfers will impel individuals to leave the work force; where they differ is in regard to the magnitude of the disincentive effect. Most of these specialists also believe that there are various second-order effects of significance on disability policy. Berkowitz (1981), for instance, has argued that the availability of transfer income also deters individuals with disabilities from seeking the services of rehabilitation agencies or of completing rehabilitation programs once started (cf. Better et al. 1979; Conley, Noble, and Elder 1986; and Walls, Zawlocki, and Dowler 1986).

A host of complex methodological issues has been raised by research on the relative effects of poor health and economic incentives on the labor-market behavior of persons with disabilities, most of which are beyond the scope of the present discussion (cf. Stern 1989). Yet, two of these issues warrant brief mention here because they bear significantly on the economics of title I.

One is the degree to which economic incentives condition the self-perception of disability or the likelihood that individuals will declare themselves disabled in sample surveys. Chirikos and Nestel (1984) produced convincing evidence that the probability of middle-aged men and women reporting themselves as work disabled is affected by their potential earnings, controlling for impairment status, job requirements, and other sociodemographic characteristics. Individuals with more to lose from time spent out of the work force are significantly less likely to report themselves disabled. Chirikos (1986) estimated that approximately one-third of the annual growth rate in the prevalence of work disability in the postwar period is attributable to changes in economic circumstances that determine whether individuals with impairments declare themselves disabled. Among others, these results are consistent with earlier research demonstrating that application rates for disability benefits rise and fall countercyclically, with periods of recession witnessing substantial relative increases in application rates (Berkowitz, Johnson, and Murphy 1976). The findings also underscore the frequent observation of disability specialists that many impairments are "invisible" and that many persons with disabilities choose not to identify themselves either as disabled or even in need of certain accommodations for fear of possible discriminatory responses (Spiegel and Podair 1981; Rusch, Mithaug, and Flexer 1986). These effects do not bode well for enumerating the supply of persons with disabilities or measuring progress toward their employment goals.

The other issue is the degree to which the emphasis in the economics literature on the replacement rate of predisability income per se adequately accounts for the disincentive effects of disability-transfer programs. Perhaps of greater significance in this regard is eligibility for medical-care insurance benefits such as Medicare or Medicaid, particularly in view of the accommodations that have been made in recent years to increase the probabilities that persons with disabilities return to work. For example, after a six-year demonstration project, section 1619 was made a permanent part of the Social Security Act (PL99–643) in 1986. The provisions encourage individuals with disabilities who are eligible for SSI benefits to make efforts to return to the labor market by, among other things, continuing Medicaid coverage when they do so. Impact analysis of the section 1619 demonstration suggests that the continuation of medical-care insurance benefits increases the likelihood that SSI beneficiaries return to work (Andrews et al. 1988).[9] The countervailing influence of these provisions on the measured effect of the replacement rate on labor-force participation has thus far been ignored in econometric studies on this topic. When they are taken into account, the magnitude of disincentive effects of transfer programs should be lower than the estimates published thus far.

Despite the emphasis on disincentive effects, we should not lose sight of the fact that the economic literature on the labor supply of persons with disabilities also provides compelling empirical evidence that impaired health causes involuntary exits from the job market. The primary determinants of early withdrawal from the work force are impairments due to chronic diseases, particularly coronary heart disease. Studies show consistently that the probability of involuntary departures rises significantly with the severity level of those impairments. As a result, many individuals who have withdrawn cannot be expected to work nor, by implication, can they be accommodated even with great difficulty or expense. Others have sufficiently severe impairments to raise the cost of accommodation well beyond the commensurate level of economic benefits, even when accommodation is possible. Projections of the potential labor supply of persons with disabilities must account realistically for the segment of the population that is severely impaired (cf. Vachon 1987). The widely reported ICD/Harris poll results (Harris 1986) that two-thirds of all persons with disabilities wish to work must be interpreted cautiously from this vantage point. Ignoring the fact that health conditions rule out work for some severely impaired persons runs the risk of creating a new "myth" about persons with disabilities akin to the old "myth" that few, if any, of these persons are capable of work (Daniels 1985).

Labor-supply research also indicates that impaired health compounds other factors associated with lower probabilities of labor-force participation like formal schooling. Thus, persons with disabilities and low levels of educational attainment are proportionately even less likely to work than their less-educated but nondisabled counterparts. Interestingly, little economic research has been conducted on the impact of early onset of disability on schooling or other factors that correlate with increased labor-force participation. Yet, such research is important because improvements in life expectancy at younger ages have been substantial in recent years, and a growing proportion of the population with disabilities represents individuals in their twenties who were chronically impaired at birth or as young children (Lubitz and Pine 1986). Recall, nonetheless, that the highest rates of disability prevalence and work withdrawal are in the age group 45 to 64 years (Chirikos 1989). This group is most often disabled after a significant period of time spent in gainful employment, thus mitigating somewhat the influence of formal schooling and job skills on the prospects of returning to the work force.

DISCRIMINATION IN THE DEMAND FOR WORKERS WITH DISABILITIES

There has been even less economic research on the demand for workers with disabilities than on supply. Published studies have focused naturally enough on the effects of discrimination on the demand for workers with disabilities. Several small-scale investigations concluded that persons with disabilities obtain employment only in secondary labor markets where jobs are characterized by low pay and dead-end career opportunities (Barnartt and Christiansen 1985; Craft, Benecki, and Shkop 1980); this occupational segregation is frequently compounded by other kinds of job discrimination as well (Angel 1984). Several other studies have examined wage discrimination against persons with disabilities.[10] The most careful and recent of these is the analysis carried out by Johnson and Lambrinos (1985).

These investigators used data from the 1972 Social Security Survey of Disabled and Nondisabled Adults to estimate the determinants of the earnings of "handicapped and nonhandicapped" workers and, by so doing, compute the degree to which employers practice wage discrimination against the "handicapped." Their methodology allowed them to calculate the extent to which wage differentials between the disabled and nondisabled arise from differences in the correlates of economic performance (say, schooling) and then how much can be attributed to discriminatory job practices. Johnson and Lambrinos define the "handicapped" as individuals with "visible" impairments that "affect the ability to communicate. . ., alter bodily movements. . ., or are in some way deforming"; nonhandicapped persons are either unimpaired or nonvisibly impaired. Earnings data are carefully controlled for impaired functional capacities, work experience, education, and other factors affecting labor demand such as the capital intensity of the industry; in contrast to other studies, the researchers also made allowances methodologically for the lower probability that persons with disabilities will be at work. The results demonstrated that "handicapped" workers received lower wages than the comparison group, and that only a fraction of this differential is attributable to differences in the correlates of higher earnings. Approximately one-third of the observed wage differential of men, and about 40 percent of the differential for women, can be traced to discriminatory behavior. Furthermore, significant interaction effects of disability status were detected, including a lower relative pay-off to the amount of formal schooling that "handicapped" persons obtain and, in the case of females, an exacerbation of gender-related discrimination.

Perhaps the most important result of the Johnson and Lambrinos study was evidence that wage differentials do not narrow as the length of time "handicapped" persons are employed by the same firm increases. This is important because it reduces the likelihood that the gap in earnings resulted simply from what economists call "statistical discrimination," and simultaneously increases the likelihood that employers either exploited workers with disabilities and/or exacted some of the costs of accommodation from them.

The "statistical" theory of discrimination posits that employers can obtain only imperfect information about the potential productivity of any given job applicant, so they rely on various indicators of success of the average applicant and offer a wage commensurate with the average level of productivity of the applicant pool (Aigner and Cain 1977; Stiglitz 1987). Because the variation of persons with disabilities on most commonly used job screens (for example, the amount of job experience) is likely to be greater, their mean value is likely to be lower and they are paid correspondingly less. Given this logic, however, workers with disabilities who have been employed for a long period of time with the same employer, and whose actual productivity levels are accordingly better known to that employer, should have higher relative wages than newly hired workers, all else being equal. However, Johnson and Lambrinos find no evidence of such narrowing of the wage differential as these workers gain more firm-specific work experience. In fact, they find that the wage gap actually widens as the length of time "handicapped" workers are on the job increases.

This result casts doubt not only on the application of "statistical" discrimination theory to the issue of the earnings differential between persons with disabilities and persons without disabilities, but also on the effectiveness of disseminating information on the productivity and work virtues of persons with disabilities to employers as a means of increasing employment opportunities (Kokaska and Maslow 1986; Parent and Everson 1986; Rabby 1985; Schroedel and Jacobsen 1978). Yet, conclusions about this issue should be drawn cautiously, and the hypothesis should be tested in other studies and data sets in order to rule out the possibility that it is simply an artifact of the Johnson and Lambrinos analysis. A more detailed examination of wage profiles by firm-specific experience and disability status is also needed to ascertain whether employers attempt to recoup expenses associated with hiring and accommodation through the amount they pay workers with disabilities. Such knowledge is crucial in judging whether the employment of these workers would be substantially increased if the employer and employee shared in the costs of hiring and accommodation (Johnson 1986).

MONITORING THE PROGRESS OF TITLE I

Clearly, more research on labor demand-and-supply conditions of persons with disabilities is needed to gauge the impact of title I on the economic well-being of this target population. Efforts to obtain the data needed to support priority research should be initiated as soon as possible. This section sketches some of what is needed.

DEMAND

More detailed information on the current level and distribution of the employment of persons with disabilities by industry group and occupation is vitally needed to provide a benchmark against which to judge the future employment effects of the ADA. Empirical studies of variations in accommodation costs, wages, and employment by disability status must be carried out to estimate the responsiveness of demand to accommodation costs. Factors that shift the demand for workers with disabilities also must be studied in more detail.

The literature reviewed above suggests generally that this data-collection effort will not be an easy task. Unlike race and gender groups subjected to job discrimination, members of the population with disabilities are not easily identified nor do they always comply with requests for self-identification. The reliability of disability data, as a result, is a matter of serious concern. The ability and willingness of employers to provide relevant data is also a major stumbling block. As

Collignon (1986) observes, the imposition of heavy data demands on employers could be counterproductive because it may reduce the general good will in the private sector toward hiring persons with disabilities. Moreover, what in principle can be learned from employers who have hired such workers is limited because of the problem of selection bias discussed in an earlier section.

SUPPLY

Additional and more detailed information on the sociodemographic, health/impairment, and economic characteristics of persons with disabilities must be acquired. To do so, an especially important hurdle must be overcome: to generate consistency and comparability in the definitions of disability and the population with disabilities in ongoing compilations of population statistics. At the moment, each of the available sources of data on households in the United States uses somewhat different definitions or criteria of disability and thus enumerates different populations of persons with disabilities. Incorporating the three-prong ADA disability definition in the data sets regularly maintained by the federal government should be established now as a goal to be fulfilled by the end of the decade. Of primary importance is to incorporate comparable disability definitions in the ongoing Current Population Survey (CPS) and the National Health Interview Survey (NHIS).[11] These design modifications can be effected at minimal cost and will pay handsome dividends in the form of empirical analyses of the labor-market behavior, health-care utilization, and economic status of persons with disabilities.

SPECIAL SURVEYS

Although comparable definitions of disability in ongoing surveys will expand the database about the population with disabilities, other needs remain. One reason is that the sample size of persons with disabilities in the CPS or the NHIS is too small to draw reliable inferences about subgroups of this population. Special surveys linked to the sampling schemes of either of these major data sources and using a longitudinal design are needed to provide the requisite detail or disaggregation. I have in mind a special survey linked to the overall sampling frame of the CPS or NHIS but utilizing complex, multistage sampling techniques to ensure appropriate representation of persons with lifelong and recently acquired disabilities; with various types of disabilities and in different degrees of severity; with various patterns of work and labor-market experience; and with various patterns of rehabilitation, among others. The survey design, in other words, should reflect the characteristics common to all persons with disabilities, while simultaneously gauging the considerable heterogeneity within this population. Drawing this sample of persons with disabilities within the framework of a larger, representative sample of Americans allows the socioeconomic differentials of the two groups to be measured with greater precision.

The design of the proposed survey should be longitudinal to permit, among other things, changes in the severity and course of disability episodes as well as the socioeconomic consequences of these episodes to be charted in detail. It must be noted in this context that not all episodes of disability or functional impairment are permanent, and the status of some persons will change over time. Similarly, not all disabilities yield the same employment outcomes over time: some impairments may be rehabilitated or ameliorated by reasonable accommodation on the job; others may grow more severe as chronic conditions or the aging process interact and work activity becomes more difficult or impossible. Single cross-sectional surveys such as the ICD/Harris Survey (Harris 1986) are clearly limited in these terms because they provide only the equivalent of a "snapshot" whereas what is required is a "moving picture" of the economic behavior and outcomes of persons with disabilities over time. In my judgment, implementing a longitudinal or panel survey of a representative sample of persons with disabilities should be accorded very high priority for research and evaluation funds in the disability field over the next few years.

Such a panel survey should focus on priority areas of required data about the demand and supply of workers with disabilities: First, data on the behavior of these persons who are at work must be acquired, including detailed information on job requirements, performance, accommodations, and mobility. For those not at work, information on job-search behavior, employment barriers, and potential accommodation costs must be collected. Attitudinal probes about the "desire" to work should be minimized in favor of more detailed behavioral descriptions of what persons with disabilities actually did to look for work during a defined reference period and/or the factors that may have discouraged them from doing so.

Second, information must be obtained on the health and medical-care utilization of persons with disabilities. Panel respondents should be questioned about temporal changes in pathology or residual functional impairment and improvements in their ability to carry out role functions attributable to health-care and rehabilitative interventions. Their answers should clarify the picture we now have of the impact of impairments on the duration of departures from work roles and, thereby, the health-related determinants of accommodation costs.

Finally, the panel survey should obtain information on the indirect costs of accommodation to the families of persons with disabilities. How families respond to the economic losses arising from the disability of one of its members is unclear (Berger 1982; Chirikos 1989; Parsons 1977). Family members sometimes substitute their own market time for the lost time of the person with a disability, but not always. Exceptions occur when family members stay at home in order to care for the person with a disability or when they themselves have a disability. The panel survey proposed here would be an appropriate vehicle for obtaining additional information about the economic and health status of family members of persons with disabilities.

CONCLUSIONS

Despite the pivotal role that accommodation costs will play in the future success of title I, not much is known at the moment about their level or distribution across the economy or population of persons with disabilities. Available evidence suggests that many workers have been accommodated in the past at little or no expense. Extrapolation of these data leads straightforwardly to the conclusion that accommodation costs will neither impede the employment of workers with disabilities nor run the risk of imposing an unfair burden on some employers as the ADA is implemented over time. Such extrapolation, however, may not be entirely warranted. Available estimates are based on definitions that tend to minimize cost levels. More important, these estimates fail to adjust for the likelihood that persons with disabilities who have been successful in finding jobs can be accommodated more readily and inexpensively than persons with disabilities who have attempted unsuccessfully to find work. Put differently, evidence of negligible accommodation costs would be more compelling if a very large fraction of the population of persons with disabilities was already employed and/or if a plausible case could be made for constancy in the level of costs across the distribution of disabilities in the population.

In fact, however, employment levels of these persons are low, and various indicators suggest both that accommodation costs vary directly with the severity of impairment and that persons with more severe impairment are less likely to be working. Although these matters do not completely vitiate the results of past studies, they do argue for the need for additional information related to the costs of accommodation, which could be used by regulation writers for title I.

Three main inferences follow from the analysis in this article:

1. Average accommodation costs should be expected to increase as more persons with disabilities enter the market. Although this may not happen immediately because of the slack attributable to past job discrimination experienced by this group of persons, it should take place in the future if title I is successful. Indeed, not unlike the "no pain, no gain" credo of body builders, rising supply cost may be used as an indicator of the impact of the ADA legislation.

2. The mix and severity level of disabilities in the population of persons with disabilities must be carefully quantified and monitored. Additional research on their functional capacities and willingness to work must be carried out as soon as possible.

3. Even though the benefits of employing more persons with disabilities are expected to outweigh the added costs of accommodation, this too must be carefully monitored. If benefit–cost ratios prove to be lower than what is now expected, redistributive issues in generating employment for persons with disabilities will have to be faced more squarely. Policy tools beyond the scope of the ADA may have to be used to ensure that persons with disabilities are fully integrated into the American economy, including the expanded use of subsidies and alternative means of sharing the burden between the employer and employee.

NOTES

1. Adopting the "persons with disabilities" terminology of the ADA, as this article does, presents several challenges. One is that it is a cumbersome construction grammatically, and it admits to few, if any, acceptable synonyms. Another is that it leads frequently to imprecision in the exposition. The difficulty in this latter and more important case is that the three-prong ADA definition of disability (an impairment that limits major life activities, a record of such an impairment, or being regarded as having such an impairment) encompasses a somewhat different population from the ones enumerated in statistical compilations as "the disabled" or even "disabled persons." In the context of the present paragraph, for example, "disabled" Americans refer essentially to individuals who are limited in work activity. Persons with an impairment who are either gainfully employed and/or choose not to report themselves as work disabled are *not* counted as "disabled" in these data. Because the number of such persons is quite large, and because the likelihood of reporting a work disability is itself related to economic status, the issue here is more than semantic quibbling. The article considers later on the need to obtain data comparing "persons with and without disabilities" in the ADA sense that are equivalent to available data comparing the "disabled and nondisabled."

   In order to avoid confusion in the remainder of the article, I adopt the convention of using "persons with disabilities" in the three-prong ADA sense in all circumstances except where the original data source or citation to the literature employs alternative terminology or disability definition. In a few cases where this terminology fails to conform to the current mode of acceptable practice, such as references to "handicapped persons," I have put the source material in quotation marks.

2. Present-value computations are required if streams of costs (or benefits) are to be compared at a point in time. Present-value costs (PVC) are calculated as the sum of all discounted annual cost values, that is,

$$PVC = \Sigma_t c(t) / (1 + r)^t$$

   where c(t) = costs in year *t*, *r* = the discount rate, and *t* indexes each year of the continuing stream of costs over the work life of the employee.

3. Economists define marginal productivity as the addition to total output brought about by hiring the last unit of any factor of production such as labor, all other factors being constant. In simple terms, this marginal contribution is expected to fall as more units are hired because of the law of diminishing returns, that is, the technical conditions governing the production process. Assuming that all units of this extra output can be sold in competitive markets at the same price, profit maximization requires that the dollar value of the marginal product be equated to the wage rate and other hiring costs to the employer; the ratios of these two variables for all factors of production are thus equalized. This results in the downward-sloping demand curve for factor inputs presented in most elementary economics textbooks.

Economists will recognize that the matter is a bit more complicated than this, particularly in the case of delineating demand functions for workers with or without disabilities. I assume in the following that the demand for particular categories of labor are efficiency adjusted over the expected years of work life in that category at constant wage rates. If workers with and without disabilities are equally productive at the margin at all time points in their (assignment-specific) work lives, workers with disabilities will be hired at the same rate as workers without disabilities if accommodation costs are zero (or negligible) or at a lower rate corresponding to the difference in accommodation costs between the two groups. However, if persons with disabilities are more efficient over time than persons without disabilities (e.g., because their turnover rates are lower), their employment rate may be higher than persons without disabilities if accommodation costs are zero or proportionately higher if accommodation costs are positive but nonetheless offset by the value of the additional output.

4. This could be portrayed as the intersection of supply and demand curves akin to those commonly found in elementary economic textbooks. If accommodation costs (or efficiency-adjusted costs) are measured on the vertical axis and employment of persons with disabilities is measured on the horizontal axis, the demand curve will slope downward to the right and the supply (marginal cost) curve will slope upward to the right. Cost and employment levels will be jointly determined at the point at which the two curves intersect. Clearly, any policy that affects either the slopes of these curves or their respective positions in the plane of costs and employment will result in some change in costs and the number of workers with disabilities who are hired.

5. However, this may not necessarily be the way undue hardship will be interpreted by the courts. The reason is that the legislation mandates due consideration of the size and financial resources of the covered entity in judging undue hardship. If employment of persons with disabilities is expanded beyond the intersection of supply and demand, the ADA will become redistributive in nature. It will expand the employment of persons with disabilities at the expense of those without disabilities, and it will impose unfair burdens on some firms by requiring them alone to pay for that expansion. Generally speaking, economists oppose such implicit redistributive schemes, recommending instead that efforts to redistribute resources be acknowledged explicitly and be financed in some equitable fashion through the tax system. In the case of title I, this means that the costs of accommodation exceeding the value of the marginal product of workers with disabilities be defrayed through public budgets and that the "displacement effect" of workers without disabilities be accounted for in any estimate of the benefits of the legislation. From a practical point of view, moreover, significant variations in the incidence of accommodation costs across firms and industries will afford a competitive advantage for noncompliance and, accordingly, will raise the costs of surveillance and regulation.

6. In economic parlance, reasonable accommodation attempts to change the elasticities of the demand and supply functions. Elasticities, in this case, gauge the proportional change in either the demand for, or supply of, workers with

disabilities stemming from some given proportional change in accommodation costs, all other things being constant.

7. In economic terminology, the ADA is designed to shift the demand and supply curves of workers with disabilities in addition to changing the elasticities at relevant points along these functions.

8. For purposes of comparability and exposition, I used the Consumer Price Index to update the cost estimates reported here and elsewhere in the article in terms of current purchasing power.

9. Changes with similar goals have also been made in Medicare coverage for SSDI beneficiaries. Some propose that the current 24-month waiting period also be eliminated for these beneficiaries on the assumption that early receipt of medical care may reduce the duration of disability episodes. See, for example, Bye and Riley (1989).

10. A number of economic studies have investigated wage differentials between persons with disabilities and persons without disabilities, although not all necessarily attempt to gauge the impact of discrimination on those differentials. See, for example, Luft (1975). Many of the early studies are flawed methodologically by the selection biases arising from the problem of observing a wage for persons with disabilities who are out of the labor force. More recent studies use newer techniques that eliminate these biases. See, for instance, Burkhauser et al. (1986). These difficulties also arise in cost–benefit evaluations of vocational-rehabilitation programs (see Hall-Kane and Gibbs 1988).

11. Each survey has different strengths. The CPS provides more detailed labor market and economic data for persons of working age. The NHIS provides detailed data on health status and role functioning for all age groups. Comparable definitions would, of course, facilitate comparisons between the two data sets.

REFERENCES

Aigner, D.J., and G.G. Cain. 1977. Statistical Theories of Discrimination in Labor Markets. *Industrial and Labor Relations Review* 10(April):175–87.

Andrews, R.A., M. Ruther, D.K. Baugh, P.L. Pine, and M. P. Rymer. 1988. Medicaid Expenditures for the Disabled under a Work Incentive Program. *Health Care Financing Review* 9(3):1–8.

Angel, R. 1984. The Costs of Disability for Hispanic Males. *Social Science Journal* 65(2):426–43.

Applied Management Sciences. 1985. Literature Review of Key Issues Relevant to OFCCP Regulations Regarding the Employment of the Handicapped. Silver Spring, Md.: AMS.

Barnartt, S. N., and J.B. Christiansen. 1985. The Socioeconomic Status of Deaf Workers: A Minority Group Perspective. *Social Science Journal* 22(4):19–32.

Bellamy, G.T., L.E. Rhodes, and J.M. Albin. 1986. Supported Employment. In *Pathways to Employment for Adults with Developmental Disabilities*, ed. W.E. Kiernan and J.A. Stark, 129–38. Baltimore, Md.: Paul H. Brookes.

Bennefield, R.L., and J.M. McNeil. 1989. Labor Force Status and Other Characteristics of Persons with a Work Disability: 1981–1988. *Current Population
Reports*, series P-23, no. 160. Washington.

Berger, M.C. 1982. Family Allocation of Time: The Effects of Health on Labor
Supply. *Atlantic Economic Journal* 10(4):14–24.

Berkeley Planning Associates. 1982. *A Study of Accommodations Provided to
Handicapped Employees by Federal Contractors*. Two Volumes. Berkeley,
Calif.: BPA.

Berkowitz, M. 1981. Disincentives and the Rehabilitation of Disabled Persons. In
Annual Review of Rehabilitation, ed. E. Pan, T. Backer, and C. Lash, 40–57.
New York: Springer.

Berkowitz, M., W.G. Johnson, and E.H. Murphy. 1976. *Public Policy toward
Disability*. New York: Praeger.

Better, S.R., P.R. Fine, D. Simison, G.H. Doss, R.T. Walls, and D.E. McLaughlin.
1979. Disability Benefits as Disincentives to Rehabilitatiion. *Milbank Memorial Fund Quarterly/Health and Society* 57(3):412–27.

Bound, J. 1989. The Health and Earnings of Rejected Disbility Insurance Applicants. *American Economic Review* 79(June): 482–503.

Burkhauser, R.V., J.S. Butler, J.M. Mitchell, and T. Pincus. 1986. Effects of Arthritis on Wage Earnings. *Journal of Gerontology* 41(2): 277–81.

Bye, B.V., and G.F. Riley. 1989. Eliminating the Medicare Waiting Period for
Social Security Disabled-Worker Beneficiaries. *Social Security Bulletin*
52(May):2–15.

Chirikos, T.N. 1986. Accounting for the Historical Rise in Work-Disability Prevalence. *Milbank Quarterly* 64(2):271–301.

———. 1989. Aggregate Economic Losses from Disability in the United States: A
Preliminary Assay. *Milbank Quarterly* 67(suppl. 2, part 1): 59–91.

Chirikos, T.N., and G. Nestel. 1981. Impairment and Labor Market Outcomes: A
Cross-sectional and Longitudinal Analysis. In *Work and Retirement: A Longitudinal Study of Men*, ed. H.S. Parnes, 93–131. Cambridge: MIT Press.

———. 1984. Economic Determinants and Consequences of Self- Reported Work
Disability. *Journal of Health Economics* 3(August): 117–36.

———. 1985. Further Evidence on the Economic Effects of Poor Health. *Review of
Economics and Statistics* 67(February): 61–69.

Collignon, F.C. 1986. The Role of Reasonable Accommodation in Employing
Disabled Persons in Private Industry. In *Disability and the Labor Market*, ed.
M. Berkowitz and M.A. Hill, 196–241. Ithaca, N.Y.: ILR Press.

Conley, R.W., J.H. Noble, Jr. and J.K. Elder. 1986. Problems with the Service
System. In *Pathways to Employment for Adults with Developmental Disabili-
ties*, ed. W.E. Kiernan and J.A. Stark, 67–83. Baltimore, Md.: Paul H.
Brookes.

Craft, J.A., T.J. Benecki, and Y.M. Shkop. 1980. Who Hires the Seriously Handicapped? *Industrial Relations* 19(1):94–99.

Daniels, S.M. 1985. Attitudinal Influences on Affirmative Action Implementa-
tion. In *Complete Guide to Employing Persons with Disabilities*, ed. H.
McCarthy, 31–47. Albertson, N.Y.: National Center on Employment of the
Handicapped at Human Resources Center.

Hall-Kane, A.G., and E. Gibbs. 1988. Correcting for Zero Wages at Referral. In *Measuring the Efficiency of Public Programs*, ed. M. Berkowitz, 119–39. Philadelphia: Temple University Press.

Harris, L., and Associates. 1986. *The ICD Survey of Disabled Americans: Bringing Disabled Americans into the Mainstream*. New York: Louis Harris and Associates.

———. 1987. *The ICD Survey II: Employing Disabled Americans*. New York: Louis Harris and Associates.

Haveman, R.H., and B.L. Wolfe. 1984. The Decline in Male Labor Force Participation: Comment. *Journal of Political Economy* 92(3): 532–49.

———. 1989. The Economic Well-Being of the Disabled. *Journal of Human Resources* 25(1):32–54.

JAN. 1987. Job Accommodation Network Evaluation Study; Executive Summary. Washington.

Johnson, W.G. 1986. The Rehabilitation Act and Discrimination against Handicapped Workers: Does the Cure Fit the Disease? In *Disability and Labor Markets*, ed. M. Berkowitz and M.A. Hill, 242–61. Ithaca, N.Y.: ILR Press.

Johnson, W.G., and J. Lambrinos. 1985. Wage Discrimination against Handicapped Men and Women. *Journal of Human Resources* 20(2):264–77.

Kokaska, C.J., and P. Maslow. 1986. Employment of People with Epilepsy: A Review of Employer Attitude Surveys. *Journal of Rehabilitation* 52(October):31–33.

Leonard, J.S. 1986. Labor Supply Incentives and Disincentives for Disabled Persons. In *Disability and the Labor Market*, ed. M. Berkowitz and M.A. Hill, 64–94. Ithaca, N.Y.: ILR Press.

Lubitz J., and P. Pine. 1986. Health Care Use by Medicare's Disabled Enrollees. *Health Care Financing Review* 7(Summer): 19–31.

Luft, H.S. 1975. The Impact of Poor Health on Earnings. *Review of Economics and Statistics* 57(February):43–57.

O'Neill, D.M. 1976. Discrimination against Handicapped Persons. *Federal Register* 41(96):20314–76.

Parent, W.S., and J.M. Everson. 1986. Competencies of Disabled Workers in Industry: A Review of Business Literature. *Journal of Rehabilitation* 52(October):16–23.

Parsons, D.O. 1977. Health, Family Structure, and Labor Supply. *American Economic Review* 67(September):703–12.

———. 1982. The Decline in Male Labour Force Participation. *Journal of Political Economy* 88(February):117–34.

———. 1984. Disability Insurance and Male Labor Force Participation: A Response to Haveman and Wolfe. *Journal of Political Economy* 92(3):542–49.

Percy, S.L. 1989. *Disability, Civil Rights, and Public Policy*. Tuscaloosa: University of Alabama Press.

Poole, D.L. 1987. Competitive Employment of Persons with Severe Physical Disabilities: A Multivariate Analysis. *Journal of Rehabilitation* 53(January):20–25.

Rabby, R. 1985. Innovative Outreach Strategies in Affirmative Action Programs for

Handicapped Persons. In *Complete Guide to Employing Persons with Disabilities*, ed. H. McCarthy, 51–64. Albertson, N.Y.: Human Resources Center.

Rusch, F.R., D.E. Mithaug, and R.W. Flexer. 1986. Obstacles to Competitive Employment and Traditional Program Options for Overcoming Them. In *Competitive Employment Issues and Strategies*, ed. F.R. Rusch, 7–21. Baltimore, Md.: Paul H. Brookes.

Sammartino, F. 1987. The Effect of Health on Retirement. *Social Security Bulletin* 50(February):31–47.

Schroedel, J.G., and R.J. Jacobsen. 1978. *Employer Attitudes Towards Hiring Persons with Disabilities*. Albertson, N.Y.: National Center on Employment of the Handicapped at the Human Resources Center.

Spiegel, A.D., and S. Podair. 1981. *Rehabilitating People with Disabilities into the Mainstream of Society*. Park Ridge, N.J.: Noyes Medical Publications.

Stern, S. 1989. Measuring the Effect of Disability on Labor Force Participation. *Journal of Human Resources* 24(3): 361–95.

Stiglitz, J.E. 1987. The Causes and Consequences of the Dependence of Quality on Price. *Journal of Economic Literature* 25(March): 1–48.

U.S. Commission on Civil Rights. 1983. *Accommodating the Spectrum of Individual Abilities*. Washington.

U.S. General Accounting Office. 1990. *Persons with Disabilities: Reports on Costs of Accommodations*. Washington.

U.S. Senate. 1989. *The Americans with Disabilities Act of 1989*. Senate Report 101–116. Washington.

Vachon, R.A. 1987. Inventing A Future for Individuals with Work Disabilities: The Challenge of Writing National Disability Policies. In *The Changing Nature of Work, Society and Disability: The Impact on Rehabilitation Policy*, ed. D.E.Woods and D.Vandergoot, 19–45. New York: R.P. Donnelley and Sons.

Walls, R.T., R.J. Zawlocki, and D.L. Dowler. 1986. Economic Benefits as Disincentives to Competitive Employment. In *Competitive Employment Issues and Strategies*, ed. F.R. Rusch, 317–29. Baltimore, Md.: Paul H. Brookes.

Wehman, P. 1981. *Competitive Employment*. Baltimore: Paul H. Brooks.

Yelin, E. 1986. The Myth of Malingering: Why Individuals Withdraw from Work in the Presence of Illness. *Milbank Quarterly* 64(4): 622–49.

III. An Inclusive Infrastructure

*When I tried to go to the Bijou Theater in Tacoma, Washington . . .
the owner would not let me. She would not let me come in because of
what I am. A person with cerebral palsy. I was sad for me — but more
sad for her because she would not see me, only my C.P.*

Lisa Carl, testifying before Congress on
May 10, 1989

Equal Access to Public Accommodations*

Robert L. Burgdorf Jr.

EDITOR'S NOTE

Lack of access to the daily commerce of public life has promoted the persistent social isolation of persons with disabilities. The guarantee of access to public accommodations is an historical cornerstone of civil-rights law that now extends to persons with disabilities. The provision of accessibile public accommodations can draw on the wealth and breadth of experience to date, experience that Robert L. Burgdorf Jr. describes as extending from restaurants and hotels to national parks and fishing piers. With the development of an accessible society posing particular challenges to small businesses, the law has been crafted to be flexible and to accommodate the particular needs of small businesses.

Currently associate professor at the District of Columbia School of Law, Burgdorf was involved in the development of the Americans with Disabilities Act (ADA) from its inception. He was the staff author for the National Council on Disability's report, Toward Independence, *in which the concept of an ADA was first proposed. He was the chief draftsperson of the original* Americans with Disabilities Act *introduced in Congress in 1988 and has published widely on disability law. In 1983, he coauthored the U.S. Commission on Civil Rights report on disability discrimination,* Accommodating the Spectrum of Individual

---

*Portions of this article have been published in the *Temple Law Review* symposium issue (winter 1990/1991) on the Americans with Disabilities Act.

Abilities, *and he wrote the first law-school casebook on disability-rights law,* The Legal Rights of Handicapped Persons: Cases, Materials, and Text. *His article, "Second General Civil Rights Statute: The Americans with Disabilities Act and Its Implications for Future Civil Rights Laws," will be published in the spring 1991 issue of the* Harvard Civil Rights/ Civil Liberties Law Review. *He is working with Chai R. Feldblum on a major legal treatise,* Disability Discrimination Law, *to be published by the Bureau of National Affairs in 1992. Burgdorf received his J.D. from the University of Notre Dame.*

Nearly three decades ago, four black students sat down at a lunch counter at a Woolworth's store in Greensboro, North Carolina, ordered a cup of coffee, and refused to move until they were served.[1] Unknown to the four young men at the time, their act of courage would help precipitate a series of sit-in protests and other forms of civil disobedience challenging racial segregation at lunch counters, restaurants, parks, hotels, motels, and other facilities. The segregation of such places was a principal target of civil-rights protests, lawsuits, and proposals for legislative reform during the early sixties.

Equal opportunity to use and obtain the benefits of places of public accommodation is a long-cherished right in American law. In the *Civil Rights Cases*,[2] decided in 1883, the Court posited without deciding that "a right to enjoy equal accommodation and privileges in all inns, public conveyances, and places of public amusement, is one of the essential rights of the citizen . . . " In 1964, in his separate opinion in *Bell v. Maryland*,[3] Justice Douglas stated that "the right to be served in places of public accommodations is an incident of national citizenship."[4] In another opinion in that case, Justice Goldberg declared his belief that all Americans are guaranteed "the right to be treated as equal members of the community with respect to public accommodations."[5] In the view of both Justice Douglas and Justice Goldberg, access to public accommodations should be legally protected as a "civil right."[6] Their characterization was endorsed by the enactment of the Civil Rights Act of 1964, title II of which prohibits discrimination based upon race, color, religion, or national origin in "places of public accommodation."[7]

For individuals with disabilities, title III of the Americans with Disabilities Act (ADA) of 1990 provides an analogous, but broader, prohibition of discrimination by public accommodations. Justice Goldberg's concept of a right of equal membership in the community is the foundational premise that undergirds the public accommodations provisions of the ADA. This article traces the purposes and origins of the public accommodations provisions of the ADA, outlines the major legal concepts and legislative background of these provisions, and examines relevant experiences to date in providing accessible public accommodations.

EXTENT AND IMPACT OF DISCRIMINATION ON THE BASIS OF DISABILITY IN PUBLIC ACCOMMODATIONS

In the first nationwide poll of people with disabilities conducted in 1986, the Louis Harris organization asked a number of questions regarding the social integration and activities of Americans with disabilities (Louis Harris and Associates 1986). The pollsters discovered that people with disabilities are an extremely isolated segment of the population.

Specific findings of the poll included the following:

- Nearly two-thirds of all disabled Americans never went to a movie in the past year.
- Three-fourths of all disabled persons did not see live theater or a live music performance in the past year.
- Two-thirds of all disabled persons never went to a sports event in the past year, compared with 50 percent of all adults.
- Disabled people are three times more likely than are nondisabled people never to eat in restaurants. Seventeen percent of disabled people never eat in restaurants, compared with 5 percent of nondisabled people. (Louis Harris and Associates 1986, 3)

Why do people with disabilities not frequent places of public accommodation and stores as often as other Americans? The Harris poll shed some light on the reasons for this isolation and nonparticipation by persons with disabilities in the ordinary activities of life.

The preeminent reason why people with disabilities do not participate in various aspects of commercial, social, and recreational activities that are a routine part of ordinary life for most other Americans is that they do not feel welcome and able to participate safely. In the Harris poll, 59 percent of persons with disabilities reported fear as a reason for nonparticipation and 40 percent reported self-consciousness (1986, 63–64). To a disturbing degree, people with disabilities do not feel safe or welcome to attend or visit ordinary places open to the public for socializing, doing business, or engaging in recreation and other major activities in our society.

In addition, physical barriers prevent people with disabilities from visiting social, commercial, and recreational establishments. Many people with mobility impairments, particularly those who use wheelchairs, cannot enter or use a facility that has steps, narrow doorways, inaccessible bathrooms, and other architectural barriers. People having visual and hearing impairments are often unable to make effective use of or to participate safely in activities and services if the facility in which they occur has included no features for communication accessibility. According to the Harris poll, 40 percent of individuals with disabilities reporting curtailments of their activities said that an important limitation is inaccessibility of buildings and restrooms (Louis Harris and Associates 1986, 64).

People with various disabilities are turned away from public accommodations because proprietors say that their presence will disturb or upset other customers. During Senate committee hearings on the ADA legislation in 1989, Lisa Carl, a 21-year-old woman with cerebral palsy, gave dramatic testimony about her exclusion from a local movie theater in Tacoma, Washington, by a manager who simply refused to allow her to enter due to her disability.[8] (President Bush made an explicit reference to Lisa in his remarks at the ADA signing ceremony.)[9] At the height of civil-rights confrontations in the early 1960s, entrenched authorities closed some parks and zoos rather than permit them to be integrated. Nearly 30 years later, people with disabilities were still having trouble gaining admission to many such establishments. In 1988, the *Washington Post* reported that a New Jersey zookeeper refused children with Down syndrome admission to his zoo because he was afraid they would upset his chimpanzees (Shapiro 1988).

SCOPE OF PUBLIC ACCOMMODATIONS COVERED
BY THE ADA

Title II of the Civil Rights Act of 1964, which prohibits discrimination on the basis of race, color, religion, or national origin in places of public accommodation, defines the phrase "place of public accommodation" to include a range of establishments that had generated serious problems of segregation.[10] These include inns, hotels, motels, and other lodging establishments; restaurants, cafeterias, lunch rooms, lunch counters, soda fountains, and other facilities selling food for consumption on the premises; gasoline stations; and motion-picture houses, theaters, concert halls, sports arenas, stadiums, and other places of exhibition or entertainment. Since 1964 it has been illegal for any of these establishments to discriminate on the basis of race, color, religion, or national origin. Under the ADA, it is now unlawful for these same establishments to exclude, segregate, or otherwise discriminate against people because of their disabilities.

The ADA, however, goes beyond the 1964 Civil Rights Act list of public accommodations, and takes a much broader view of the concept. Title III of the ADA establishes the following 12 categories of entities that constitute public accommodations:

1. Places of lodging—inns, hotels, motels
2. Establishments serving food or drink—restaurants, bars
3. Places of exhibition or entertainment—motion picture houses, theaters, concert halls, stadiums
4. Places of public gathering—auditoriums, convention centers, lecture halls
5. Sales or rental establishments—bakeries, grocery stores, clothing stores, hardware stores, shopping centers
6. Service establishments—laundromats, dry-cleaners, banks, barber shops, beauty shops, travel services, shoe repair services, funeral parlors, gas stations, offices of accountants or lawyers, pharmacies, insurance offices, professional offices of health care providers, hospitals
7. Transportation stations—terminals, depots
8. Places of public display or collection—museums, libraries, galleries
9. Places of recreation—parks, zoos, amusement parks
10. Places of education—nursery schools, elementary schools,

secondary schools, undergraduate schools, postgraduate
schools
11. Social service establishments—day care centers, senior citizen
centers, homeless shelters, food banks, adoption agencies
12. Places of exercise or recreation—gymnasiums, health spas,
bowling alleys, golf courses[11]

This list of covered entities is obviously much more comprehensive
than the formulation in title II of the Civil Rights Act of 1964. With
the exception of sales or rentals of residential housing, the 12 categories
include almost every type of operation that is open to business or
contact with the general public.

Although the definition of public accommodations in the ADA is
broad, it applies only to private entities.[12] Buildings owned by state and
local governments are not within the definition of public accommodation, but most will be covered by the "public service" provisions in title
II of the ADA. Specifically exempted from the coverage of this title of
the Act are private clubs, religious organizations, and entities controlled by religious organizations.[13] The exemption for private clubs is
accomplished through a cross-reference to the exemption for private
clubs or establishments in title II of the Civil Rights Act of 1964.[14] The
exemption for religious organizations was prompted by a Bush administration conviction that such an exception from statutory coverage was
necessary to protect the free exercise of religion—a concern that the
legislation should "avoid potential confrontation with the First Amendment to the Constitution that might arise with the coverage of religious
institutions."[15] Private homes, apartments, condominiums, coopera-
tives, and other private housing facilities and residences are also not
included in the concept of public accommodations.[16]

In addition to public accommodations, the requirements regarding
accessibility of new construction and alterations in title III apply to all
"commercial facilities."[17] The definition of "commercial facilities"
encompasses facilities "(A) that are intended for nonresidential use;
and (B) whose operations will affect commerce."[18] The concept of
"affecting commerce" has been interpreted extremely broadly in American jurisprudence.[19] The ADA definition does not circumscribe this
expansive formulation, but only adds that it does not apply to residential uses; the result is an extraordinarily broad definition of "commercial facilities."

ADA REQUIREMENTS RE PUBLIC ACCOMMODATIONS

The substantive requirements of title III establish a paramount, broad "general rule" proscribing discrimination "on the basis of disability in the full and equal enjoyment of the goods, services, facilities, privileges, advantages, or accommodations of any place of public accommodation."[20] Subsequent provisions outline various more specific requirements that the general prohibition entails. Public accommodations are prohibited from subjecting, by direct or indirect means, an individual or class of individuals with disabilities to any of the following forms of discrimination:

1. Denying participation in or benefit from an opportunity
2. Affording an opportunity that is not equal to that made available to other individuals
3. Providing an opportunity that is different or separate, unless such separation or difference is necessary to provide an individual with a disability an opportunity that is as effective as that provided to others
4. Providing opportunities that are not in "the most integrated setting appropriate to the needs of the individual"
5. Using standards or methods of administration, directly or through contractual arrangements, that have the effect of discriminating or that perpetuate the discrimination of others who are subject to common administrative control
6. Excluding or denying an individual equal treatment because of that person's association or relationship with a person who has a disability[21]

Title III also establishes what are termed "specific prohibitions"[22] that delineate five major elements of the prohibition of discrimination on the basis of disability:

1. Discriminatory Eligibility Criteria. Places of public accommodation are prohibited from imposing or applying "eligibility criteria that screen out or tend to screen out" individuals or classes of individuals with disabilities, unless these criteria "can be shown to be necessary for the provision of the goods, services, facilities, privileges, advantages, or accommodations being offered."[23] The "necessary" test is similar to the stringent "business necessity" and "job-related" standards ADA imposes on tests and selection criteria in the employment context.[24]

2. Reasonable Modifications. Public accommodations are required to make "reasonable modifications to policies, practices, or procedures," to permit an individual with a disability opportunity to obtain the goods, services, facilities, privileges, or accommodations being offered; a business is not required, however, to make modifications that it "can demonstrate . . . would fundamentally alter the nature of such goods, services, facilities, privileges, or accommodations."[25] Although the "reasonable modifications" requirement is generally equivalent to the "reasonable accommodation" requirement in employment,[26] the fundamental alteration limit imposes a much higher level of obligation upon a public accommodation than does the "undue hardship" limit upon employers. Consequently, although the objectives and nature of the modifications required as a "reasonable modification" or a "reasonable accommodation" are conceptually the same, the amount or degree of required change is substantially more for the public accommodation because its limiting standard is higher.

The fundamental alteration concept in the disability discrimination context derives from the Supreme Court's decision in *Southeastern Community College v. Davis*,[27] under section 504 of the Rehabilitation Act, in which the Court ruled that a university did not have to modify its clinical nursing program by converting it into a program of academic instruction in order to accommodate a woman with a hearing impairment. The Court declared that "[s]uch a fundamental alteration is far more than the 'modification' the regulation requires."[28] Lower courts have further outlined the dimensions of the "fundamental alteration" concept: accommodations are not mandated if they would endanger a program's viability;[29] "massive" changes are not required;[30] nor are modifications that would "jeopardize the effectiveness" of a program or would involve a "major restructuring" of an enterprise;[31] and modifications that would so alter an enterprise as to create, in effect, a new program are not required.[32] A colleague and I have elsewhere proposed the following definition of "fundamental alteration": "(1) a substantial change in the primary purpose or benefit of a program or activity; or (2) a substantial impairment of necessary or essential components required to achieve a program or activity's primary purpose or benefit."[33]

3. Auxiliary Aids and Services. Covered entities must "take such steps as may be necessary" to assure that no person with a disability "is excluded, denied services, segregated, or otherwise treated differently . . . because of the absence of auxiliary aids or services."[34] "Auxiliary aids and services" are defined in the statute to include:

1. Qualified interpreters or other effective methods of making aurally delivered materials available to individuals with hearing impairments
2. Qualified readers, taped texts, or other effective methods of making visually delivered materials available to individuals with visual impairments
3. Acquisition or modification of equipment or devices
4. Other similar services and actions[35]

A public accommodation is not required to provide such aids and services if it is able to demonstrate that doing so would "fundamentally alter the nature of the good, service, facility, privilege, advantage, or accommodation being offered or would result in an undue burden."[36] Thus, the fundamental-alteration limit on provision of auxiliary aids and services is supplemented by an undue-burden limitation, a concept for public accommodations that is analogous to the undue-hardship limitation within the employment context.[37]

4. Readily Achievable Barrier Removal in Existing Facilities. Public accommodations must remove "architectural barriers, and communication barriers that are structural in nature, in existing facilities . . . where such removal is readily achievable."[38] "Readily achievable" means "easily accomplishable and able to be carried out without much difficulty or expense."[39] In determining whether an action is readily achievable, the ADA indicates some of the factors to be considered:

1. The nature and cost of the action needed under this Act
2. The overall financial resources of the facility or facilities involved in the action; the number of persons employed at such facility; the effect on expenses and resources, or the impact otherwise of such action upon the operation of the facility
3. The overall financial resources of the covered entity; the overall size of the business of the covered entity with respect to the number of its employees; the number, type, and location of its facilities
4. The type of operation or operations of the covered entity, including the composition, structure, and functions of the workforce of such entity; the geographic separateness, administrative or fiscal relationship of the facility or facilities in question to the covered entity[40]

Inclusion of "geographic separateness" in the list of factors was a legislative compromise. Some business interests contended that consideration of resources should be limited to those of the particular facility and not of the parent company, arguing that readily achievable changes should not be permitted to justify changes that would make a particular facility at a particular location unprofitable and thus cause a company to close it. Disability rights advocates maintained that the full amount of resources available to a facility through a parent company should be controlling, arguing that more should be required of a large corporation with multiple sites than of a small, local, one-site operation. The final language provides that both the site-specific and parent-company resources are to be considered.[41]

The ADA committee reports list, as examples of barrier removal that would be readily achievable, "the addition of grab bars, the simple ramping of a few steps, the lowering of telephones, the addition of raised letter and braille markings on elevator control buttons, the addition of flashing alarm lights, and similar modest adjustments."[42]

5. Alternative Methods. Where measures to remove barriers are not required because a public accommodation can demonstrate that they are not "readily achievable," the entity must still make its goods, services, facilities, privileges, advantages, or accommodations available through "alternative methods" if such methods are readily achievable.[43] Examples of "alternative methods" are provided in the committee reports: "coming to the door to receive or return drycleaning; allowing a disabled patron to be served beverages at a table even though nondisabled persons having only drinks are required to drink at the inaccessible bar; providing assistance to retrieve items in an inaccessible location; and rotating movies between the first floor accessible theater and a comparable second floor inaccessible theater."[44]

The requirements to remove barriers in existing facilities and to provide alternative methods where doing so is readily achievable applies to "communication barriers" as well as to "architectural barriers."[45] Thus, where structural changes to signage, loudspeaker systems, or visual displays in existing facilities to benefit people with visual, hearing, or cognitive impairments are not readily achievable (and are not otherwise required as an auxiliary aid), places of public accommodation may nonetheless be required to undertake readily achievable alternative actions such as providing a person to read information, to write down oral communications, or to escort an individual to the location of goods, facilities, or programs that might otherwise be difficult or impossible for the individual to find.

In addition to the "general prohibition" and the "specific prohibitions," title III also includes some particular provisions for new construction and alterations. Both newly constructed public-accommodation facilities and commercial facilities for first occupancy 30 months or more after the ADA's enactment must be accessible, unless an entity can demonstrate that doing so is "structurally impracticable."[46] "Structurally impracticable" is a very narrow exception applying primarily to buildings required to be built on stilts over water or marshes.[47] A small-building elevator exception is established as an exception to the Act's accessibility requirements, and provides that an elevator is not required in facilities that are less than three stories high or have less than 3,000 square feet per story, unless the facility is a shopping center, shopping mall, office of a health-care provider, or some other type of facility in a category that the Attorney General determines, based upon its usage, requires the installation of elevators.[48]

When public accommodations and commercial facilities are altered, the altered portions must be accessible.[49] If alterations are made to an area of a facility containing a primary function, the entity must provide an accessible path of travel to the altered area, and accessible bathrooms, telephones, and drinking fountains serving the altered area, unless doing so would be "disproportionate" to the overall cost and scope of the alterations.[50] The ADA gives the Attorney General the responsibility of establishing standards for the disproportionality criterion.[51] House-committee ADA reports suggest that a level of 30 percent of the alteration costs would be an appropriate standard for distinguishing what is or is not disproportionate.[52]

PRECEDENTS AND EXPERIENCES PROVIDING GUIDANCE FOR THE IMPLEMENTATION OF ADA PUBLIC ACCOMMODATIONS REQUIREMENTS

ACCESSIBILITY REQUIREMENTS

The ADA's accessibility provisions make use of terms of art under prior statutes and federal regulations—facilities and vehicles must be made "readily accessible to and usable by" individuals with disabilities.[53]

Under previous legislation and regulations, relatively specific standards and schematic drawings have been devised and issued to flesh out the application of the readily-accessible-to and usable-by standard.[54] The ADA committee reports provide guidance to the basic implications of the concept:

> The term is intended to enable people with disabilities (including mobility, sensory, and cognitive impairments) to get to, enter and use a facility. While the term does not necessarily require the accessibility of every part of every area of a facility, the term contemplates a high degree of convenient accessibility, entailing accessibility of parking areas, accessible routes to and from the facility, accessible entrances, usable bathrooms and water fountains, accessibility of public and common use areas, and access to the goods, services, programs, facilities, accommodations and work areas available at the facility.[55]

The ADA's legislative history provides some additional clarifications regarding the application of accessibility requirements in particular situations.[56] For example, the legislative history indicates that all newly constructed buildings must have an accessible ground floor, even if they are not mandated to have elevators pursuant to the previously noted exception for certain small buildings.[57]

Another important concept for the ADA's coverage of places of public accommodation is the term "facility," which the Senate report indicates should be interpreted to refer to "all or any portion of buildings, structures, sites, complexes, equipment, roads, walks, passageways, parking lots, or other real or personal property or interest in such property, including the site where the building, property, structure, or equipment is located."[58] This is based upon the definition in section 504 regulations,[59] and similar definitions can be found in other sets of standards.[60] The definition applies to both indoor areas and all outdoor areas where human-constructed improvements or items have been added to the natural environment. It includes buildings and other erected structures, as well as equipment, apparatus, and parking lots, walkways, sidewalks, roadways, and passageways, plus the sites, areas, or settings in which such things are located.

The ADA authorizes the Attorney General to promulgate regulations for the implementation of title III.[61] These regulations are to be consistent with minimum guidelines regarding accessibility to be issued by the Architectural and Transportation Barriers Compliance Board (ATBCB).[62] ATBCB has previously developed minimum guidelines for accessibility under the Architectural Barriers Act of 1968 and section 504 of the Rehabilitation Act of 1973—the Minimum Guidelines and Requirements for Accessible Design (MGRAD),[63] and these guidelines are to be supplemented and revised as necessary to develop minimum guidelines under the ADA.[64]

On several occasions prior to the ADA, the federal government recognized that protecting people with disabilities from discrimination requires regulation of the built environment. In the Fair Housing Amendments Act of 1988, Congress directed the Secretary of HUD to encourage but not require state and local governments to issue accessibility requirements consistent with the minimum access requirements set out in the Act.[65] The approach through encouragement in the Fair Housing legislation provided a useful model for the ADA. The ADA pursued this approach further by authorizing states and local governments to apply voluntarily to the Attorney General for certification that a state law, local building code, or similar ordinance meets or exceeds the minimum requirements of the Act for accessibility.[66]

The voluntary certification process notwithstanding, the ADA does not establish any direct mandate for including its minimum accessibility standards in state and local building codes and ordinances. As a practical matter, however, because entities that fail to comply with the minimum accessibility requirements of ADA may be subject to legal liability under the ADA, state and local regulatory agencies will probably begin to make their requirements consistent with the accessibility provisions of the ADA. State and local governments can continue to select and/or develop their own codes, but they will probably not want their standards to fall below the minimum guidelines established by the ADA.

Ready Achievability. Under the ADA, existing facilities are only required to make structural changes that are "readily achievable," a phrase that is defined to mean "easily accomplishable and able to be carried out without much difficulty or expense."[67] As discussed above, the Act establishes a list of factors to be considered in determining whether a particular change is readily achievable by a particular business. This requires physical access that can be achieved without extensive restructuring or burdensome expense. For example, a public accommodation that has one or two steps may be required to install a simple ramp. A public accommodation would generally not be required to provide access if there is a flight of steps that would require extensive ramping or an elevator. The agency or business would still have to take other "readily achievable" steps to provide program access. For example, a real-estate agency doing business with the general public at a three-story walk-up office would not be required to install an elevator to provide access to the upper floors. The agency would be required, however, to install a simple ramp over a few steps to its entrance, in order to provide its services to customers with mobility impairments in the first-floor accessible offices, and to add glue-on, raised-letter, and braille markings to its elevator panels (if there are elevators) and floor numbers.

Topological Problems. The ADA recognizes that sometimes accessibility poses topological problems by allowing for exceptional cases where access would be impracticable or infeasible. Thus, the ADA does not require full accessibility when (1) in the case of new facilities, access would be "structurally impracticable;" or (2) in the case of altered facilities, access would be beyond the "maximum extent feasible." Such limitations will apply only in rare and unusual circumstances where unique characteristics of terrain make full accessibility unusually difficult. Such limitations for topological problems are analogous to an acknowledged limitation in the application of the accessibility requirements of the Fair Housing Amendments Act of 1988. In the House Committee Report accompanying the Housing Act, the House Committee on the Judiciary noted:

> Certain natural terrain may pose unique building problems. For example, in areas which flood frequently, such as waterfronts or marshlands, housing may traditionally be built on stilts. The Committee does not intend to require that the accessibility requirements of this Act override the need to protect the physical integrity of multifamily housing that may be built on such sites.[68]

Likewise, provisions in the existing Uniform Federal Accessibility Standards contain special requirements for alterations in cases where meeting the general standards would be impracticable or infeasible.[69]

Delineation of the narrow circumstances in which such topological limitations can be invoked in the context of public accommodations will occur in regulations implementing the Act. In such circumstances, a place of public accommodation will not be required to exceed these limits in order to achieve full accessibility. Such an entity will, however, be required to take less extensive steps in order to achieve accessibility. Even where full architectural accessibility is not mandated, there is still a requirement of "alternative methods," such as arranging for services or goods to be delivered at a portion of a facility that *is* accessible.

ENVIRONMENTAL IMPACT OF ACCESSIBILITY

The limitations on accessibility requirements minimize the possible disruptive or burdensome effect of such requirements. It is a common misconception, however, that making facilities accessible may have an adverse effect on the environment, particularly in environmentally sensitive areas. Experience indicates that proper planning and design, and proper construction and renovation of facilities should protect and maintain the integrity of the natural environment.

National Park Service Experience. An agency with considerable experience in providing access to people with disabilities while protecting environmental interests is the National Park Service. In implementing the requirements of section 504 of the Rehabilitation Act of 1973, the National Park Service (NPS) has spent the last decade and a half developing ways to make parks and recreation areas accessible to all persons with disabilities. At first blush, park and recreation facilities seem to pose challenging design questions: how can the Grand Canyon, Rocky Mountains, Cape Cod National Seashore, or Hawaiian Volcanoes be made accessible? In fact, through the application of a few simple principles, the National Park Service has found it feasible to provide an effective level of accessibility at almost all of its parks and facilities without undercutting environmental integrity.

NPS has stated as one of its guiding principles: "The degree of accessibility provided will be proportionately related to the degree of man-made modifications made to the area or facility and to the significance of the facility."[70] Visitors' centers, for example, have a high degree of importance and are highly man made, so accessibility should be optimal. In areas like campgrounds, which have some man-made modifications, it may be appropriate only to make a few campsites accessible. In certain natural areas with extreme slopes, rugged terrain, and no man-made modifications, accessibility features required will be minimal. Even in these areas, park staff are required to take steps to assist visitors with disabilities to experience, as nearly as is feasible, the type of recreation experience available at the site.

The common-sense accessibility policies of the National Park Service are consistent with the ADA. Full access is not required when (1) in the case of new facilities, access would be "structurally impracticable;" (2) in the case of existing facilities, access is not "readily achievable;" or (3) in the case of altered facilities, access would be beyond the "maximum extent feasible."

When full accessibility is not possible, the ADA requires alternative methods of providing access. A similar approach has already been implemented in many programs under the jurisdiction of the Park Service. The Statue of Liberty is a good example. While the Statue was undergoing renovation, the architects determined that it was structurally impossible to provide an elevator to the lookout area in the crown. Yet, being in the crown area and the view from it constitute one of the major experiences available to visitors at the park. To compensate for the inaccessibility of that area for persons unable to climb the stairs to the top, a full-scale model of the crown was developed and displayed in the museum at the site, so that people can enter it and get an idea of its size. A video presentation of the view from the top is also provided. Of course, such alternative methods must be used with some caution to avoid superficial, unequal solutions—seeing a picture of a wild and scenic river is no substitute for rafting the river. People with disabilities should have the opportunity for the first-hand experience whenever possible.

Other Agencies. In addition to the National Park Service, other federal agencies such as the U.S. Forest Service, the Fish and Wildlife Service, and the U.S. Army Corps of Engineers are also experienced in developing accessible facilities. A number of states have passed legislation mandating accessibility in their park and recreation facilities.[71] The experiences of all these agencies have demonstrated that making facilities accessible can be accomplished through means that are in harmony with the environment.

STANDARDS, GUIDELINES, AND TECHNICAL ASSISTANCE
REGARDING ACCESSIBILITY OF PUBLIC ACCOMMODATIONS

PUBLIC ACCOMMODATIONS GENERALLY

A variety of standards, guidelines, technical-assistance documents,and how-to guides are already available regarding access for people with disabilities to various types of public accommodations.

At the time the ADA was enacted, considerable guidance for applying accessibility requirements to particular circumstances was available under existing standards: the ANSI standards (promulgated by the American National Standards Institute)[72] and the UFAS (Uniform Federal Accessibility Standards)[73] are two examples. ANSI, as a private standards-setting organization, has promulgated codes covering many aspects of the built environment that are used in most parts of the country. The large majority of states already have some form of accessibility requirements,[74] and ANSI's accessibility standards are the standards most often referenced by existing local and state accessibility laws.[75]

UFAS are similar in many respects to ANSI, but have been carefully reworked by the four principal standard-setting federal departments (HUD, GSA, DOT, and the Postal Service) for use in enforcing existing federal rules requiring nondiscrimination on the basis of handicap. UFAS is particularly pertinent as a starting point for standards under the ADA, because UFAS includes thorough scoping requirements that clarify exactly what standards apply in what situations. UFAS specify for designers exactly what is required, and eliminate potential confusion that might be engendered by a less detailed set of standards.

The ADA provides that the Department of Justice will issue standards consistent with minimum guidelines developed by the ATBCB, which shall extrapolate upon existing Minimum Guidelines and Requirements for Accessible Design and apply them to the various types of facilities and places of public accommodation and public services covered by titles II and III of the Act. In addition to formal standards such as UFAS that apply to places of public accommodation, there are a variety of technical assistance manuals and how-to guides that give nuts-and-bolts descriptions of how to achieve accessibility. A number of guides are available for the hotel and motel industry. Manuals on how to conduct an accessible conference or meeting are also available. A sample list of such guides appears at the conclusion of this chapter.

PARKS AND RECREATIONAL FACILITIES

PARKS AND RECREATIONAL FACILITIES

There are a number of sets of standards and how-to guides regarding access for people with disabilities to park and recreational facilities.

Existing accessibility standards, UFAS and ANSI, are applicable to the majority of such facilities either directly or indirectly. Both UFAS and ANSI include standards for buildings, bathrooms, parking lots, entrances, and so forth. Nature centers, visitors' centers, and many other park and recreational facilities are buildings, and as such are subject to accessibility standards applicable to other buildings. Requirements regarding bathroom and parking facilities are the same. UFAS has standards for certain special uses, such as restaurants, housing, and assembly and mercantile areas. These standards can be applied to recreational facilities.

Even where existing accessibility standards do not apply directly, they may provide substantial guidance indirectly. For facilities such as fishing piers, campgrounds, and nature trails, UFAS and ANSI can lend significant direction. Major elements of accessible design under UFAS, including parking, accessible route, entrance and egress, bathrooms, and water fountains, can be applied or adapted to such facilities. Specifications for access to a pier, for example, can be extrapolated from UFAS simply by considering the pier as an extension of the pathway, and applying appropriate criteria for making a pathway accessible.

Because accessibility was required by section 504 of the Rehabilitation Act of 1973, guidelines for federally assisted and federally conducted programs in the areas of parks and recreation have been available since the mid-1970s. Examples include guides to making parks accessible for persons with physical impairments and hearing and speech impairments and guides for accessible fishing (U.S. Department of Housing and Urban Development 1976; National Park Service 1986; Nordhaus, Kantrowitz, and Siembieda 1984). A national directory of accessible parks is also available (Northern Cartographic 1988). In addition, the National Park Service has produced two videotapes on accessibility. (They are listed at the end of the chapter.)

HISTORIC BUILDINGS

If an existing historic building is not being otherwise altered or reno-
vated, barriers must be removed when doing so is "readily achievable."
This standard leaves considerable room for balancing the need for
accessibility with maintaining the integrity of the building's historically
significant features. Under existing law, providing access to historic
properties has generally been found to be achievable without destroy-
ing a property's historic significance. The National Park Service has
established an accessibility policy, which may be summarized as follows: "The issue is not *if* we should make historic properties accessible
but *how* to provide the *highest* level of access with the *lowest* level of
impact."[76]

Section 504(c) of the ADA requires the ATBCB to develop minimum
guidelines for "qualified historic properties."[77] These guidelines are to
be generally consistent with the standards for accessibility of historic
properties under UFAS. UFAS contains provisions that allow access to
be provided to certified historic buildings in alternative ways.[78] For
example, if it would impair the historic facade of a building to make
the primary entrance accessible, another entrance can be made
accessible.

COST CONSIDERATIONS

MAKING NEW FACILITIES ACCESSIBLE

The regulatory-impact statement issued in connection with the section
504 rule by the Department of Health, Education and Welfare in 1977
estimated that a new building could be made accessible at an additional cost of one half of one percent (.5 percent) of the total cost of
construction.[79] Other studies, prior and subsequent to the 1977 estimate, have lent support to the conclusion that accessibility costs in the
construction of new buildings are extremely low. In the mid 1960s the
National League of Cities studied costs of access for people with disabilities when considering a national commission on architectural barriers;
the study showed that when planned into the initial design, accessibility features usually cost less than one-half of one percent.[80] A Syracuse
University study conducted for HUD reached the same conclusion.[81] In
1975, the General Accounting Office estimated that accessibility in a

new building can be accomplished for less than one-tenth of one percent of overall costs.[82]

Other authorities have concurred with these estimates that accessibility
in a new building should not cost more than one-tenth to one-half of one
percent of construction costs.[83] In 1981 the ATBCB prepared for the
Office of Management and Budget a report of cost information based
upon data provided by the federal accessibility standard-setting agencies.
The report noted that whereas accessibility can generally be achieved at
.5 percent of the constuction cost, "this percentage would be even lower
if the total costs were considered (i.e., architectural and engineering fees,
cost of land, landscaping, and the like)."[84]

Studies and authorities generally agree that the costs of accessibility
in new construction are quite low. In its ADA cost estimates in 1990,
the Congressional Budget Office referred to a study conducted by the
Department of Housing and Urban Development in 1978, which had
found that the cost of making a building accessible is less than one
percent of total construction costs if the accessibility features are
included in the original building design.[85] The CBO also noted that
"[a]ll states currently mandate accessibility in newly-constructed, state-
owned buildings and therefore would incur little or no costs if this bill
were to be enacted."[86]

COSTS OF MAKING EXISTING INACCESSIBLE BUILDINGS ACCESSIBLE

The costs of alterations to render existing buildings accessible vary
widely, depending upon the type and age of the building, the extent of
architectural and communication barriers present, and other factors.
While Congress was considering the ADA, the National Federation of
Independent Business (NFIB) presented cost figures to demonstrate its
claim that costs of making existing buildings accessible would be substantial and hard for small business to bear; NFIB stated that the
following figures were "based upon several studies and reputable news
articles published during 1988":

- $1,000 to $10,000 for a concrete ramp (cost depending on the
  number of steps to be ramped)
- $3,000 to widen and install a new exterior door
- $300 to $600 to widen and install a new interior door
- $200 to lower an existing water fountain
- $300 to $3,000 to modify an existing public restroom[87]

Generally, renovations to make buildings accessible are estimated to vary between one-half to three percent of construction costs of an overall renovation or of a building's underlying value.[88] The GAO has concluded that the cost of altering existing buildings to make them accessible "is relatively small."[89]

DEFERENCE TO NEEDS OF SMALL BUSINESSES

During congressional consideration of the legislation, the small-business community expressed a great deal of concern that the requirements of the ADA would impose serious hardships upon small businesses.[90] In response, the ADA was carefully crafted so that each of the major requirements of the Act considers and makes allowances for the important and unique needs of the small-business operator. The following are some of the ways in which the public-accommodations provisions[91] of the ADA defer to the characteristics and needs of small businesses.

THE READILY ACHIEVABLE LIMITATION

As noted previously, the ADA places a limit on the requirement for removing architectural and communication barriers in existing public accommodations—such barriers need not be removed unless doing so is "readily achievable," that is, is "easily accomplishable and able to be carried out without much difficulty or expense."[92] The size and budget of a business are explicitly considered in determining what is readily achievable. A Mom-and-Pop store is clearly held to a much lower standard than is a highly financed, national enterprise. A struggling small business will be required to do much less than a bigger, more well-to-do establishment.

UNDUE BURDEN LIMITATION REGARDING AUXILIARY AIDS AND SERVICES

The requirement that places of public accommodation make available "auxiliary aids and services" does not apply in circumstances where the provisions of such aids and services would "fundamentally alter" or would "result in undue burden."[93] The committee reports note that the term "undue burden" is analogous to the phrase "undue hardship" in the employment section of the ADA, and that "the determination of whether the provision of an auxiliary aid or service imposes an undue burden on a business will be made on a case-by-case basis, taking into account the same factors used for purposes of determining 'undue hardship.' "[94] In determining whether providing an auxiliary aid or service amounts to an undue burden, the size, budget, and circumstances of a business are expressly relevant. A struggling small business will be excused from providing an auxiliary aid or service in circumstances where a larger, more prosperous business might be required to provide it.

THE ELEVATOR EXCEPTION FOR NEW CONSTRUCTION
AND ALTERATIONS

The inclusion of accessibility features in the design and construction of new facilities and in renovation projects can usually be accomplished at relatively little expense. To further protect small businesses, however, the Senate compromise bill incorporated a specific exception to accessibility requirements with regard to elevators in small buildings. Whereas the previous version of the bill would have required elevators where necessary for accessibility of upper floors in new construction and certain major renovations, the Senate compromise specifically provided that elevators are not required "for facilities that are less than three stories or that have less than 3,000 square feet per story."[95] Arguably, elevators in such circumstances might constitute only a small and manageable percentage of overall building and renovation costs, but to make absolutely sure that small-building owners and builders would not be unduly burdened, the Act excepts small buildings from the elevator requirement—the single most potentially costly accessibility feature.

THE "READILY-ACCESSIBLE-TO-AND-USABLE-BY"
ACCESSIBILITY STANDARD

The ADA does not require total or universal accessibility, even for newly constructed buildings subject to its requirements, but incorporates a standard of accessibility developed under federal statutes and regulations—"readily accessible to and usable by." This standard imposes accessibility obligations that are tailored to the type and use of each particular facility. The committee reports note that "the term does not necessarily require the accessibility of every part of every area of a facility."[96] The term is intended to enable people with disabilities "to get to, enter, and use a facility."[97]

Making facilities readily accessible to and usable by persons with disabilities is a case-by-case process that considers a facility's physical structure and the nature of its current and projected activities. A small facility will have fewer areas and services to make accessible.

Complying with the readily-accessible-to-and-usable-by requirement of the ADA will require a business to make its services and facilities accessible to persons with disabilities, but will not require it to add additional features not made available to persons without disabilities. For example, a business that does not provide drinking fountains or restroom facilities for the use of its customers will not be forced to add accessible fountains or toilets for customers with disabilities. Under this standard, small businesses with the fewest "frills" will have fewer such services and conveniences to make accessible.

ALTERNATIVE MEANS TO SERVE CUSTOMERS

Where the removal of an access barrier is not required under the ADA because such removal is not readily achievable, the ADA permits businesses to make goods and services available "through alternative methods."[98] Such methods involve means by which small businesses can accommodate the needs of customers with disabilities without hurting their businesses or incurring extensive expenses.

TELECOMMUNICATIONS RELAY SERVICES

Title IV of the ADA provides for the establishment of a system of telecommunications relay services for individuals with speech or hearing impairments. Although it may not be apparent on its face, the development of this relay service is an accommodation to the interests of small businesses. In prior versions of the ADA where there was no relay-service requirement, one of the potential obligations upon places of public accommodation was the purchase and operation of a Telecommunications Device for the Deaf (TDD) so that customers and potential customers could call on their TDDs to make reservations, purchase tickets, inquire about products and prices, and check on store hours.

Although portable TDDs are relatively inexpensive (a good unit can usually be purchased for around $200), there was some concern that it was too burdensome for small businesses to require that all such businesses must have TDDs. As an alternative, the relay-service provisions were developed. Under the requirements of title IV, each area and locality of the country will be served by a telecommunications relay service, and individuals using TDDs will be able to call the relay service and have their inquiries and reservations passed on by voice to the business. Small businesses were thus spared the requirement that all of them incur the modest costs of obtaining TDDs.

Table 1 summarizes the provisions related to public accommodations that are tailored to consider the concerns of small businesses.

It is clear that the ADA was molded with an eye toward accommodating the interests of small businesses. In his remarks at the signing of the bill, President Bush declared:

> I know there have been concerns that the ADA may be vague or costly, or may lead endlessly to litigation. But I want to reassure you right now that my administration and the United States Congress have carefully crafted this Act. We've all been determined to ensure that it gives flexibility . . . and we've been committed to containing the costs that may be incurred.[99]

THE FRUITS OF PUBLIC ACCOMMODATIONS ACCESS REQUIREMENTS

A widely accepted premise of the American system of government is that the nation has an obligation to guarantee equal opportunity for its citizens, to prohibit discrimination, and to regulate facilities in the public interest. Consequently, access for people with disabilities has increasingly gained recognition and acceptance as a legitimate public and governmental interest. Given that a significant portion of the populace has a disability or will experience one at some point, such requirements do not represent a fiscal sacrifice for a select few, but a basic insurance policy provided by our entire society on behalf of the entire society.

ADA access requirements represent a crystallization of conviction that at this point in the development of our society, we have enough understanding of the significant life limitations posed by attitudinal, architectural, and communications barriers to millions of our citizens that it is folly to continue to tolerate such barriers. To continue to erect inaccessible public facilities, for example, when access can be provided

TABLE 1

Accommodations to the Interests of Small Business

Obligation	Accommodation to Small business	Effect
Removing architectural and communications barriers in existing facilities	Readily achievable limitation	Do not have to make changes that involve much difficulty or expense; takes into account financial resources and size of the business
Providing auxiliary aids and services	Undue burden and fundamental alterations	Do not have to provide if doing so would unduly burden or fundamentally alter a business; takes into account financial resources and size of the business
Making new and renovated facilities accessible	Small building elevator exception	Do not have to install elevator in buildings under 3 stories or having fewer than 3,000 square feet per story
	Readily-accessible-to-and-usable-by concept	Tailored to each type of facility; does not require full accessibility of all features, but a reasonable number; facilities having fewer areas and amenities will have fewer to make accessible
Providing access to goods and services	Alternative methods	Where changes to ensure access not readily achievable, permits businesses to use alternative methods
Communications access for TDD users	Relay services	Rather than requiring each business to have a TDD, establishes a relay system

so cheaply, is to continue a form of discrimination that can be characterized as ignorant, at best, or, at worst, as intentional. The ADA
inaugurates a new strand of public policy for the 1990s and beyond that
takes cognizance of the increasing age of our society, of the many
groups of people with disabilities whose talents are needed by our
culture and economy, and of the need to decrease the percentage of our
citizenry surviving on benefits and entitlements because of discrimination and an inaccessible environment. Such positive objectives provide
ample justification for regulating the operations of public accommodations to impose modest nondiscriminatory obligations.

The ADA represents an important advance toward assuring that
places of public accommodation will begin to include people with
disabilities as full and equal parts of the "public" they serve; people
with disabilities will be afforded "the right to be treated as equal
members of the community with respect to public accommodations"
that Justice Goldberg advocated for all Americans in the 1960s in *Bell
v. Maryland.*[100]

NOTES

1. In introducing the original Americans with Disabilities Act bill in the Senate
   in 1988, Senator Lowell Weicker noted that the roots of public accommodations civil-rights laws could ultimately be traced to the Greensboro sit-ins.
   134 Cong. Rec. S 5107 (Daily Edition) (April 28, 1988).
2. 109 U.S. 3, 19 (1883).
3. 378 U.S. 226 (1964).
4. Id., at 250 (opinion of Douglas, J.).
5. Id., at 286 (Goldberg, J., concurring).
6. Id., at 252; 294–95.
7. 42 U.S.C. §2000a et seq.
8. *Americans with Disabilities Act of 1989: Hearings on S. 933 before the
   Senate Committee on Labor and Human Resources,* 101st Cong., 1st Sess.,
   64–65 (1989).
9. Remarks by the President during Ceremony for the Signing of the Americans
   with Disabilities Act of 1990, July 26, 1990, at 2.
10. 42 U.S.C. §2000a.
11. 42 U.S.C. §12181(7). Entities are covered by title III if they are on the list and
    their operations "affect commerce."
12. 42 U.S.C. §§301(6) and (7).
13. 42 U.S.C. §§12187.
14. 42 U.S.C. §2000a(e).
15. *Hearings on S. 933 before the Senate Committee on Labor and Human*

Resources, 101st Cong., 1st Sess., 815 (1989) (testimony of Attorney General Thornburgh).

16. Many multifamily residences are subject to the accessibility requirements of the Fair Housing Amendments Act.
17. 42 U.S.C. §12183(a).
18. 42 U.S.C. §12181(2).
19. See, e.g., *United States v. Darby*, 312. U.S. 100 (1941); *Wickard v. Filburn*, 317 U.S. 111 (1942); *Atlanta Motel v. United States*, 379 U.S. 241 (1964); *Katzenbach v. McClung*, 379 U.S. 294 (1964); *Perez v. United States*, 402 U.S. 146 (1971); *Hodel v. Virginia Surface Mining and Reclamation Association*, 452 U.S. 264 (1981); *Hodel v. Indiana*, 452 U.S. 2376 (1981).
20. 42 U.S.C. §12182(a).
21. 42 U.S.C. §12182(b)(1).
22. 42 U.S.C. §12182(b)(2).
23. 42 U.S.C. §12182(b)(2)(A)(i).
24. 42 U.S.C. §§102(b)(6) and 103(a).
25. 42 U.S.C. §12182(b)(2)(A)(ii).
26. 42 U.S.C. §§102(b)(5)(A) and 101(9). In *Alexander v. Choate*, 469 U.S. 287, 299–301 (1985), the Supreme Court made interchangeable use of the phrases "reasonable accommodations" and "reasonable modifications."
27. 442 U.S. 397, 410 (1979).
28. Id.
29. *New Mexico Association of Retarded Citizens v. State of N.M.*, 678 F.2d 847, 855 (10th Cir. 1982).
30. *Dopico v. Goldschmidt*, 687 F.2d 644, 653 (2d Cir. 1982); *American Public Transit Association v. Lewis*, 655 F.2d 1272, 1278 (D.C.Cir. 1981).
31. *Rhode Island Handicapped Action Commission v. Rhode Island Public Transit Authority*, 549 F.Supp. 592, 607, 611 (D.R.I. 1982).
32. *Doe v. Colautti*, 592 F.2d 704, 707–09 (3d Cir. 1979); *Turillo v. Tyson*, 535 F.Supp. 577, 587 (D.R.I. 1982); *Lynch v. Maher*, 507 F.Supp. 1268, 1280 (D.Conn. 1981); *Colin K. v. Schmidt*, 536 F.Supp. 1375, 1388 (D.R.I. 1982); *R.I. Handicapped v. Transit Authority*, 549 F.Supp. 592, 607 (D.R.I. 1982).
33. R.L. Burgdorf Jr. and C.G. Bell. 1984. Eliminating Discrimination against Physically and Mentally Handicapped Persons: A Statutory Blueprint. 8 *Mental and Physical Disabilities Law Reporter* 64, 70 (Jan./Feb.)
34. 42 U.S.C. §12182(b)(2)(A)(iii).
35. 42 U.S.C. §12102(1). The list is not exhaustive according to the Committee reports. S. Rep. No. 101–116, 101st Cong., 1st Sess., 63 (1989); H. Rep. No. 101–485, Part 2, 101st Cong., 2d Sess., 107 (1990).
36. 42 U.S.C. §12182(b) (2) (A) (iii).
37. 42 U.S.C. §§102(b)(5)(A) and 101(10). See S. Rep. No. 101–116, 101st Cong, 1st Sess., 63 (1989); H. Rep. No.101–485, Part 2, 101st Cong., 2d Sess., 106–107 (1990); H. Rep. No.101–485, Part 3, 101st Cong., 2d Sess., 59 (1990).
38. 42 U.S.C. §12182(b)(2)(A)(iv)
39. 42 U.S.C. §12181(9).

40. 42 U.S.C. §12181(9).
41. See, e.g., H. Rep. No.101–485, Part 2, 101st Cong., 2d Sess., 109, 68 (1990); Part 3, 55.
42. S. Rep. No. 101–116, 101st Cong, 1st Sess., 66 (1989); H. Rep. No.101–485, Part 2, 101st Cong., 2d Sess., 110 (1990).
43. 42 U.S.C. §12182(b)(2)(A)(v).
44. S. Rep. No. 101–116, 101st Cong, 1st Sess., 66 (1989); H. Rep. No.101–485, Part 2, 101st Cong., 2d Sess., 110–111 (1990). The House Committee on Education and Labor adds that the theater in the last example is responsible for "notifying the public of the movie's location in any advertisements." H. Rep. No.101–485, Part 2, 101st Cong., 2d Sess., 111 (1990).
45. 42 U.S.C. §12182(b)(2)(A)(iv).
46. 42 U.S.C. §12183(a).
47. See S. Rep. No. 101–116, 101st Cong, 1st Sess., 70–71 (1989); H. Rep. No.101–485, Part 2, 101st Cong., 2d Sess., 120 (1990)
48. 42 U.S.C. §12183(b).
49. 42 U.S.C. §12183(a)(2). The exception regarding elevators in small buildings just discussed applies to alterations as well as new construction.
50. Id.
51. Id.
52. H. Rep. No.101–485, Part 2, 101st Cong., 2d Sess., 113 (1990); H. Rep. No.101–485, Part 3, 101st Cong., 2d Sess., 64 (1990).
53. See, S. Rep. No. 101–116, 101st Cong, 1st Sess., 69 (1989); H. Rep. No.101–485, Part 2, 101st Cong., 2d Sess., 117 (1990), in which the committees observe: "The phrase 'readily accessible to and usable by' is a term of art which, in slightly varied formulations, has been applied in the Architectural Barriers Act of 1968 ('ready access to, and use of'), the Fair Housing Act of 1968, as amended ('readily accessible to and usable by'), and the regulations implementing section 504 of the Rehabilitation Act of 1973 ('readily accessible to and usable by'), and is included in standards used by Federal agencies and private industry, e.g., the Uniform Federal Accessibility Standards (UFAS) ('ready access to and use of') and the American National Standard for Buildings and Facilities—Providing Accessibility and Usability for Physically Handicapped People (ANSI A117.1) ('accessible to, and usable by')."
54. In particular, see General Services Administration, Department of Defense, Department of Housing and Urban Development, and U.S. Postal Service, *Uniform Federal Accessibility Standards* (U.S. Government Printing Office, 1985), originally published at 49 Fed. Reg. 31528 (Aug. 7, 1984) (hereinafter referred to as UFAS).
55. S. Rep. No. 101–116, 101st Cong, 1st Sess., 69 (1989); H. Rep. No.101–485, Part 2, 101st Cong., 2d Sess., 117–118 (1990).
56. See, e.g., S. Rep. No. 101–116, 101st Cong, 1st Sess., 69–70 (1989); H. Rep. No.101–485, Part 2, 101st Cong., 2d Sess., 117–119 (1990).
57. 42 U.S.C. §12183(b).
58. S. Rep. No. 116, 101st Cong., 1st Sess. 67 (1989).
59. See, e.g., 45 CFR 84.3(i).
60. American National Standards Institute, *American National Standard for*

Buildings and Facilities — Providing Accessibility and Usability for Physically Handicapped People (1986) at 15, §3.5 and *Uniform Federal Accessibility Standards*, note 54 supra, at 4, §3.5.

61. 42 U.S.C. §12186(b).
62. 42 U.S.C. §12186(c).
63. Architectural and Transportation Barriers Compliance Board, "Minimum Guidelines and Requirements for Accessible Design," 36 CFR Part 1190, originally published at 47 Fed. Reg. 33862 (Aug. 4, 1982) (hereinafter referred to as MGRAD).
64. 42 U.S.C. §12204.
65. 42 U.S.C. §3604(f)(5)(C).
66. 42 U.S.C. §12188(b)(1)(A)(ii). Such certification can take place only after prior notice and a public hearing, and in consultation with the ATBCB.
67. 42 U.S.C. §12181(9).
68. H. Rep. No. 711, 100th Cong., 2d Sess. 27 (1988).
69. UFAS, note 54 supra, §§4.1.6(2), (3), (4)(c)(ii), (e), and (f) and 4.17.3 at 12–13, 38.
70. National Park Service, Special Directive 83-3.
71. See, e.g., Ill. Ann. Stat. ch. 111 1/2 §3713(r)(2) (Smith-Hurd); Mich. Stat. Ann. §3.550(301); N.C. Gen. Stat. §168-3.
72. See, note 60 supra.
73. See, note 54 supra.
74. See, e.g., Cal. Government Code §4450 (West); Fla. Stat. Ann. §553.45 et seq. (West). State architectural accessibility statutes are discussed in 82 ALR 4th 121.
75. See, e.g., Fla. Stat. Ann. sec. 553.481 (West Cumm. Supp. 1990).
76. See note 70 supra.
77. 42 U.S.C. 12204(c).
78. UFAS, note 54 supra, §4.1.7. at 13–14.
79. 41 Fed. Reg. 20,333.
80. The results of this study are discussed in a pamphlet issued by the Architectural and Transportation Barriers Compliance Board (Architectural and Transportation Barriers Compliance Board 1982, 5).
81. See U.S. General Accounting Office 1990: *Persons with Disabilities: Report on Costs of Accommodations*, January 4, at 15.
82. See id., at 14–15.
83. See, e.g., ATBCB 1982: *About Barriers*, p. 5; National Council on Disability 1986: *Toward Independence*, Appendix, pp. F-28 and F-29; U.S. Commission on Civil Rights 1983: *Accommodating the Spectrum of Individual Abilities*, pp.81–82; *Congressional Record*, April 29, 1988 (Remarks of Representative Owens).
84. ATBCB 1981: ATBCB Minimum Guidelines and Requirements — Cost Information. Memorandum to James C. Miller III, March 20.
85. H. Rep. No.101–485, Part 3, 101st Cong., 2d Sess., 80 (1990).
86. Id.
87. *Americans with Disabilities Act: Hearings on H.R. 2273 before the House Committee on the Judiciary*, 101st Cong., 1st Sess. 88.

88. See, e.g., ATBCB 1981: ATBCB Minimum Guidelines and Requirements—
    Cost Information. Memorandum to James C. Miller III, March 20, pp. 5 and
    9; U.S. Commission on Civil Rights 1983: *Accommodating the Spectrum of
    Individual Abilities*, p. 81; Senator Paul Simon 1981: Defending the Handi-
    capped, *National Journal*, March 14.
89. See U.S. General Accounting Office 1990: *Persons with Disabilities: Report
    on Costs of Accommodations*, January 4 at 15, citing a 1975 GAO report.
90. The National Federation of Independent Business, for example, testified that
    the legislation would create "onerous requirements," and that "the practical
    implications could well be overwhelming for many small firms." *Americans
    with Disabilities Act: Hearings on S. 933 Before the Senate Committee on
    Labor and Human Resources*, 101st Cong., 1st Sess. 507, 505 (1989).
91. This article focuses upon the public accommodations requirements of the
    ADA, but small business concerns are well-accounted for in other parts of the
    Act as well, for example, in the employment title and various requirements
    regarding transportation.
92. 42 U.S.C. §12181(9).
93. 42 U.S.C. §12182(b)(2)(A)(iii).
94. S. Rep. No. 101–116, 101st Cong, 1st Sess., 63 (1989); H. Rep. No.101–485,
    Part 2, 101st Cong., 2d Sess., 106–107 (1990).
95. 42 U.S.C. §12183(b).
96. S. Rep. No. 101–116, 101st Cong, 1st Sess., 69 (1989); H. Rep. No.101–485,
    Part 2, 101st Cong., 2d Sess., 117–118 (1990).
97. S. Rep. No. 101–116, 101st Cong, 1st Sess., 69 (1989); H. Rep. No.101–485,
    Part 2, 101st Cong., 2d Sess., 117–118 (1990).
98. 42 U.S.C. §12182(b)(2)(A)(v).
99. Remarks by the President during Ceremony for the Signing of the Americans
    with Disabilities Act of 1990, July 26, 1990, at 3.
100. 378 U.S. 226, 286 (1964) (Goldberg, J., concurring).

REFERENCES

Architectural and Transportation Barriers Compliance Board. 1982. *About Barri-
    ers*. Washington.
Louis Harris and Associates. 1986. *The ICD Survey of Disabled Americans: Bring-
    ing Disabled Americans into the Mainstream*. New York.
National Park Service. 1986. *Interpretation for Disabled Visitors in the National
    Park System*. Washington.
Nordhaus, R.S., M. Kantrowitz, and W.J. Siembieda. 1984. *Accessible Fising: A
    Planning Handbook*. Santa Fe, N. Mex.: Natural Resources Department.
Shapiro, J.S. 1988. A New "Common Identity" for the Disabled. *Washington Post*
    (March 29):19 (Health Section).
U.S. Department of Housing and Urban Development. 1976. *Barrier Free Site
    Design*. Washington.

ADDITIONAL RESOURCES

Readings

American Hotel and Motel Association. 1986. *Handicap Accessibility in Newly Constructed Hotels & Motels: An Interpretation of ANSI A117.1*. New York.

Arkansas Rehabilitation Continuing Education Program. 1981. *Accessibility Guidelines for Meeting and Lodging Facilities*. Hot Springs, Ark.

Davies T.D., and K.A. Beaslely. 1988. *Design for Hospitality: Planning for Accessible Hotels and Motels*. New York: Nichols Publishing.

Eastern Paralyzed Veterans Association. 1984. *Curb Cuts*. New York.

Federal Government Working Group on Access to Recreation. 1985. *Access to Outdoor Recreation Planning and Design*. Washington.

Northern Cartographic. 1988. *Access America: An Atlas and Guide to the National Parks for Visitors with Disabilities*. Burlington, Vt.

Redden, M.R., S. Fortunato-Schwandt, and J.W. Brown. 1976. *Barrier-Free Meetings: A Guide for Professional Associations*. Pub. No. 76-7. Washington: American Association for the Advancement of Science.

Videotapes

National Park Service. 1988. *Access to Parks and Recreation: Disabled People Speak*.

_____. 1989. *Access to Park and Recreation Facilities*.

Transportation Policy

Robert A. Katzmann

EDITOR'S NOTE

The complex mesh of private and public systems of transportation is an essential component of our societal infrastructure. Usable public and private transportation systems are particularly important for persons with disabilities for whom driving a car may not be a viable option. Exercising the right to pursue employment in a discrimination-free environment and to utilize accessible services is a vacuous opportunity if there is no usable transportation to that job or service.

With a gradual phase-in of accessibility requirements, the Americans with Disabilities Act (ADA) ensures that the building and updating of systems will take place in a manner that renders them accessible and distributes the costs over time. With more than a decade of experience in developing accessible transportation for persons with disabilities (e.g., the Washington, D.C., and San Francisco Metro systems), we have significant experience to build on.

Robert A. Katzmann has contributed one of a handful of comprehensive disability policy studies to the field: Institutional Disability: The Saga of Transportation Policy for the Disabled, *published by the Brookings Institution 1986. In this article he picks up where the Brookings book left off, analyzing both the transportation-related requirements of the ADA and the relevant regulations issued by the Department of Transportation. Katzmann has been associated with the Brookings Institution in Washington, D.C., since 1981 as a research associate and senior fellow. He is currently a visiting fellow in the Brookings governmental studies program and is president of the Governance Institute, a nonprofit organization focusing on law and policy making. Fortified by a Ph.D. in government from Harvard University and a J.D. from Yale Law School, Katzmann has written a number of books on regulation, judicial-congressional relations, and court reform.*

If persons with disabilities are to be wholly integrated into society — if they are to enter the work force to the fullest extent possible and to enjoy their rights of citizenship more generally — then they must have access to transportation. Yet, a segment of the American population has been thwarted from using transportation because the public and private sectors have not taken their needs into account. Over the last 20 years, society has decided to remedy this circumstance. How and at what level are highly debatable (Berkowitz 1987; Katzmann 1986; Percy 1989; Skotch 1989; Zola 1989). Policy has been far from consistent, moving back and forth between concepts of "effective mobility" and "full accessibility." The former seeks to provide transportation by any presumably practical mode, and would accept special transit service, even if it were not integrated. The latter maintains that each individual has a right to be fully integrated into society, and thus integrated transportation must be available to everyone. With the passage of the Americans with Disabilities Act (ADA), the federal government has moved decisively to support the full-accessibility conception, significantly extending it to both the public and private spheres.[1]

Our discussion will cover the following points: (1) what we know; (2) the requirements of the ADA; (3) the historical regulatory context; (4) DOT regulations regarding the acquisition of vehicles (based on a full review of the regulatory docket); (5) the regulatory challenge; and (6) what research tells us.

WHAT WE KNOW: A SUMMARY

In summarizing "what we know" about transportation policy for persons with disabilities, we could as aptly describe "what we don't know." For the most part, information gathering and rigorous analysis has followed the passage of the ADA rather than preceded it. A recent

Project ACTION study went so far as to claim that, with respect to
transportation needs, "there is no solid data base for identifying persons with disabilities" (Project ACTION 1990). However, some comments are in order about the population of persons with disabilities and
the views of the community of persons with disabilities, manufacturers,
and operators.

POPULATION

The last comprehensive Department of Transportation (DOT) survey of
persons with disabilities was undertaken in 1977 (Cannon and Rainbow
1980; U.S. Department of Transportation 1978). It identified a total
population of 7.4 million persons over the age of five who live in urban
areas and are constrained to some extent from using public transportation. Of that total, 1.4 million were unable to use public transit at all.
More recent national surveys, although not specifically dealing with
transportation, suggest that the population is higher than the 1977
survey would indicate (National Center for Health Statistics 1984). As
it undertakes its regulatory responsibilities consistent with the ADA,
DOT, through its consultant, David Lewis, expects to draw upon data
prepared for the Canadian Health and Disability Survey (Hickling Consultants 1984; Lewis 1984). That study found that an estimated 0.11
percent of the general population cannot be expected to use an accessible bus, even if access to and from the bus stop were not a problem.
Among this group, 0.03 percent could use paratransit without traveling
in the company of an attendant, whereas 0.04 percent could only use
paratransit if accompanied by an attendant. If each of the 0.04 percent
is accompanied by an attendant, the total eligible group is 0.11 percent
of the population, according to the study.

VIEWS OF PERSONS WITH DISABILITIES

Nationwide, persons with disabilities are very much concerned about
the lack of adequate transportation services. The Harris Survey of Disabled Americans, for example, reported that 28 percent of nonworking
people with disabilities asserted that a dearth of accessible or affordable
transportation was an important reason why they were not employed
(Louis Harris and Associates 1986).

MANUFACTURERS

Anecdotal evidence indicates that, where the incentive exists, usually in the form of governmental requirements, manufacturers can be spurred to develop accessible vehicles. Certainly, over the last several years, there has been a variety of technological advancements. The absence of standards for securement devices, however, has complicated the task for manufacturers seeking to create accessible vehicles.

TRANSIT OPERATORS

Localities vary in the nature and level of transportation services. Some cities, for instance Denver and Seattle, are widely regarded as leaders in providing accessible fixed-route bus services. Nationwide, 35 percent of the national transit fleet was equipped with accessible features in 1990, according to DOT (U.S. Department of Transporation 1990b).

Cost estimates for implementing the transportation requirements of the ADA vary. Nationwide, DOT calculates that the lift-equipped buses will range from $675 million to $735 million over 30 years on a present-value basis (U.S. Department of Transportation 1990a). The American Public Transit Association, representing local mass-transit systems, estimates that the costs of lifts fall somewhere between $10,000 and $15,000 per bus, with an additional $1,000 to $8,000 per year, per bus, in operating and maintenance costs (U.S. Congress 1990). At the same time, various consumer groups assert that the costs are considerably less.

The cost of paratransit varies, depending upon the amount of time in advance services must be reserved (generally referred to as "response time"). DOT estimates that the provision of paratransit services on a 24-hour response-time basis nationwide would cost $1.1 billion.

Many private operators assert that the costs of complying with the ADA, added to other economic woes, could force them to cease operations altogether. Greyhound, for instance, has calculated annual costs stemming from the ADA in the range of between $40,4000,000 and $133,200,000 (U.S. Congress 1990).

Estimates of costs of rail-transit accessibility also differ, ranging from $21,334,057 (ten-year annualized) to $72,669,809 (ten-year realized) (Reuter 1990). Some rail systems, for example, Washington, D.C.'s METRORAIL and San Francisco's BART are already in full compliance with the ADA.

THE HISTORICAL REGULATORY CONTEXT

DOT has, since 1976, promulgated a series of regulations to implement section 504 of the Rehabilitation Act of 1973, section 16 of the Urban Mass Transportation Act (UMTA) of 1970, and related statutes pertaining to transportation for persons with disabilities (Katzmann 1986). Section 504 declared that "no otherwise qualified handicapped individual in the United States . . . shall solely by reason of his handicap, be excluded from participation in, be denied the benefits of, or be subjected to discrimination under any program or activities receiving Federal financial assistance."[2] Section 16 of the 1970 UMTA decreed as national policy that "elderly and handicapped persons have the same right as other persons to utilize mass transportation facilities and services, that special efforts shall be made in the planning and design of mass transportation so that the availability to handicapped persons of mass transportation which they can effectively utilize will be assured."[3]

The first set of regulations, embodying the effective mobility approach, required that federally supported local governments make "special efforts" to provide transportation for such persons.[4] A few years later, in 1979, the department changed course, adopting a policy of full accessibility, pursuant to section 504 of the Rehabilitation Act of 1973; regulations would have required the purchase of accessible buses and the retrofitting of rail mass-transit systems.[5] A successful court challenge to those regulations by the transit industry, contending that the department went beyond its authority by imposing "undue financial burdens" on transit authorities, led in 1981 to an interim rule that resurrected the 1977 special-efforts approach.[6] Dissatisfied with the interim rule, Congress added a new section 16(d) to the UMTA Act in 1983, requiring the DOT to issue a new rule setting out minimum service criteria for transportation for persons with disabilities (although the law did not mandate comparable service or equal access to transit for persons with disabilities).[7]

In 1986, the department issued a rule, implementing the statute, consisting of six service criteria to measure adequate service.[8] To resolve the "undue burdens" problem, which led the court to strike down the 1979 section 504 regulations, the regulations included a "cost cap." That is, a transit authority did not have to spend more than 3 percent of its operating budget to satisfy the rule, even if, as a consequence, the transit authority did not completely satisfy all the service criteria.

The United States Court of Appeals for the Third Circuit concluded in 1989 that, although the department could take costs into consideration in formulating the rule, the 3 percent cost cap was arbitrary.[9] According to court order, the department agreed to issue a final rule, consistent with the Third Circuit opinion, by September 21, 1990.

At the same time that the litigation was winding its way through the courts, disability groups were pressing for passage of what would become the Americans with Disabilities Act. The Bush administration's decision to support those efforts led DOT to broaden its commitment to persons with disabilities. DOT anticipated the ADA when, in response to the Third Circuit opinion, its notice of proposed rule making, on March 26, 1990, stated support for policies requiring all new buses to be accessible, and supplemental paratransit that was comparable to service for the general public for persons who could not use the fixed-route transit service.[10] DOT also announced that it intended to address problems of undue financial burdens of supplemental paratransit.

THE REQUIREMENTS OF THE ADA

With enactment of the ADA, these policy pronouncements became law. Titles II and III of the Act are most concerned with transportation.[11] The Act defines "fixed-route system" as a system of providing public transportation on which a vehicle is operated along a prescribed route according to a fixed schedule; and "demand-responsive system" as any system that is not a fixed-route system.

TITLE II – PUBLIC TRANSPORTATION

Title II provides that "no qualified individual with a disability shall, by reason of such disability, be excluded from participation in or be denied the benefits of the services, programs, or activities of a public entity, or be subjected to discrimination by any such entity."[12] A "qualified individual with a disability" is defined as "an individual with a disability who, with or without reasonable modifications to rules, policies, or practices, the removal of architectural barriers, or the provision of auxiliary aids and services, meets the essential eligibility requirements for the receipt of services or the participation in programs or activities provided by a public entity."[13] A "public entity" means any state or local government, any instrumentality of a state or local govern-

ment, the National Railroad Passenger Corporation, and any commuter
authority (as defined by the Rail Passenger Act). The title also pertains
to intercity rail.

Fixed-Route Systems. The Act does not require the retrofitting of
existing buses, but does mandate that all new vehicles purchased or
leased by a public entity, operating a fixed-route system, be accessible.
Moreover, the public entity must make "demonstrated good faith
efforts" when purchasing or leasing used vehicles.[14] The law also holds
that a public entity operating a fixed-route system, other than a system
that solely provides commuter bus service, must offer paratransit and
other special transportation services to individuals with disabilities.
That level of service must be "comparable to the level of designated
public transportation services provided to individuals without disabilities using such a system;" or, in the case of response time, "comparable
to the extent practicable, to the level of designated public transportation services provided to individuals without disabilities using such
system."[15] Not later than one year after the effective date of the law—
July 26, 1991—the Secretary of DOT is to issue final regulations implementing the paratransit section.

Paratransit. Those eligible for paratransit and other special transportation services, to be provided by public entities, are persons who are
"unable, as a result of a physical or mental impairment and without
the assistance of another individual" (except a wheelchair lift operator
or other boarding assistance device) "to board, ride, or disembark from
any vehicle on the system which is readily accessible to and usable by
individuals with disabilities." Also eligible are individuals for whom
accessible fixed-route transit is not being provided, although such service could be used if available; and persons with disabilities who have
"specific impairment-related condition[s]" that prevent them from
"traveling to a boarding location or from a disembarking location on
such a system." Paratransit eligibility criterion also applies under this
law to one other individual accompanying the person with the disability, and to other companions, provided that space is available and other
people with disabilities are not displaced.[16] Proponents of this last
eligibility criterion argued that persons with disabilities must have the
opportunity to travel together with friends and business associates in
order to achieve integration into society.

In a section entitled "undue financial burden limitation," the legislation provides that when it is demonstrated to the satisfaction of the
Secretary that the provision of paratransit and other special transporta-

tion services would impose an undue financial burden on the public entity, then it will "only be required to provide such services to the extent that providing such services would not impose such a burden."[17]

Demand-Responsive Systems. With respect to demand-responsive systems, the ADA declares that it "shall be considered discrimination . . . [for a public entity] to purchase or lease a new vehicle . . . for which a solicitation is made after the 30th day following the effective date [of this law] . . . that is not readily accessible to and usable by individuals with disabilities . . . unless such a system, when viewed in its entirety, provides a level of service to such individuals equivalent to the level of service such system provides to individuals without disabilities."[18]

Bus Lifts. When bus lifts are unavailable for new buses, the Secretary may grant the public entity temporary relief if that entity shows that it made good-faith efforts to locate a qualified manufacturer in sufficient time to comply with the solicitation, and that further delay in purchasing new buses would "significantly impair transportation services in the community served by the public entity."[19]

New Facilities and Alterations. New facilities used in the provision of public transportation must also be accessible. The law further states as a general rule that "[w]here the public entity is undertaking an alteration that affects or could affect usability of or access to an area of the facility containing a primary function, the entity shall also make the alteration in such a manner that, to the maximum extent feasible, the path of travel to the altered area, is readily accessible to and usable by individuals with disabilities . . . where such alterations to the path of travel or the bathrooms, telephones, and drinking fountains serving the altered area are not disproportionate to the overall alterations in terms of cost and scope (as determined under criteria established by the Attorney General)."[20]

Special Rules for Rail Stations and the One-Car-per-Train Rule. "Key" rapid-rail and light-rail stations (with the DOT Secretary determining the criteria for key stations) are to be accessible as soon as practicable, but "in no event later than the last day of the 3-year period" beginning on the effective date of the law. However, with regard to "extraordinarily expensive structural changes," the Secretary may extend the three-year period up to a 30-year period, but by the last day of the 20th year following the date of the Act's passage, "at least 2/3 of such key stations must be readily accessible to and usable by individuals with disabilities."[21] As a general rule, a public entity must provide "at least one vehicle [car] per train that is accessible to individuals with disabilities . . . as soon as practicable but in no event later than the last day of the 5-year period beginning on the effective date" of the act.[22] No later than one year after the date of the ADA's enactment—July 26, 1991—the Secretary is to issue implementing regulations.

Intercity and Commuter Rail Transit. Some of the requirements for rapid-rail and light-rail transit also apply to intercity and commuter-rail transit—for instance, the one-car-per-train rule and provisions for alterations of primary-function areas. New intercity cars must be "readily accessible to and usable by individuals with disabilities;"[23] purchase or lease of any new rail-passenger car for use in inaccessible intercity-rail transportation for which a solicitation is made 30 days after the effective date of the section shall be considered discrimination. Single-level coaches are to provide a number of spaces to park and secure wheelchairs (to accommodate persons who wish to remain in their wheelchairs) equal to not less than one-half the number of single-level rail-passenger coaches in such train, and space to fold and store wheelchairs (to accommodate individuals who wish to transfer to coach seats) "equal to not less than one-half of the number of single-level rail passenger coaches in such train."[24] These coaches are also required to have a restroom accessible to individuals who are wheelchair users. These provisions must be in place as soon as practicable, but in no event later than five years after the enactment of the ADA.

The law also addresses food service on these intercity and commuter-rail trains. For instance, table service in single-level dining cars shall be provided to a passenger who uses a wheelchair, with appropriate auxiliary aids and services (to ensure equivalent food service to individuals with disabilities), if the car adjacent to the end of the dining car through which a wheelchair may enter is itself accessible to a wheelchair, space to park and secure a wheelchair is available in the dining car at the time such passenger wishes to eat, "or space to store and fold a wheelchair is available in the dining car at the time such passenger wishes to eat (if such passenger wishes to transfer to a dining-car seat)."[25] Unless it is "not practicable," a car that is accessible to wheelchairs should be placed adjacent to the end of a dining car.

The ADA requires a purchaser or leasor of used rail cars to make "demonstrated good faith efforts" in obtaining vehicles that are readily accessible to and usable by individuals with disabilities.[26]

All existing intercity rail stations are to be readily accessible to individuals with disabilities no later than 20 years after the passage of the Act. "Key" commuter rail stations (as designated by the commuter authority in consultation with individuals with disabilities) are to be accessible no later than three years after the ADA's enactment, although the Secretary of Transportation may extend the deadline "where the raising of the entire passenger platform is the only means available of attaining accessibility or where other extraordinarily expensive structural changes are necessary to attain accessibility."[27] These parts of the law concerned with intercity and commuter rail transit are effective 18 months after the date of the ADA's enactment.

TITLE III – PRIVATE ENTITIES

Title III of the ADA contains sections forbidding discrimination in certain public transportation services provided by private entities: "No individual shall be discriminated against on the basis of disability in the full and equal enjoyment of specified public transportation services provided by a private entity that is primarily engaged in the business of transporting people and whose operations affect commerce."[28] The term "specified public transportation" means "transportation by bus, rail, or any other conveyance (other than by aircraft) that provides the general public with general or special service (including charter service on a regular and continuing basis)."[29]

Discrimination includes the imposition or application of eligibility criteria that screen out or tend to screen out an individual with a disability, "unless such criteria can be shown to be necessary for the provision of the services being offered;" the failure to make reasonable modifications, provide auxiliary aids and services, and remove barriers; and the purchase or lease of a new or remanufcatured rail passenger car that is not accessible to and usable by individuals with disabilities. Moreover, with regard to discrimination, the legislation includes a special rule for vans with a seating capacity of fewer than eight passengers. Such vans need not be accessible if the van is to be used solely in a demand-responsive system, and if the private entity can demonstrate that the system for which the van is being purchased or leased, when viewed in its entirety, provides a level of service to individuals with disabilities equivalent to the level of service provided to the general public.[30] The DOT Secretary is to issue regulations implementing this part of the ADA not later than one year after the date of its enactment.

Over-the-Road Buses. The ADA charges the Office of Technology Assessment (OTA) with undertaking a comprehensive examination of over-the-road bus service. In conducting the study, OTA is to establish an advisory committee, consisting of private operators and manufacturers of over-the-road buses, persons with disabilities, and technical experts. OTA is also to provide a preliminary draft of the study to the Architectural and Transportation Barriers Compliance Board; any written comments made by the board within 120 days after its receipt of the draft study are to be incorporated as part of OTA's final study. Within 36 months after the ADA's enactment, OTA is to submit the study and recommendations, including options for legislative action, to the president and Congress. Not later than one year after the submission of the study, the Secretary is to issue regulations pertaining to over-the-road bus service. Regulations for "small providers of transportation" (as defined by the DOT secretary) will take effect seven years after the ADA's enactment, and for "other providers of transportation," six years after that date. If the president determines that compliance with the DOT's regulations will result in "a significant reduction" in intercity over-the-road bus service, then the chief executive shall extend the relevant deadlines by one year.[31]

DOT REGULATIONS REGARDING VEHICLE ACQUISTION

Since the passage of the ADA, the Department of Transportation has issued two sets of final regulations. The first directly responds to the 1989 ruling of the U.S. Court of Appeals for the Third Circuit.[32] The second seeks to implement those portions of the ADA of 1990 that require private and public transportation providers to acquire accessible vehicles beginning August 26, 1990.[33]

In the first set of regulations, the DOT deleted the cost cap, which provided that a transit authority did not have to spend more than 3 percent of its operating budget to comply with the 1986 rule, even if, as a result, the transit authority did not fully meet all of the service criteria for transporting persons with disabilities. The effect of the new rule is to require UMTA recipients that have a special service system to meet all service criteria, regardless of the cost. The rule also contains a "maintenance-of-effort" provision, requiring any UMTA grantee that changes the mode of service from special to accessible to maintain at least its current level of special service. This amendment "is intended to prevent a transit authority from eliminating or severely curtailing paratransit service, only to have to build it up again when the department's rule implementing the ADA's supplemental paratransit requirement goes into effect."[34]

The second set of regulations, issued the same day as the first, is consistent with the ADA's requirements for acquiring accessible vehicles, beginning August 26, 1990. DOT makes it clear that the rules apply to both public and private entities that offer transportation service, whether or not they are primarily engaged in providing those services. A private entity contracting with a public entity "stands in the shoes of the public entity."[35]

As part of its nondiscrimination provisions, DOT rules state that each covered entity shall train and supervise personnel to operate vehicles safely and treat individuals with disabilities in a "courteous and respectful way."[36] Those entities are also charged with ensuring that adequate assistance and information about the service is available to individuals, including those with vision or hearing impairments.

Regulatory sections for the purchase or lease of new vehicles by public entities operating fixed-route systems track the ADA, as already described: After August 25, 1990, any new vehicle that is purchased or leased by public entities has to be accessible. The regulations follow the ADA's requirements for granting a temporary waiver to purchase lift-equipped buses, but adopt language that better fits the relationship among lift manufacturers, bus manufacturers, and the public authority. One of the ADA's statutory conditions for granting a waiver—that a public entity has made good-faith efforts to locate a qualified manufacturer to supply the lifts—assumes a direct relationship between the transit provider and the lift manufacturer. "In fact, it is the bus manufacturer, rather than the transit provider directly, which would have the task of looking for a supplier of lifts to meet the transit provider's specifications."[37]

To ensure that the waiver provision does not create a loophole, the regulations make clear that relief will only apply to a particular procurement, and only on a temporary basis. Vehicles purchased under a waiver must be capable of accepting a lift, and that lift should be installed as soon as it becomes available.[38]

In the case of purchase or lease of used vehicles by public entities operating a fixed-route system, DOT notes the ADA's "demonstrated good-faith efforts" exception to the requirement. Good-faith efforts include specifying accessible vehicles in bid solicitations; engaging in a *national* search for accessible vehicles during which specific inquiries are made to other transit providers; advertising in trade publications; and contacting trade associations.[39]

With regard to remanufactured vehicles, DOT, interpreting the ADA's "to the maximum extent feasible" proviso, determined that "it shall be considered feasible to remanufacture a bus or other motor vehicle so as to be readily accessible to and usable by individuals with disabilities including individuals who use wheelchairs, unless an engineering analysis demonstrates that including accessibility features required [by the regulations] would have a significant adverse effect on the structural integrity of the vehicle."[40]

In its regulations, DOT also fleshed out the requirements for the purchase or lease of new vehicles by public entities operating a demand-responsive system for the general public. As the department interpreted the ADA, a demand-responsive system was defined as one that a user must request before it is provided. Thus, a vehicle used in "fixed route service (even if as part of a mixed fixed route/demand responsive system) meets the requirements of other sections for the acquisition of fixed route systems."[41] Moreover, the regulations state that a demand-responsive system, "when viewed in its entirety, shall be deemed to provide equivalent service if the service available to individuals with disabilities, including wheelchair users is provided in the most integrated setting feasible and is equivalent to the service provided other individuals with respect to the following service characteristics: (1) Response time; (2) Fares; (3) Geographic area of service; (4) Hours and days of service; (5) Restrictions based on trip purpose; (6) Availability of information and reservations capability; and (7) Any constraints on capacity or service availability."[42]

DOT regulations also specifically cover private entities, including those not "primarily engaged" in the business of transporting people. The "primarily engaged" test, the DOT preamble notes, "distinguishes between entities whose principal business is providing transportation (e.g., a charter bus company) and entities whose provision of transportation is tangential to their main business (e.g., airport shuttles operated by hotels, customer and employee shuttle services operated by private companies or shopping centers, shuttle operations of recreational facilities such as stadiums, ski resorts, zoos, and amusement parks.)"[43]

The section applies different requirements depending upon whether vehicles with a certain seating capacity are involved. A private entity that is not primarily engaged in transporting people, which operates a fixed-route system and makes a solicitation after August 25, 1990 to purchase or lease a vehicle with a seating capacity of 16 passengers (including the driver), must ensure that the vehicle is readily accessible to and usable by individuals with disabilities. Such an entity is not to purchase a vehicle with a seating capacity of 16 passengers or less (including the driver) unless the system, "when viewed in its entirety, ensures a level of service to individuals with disabilities, including individuals who use wheelchairs, equivalent to the level of service provided to individuals with disabilities."[44]

The criteria for "equivalent service" are the same as those for public entities operating a demand-responsive system, except that for fixed-route service, schedules/headways (that is, the interval between buses on a route) are substituted for response time. Private entities operating a demand-responsive system are held to the same criteria when seeking to purchase or lease a new vehicle with a seating capacity in excess of 16 passengers (including the driver). A private entity that is "primarily engaged" in transporting people and makes a solicitation to purchase or lease a new vehicle ("other than an automobile, a van with a seating capacity of less than eight persons, including the driver, or an over-the road bus")[45] must ensure that the vehicle is readily accessible to and usable by individuals with disabilities. Where that entity operates a demand responsive system, it can purchase a new vehicle that is not readily accessible to and usable by individuals with disabilities, if it offers equivalent service.

DOT's regulations with respect to rapid-and light-rail systems and intercity and commuter rail service[46] closely follow the ADA, as discussed earlier.

THE REGULATORY CHALLENGE

The critical challenge is to ensure that the ADA is implemented in ways that achieve its goals. The focus will continue to be on the regulatory process—mainly DOT—as the legislative framework of the ADA is translated into specific policies (Katzmann 1990).

In determining how best to devise regulations, it would be useful to draw upon rigorous studies about experiences under previous regulations. Although there are a number of surveys and valuable case studies, there are no comprehensive analyses of transportation policy for persons with disabilities, a situation that DOT is seeking to remedy through its recent commissioning of a study. The task of implementing the ADA is more difficult because of the absence of fundamental information about the population to be served, the needs of particular geographic regions, or the services in those regions. We can, for example, be only highly speculative as to cost. Of course, the nature of costs changes as technological developments make improvements available at a lower price.

Still, we can say a good deal about the challenge ahead and the problems to be confronted. We will discuss some of these problems and in the succeeding section will highlight various research findings that could be helpful in analyzing these issues.

DOT'S ACQUISITION OF VEHICLE RULES

An important unresolved issue is how transit providers should address nonstandard or nontraditional wheelchairs or mobility devices (for instance, three-wheel scooters, unusually heavy electric wheelchairs, and devices with cambered or small wheels). Transit authorities point to a variety of problems: many scooters are not readily securable by some types of securement systems, others lack arm rests to stabilize sideward motion of the occupant; some device/passenger loads are too great for some lifts; various securement systems do not work adequately with light-weight chairs, power wheelchairs that have four small wheels, and small stroller-type chairs used for children with disabilities.

Transit authorities deal with these problems in at least two ways: some have found or devised securement systems (typically four-point belt systems or combined wheel-clamp and belt systems) that can restrain a variety of mobility devices; others either refuse to carry scooters and nonstandard devices or else require the passenger to transfer out of his or her own device to a vehicle seat.

Many persons with disabilities charge that it is discriminatory for transit providers to require securement for mobility device users when they do not make such demands on other persons (for instance, standees, people with grocery carts and packages, infants in strollers).

The ADA mandates that the Architectural and Transportation Barriers Compliance Board (ATBCB) complete standards for lifts by April 1991. Those standards should resolve some of the issues by setting requirements for the dimensions and weight bearing capacity of lifts. Once the lift standard is promulgated, DOT will still have to determine, as a policy matter, whether transit providers should be required to transport other types of mobility devices, and under what criteria. Other standards may not be ready for some years. While DOT and ATBCB are addressing these issues, they should refer to the work of organizations like the International Standards Organization, Society of Automotive Engineers, and the National Highway Traffic Safety Administration, and study the efforts to develop standards in Australia and a number of European countries. Moreover, further tests of non-standard mobility devices and securement systems need to be done.

In order to address the issue of providing services in a nondiscriminatory manner, we need more data from communities about the training of personnel.

PARATRANSIT

The ADA defines who is eligible for paratransit services, but service criteria for paratransit are still undefined. Some of the criteria of the 1986 rules provide a point of departure: no restrictions or priorities can be based on trip purpose; hours and days of service availability will be the same as on the fixed-route bus system. Two unresolved issues have to do with criteria based on *fare* and *response time*.[47]

At least two approaches might be taken with regard to *fare* criterion. One, following the 1986 rule, would require that fares for supplemental paratransit be comparable to the fares charged a user of the fixed-route system for a trip of similar length at a similar time of day. This approach would not necessarily require equal or equivalent fares. Rather, fares could be different based on the differences between special-service and fixed-route systems. In this formulation, DOT would apply a rule of reason: for example, a $1.50 paratransit fare might be thought comparable to an 80-cent bus fare, but a $20 paratransit fare would not.[48] A second approach would maintain that the fare for paratransit service could not exceed the fare on the fixed-route system for a trip of comparable length at the same time of day.

A variety of approaches might be taken to *response time*. One approach, following the 1986 rules, would mandate a 24-hour response time. Another would be for the department to mandate a shorter response time — for instance, eight or four hours, or a time equivalent to bus headways on the relevant bus route at the requisite time of day. As the supplemental paratransit system develops, response times could shorten over a period of years. DOT has relied on studies indicating that the costs of providing paratransit may increase significantly as response times fall below 24 hours. DOT estimates, for instance, that requiring response time in 2 hours, rather than 24 hours, could increase annual paratransit costs on average by about 68 percent (over the base cost assumed for the "minimal" system) (U.S. Department of Transportation 1990a).

DEFINING "UNDUE FINANCIAL BURDENS"

A particularly difficult issue has to do with determining what constitutes an "undue financial burden" under the ADA. Some limited guidance comes from *American Public Transit Association v. Lewis*,[49] reviewing DOT's full accessibility regulations under section 504 of the Rehabilitation Act of 1973. In that case, the U.S. Court of Appeals indicated that DOT could not require extensive modifications of existing systems, which imposed heavy financial burdens. At the same time, case law suggests that DOT cannot assume that imposing some financial burden is impermissible.

The department has already indicated that an undue burden waiver would be available only with regard to the *cost* of providing *supplemental paratransit*.[50] The costs of providing other services for persons with disabilities would not be relevant. What constitutes an undue burden is the "magnitude of [the] effect [of its cost] on the recipient's overall operation."[51]

Still unanswered is a determination as to which approach to take in ascertaining an undue burden. One approach could focus on the extent to which a fare increase for the entire transit system would be necessary to cover the costs of supplemental paratransit. Another angle might be how the recipient's overall ridership would be affected by service cutbacks brought on by the paratransit costs. One could also ask the extent to which the recipient's deficit would be increased, on an overall per rider basis, by the cost of paratransit and, if so, by how much. In each case, questions would remain as to what degree of fare increase, deficit increase, or ridership loss should be involved before a burden becomes undue (for instance, 10, 20, or some other percentage). Perhaps one or more of the three approaches (for instance, fare increases and/or ridership loss) would be combined. It might be worth exploring whether it is practicable to construct a formula, using such factors as population, current paratransit service levels, residential patterns, and current level of accessible fixed-route service.

OVER-THE-ROAD BUS SERVICE

The mandate of the Office of Technology Assessment (OTA) with regard to over-the-road bus service is clear. OTA must determine "the access needs of individuals with disabilities to the over-the road buses and over-the-road bus service; and . . . the most cost-effective methods for providing access to over-the-road bus service to individuals with disabilities, particularly individuals who use wheelchairs, through all forms of boarding options."[52] Such a study should include analysis of the population to be served; the regions to be served; the anticipated demand by individuals with disabilities; the current state of accessibility; the effectiveness of various means of providing accessibility; possible design changes that could improve accessibility; and the cost of providing such service, taking into account technological and cost-saving developments. Under the ADA, OTA must also examine the "impact of accessibility requirements on the continuation of over-the-road bus service, with particular consideration of the impact of such requirements on such service to rural communities."[53]

The OTA study is being undertaken in response to the claims of private operators that their current economic situation is dire, that a decision to require full accessibility would be so costly as to force them out of business altogether. If the study results support those claims, then the challenge for decision makers will be a political one: to ensure that buses are fully accessible while providing assistance, through tax and other policies, so that the private operators do not cease to exist because of added costs.

WHAT RESEARCH TELLS US

Although comprehensive analyses of transportation policy for persons with disabilities are virtually nonexistent, a number of studies can provide some guidance to decision makers. What follows is a review of surveys, case studies, and technological research that addresses those problems.

SURVEYS

More than a dozen years have passed since the last federally sponsored comprehensive transportation survey of the *population* of persons with disabilities, and that was subject to criticism (Cannon and Rainbow 1978; U.S. Department of Transportation 1978). For its forthcoming round of regulatory proceedings, DOT may extrapolate from a 1984 Canadian Health and Disability Survey (Hickling Consultants 1984). To undertake that analysis, DOT has employed David Lewis, the principal author of the 1979 Congressional Budget Office report, which raised questions about the costs of the full accessibility approach (Congressional Budget Office 1979). The 1990 Bureau of the Census survey may also provide some limited information about the population of persons with disabilities.

Perhaps the best *survey of programs* underway in the United States was conducted by Project ACTION of the National Easter Seal Society (Project ACTION 1990 a; b). Project ACTION surveyed 112 selected *bus* transit systems, urban and rural, across the country. A significant finding of the study was that a "substantial" number of systems have already adopted a policy to purchase only accessible buses. At the same time, Project ACTION pointed to a variety of obstacles to effectively providing these services, such as inadequate outreach and marketing programs and the lack of trained personnel to communicate with and assist people with disabilities. Another, more limited, survey of compliance with specialized transit requirements found systems responsive to the law (Walther 1988).

With respect to *rail transit*, a study found that many operating systems have made significant improvements over the past ten years resulting in apparent compliance with the ADA (Reuter 1990). San Francisco's BART system and Washington, D.C.'s METRO system are among those that appear to be in full compliance.

CASE STUDIES

Although communities differ in the kinds and level of services they need to provide, case studies of a particular locality may be illuminating to other cities or townships.

Needs Study. The Toronto Transit Commission undertook a particularly comprehensive analysis of various options, recommending among other things that all new rail stations be made accessible, that 20 key stations be retrofitted, all future buses be equipped with a kneeling feature, and that demand-responsive (24-hour) paratransit be provided (Toronto Transit Commission 1989). One interesting finding was that persons with disabilities in Toronto make half as many trips as the general population, and, like the general population, prefer the convenience and reliability of door-to-door transportation (automobiles, taxis, vans) (Toronto Transit Commission 1989).

Problems of Coordination. A report of the Legislative Budget and Finance Committee of the Pennsylvania General Assembly documented the problems that can develop when the administration and delivery of services is fragmented (Pennsylvania General Assembly 1990).

Barriers to Transit. A study of the Houston Metro found that the lack of accessible sidewalks imposed barriers to fixed-route transit, regardless of how accessible the buses themselves were (Houston Metro 1989). In contrast, Seattle and Denver have systems whose accessible facilities and sidewalks make them far more attractive to consumers.

Bus-lift Maintenance. Although weather conditions can affect bus lifts, experience shows that preventive service maintenance permits them to operate effectively. A case in point is Denver's Regional Transportation District. Moreover, over time, costs have gone down as operators have learned to anticipate and prevent problems (Project ACTION 1990).

Training. Austin (Texas), Dayton (Ohio) and the state of Oregon have innovative training programs for transit personnel, which focus on attitude and awareness, and offer instruction on how to detect problems of bus lifts (Project ACTION 1990).

TECHNOLOGICAL RESEARCH

A conference at Oregon State University sponsored by the Transportation Research Institute (1990) reported on the important issue of how transit providers should deal with so-called nonstandard or nontraditional wheelchairs or mobility devices. The report documented many devices apart from the standard manual or electric wheelchairs that are unfamiliar to transit operators. Commentators also described the inadequacies of present securement systems.

British Columbia Transit videotaped eight crash test trials in which a relatively small paratransit van was driven into a barrier at 20 miles per hour carrying a scooter ridden by an anthromorphic dummy (British Columbia Transit 1990). Although securement systems generally prevented the scooters from leaving the securement area, the upward and rearward motion of the dummies could have caused death or serious injury to human occupants.

CONCLUSION

In this paper, I have sought to present the statutory requirements of the ADA and the regulatory problems to be confronted. Those challenges are indeed great. However, if one considers the progress (however limited) made over the last 20 years, in spite of an often unclear mandate, then there is perhaps no telling how much can be accomplished with an explicit charge to provide fully accessible transportation for persons with disabilities.

NOTES

1. P.L. 101–136 (1990), 104 Stat. 327 (1990).
2. 87 Stat. 355 (1973).
3. 84 Stat. 962 (1970).
4. 41 Fed. Reg. 18234 (1976).
5. 44 Fed. Reg. 31442 (1979).
6. 46 Fed. Reg. 37489 (1981).
7. 96 Stat. 2154 (1983).
8. 51 Fed. Reg. 18994–19038 (1986).
9. *ADAPT v. Skinner*—F.2d—(3d Cir. 1989).
10. 55 Fed. Reg. 11120 (1990).
11. On the legislative history of the Americans with Disabilities Act with regard to transportation, especially *Americans With Disabilities Act*, Hearings before the Subcommittee on Surface Transportation of the House Committee on Public Works and Transportation, 101 Cong. 1st sess. (1990); *Americans with Disabilities Act*, H. Rep. 101–485, pt. 1, 101 Cong. 2d sess. (1990); *Americans with Disabilities Act*, H. Rep. 101–485, pt. 2, 101 Cong. 2d sess. (1990); *Americans with Disabilities Act*, S. Rep. 101–116, 101 Cong. 1st sess. (1989); and *Americans with Disabilities Act of 1990*, Conference Report to Accompany S. Rep. 993, Joint Explanatory Statement of the Committee of   Conference, title II and title III, 101 Cong. 2d sess. (1990).
12. 104 Stat. 337.
13. Id.
14. 104 Stat. 339.
15. 104 Stat. 340.
16. 104 Stat. 340–41.
17. Id.
18. 104 Stat. 342–43.
19. 104 Stat. 343.
20. 100 Stat. 344.
21. Id.
22. 104 Stat. 345.

23. 104 Stat. 347.
24. 104 Stat. 348.
25. 104 Stat. 349.
26. Id.
27. 104 Stat. 351.
28. 104 Stat. 355.
29. 104 Stat. 355.
30. 104 Stat. 356–57.
31. 104 Stat. 360–63.
32. 55 Fed. Reg. 40762 (1990).
33. 55 Fed. Reg. 40764 (1990).
34. 55 Fed. Reg. 40763 (1990).
35. 55 Fed. Reg. 40766 (1990).
36. Id.
37. Id. at 40770.
38. Id. at 40771.
39. Id. at 40770.
40. Id. at 40778.
41. Id. at 40773.
42. Id. at 40778–79.
43. Id. at 40774.
44. Id. at 40779.
45. Id.
46. Id. at 40780–81.
47. Fed. Reg. 11121–22 (1990).
48. Id. at 11121.
49. 556 F. 2d 1271 (D.C. Cir. 1981).
50. Id.
51. Id.
52. 52. 104 Stat. 360 (1990).
53. Id. at 361.

REFERENCES

Berkowitz, E. 1987. *Disabled Policy: American Programs for the Handicapped.* New York: Cambridge University Press.

British Columbia Transit. 1989. *Report on Crash Testing of Securement Systems.* Vancouver: BC Transit.

Cannon, D., and F. Rainbow. 1980. *Full Mobility: Counting the Costs of the Alternatives.* Washington: American Coalition of Citizens with Disabilities.

Congressional Budget Office. 1979. *Urban Transportation for Handicapped Persons: Alternative Federal Approaches.* Washington.

Harris, Louis, and Associates 1986. *ICD Survey of Disabled Americans.* New York.

Hickling Consultants. 1984. *Canadian Health and Disability Survey.* Ottawa: James F. Hickling Management Consultants.

Houston METRO 1989. Analysis of Fixed Route Accessibility and Paratransit Services. Houston. (Unpublished.)

Katzmann, R. 1986. *Institutional Disability: The Saga of Transportation Policy for the Disabled*. Washington: Brookings.

――――. 1990. New Disability Protections Have Method in Murkiness. *Los Angeles Times* (August 7): B7.

Pennsylvania General Assembly, Legislative Budget and Finance Committee. 1990. *Report on a Study of the Need for and Availability of Transportation Services for Persons With Disabilities*. Harrisburg. (Unpublished.)

Lewis, David 1984. *Analysis of the Department of Transportation's Regulations Regarding Transportation of Disabled and Elderly Persons*. Ottawa: James F. Hickling Management Consultants.

National Center for Health Statistics 1984. *Survey of Population of Persons with Disabilities*. Princeton: Mathematica Policy Research.

Percy, S. 1989. *Disability, Civil Rights and Public Policy: The Politics of Implementation*. Montgomery: University of Alabama Press.

Project ACTION 1990a. *Combined Research Results*. Washington: National Easter Seal Society.

――――. 1990b. *Reconnaissance Survey of Selected Transit Agencies*. Washington: National Easter Seal Society.

Reuter, R. 1990. Rail Transportation: Costs of Compliance with the ADA. Baltimore: Access Systems.

Skotch, R. 1989. Politics and Policy in the History of the Disability Rights Movement. *Milbank Quarterly* 67 (part 2): 380–400.

Toronto Transit Commission 1989. *Transit Services for Disabled and Elderly Persons: Choices for the Future*. Toronto:

Transportation Research Institute. *Conference on Securement Devices*. Oregon State University. (Unpublished.)

U.S. Congress. 1990. *Americans with Disabilities Act*. Hearings before the Subcommittee on Surface Transportation of the House Committee on Public Works and Transportation, 101 Cong., 1st sess. Washington.

U.S. Department of Transportation. 1978. *National Survey of Transportation of Handicapped Persons* (Grey Advertising Study). Washington.

――――. 1990a. *Preliminary Regulatory Impact Analysis: The Department of Transportation's Regulation Implementing Section 504 of the Rehabilitation Act of 1973 in the Urban Mass Transit Program*. Washington.

――――. 1990b. *Preliminary Regulatory Cost Analysis: The Department of Transportation's Regulation Implementing ADA Vehicle Accessibility Requirements*. Washington.

Walther, E. 1983. *Case Study Report: Seattle METRO Elderly and Handicapped Service*. Greensboro, N.C.: Transportation Institute, N.C. A&T State University.

――――. 1988. *Section 504: Realized Impact and Projected Impacts*. Greensboro, N.C.: Transportation Institute, N.C. A&T State University.

Zola, I.K. 1989. Toward the Necessary Universalizing of Disability Policy. *Milbank Quarterly* 67 (part 2): 401–28.

ACKNOWLEDGMENTS

I would like to acknowledge Lani Florian for her assistance with this article and
Robert Ashby, Donald Trilling, and Nancy Ebersol of the Department of
Transportation and Dennis Cannon of the Architectural and Transportation
Barriers Compliance Board for discussions about the future of the Americans
with Disabilities Act in terms of transportation policy. In addition, David
Capozzi of Project Action afforded generous access to his files.

Implementing the Telecommunications Provisions

Karen Peltz Strauss

EDITOR'S NOTE

One of the cornerstones of participation in the mainstream of American society is communication. The combination of a hearing or speech impairment and a society so notably dependent upon the telephone system for day-to-day living has generated tremendous frustration on the part of individuals with speech and hearing impairments. A significant potential market has thus been untapped by telephone companies and telephone-linked businesses. With the enactment of the Americans with Disabilities Act (ADA), political will has moved one step closer to supporting full utilization of available technology.

Karen Peltz Strauss holds that the establishment of nationwide relay service mandated by title IV will ensure that individuals with hearing and speech impairments have the opportunity to exercise the civil rights specified by the other sections of the ADA. Examining the state of the art in one of the more technical of the ADA mandates, Strauss concludes that approximately 40 states are well on their way to providing statewide relay services. Utilizing their experience will make compliance with the ADA a relatively easy job.

With over a decade of advocacy for the rights of persons with disabilities, Strauss is currently supervising attorney for the National Center for Law and the Deaf at Gallaudet University in Washington, D.C. Strauss was actively involved in the congressional deliberations of title IV of the ADA and testified before Congress a number of times. She has pub-

lished numerous articles on the legal rights of persons who are deaf and hearing impaired.

More than 55 years ago, Congress set forth what has since become known as the "universal service" mandate, which stipulated that communication by wire or radio be made available to all Americans so far as is possible.[1] This congressional objective, originally pronounced in the Communications Act of 1934, may finally become a reality for deaf, hard-of-hearing, and speech-impaired individuals as a result of the enactment of the Americans with Disabilities Act (ADA). Title IV of the ADA requires all common carriers that provide intra- or interstate telephone service to offer dual party relay services for all local and long-distance telephone calls by July 26, 1993.[2] Relay services enable users of telecommunication devices for the deaf (TDDs) and other nonvoice terminal devices to communicate, through a third party, with users of conventional telephones. When fully implemented, title IV of the ADA should enable individuals who are deaf, hard-of-hearing, and speech impaired to overcome the isolation and dependence they have experienced without use of the telephone system. The establishment of nationwide relay services mandated by title IV will help to ensure that individuals with hearing and speech impairments have the opportunity to exercise the civil rights promised by the other sections of the ADA.

DEFINITIONS OF TDDs AND RELAY SERVICES

A TDD is a device with a keyboard, resembling a small typewriter, that is used to send and receive written messages over the telephone lines. TDDs typically have light-emitting diodes (LEDs) to display visually the messages transmitted and received, and sometimes have printers to record those messages on special paper. A TDD uses an acoustic coupler, into which one places the handset of a conventional telephone, or a computer modem connected to the telephone by direct coupling, to convert outgoing TDD impulses into acoustic tones and incoming acoustic tones into TDD impulses.[3] TDDs may also have a variety of optional features, including memory capability, rechargeable battery packs, and flashing light signalers to alert individuals to incoming calls.

TDDs enable deaf, hard-of-hearing, and speech-impaired individuals to use the telephone network to communicate with friends, employers, and business establishments that also have TDDs. Without relay services, however, TDD users generally cannot use the public-switched telephone network to access individuals who have conventional voice telephones. As a result, simple tasks, such as making a dinner reservation, arranging a job interview, or calling a plumber can mean long and arduous trips throughout town, or continued dependence on a friend or neighbor.

A dual party relay service currently enables persons who use TDDs or other nonvoice terminal devices to carry on near simultaneous conversations with persons who use conventional voice telephones. It accomplishes this task in the following manner: A TDD user calls the relay service, which is answered by a relay operator. The operator places the call, via voice, to the called party and then converts all TDD messages from the caller into voice and all voice messages from the called party into typed text for the TDD user. The same process can be performed in reverse, when the call is initiated by a hearing person.

WHERE WE ARE AT PRESENT

Although the ADA gives common carriers three years to establish nationwide relay operations, it is unlikely that common carriers in more than a handful of states will need or use all of that time to begin relay operations. Indeed, to a large extent, the mere introduction and movement of the ADA through Congress has already provided enough of an incentive for telephone companies and the states in which they are housed to develop a solid infrastructure of relay services throughout the United States. The facts are self-evident: only 17 states had formal statewide relay systems operating (with 6 additional states expecting operations to begin within the following year) as of May 1989, when the ADA was introduced in the 101st Congress.[4] By July 1990, when the ADA was signed into law, as many as 40 states either had statewide systems in place or concrete plans to have those systems begin operations within the next year and a-half (National Center for Law and the Deaf [NCLD] 1990). Many of these systems impose restrictions or suffer from blockage rates that will be unacceptable under the minimum standards established by title IV. The ADA will now require increased funding to achieve "functionally equivalent" telephone service.

RELAY SERVICE STANDARDS REQUIRED BY TITLE IV

Title IV of the ADA is intended to further the goal of universal telephone service for deaf, hard-of-hearing, and speech-impaired individuals.[5] It requires common carriers to provide interstate and intrastate telephone relay services that are functionally equivalent to telephone services available to hearing persons. The ADA charges the Federal Communications Commission (FCC) with establishing minimum standards—to be met by all relay-service providers—that will define functional equivalence between dual party relay services and voice telephone services.[6] Some of these standards are delineated in the statute itself and others are articulated in committee reports.

STATUTORY REQUIREMENTS

Continuous Service. All relay services must operate 24 hours per day, 7 days a week.[7] Clearly, an essential aspect of functional equivalence is for deaf, hard-of-hearing, and speech-impaired individuals to have the telephone system available to them at all times.

No Content Restrictions. The ADA prohibits "relay operators from failing to fulfill the obligations of common carriers by refusing calls or limiting the length of [those] calls."[8] Just as a hearing person can use the telephone to communicate any message without limitation, so too does Congress intend relay users to have this right.

Many statewide relay programs have recognized the importance of relaying all calls regardless of content, and are therefore already in compliance with this relay specification. In Minnesota, for example, the relay contract requires that all calls, including those that are obscene or illegal, be relayed.[9] Similarly, the California, Delaware, New York, Pennsylvania, and Washington relay services forbid operators from passing judgment on the nature of any conversation or making decisions about whether such conversations should be relayed.[10]

Other states will likely need to revise their policies to come into compliance with this title IV requirement. In Arizona and Virginia, for example, operators are permitted to terminate calls and notify police authorities about calls that pertain to certain illegal activities.[11] Such a policy appears to be in direct conflict with the ADA requirement. In regulations, the FCC should clarify that such content restrictions are prohibited by the ADA.

Confidentiality. Somewhat related to the content issue is the question of the confidentiality of relayed calls. The ADA "prohibit[s] relay operators from disclosing the content of any relayed conversation and from keeping records of the content of any such conversation beyond the duration of the call."[12] Most, if not all, of the states that have established relay programs already adhere to a policy of assuring strict confidentiality of relayed communications. Some states, such as Pennsylvania, Delaware, and Minnesota, require relay operators to take a pledge of confidentiality before they can assume their operator duties. Moreover, Connecticut's relay law considers all relayed communications to be "privileged" and specifically prohibits relay operators from disclosing such communications "in any civil or criminal case or proceeding or in any legislative or administrative proceeding, unless the person making the confidential communication waives such privilege."[13]

Again, however, the practices of some state relay programs may not comply with the ADA's mandate of confidentiality. For example, Colorado legislation requires operators to preserve the confidentiality of all calls, except in such instances as would constitute a furtherance of a violation of law.[14] Similarly, in Texas, relay law is silent on this issue, but the state has a separate statute requiring any individual with knowledge of child-abuse practices to report such practices to the state. This has caused that state's provider—Sprint Services—to require its operators to report conversations containing information about child abuse.

The ADA is unequivocal in its requirement that calls be kept confidential. To the extent that it has such authority, the FCC should therefore prescribe rules to ensure the privileged status of all communications made through a relay service.[15] In the future, relay services may be automated through voice synthesis, speech-to-text, and other technologies. Until such time that these technologies replace relay operators, the operators should act as a transparent conduit between the relay parties.

Unaltered Messages. The ADA directs the FCC to "prohibit relay operators from intentionally altering a relayed conversation."[16] Initially, this means that relay operators may not interject any opinion or comment into a relayed conversation (Conlon-Mentkowski 1988). Most consumers of relay services wish to have their messages relayed verbatim. The only exception to this rule applies to deaf individuals who use American Sign Language (ASL)—a language that differs in grammar and syntax from English. These individuals may want their messages interpreted into English for hearing people and may want English messages from those persons interpreted into ASL. Because, at times, either party may be unaware that the operator is able to perform the interpreting service, some experts in the field consider it a good practice to alert each party to the availability of this particular service.[17].

Charges Billed to Relay Users. Under the ADA, users of relay services will "pay rates no greater than the rates paid for functionally equivalent voice communication services with respect to such factors as the duration of the call, the time of day, and the distance from point of origination to point of termination."[18] In other words, the toll charges billed to relay users for long-distance calls must be equal to the charges that the users would have incurred had they made those calls directly, without any charges for routing by the relay system. Here, it is important to note that completion of a TDD call takes much longer than does a voice call. Relay services add even more time to the total length of the call. For this reason, some states and long-distance telephone companies offer TDD discounts on the toll charges of relayed telephone calls.[19] Although a toll discount is not required by the ADA, the FCC does have the option of mandating a reduced toll rate nationwide for relayed telephone calls.[20]

DIRECTIVES IN CONGRESSIONAL REPORTS

Equal Blockage Rates.[21] The repeated delays and busy signals that TDD users confront when attempting to access relay services remain their biggest grievance with these services. Congress recognized that a functionally equivalent relay service will be one in which the blockage rates are "no greater than standard industry blockage rates for voice telephone services," and Senate report language directs the FCC to issue a rule requiring that this standard be met by relay providers.[22] The California relay comes closest to this standard, allowing for a blockage rate of only .003 to .18 percent. New York and Delaware relays also approximate this objective by allowing for a 1 percent blockage rate, the same rate of blockage that voice users confront when trying to access operator assistance through the regular telephone dialing network (Taylor 1988).[23] With improvements in relay service, it is more than likely that equal blockage rates will become the standard of high-quality relay service in the future. By clarifying that equal blockage rates are a requirement of the functional equivalency mandate, FCC regulations would bring relay services one step closer to a telephone system that provides access to deaf, hard-of-hearing, and speech-impaired persons equivalent to that enjoyed by the general population.

Qualified Operators. The Senate report and subsequent congressional statements on title IV direct the FCC to issue specific regulations requiring relay operators to "be sufficiently trained in the specialized communications needs of individuals with hearing and speech impairments, [and in] typing, grammar and spelling."[24] Indeed, given the unique nature of a relay operator's duties, some have urged the creation of a new job classification for these operators, one that would require semiprofessional skills and a salary commensurate with those skills (White 1990).

Most states with relay systems have, in fact, developed their own training programs. A review of the literature on this issue suggests that the following components can be included in an operator training program (Shapiro 1988):

- information about and sensitivity to the cultural and linguistic differences between the deaf, hard-of-hearing, and speech-impaired communities and the hearing community
- instruction on proper ethics and etiquette, covering issues of confidentiality and the use of varying inflections and tones of voice to convey TDD messages
- information on the mechanics of handling calls, including instruction on relay equipment and billing methods
- instruction on coping with difficult situations, including emotionally charged telephone calls[25]

A review of the various state training programs that already exist would enable the FCC to establish minimum guidelines for a comprehensive training program to meet the telecommunications needs of individuals with hearing and speech impairments nationwide.

Real-Time Transmission. The Senate Committee report directs relay providers to transmit relayed conversations simultaneously or in "real time."[26]

Choice of Long-Distance Carrier. The Senate Committee report directs relay providers to give their customers the opportunity to choose a long-distance carrier whenever possible.[27] To date, only a few states offer this option to relay users.[28]

THE EXPERIENCES OF STATE RELAY PROGRAMS

The experiences of the states that have operated relay systems should provide invaluable information to other states and to common carriers that will establish these systems. This section first examines the experiences of the existing state programs, placing special emphasis on relay costs, volume, and service restrictions, and then goes on to discuss some of the changes that will be needed to bring these systems into compliance with the ADA.

COSTS OF PROVIDING RELAY SERVICES

The costs of providing relay service appear high at a glance: anywhere from $4.00 to $9.00 per minute, with the average call lasting seven minutes. The experiences of states that have begun relay operations, however, have shown these costs to be quite small when distributed among all telephone subscribers.[29] Generally these charges range from 5 cents to 20 cents per month per telephone subscriber (NCLD 1990). In most states, a specified amount of money used to pay for relay services is added to the consumer's monthly telephone bill, sometimes printed as a separate item on the bill itself, and other times incorporated with normal operating expenses into the general telephone rates. Oftentimes, the specified sum of money pays not only for relay services, but for state TDD distribution programs as well.

The cost of starting up relay operations varies from state to state. Figures regarding these start-up costs were generally unavailable, in large part because of their proprietary nature. However, one estimate of $3 million as the potential start-up cost of interstate relay services was provided by the FCC in a prior proceeding on that subject.[30]

DEMAND FOR SERVICES

The demand for relay services in states that have initiated programs has been truly astonishing. The experience in California perhaps best exemplifies the unexpected growth that has taken place (Shapiro 1988). The California relay system was originally designed with the expectation that the service would receive 50,000 calls per month. However, in the first month alone, 87,511 calls were received. By December 1987, the end of the first year, the number of calls had increased by 205 percent, and by July 1988, some 19 months after the system began operating, the California program was handling nearly 250,000 calls per month.

Other states, too, have experienced dramatic growth in relay volume over a very short period. In March 1987, the Arizona Relay Service started its relay operations with 10,000 calls per month. Currently, the service relays 37,500 per month (NCLD 1990).[31] Similarly, in Washington state, the number of calls received by the relay service increased by 2,000 in just a two-week period after the system began operations. Finally, approximately 42,000 calls were relayed by the New York relay system in January 1989, its first month of operation. By May 1990, 112,000 calls, representing a 167 percent increase, were relayed in New York (NCLD 1989; 1990). It is worth noting that call volumes in some of the state programs may have been even greater had funding restrictions not been placed on them.

There are various reasons for the tremendous growth in relay volume. Primarily, it is apparent that relay services are improving. In the past, limited volunteer relay services, operating on threadbare budgets, provided little incentive for TDD users to turn to them. However, the gradual reduction in blockage rates and improvements in relay-service quality in many of the states have prompted more individuals to utilize this mode of communication. As one telecommunications expert noted, the increased demand is attributed to "customer acceptance and satisfaction with the new service, coupled with the sudden freedom to place a call when needed, not only when . . . able to penetrate the busy signals or find an interpreter" (Heil 1988).

Second, the hearing population has come to use relay services more than they did when the services first became available. In Minnesota, for example, when the system first began operations in March 1989, approximately 98 percent of all calls were initiated by TDD users. By April 1990, only 82 percent of the calls in that state were TDD initiated, while 18 percent were initiated by voice telephone users.[32] Similarly, in California, as many as 20 to 25 percent of the calls are initiated by hearing callers (Heil 1988; Shapiro 1988).

STATE RESTRICTIONS

Although numerous states have begun efforts to provide relay services, many of the existing state programs impose restrictions on the number, length, and types of calls that they will relay. These restrictions have resulted in dependence, hardship, and frustration for deaf, hard-of-hearing, and speech-impaired individuals. Insufficient funding is most often the reason for these restrictions. For example, until May of 1990, limited funding required the relay program in Kansas to accept calls only Monday through Friday, from 8 A.M. to 5 P.M., and no calls at all on state holidays (NCLD 1989). Kansas has since established a full service relay, and incorporates the costs of operating relay services with other normal operating expenses of the state's telephone companies (NCLD 1990).[33]

State appropriations of only $215,000 per year in Arkansas still require that state to limit its users to a period of 15 minutes per call and to disallow personal ("chatty") telephone calls. Massachusetts — another state that relies on state appropriations to fund its relay program — almost had to shut down its operations as a result of its inability to meet relay demand. Although that state's legislature had appropriated $680,000 for the year beginning July 1989, this amount enabled its relay program to handle only 60 to 65 percent of all incoming calls, and forced the program to place a 10-minute limit on personal calls and a 20-minute limit on business calls. Moreover, nonemergency calls in Massachusetts were permitted only between 7 A.M. and 11 P.M. Recent legislation in Massachusetts promises to bring a full service relay system to that state within the near future. Finally, New Hampshire, yet another state relying on state monies to support its relay system, limits the number of calls that may be relayed by any one person to five per day with a limit of 15 minutes per call (NCLD 1990).

Even when state programs do not impose specific restrictions, their residents who use relay services continue to suffer from far more delays and blockage rates than do voice telephone users. For example, during the first few months of the Washington state program in the latter part of 1989, 74 percent of all call requests were turned away.[34] As recently as April 1990, the coordinator of the Washington relay program estimated that the blockage rate in that state remained as high as 30 percent.[35]

COMPLIANCE WITH THE ADA

Although most states have some level of relay system in place, nearly all will need to make some changes in order to comply with ADA. In California, for example, 120 operator stations allow that many incoming calls to be handled at any one time, resulting in very few delays when trying to access California relay services. Consumers are generally satisfied with the relay programs in New York and Alabama as well. However, neither California nor New York nor Alabama's relay programs accept interstate calls, a major restriction that precludes all of these programs from meeting the ADA's minimum requirements for relay services.

A handful of states that have not yet begun relay operations do promise to fulfill the ADA's objective of providing functionally equivalent services. Delaware, Georgia, Montana, Nebraska, and South Carolina all expect to begin 24-hour, 7-day-a-week relay operations in early 1991. None of these states has reported that their programs would impose any major restrictions on relay services (NCLD 1990). The relay services in Virginia and Texas, which also approach compliance with the ADA's specifications, may fall short of the Act's requirement of confidentiality. Finally, Kansas, which began operations in May 1990, will probably also comply with most of the ADA's minimum standards.[36]

The requirements of ADA's title IV will preempt the policies and practices of state programs to the extent that they fall short of meeting the minimum standards set forth in the ADA itself and the FCC's implementing regulations.

PRACTICAL CONSIDERATIONS FOR A RELAY SERVICE: TITLE IV REQUIREMENTS AND THE LESSONS OF EXPERIENCE

ESTABLISHMENT

Structure. Common carriers charged with providing relay services under the ADA are offered considerable flexibility in providing those services. A carrier may provide relay services "individually, through designees, through a competitively selected vendor, or in concert with other carriers."[37] For example, in New York, the 41 local telephone companies charged by the Public Service Commission with providing relay services to their customers joined together in a single contract with AT&T to have that company provide statewide relay services. In contrast, a single local exchange carrier in Michigan—Michigan Bell— recently agreed to provide relay services for that entire state. Other states, such as Utah and Oregon, have chosen nonprofit corporations for their service providers. Still others, like Kansas, have chosen one of the seven regional Bell companies to provide relay service.[38] Regardless of how common carriers choose to delegate the day-to-day operations of their relay obligations, they remain ultimately responsible under the ADA for ensuring that those services are provided in accordance with the minimum standards set forth by the FCC.[39]

The ADA's requirement for relay services nationwide is already resulting in the establishment of regional relay centers. Several states have teamed efforts in a single relay system to reduce the overall costs of their facilities and administration. For example, Delaware and Pennsylvania will operate a single relay system, as will Maine and New York, Texas and Colorado, and Alabama and Tennessee. Regional centers make good sense for these and other states.

Many feel that integration of the newly required interstate relay services into the local relay network is preferable to the creation of one nationwide relay system. Long-distance calls are estimated to constitute only 5 to 10 percent of total call volume. For this reason, integrating these calls into existing local systems is likely to result in a cost savings in operator and equipment expenses. One expert has noted that there are two other advantages to having multiple relay centers. First, consumers can maintain better control and supervision over a local system. Second, the costs of relaying calls may be cheaper with less costly access lines compared with more expensive toll lines (Heil 1988).

Demographic Data. Experts who have been active in the establishment of relay systems have suggested that effective relay planning by a state or telephone company should begin with demographic data on the number and location of individuals with hearing and speech impairments and TDD users in a given state. The Senate report accompanying ADA notes that there are over 24 million deaf, hard-of-hearing, individuals and 2.8 million speech-impaired individuals in the United States.[40] Unfortunately, according to Gallaudet's Center for Assessment and Demographic Studies, estimates of the deaf, hard-of-hearing, population on state and local levels are not currently available (Hotchkiss 1989).

Moreover, accurate statistics on the numbers of individuals who are likely to use relay systems nationwide in the future is very difficult to ascertain. No formal study has yet been performed to ascertain the number of TDD owners throughout the country. However, only a small fraction of deaf and hard-of-hearing individuals has been estimated to own TDDs at present. In part, this may be due to the relatively high cost of a TDD—approximately $150—for individuals with low incomes. It may also be that, in the past, TDD users were severely limited in the calls they could make with their equipment. Without relay systems in place, these individuals could only complete calls to other TDD users. The existence of relay centers should provide an incentive for other individuals to purchase TDDs in the future.

In addition, approximately 40 percent of individuals over the age of 75 have a hearing loss, compared with only 4 percent of individuals under the age of 44 (U.S. Congress 1986). Yet because these individuals often do not consider themselves to be part of the deaf population, they do not purchase equipment, like TDDs, to help with their hearing impairment, in spite of its probable usefulness to them. General availability of relay services may result in an increased demand from these individuals for services.

In any event, the use of estimates of the number of TDD owners to measure potential relay volume can be unreliable for a variety of reasons. First, several deaf, hard-of-hearing, and speech-impaired people, who each make numerous relay calls, may live in a single household, yet only own one TDD. Second, many non-hearing-impaired individuals and organizations own TDDs; yet these individuals may not use relay services. Finally, relay services are for the use of both hearing and deaf, hard-of-hearing, individuals. Therefore, a proper calculation of potential relay users must necessarily take into account members of the hearing population as well.

Information from states that have operated programs can, however, provide useful information for relay planners. General population size of a state already operating a program can offer some guidance to a state with a comparable population that plans to begin relay operations. In addition, some of the states that have operated programs have gathered a variety of data about their operations—including the number of calls relayed, average call holding times, percentage of busy signals, and information about calls queued, connected, or abandoned—broken down by minute, hour, or day (Shapiro 1988). It is important to note, however, that projections based on the volumes of calls handled by existing relay centers may be unreliable if the funding for those centers is limited in any way. As one expert explained, "Planners should understand that until the deaf users' calling rates match those of other residential telephone customers there is every reason to expect the volumes to expand rapidly" (Heil 1988).[41]

Funding. The ADA permits common carriers to recover the costs of providing relay service in any manner they wish, so long as users of the service pay rates no greater than the rates paid for the functionally equivalent service offered to the general population.[42] There are at least three ways in which the costs of providing relay services have been recovered: state appropriations, surcharges, and integration into normal operating expenses (Ransom 1988). Each of these is considered below.

State Appropriations. Some states, such as Arkansas, Maryland, Massachusetts, New Hampshire, Virginia, and Wisconsin, have funded all or part of their programs with specific or general state appropriations (NCLD 1989; 1990). Typically, the funding in these states has been insufficient to meet the relay needs of their residents, resulting in restrictions on the service provided to those individuals. Moreover, appropriations in these states remain at the discretion of state legislatures. Relay users are placed in the unsettling position of not knowing if the relay services will continue from year to year, and if they do, with what restrictions.

Surcharge. Probably a majority of the states that currently have relay programs fund their programs with a monthly surcharge of anywhere from 3 to 20 cents on each subscriber access line (NCLD 1990). There are two kinds of relay surcharges. The first of these places a "ceiling" or a "cap" on the amount of surcharge that can be collected. Funding through a capped surcharge does not provide much more financial security than do state appropriations. States employing this mechanism have typically encountered difficulties in handling the increased relay expenses that accompany unexpected growth in call volume. The consequence has been severe funding crises, resulting in TDD relay users requesting increases in the surcharge cap from state legislatures. Continual requests of this nature may trigger complaints from general taxpayers, who might seek to cut back services in order to lower costs (Ransom 1988).

California's experiences illustrate best the drawbacks of a capped surcharge (Ransom 1988). At its inception in January 1987, the California relay program began with a 3-cent surcharge. As early as October 1987, it became clear that the DEAF Trust Fund administering the surcharge could not meet the cost of the program. To remedy the situation, the California Public Utility Commission authorized an emergency increase in the cap to 10 cents, to become effective on January 1, 1988, and expanded the surcharge to include private-line and WATS/800 telephone services. In July 1988, the Commission again had to raise the surcharge in order to meet relay expenses. This time, it ordered that .5 percent of all intrastate telephone charges be collected from October 1, 1988 to June 30, 1990 to support the relay. Currently,

.3 percent of each subscriber's total bill on tariffed intrastate services is collected for the California relay fund. During all these proceedings, relay users faced the continual threat that the California relay system would be shut down for lack of sufficient funding, leaving them without telephone access.[43]

The second type of surcharge is one that is flexible and can be adjusted, depending on the actual costs of the relay operations. Illinois is one state that started with a 3-cent cap and changed to this flexible surcharge (NCLD 1989; 1990). Mississippi's relay statute offers a good example of language providing for a flexible surcharge. There, the monthly maintenance surcharge on all residential and business local-exchange access facilities "shall be determined by the commission based upon the amount of funding necessary to accomplish the purposes of [the Mississippi] act and provide dual party telephone relay services on a continuous basis."[44]

Some experts have questioned whether any surcharge at all is cost-effective or equitable (Ransom 1988). At least one public-service commission has concluded that treatment of relay expenses as a distinct and separate item violates principles of traditional rate making.[45] States that use a surcharge typically allow recovery of relay costs on a dollar-by-dollar basis. But usual rate-making procedures offer no guarantee that the utility will make a full recovery of a particular expense. In this fashion, traditional rate-making proceedings provide an incentive for companies to undertake cost-containment measures, an incentive that is absent when the surcharge mechanism is adopted. In addition some states, such as Illinois, have created separate corporations to collect and administer the surcharge funds, thus adding administrative costs and a layer of bureaucracy to the system.

A final issue related to the surcharge funding mechanism is that often the surcharge appears on residential telephone bills as a distinct item. This highlights to the hearing public that they are paying for a "special" service.[46] For example, in California, a portion of each subscriber's bill is allocated for "Communication Devices Funds for the Deaf and Disabled," while in Montana, subscribers see "MT Telecommunications for the Handicapped" on their telephone bills. Singling out relay services in this fashion also causes these services to be an easy target for cutbacks. Both the House and Senate noted their disapproval of such labeling in the committee reports.[47]

Normal Operating Expenses. Many states have adopted the practice of treating the costs of providing relay services as part of the normal operating expenses of providing general telephone service. The integration of the costs in this manner offers several advantages. First, it provides a flexible funding source for the relay operations, which can fluctuate with the costs of those operations. Second, this approach allows costs to be distributed across all rate-payers and allows recovery of these costs through normal rate-making proceedings. In this fashion, funding for relay services is treated like funding for other utilities by the state. Similar to water, gas, and electric, the costs of relay services are monitored by local commissions, and deaf, hard-of-hearing, and speech-impaired individuals can remain confident that these services will continue from day to day and year to year, regardless of demand (Taylor 1988). Calculating relay costs as an integrated part of overall operating expenses is likely to result in relay services being as available as telephone services are to the general population, thus meeting the test of functional equivalence.

OUTREACH AND EDUCATION

Outreach and education about relay services should inform potential consumers of the availability of relay services and how they can be accessed. Special efforts should be made to educate groups who can benefit from such services but who might otherwise not be acquainted with them, for example, elderly persons experiencing hearing losses and persons who are speech impaired, and to inform hearing persons about the existence of these relay services.

Outreach and education can be provided in a variety of ways. For example, the public commission in New York has ordered that information be placed in all local telephone directories and distributed in bill inserts to all telephone subscribers at least one time each year.[48] In Arizona, efforts are made to publicize the relay over local television shows, to appear before civic organizations, and to hold open houses and workshops on the availability and use of the relay.[49] Minnesota, borrowing an idea from Bell Canada, has printed up business cards with its relay name and logo, phone numbers, a slot for the relay user's name, and brief instructions on use of the service for relay users to distribute to business associates and other interested persons.[50] Finally, Oregon and Kansas each put together a brief videotape to be presented to various communities.[51]

In addition to general information about the relay service, specific information about relay service numbers should be readily available in any given state to enable travelers who use relay services outside of their states to access these numbers easily. The importance of facilitating such access was noted in congressional consideration of title IV when one Congressman stated that an individual should be able to obtain this information "by calling a toll-free number, by checking local telephone directories, or by calling operator information numbers."[52]

MONITORING AND ENFORCEMENT

Careful monitoring and enforcement of the nationwide relay services envisioned by the ADA will ensure that relay services function effectively. There are three levels at which such monitoring and enforcement can take place: consumer, state, and federal. The role of each of these is discussed in the following section.

Consumer Involvement. Experience throughout the United States has revealed that involvement of relay consumers with hearing and speech impairments in both designing and monitoring local relay programs can contribute significantly to the effectiveness of those programs. Advisory committees created for this purpose — with representation from deaf, hard-of-hearing, and speech-impaired relay consumers, telephone companies, and other interested parties — have become the norm in states that have relay programs.[53] The Senate Committee report on the ADA recognized the "unique and specialized needs" of consumers, and directed the FCC to pay close attention to their input through the establishment of a formal advisory committee.[54]

Among the numerous responsibilities that an advisory committee can assume at the inception of a relay program are planning and establishing the relay system design; selecting the service provider; training operators; and conducting consumer outreach programs, publicity, and education. After a relay service has begun operations, an advisory group can assist in resolving problems, mediating disputes, and evaluating and monitoring the quality of relay performance (Heil 1988). Generally, the advisory committee can and has served the very useful function of providing an ongoing dialogue among the user community, the service provider, the utility commissions, and the local exchange carriers.

State Enforcement. The FCC has overall enforcement authority for title IV of the ADA. Nevertheless, any complaint about an intrastate relay service filed with the Commission may be referred back to the appropriate state commission if the state in which the complaint was charged has been "certified" by the FCC.[55] To receive certification, a state's program and procedures must meet the FCC's minimum guidelines and standards for relay services and must provide adequate enforcement procedures and remedies to address violations of the Act.[56]

For states that have assumed responsibilty for the provision of relay services, aggressive monitoring will be necessary to ensure compliance. A number of approaches are available. In Minnesota, the state established a Civilian Review Board for the purpose of receiving complaints and grievances from the community.[57] Some states have developed a process that enables users to access a supervisor of the relay center while still on line with the relay operator.[58] States can also require tariffs to be filed with local public utility commissions so that relay consumers have the same procedural protection for disputes, including identical complaint and hearing procedures, as are provided for other telephone customers.

In order to avoid any potential conflicts of interest, many urge as well that a state entity not regularly involved with relay service be responsible for both formally evaluating relay services and acting on relay complaints. One hearing examiner in Delaware explained: "It is important that the [Public Service] Commission assume as independent and as objective a posture as feasible so that in the event that a complaint proceeding should arise concerning the provision of this telephone service, the Commission could act on any such complaint in an objective and impartial manner."[59]

FCC Enforcement. The FCC retains direct enforcement authority over relay services in all states that have not received certification. In addition, in cases where the FCC has referred a complaint back to a certified state, the Commission can still acquire jurisdiction over the complaint if (1) the state has not taken final action on the complaint within 180 days or within a shorter period if such period is prescribed by state regulations; or (2) the Commission revokes the state's certification.[60]

The ADA does not discuss the means by which the FCC is to determine, on a regular basis, whether or not a particular state program continues to merit certification. One way in which the FCC can accomplish this task would be for the Commission to gather data periodically from certified states on their program operations. Such data could include traffic studies detailing blockage rates, the number of calls in queue at given times, the average length of time those calls are in queue, the average speed of relay answer, and other information relating to the operation and standards of the state relay system.[61]

There are several other features that a relay service can offer to its telephone subscribers:

Voice Pass-Through. Recent technology has brought a technology called "voice pass-through," also referred to as "voice bridge" or "voice carryover," to relay services. With this technology, deaf and hard-of-hearing individuals who typically use their voices are able to talk directly to the hearing party and have the hearing party's message typed back in text.[62] Similarly, with a technology called "hearing pass-through," relay callers who can hear need only use the operators to type what they cannot say.

The pass-through technologies have several advantages. First, they save time, and thereby reduce the overall costs of relaying a telephone call. Second, they increase privacy, in that systems using this technology typically do not allow relay operators to listen to that part of the spoken message that does not need to be relayed. Third, they tailor the functions that the relay service can provide to the needs of the consumer, allowing for increased independence for those persons wishing to send or receive messages without any assistance from the operator. Finally, the pass-through features are likely to increase the populations of individuals who can benefit from a relay service, but who might be reluctant to allow relay operators to convey their messages. For example, hard-of-hearing individuals and senior citizens who have lost their hearing later in life are two such groups who might otherwise feel hesitant about using relay services.

Foreign-Language Relay Services. In its report on ADA, the House noted that in some American communities, there are substantial populations for whom English is a second language.[63] The report urged common carriers in these areas to provide relay services in the predominant language of these communities. Indeed, this has already been required in Arizona and Texas where Spanish-speaking operators are available to relay calls.[64]

Recorded Messages. Questions have been raised about the ability of relay operators to transmit prerecorded messages. The Senate committee report addresses this issue as follows:

The Committee recognizes that it may be technically impossible today to relay recorded messages in their entirety because TDDs can only transmit messages at a given speed. In these situations, a hearing or speech impaired individual should be given the option to have the message summarized.[65]

The manner in which prerecorded messages can best be conveyed to TDD users remains unresolved. One answer may be to require telephone companies to research new technology to provide this accommodation. At least one such technology may, in fact, already be in the making.[66] Where the information contained through these telephone services is otherwise provided to users of conventional telephones, the universal service obligation dictates that it should be made available to TDD users as well.

Time-Saving Technology. Efforts to develop technology that will result in savings in the time needed to relay calls is underway. One such technology allows software to detect TDD signals before a call to a relay service has been answered by an operator.[67] This eliminates the need to answer telephone calls by voice, and then switch to a TDD format if a TDD user is on the line. The software automatically transfers the TDD call to a TDD or computer at the relay center, reducing the number of seconds needed to answer a TDD call.

Second, some companies have begun experimenting with a technology called automatic-call set-up. With this technology, a computer at the relay center makes initial inquiries to the calling party regarding the number to be called, identifying information, and an initial message to the called party. An operator only comes on the line after this information has been obtained, thereby saving costly operator time.

RELATIONSHIP OF TITLE IV TO OTHER ADA TITLES

REASONABLE ACCOMMODATION

Although title IV sets forth the ADA's requirements for relay services, other sections of the ADA will require employers, places of public accommodation, and state and local governments to provide reasonable accommodations that ensure telephone access for deaf, hard-of-hearing, and speech-impaired individuals. For example, the covered entity may need to acquire one or more TDDs itself for calls made to or from its facilities. The entity may also be required to ensure that access to relay services is available to deaf, hard-of-hearing, and speech-impaired employees, customers, and clients. The requirements of title IV thus will have far-reaching effects for hearing-impaired and speech-impaired persons seeking to participate in the benefits and services promised under the other titles of the ADA.

Two examples can best illustrate this point. Title I of the ADA prohibits employment discrimination on the basis of disability. In the past, a deaf or speech-impaired individual may have been rejected for an employment position that included, as one of its essential functions, the making of periodic telephone calls. With the nationwide relay system in place, denial of employment to a deaf or speech-impaired individual that is based solely on the inability to use conventional telephone services would likely amount to discrimination under the ADA. Similarly, title III prohibits disability discrimination by hotels and other privately owned places of public accommodation. In the past, a hotel may not have had a TDD to accept telephone reservations from deaf and speech-impaired persons. This same hotel may now be required to familiarize its employees with relay services to enable these employees to efficiently process reservations made by deaf, hard-of-hearing, and speech-impaired consumers through a relay system.

911 SERVICES

On occasion, a relay operator may need to connect a call from a TDD user to an emergency telephone 911 service. However, relay services cannot be expected to handle calls involving serious emergencies on a regular basis. Relay operators are not sufficiently trained in handling emergency calls. Furthermore, the seconds saved in calling a 911 number directly, compared to having the call routed through a relay service, can mean the difference between life and death. The House committee report and the Conference report on the ADA directs state and local governments to provide direct access by TDDs—in both the Baudot and ASCII formats—to police, fire, ambulance, and other emergency telephone services.[68]

THE FUTURE

ASCII VERSUS BAUDOT

Two formats can be used by TDDs to transmit messages across telephone lines. The first of these, the Baudot format, was developed around the time of the invention of the telephone itself and had been considered the international standard for telegraphic communication until the 1950s (Jensema 1988). Capable of transmitting only 32 characters, however, the Baudot code could not survive the need for more sophisticated computer functions that came with the following decades.

In 1968, the rapid growth of computers led the federal government to adopt the American Standard Code for Information Interchange (ASCII) as the nationwide standard for computer transmissions (Jensema 1988). ASCII allows the transmission of anywhere from 128 to 256 characters, and permits the transmission of messages at a speed many times faster than Baudot (Starr 1989).

Another advantage to the ASCII mode is that it allows individuals using TDDs to interrupt each other's conversation. TDDs using the Baudot mode employ the "half-duplex" mode of operation, which means that when one individual is sending a message, the receiving party cannot send any messages until the first person stops keying. In contrast, most computer communication using the ASCII code allows for communication to take place in both directions simultaneously (Jensema 1988; Steel 1989). This saves both time and aggravation for the Baudot user, who is sometimes forced to wait long periods of time receiving information from the other party that he or she might not need.

Many believe that the sophisticated features offered by the ASCII format are reason enough to gradually eliminate TDDs that depend on the Baudot code. Adoption of the ASCII code for all TDDs, they say, would enable TDD users in the future to become fully integrated into a general telephone system that, over time, is becoming increasingly computerized.

The reality, however, is that, at the present time, the vast majority of TDD users use TDDs that operate in the Baudot format. The House Committee on Energy and Commerce recognized this fact, and, in order to ensure that *all* TDD users have access to the relay services

required by the ADA, directed the FCC to require access by nonvoice
terminal devices operating in both the Baudot and ASCII formats.[69]

DISTRIBUTION OF TDDS

Relay services can only serve consumers whose telephones are equipped
with TDDs or computers. Yet many deaf and speech-impaired individuals do not own their own TDDs; nor do they have computers that will
permit telephone transmissions in the ASCII mode. One reason for this
may be the high cost of TDDs and computers compared with the cost of
conventional telephones. TDDs start at approximately $150 and can go
as high as $650. Computers, of course, can be even more expensive,
going as high as several thousands of dollars.

States have begun to address this problem by implementing distribution programs through which TDDs are provided either free of cost or
at discounted rates to residents with hearing or speech impairments.
Such programs exist in approximately 25 states and consumers have
mobilized efforts in a few other states to establish additional programs.
The demand for these programs will likely grow as deaf, hard-of-
hearing, and speech-impaired people realize that, through relay services, they are now able to put their TDDs to far greater use than was
previously possible.

The future is likely to bring increased acquisition of TDDs and other
nonvoice terminals by businesses as well. As individuals with hearing
and speech impairments become more integrated into the telecommunications system, more businesses are likely to find themselves regular
recipients of relayed calls. Purchase of a TDD or terminals by these
businesses will reduce the load of relay centers and, consequently, overall telecommunication costs.

FUTURE TECHNOLOGIES

Although the ADA mandates relay services as the means to achieve
telecommunications access for individuals with hearing and speech
impairments in the immediate future, Congress recognized that
improved technology may one day require that other, superior services
be available to achieve universal access for such persons:

> Although the Committee notes that relay systems represent the
> current state-of-the-art, this legislation is not intended to discour-
> age innovation regarding telecommunications services to individ-

uals with hearing and speech impairments. The hearing-and speech-impaired communities should be allowed to benefit from advancing technology. As such, the provisions of this section do not seek to entrench current technology but rather to allow for new, more advanced, and more efficient technology.[70]

FUTURE RESERACH

Implementation of title IV presents several opportunities for research. First, demographic research should be conducted to improve our current knowledge about the number of persons with hearing and speech impairments, particularly by state and locality. Accurate demographic data can assist in planning for the expansion of relay services and in assessing the extent to which the services are being utilized.

Second, effectiveness and efficiency research should be undertaken to evaluate the relay service provided, with direction for improvements. The following are some questions this research could address: How many deaf, hard-of-hearing, and speech-impaired individuals are using the relay system? Why are some who could benefit from using the system not using it? By state, what are the statistics on call volumes, call blockage, waiting periods, and busy time periods? Are relay operators competent and available in adequate supply? What effective cost-recovery procedures have been utilized? Are consumers satisfied?

Finally, research in advancing the TDD and relay system technology should be a part of the general telecommunications research agenda. Relay system technology should keep pace with general telecommunications advances. In addition, research targeted specifically to improving the relay system itself should be continued. For example, research on new technologies that will permit reciprocal conversion of typed TDD and voice messages should be encouraged. This sort of technology, in the long run, will result in more efficient and cost-effective relay services.

CONCLUSION

Approximately 40 states are well on the way to providing statewide relay services. Common carriers in states that do not have relay programs can avail themselves of the wealth of knowledge acquired by these various states. Compliance with the ADA will be relatively easy when these companies learn about the past successes and failures of programs and incorporate those lessons in developing their programs. The FCC will also benefit from a careful review of the states' experiences as they develop regulations for title IV.

The experiences of relay systems in recent years lead to the following recommendations for implementing title IV.

- First, dual-party relay service should be fully integrated into the existing telecommunications network. This will help to ensure equal access for relay users and enable new technologies that offer improved benefits and services within the general telephone network to be available to relay users as well.
- Second, adequate funds should be available to ensure a high quality of relay services. This is best accomplished by integrating the costs of providing relay services as a part of the normal operating expenses of the telephone system. With this approach to funding, arbitrary curtailments and limitations of relay services can be avoided.
- Third, consumers should be involved in designing and monitoring relay systems that will result in more effective services.
- Fourth, efforts to educate both potential users of the relay system and businesses and the general public about the purposes and functions of relay services should be made to facilitate widespread use and acceptance of these services.
- Fifth, comprehensive monitoring of relay services, on the consumer, state, and federal levels, combined with the provision of effective grievance procedures, should be conducted to maintain a level of relay services that is functionally equivalent to general telephone services.
- Finally, aggressive and relevant research efforts should be performed to facilitate the development of a more effective and satisfying relay system.

The benefits that title IV's requirement for relay services will bring are undisputed. Integration of deaf, hard-of-hearing, and speech-impaired individuals into the telecommunications network will bring these individuals increased freedom, independence, and privacy. These individuals will be able to use the telephone to easily access businesses, colleagues, friends, and relatives, something that hearing individuals have taken for granted for approximately more than half a century. It is hoped that relay services will assist in expanding job responsibilities and opportunities for deaf, hard-of-hearing, and speech-impaired employees as well. The benefit will not only be to employees with hearing and speech impairments, but to businesses as well because they will have a wider pool of qualified persons from which to select their employees. Finally, relay services will stimulate and promote economic development by expanding markets for goods and services to the 27 million individuals with hearing and speech and impairments.

NOTES

1. The specific language of the Communications Act of 1934 directs the Federal Communications Commission ("FCC" or "Commission") "to make available, so far as possible, *to all the people of the United States* a rapid, efficient, Nation-wide, and world-wide wire and radio communication service with adequate facilities at reasonable charges. . ." 47 U.S.C. §151 (emphasis added).
2. 47 U.S.C. §225(a) and (c).
3. National Information Center on Deafness. *What are TDDs?* Washington: Gallaudet University. (Pamphlet)
4. The 17 states were Alabama, Arizona, Arkansas, California, Connecticut, Hawaii, Kansas, Massachusetts, Minnesota, New Hampshire, New York, Oklahoma, Oregon, Utah, Vermont, Virginia, and Wisconsin (NCLD 1989). Many other privately operated relay systems also existed by this time. In one survey, conducted by the Teleconsumer Hotline in the early part of 1987 through the spring of 1988, evidence of over 300 relay services was gathered (Baquis 1988).
5. S. Rep. No. 116, 101st Cong., 1st Sess. 77–78 (1989) (S. Rep.) Indeed, the language of the ADA itself incorporates the exact language of the universal service mandate. 47 U.S.C. §225(b)(1).
6. 47 U.S.C. §225(d); S. Rep at 81; H.R. Rep No. 485, Part 4, 101st Cong., 2d Sess. 66 (1990)(H.R. Rep.)
7. 47 U.S.C. 225 (d)(1)(C).
8. 47 U.S.C. §225(d)(1)(E).
9. R. Yaeger, 1990: Remarks at TDI Conference 121, Telecommunications for the Deaf, Inc. Relay Subcommittee, Tempe, Arizona 93 F, April 4; 42–44, April 5.
10. See generally, TDI Conference proceedings; P. Shapiro, Remarks during panel discussion: Relay Service Operations, Speech to Text Conference (Sept. 1988), reprinted in GRI Monograph Series B, No. 2, 114 (Operations Panel). Pennsylvania's request for a proposal setting forth the terms of its relay service further relieves relay operators from any criminal liability that might otherwise result from processing these calls. Pennsylvania RFP 10 §II (D)(2).
11. C. Foy (Arizona Relay Service) and B. Sofinski (Virginia Relay Service), 1990: Remarks at TDI Conference 158, April 4.

12. 47 U.S.C. §225(d)(1)(F).
13. Conn. Gen. Stat. Ann. §52–146m (West 1990 Cum Pkt Pt.).
14. Colo. Rev. Stat. §40–17–101 (1989).
15. Although the FCC has clear authority to supersede state *relay* laws that do not guarantee confidentiality, it is not as clear that the Commission's preemptive authority extends to state laws, such as the Texas law requiring disclosure of information about child abuse, that do not otherwise deal with the subject of relay services. Additional legal research is needed on this issue.
16. 47 U.S.C. §225(d)(1)(G).
17. See generally C. Foy (Arizona Relay Service), J. Cassell (Oregon Relay Service), and J. Ferrill (New York Relay Service) 1990: Remarks at TDI Conference 114–120, 153–154, April 4.
18. 47 U.S.C. §(d)(1)(D).
19. Alabama, Connecticut, and New York are three such states that provide a TDD discount for relayed calls (NCLD 1990).
20. Indeed, the Senate Committee on Labor and Human Resources, in reporting on the ADA, commended those states that have offered TDD discounts. S. Rep. at 82.
21. A blockage rate is defined as the number of calls receiving busy signals when trying to access the relay service.
22. S. Rep. at 81.
23. See rules and regulations of the Delaware PSC governing DPRS IV (3) (Del. PSC rules). This means that 1 out of every 100 calls would not be able to access the relay system.
24. S. Rep. at 81; 136 Cong. Rec. H2434 (daily ed. May 17, 1990), Statement of Congressman Luken.
25. In Minnesota, for example, the relay provider is currently establishing a training program in which individuals working on suicide and rape-crisis hotlines will instruct operators on the best way to handle these calls until they are relayed to the hotlines. R. Yaeger, 1990: Remarks at TDI Conference 126–127, April 4.
26. S. Rep. at 81. This compares with earlier message relay services that accepted messages from calling parties and relayed them to the called party at a later time.
27. S. Rep. at 81. Indeed this would be consistent with the divestiture of AT&T as required by the Modified Final Judgment issued in 1982, which resulted in providing users of conventional telephones with this freedom of choice. *United States v. American Telephone and Telegraph Co.*, 552 F. Supp. 1311 (D.D.C. 1982).
28. Three such states are Kansas, Delaware, and Pennsylvania.
29. Approximately 50 percent of the costs of a relayed call are estimated to be for operator wages. In addition, because a relayed call takes longer to complete than does a voice-to-voice call, the equipment costs per call are higher for relayed calls, in that these costs are distributed over fewer calls (Hurst 1988).
30. In the Matter of Access to Telecommunications Equipment and Services by the Hearing Impaired and Other Disabled Persons, *Order Completing Inquiry and Providing Further Notice of Proposed Rulemaking*, CC Dkt No. 87–124 (July

21, 1989) 21. The FCC also estimated the costs of operating two interstate relay centers to be $30 million. It is not clear how the FCC arrived at these figures.

31. S. Brackney, 1988: Remarks during Financing Panel discussion: Financing Models in State Programs, Speech to Text Conference, September. Reprinted in *GRI Monograph Serices B* 2:77.

32. R. Yaeger (Minnesota Relay Service), 1990: Remarks at TDI Conference 56–57, April 5.

33. See also Kan. Stat. Ann §75–5393(B)(10).

34. P. Hughes (Washington Relay Service), 1990: Remarks at the TDI Conference 93, April 4.

35. P. Hughes, 1990: Remarks at TDI Conference 42, April 5.

36. Of the states discussed in this section, Delaware, Kansas, and Texas will, however, only allow outgoing, but not incoming interstate calls. It is not known whether the other state programs listed will impose this restriction.

37. 47 U.S.C. §225(c).

38. The information about Kansas and the preceding states is drawn from the NCLD Summaries (NCLD 1989; 1990).

39. 47 U.S.C. §225(c); H.R. Rep. at 66.

40. S. Rep. at 77.

41. One source estimated the number of calls that each American makes per year to be 1,128, or three per day. (Department of Human Services, Oklahoma City 1986. TDDs: Their Place in the Community).

42. 47 U.S.C. §225(d)(1(D).

43. Arizona's relay service had similar experiences. Although the surcharge for that state started at .2 percent of the base charge per customer line, it has since been raised by the Arizona legislatures two times, to bring the surcharge to its current cap of .8 percent (Ransom 1988); S. Brackney, Financing Panel at 76.

44. H.B. No. 648/S.B. No. 2331(4)(1). Texas and Pennsylvania are two other states that allow their commissions to raise the surcharge whenever necessary to support the relay.

45. Delaware PSC Regulation Docket No. 24, Hearing Examiner's Interim Report 13 (Jan. 11, 1990) (Del. Rep.).

46. See, e.g., Del. Rep. at 15.

47. H.R. Rep. at 68; S. Rep. at 83.

48. See memorandum from New York Consumer Services Division & Communications Division to the New York Public Service Commission: New York memo, April 5, 1988 at 13.

49. M.B. Meenan (Arizona Relay Service), 1990: Remarks at TDI Conference 65–67, April 5.

50. R. Yaeger, 1990: Remarks at TDI Conference 73–74, April 5.

51. J. Cassell, 1990: Remarks at TDI Conference 76, April 5.

52. 136 Cong. Rec. H2635 (daily ed. May 22, 1990), statement of Congressman Bonoir. See 136 Cong. Rec. H2434 (daily ed. May 17, 1990), Colloquy between Congressman Hoyer and Congressman Luken.

53. Maine, Illinois, Michigan, Mississippi, Montana, Nebraska, New York, Oregon, South Carolina, Utah, Washington, and Wisconsin are among the states that have established or plan to establish advisory committees (NCLD 1990).

Alabama, Delaware, Pennsylvania, Texas, and Virginia also have advisory boards and require a majority of those boards to consist of relay consumers who have speech or hearing impairments. See generally R. Yaeger, 1990: Remarks at TDI Conference 96, April 4.

54. S. Rep. at 81.
55. 47 U.S.C. §225(g)(1).
56. 47 U.S.C. §225(f). However, the FCC cannot refuse to certify a state program based on the funding method chosen by the state. 47 U.S.C.§225(f)(3).
57. R. Yaeger, 1990: Remarks at TDI COnference 74, April 5.
58. See, e.g., Del. PSC Rules, §VI (2).
59. Delaware PSC Regulation Docket No. 24, Hearing Examiner's Report 7 (February 8, 1990).
60. 47 U.S.C. §225(g)(2)(A) & (B).
61. See, e.g., Pennsylvania RFP 11 Sec. II(E), listing the various records and reports that must be submitted by the Pennsylvania relay service provider on the operation of its system. In Texas, the relay provider must also report regularly to the local public utility commission.
62. According to one source, as of two years ago, more than 40 percent of all calls relayed in Norway use voice pass-through. (K. Lindberg: Remarks during Operations Panel at 114.) In America, this technology is already in place in Washington and will be required in Texas, Delaware and Virginia.
63. H.R. Rep. at 66.
64. See Meenan, 1990: Remarks at TDI Conference 26, April 5. Moreover, in the Teleconsumer Hotline survey, as many as 15 percent of the relay centers surveyed provided Spanish-speaking relay operators. See Baquis 1988 at 28.
65. S. Rep. at 82. Similarly, the inability to control the speed of a recorded message prompted the New York Commission to explicitly exclude "900" numbers, weather, and other recorded announcements from the relay service. New York memo at 6. See note 48, supra.
66. See Interactive Telephone Voice Response Systems News, in *Off Hook* 2 (1), official publication of DIRAD Technologies, Inc., which alleges that a new DiRAD TDD System enables TDD users to access and retrieve information by telephone that is otherwise transmitted only through a prerecorded voice.
67. Meenan, 1990: Remarks at TDI Conference 51, April 5.
68. H.R. Rep. No. 485, Part 2, 101st Cong., 2d Sess. 84–85 (1990); Conf. Rep. 596, 101st Cong., 2d Sess. 67–68 (1990).
69. H. R. Rep. at 66–67.
70. S. Rep. at 78.

REFERENCES

Baquis, D. 1988. TDD Relay Services across the United States. *GRI Monograph Series B* 2: 25–43.
Conlon-Mentkowski, S. 1988. Overview of State-Regulated Relay Services. *GRI Monograph Series B* 2: 19–23.

Heil, Jr., J. 1988. Planning for Statewide Relay Service. *GRI Monograph Series B* 2: 119–24.

Hotchkiss, D. 1989. *Demographic Aspects of Hearing Impairment: Questions and Answers*, 2d ed. Washington: Gallaudet Research Institute, Gallaudet University.

Hurst, M. 1988. The Process of Establishing State-Mandated Relay Services. *GRI Monograph Series B* 2: 53–57.

Jensema, C. 1988. Telecommunications for the hearing impaired: An Era of Technological Change. Paper presented to the National Conference on Deaf and Hard of Hearing People, El Paso, Texas, September 13–18.

National Center for Law and the Deaf (NCLD). 1989. *Summary of State Dual-Party Relay Services.*

———. 1990. *Summary of State Dual-party Relay Services.*

Ransom, P. 1988. Dual Party Relay Service: An Analysis of Funding Mechanisms. *GRI Monograph Series B* 2:59–71.

Shapiro, P. 1988. California Relay Service. *GRI Monograph Series B* 2: 85–88.

Singleton, P. 1988. Nationwide TDD Relay Standards: Partners in Progress. *GRI Monograph Series B* 2: 107–10.

Starr, S. 1989. Using a TDD to Communicate with a Personal Computer. *Self Help for Hard of Hearing people (SHHH) Monthly Newsletter* (January/February).

Steel, J. 1989. Phone-TTY, Practical Application of ASCII in Today's TDDs.

Taylor, P. 1988. Telephone Relay Service: Rationale and Overview. *GRI Monograph Series B* 2: 11–18.

U.S. Congress, Office of Technology Assessment. 1986. Hearing Impairment and Elderly People—A Background Paper (OTA-BP-BA-30). Washington.

White, B. 1990. Dual Party Relays . . . How Far Will They Fly? *Silent News* 22(5): 13–14.

Public Health Powers: The Imminence of Radical Change

Lawrence O. Gostin

EDITOR'S NOTE

One of the most controversial public policy challenges of recent times has been crafting policy that balances the public interest and individual rights in relation to persons with HIV and AIDS. Lawrence O. Gostin explores the convergence of the traditional exercise of public-health powers, which requires persons to be treated unequally because of communicable medical conditions, and the antidiscrimination mandate of ADA, which requires reasonable accommodation as a component of equitable treatment for persons with disabilities. Gostin concludes by proposing a set of standards that could be applied in individual cases to determine whether to draw the line on the side of public interest or individual civil rights.

Gostin is executive director of the American Society of Law and Medicine; adjunct associate professor of health law at Harvard University; and associate director of the Harvard University/World Health Organization International Center of Health Legislation. He conducted a national study for the U.S. Assistant Secretary for Health, as well as a worldwide study for the World Health Organization on AIDS law and policy. He is also co-director of the Harvard Model AIDS Legislation Project. Gostin was Legislative Counsel to the U.S. Senate Labor and Human Resources Committee, chaired by Senator Edward Kennedy, where he helped draft the Federal AIDS Policy Act. He was formerly chief executive of the National Council for Civil Liberties; legal director of the National Association for Mental Health in Great Britain; and senior fellow at Wolfson College, Oxford University. He was awarded the Delbridge Memorial Award for the person "who has most influenced Parliament and government to act for the welfare of society."

Legal controls over the unfettered exercise of public health powers have long been regarded as ineffective and idiosyncratic (Burris 1985;1989; Merritt 1986; Parmet 1989). Public health statutes (many written before the sciences of virology, bacteriology, and epidemiology had fully come of age) delegate wide-ranging powers to officials (Gostin 1987). The major check on the exercise of these powers has been constitutional review by the judiciary. The courts, however, are reluctant to interfere in public health decision making, and have not yet developed a cogent set of criteria for establishing effective boundaries around the proper exercise of public health authority.

In this article, I will argue that constitutional review—long the standard bearer for judicial activity in the public health realm—is quietly, but effectively, being replaced with a more cogent statutory review provided by the Americans with Disabilities Act (ADA). This landmark legislation will unleash a powerful review mechanism that will set effective boundaries on the historic exercise of public health powers. Ultimately, the ADA will provide a much needed impetus for states to reform fundamentally outdated statutes relevant to communicable and sexually transmitted disease (Gostin 1987). This reformation will bring state statutes into conformity with the letter and spirit of the ADA.

I will be suggesting a new way of looking at the ADA and public health law. Even some of the most astute observers do not yet recognize that, seen through the lens of the ADA, public health regulation may be regarded as discrimination against persons with disabilities. In order for public health officials to justify treating people with communicable diseases differently, they must meet strict scientific standards. In the ADA, Congress clearly asserted the preeminence of science over irrational fear and prejudice.

First, I will carefully examine the key concepts in the ADA as they apply to communicable disease. This section will reveal the clear intention of Congress to include communicable disease, even asymptomatic infection, as a disability. Second, I will explain the new "direct threat" standard in the ADA. This section will analyze how the courts and Congress have used the concept of "significant risk" as a new yardstick for reviewing public health powers. Third, I will examine how the concept of reasonable accommodations can be applied to persons with communicable disease. Finally, I will propose a systematic standard of review under the ADA for the future regulation of public health powers.

COMMUNICABLE DISEASE AS A DISABILITY

The Americans with Disabilities Act of 1990[1] (ADA) and the corpus of antidiscrimination legislation[2] appear to be unlikely sources of law to fill the doctrinal void left by deferential constitutional standards. Antidiscrimination law, on its face, is concerned with what I refer to as "pure discrimination." Pure discrimination occurs when a public or private entity treats a person unfairly, not because she lacks adequate skill, qualifications, or experience, but because of her disability. The nation's goals, according to the framers of the ADA, are to assure equality of opportunity, full participation, equal living and self-sufficiency to allow people with disabilities to compete on an equal basis.[3]

Public health regulation of communicable disease does not fit comfortably within the ADA's rubric of pure discrimination. Certainly, the annals of public health are replete with examples of pure discrimination against "discrete and insular" minorities such as prostitutes (Brandt 1985), drug-dependent people (Musto 1973), gays (Bayer 1989), and racial minorities.[4] The exercise of public health powers such as testing, screening, reporting, vaccination, treatment, isolation, and quarantine are, however, qualitatively different from the ADA's paradigm of pure discrimination: the state is regulating public health, not refusing jobs, benefits, or services because of a disability; the motive is health related, not grounded in prejudice; and the usual qualification standards of education, skill, or experience are not pertinent. Persons are treated unequally in public health regulation because of communicable medical conditions, not as a direct result of pure prejudice.

Despite the qualitative differences between a communicable disease (e.g., tuberculosis, syphilis, or hepatitis B) and a physical disability (e.g., sight, hearing, or mobility impairments), the ADA applies to each equally. The ADA, moreover, does not merely prohibit discrimination against persons with disease in employment and public accommodations. Title II of the ADA applies to public services, which are

defined broadly to encompass all actions by state and local government, including those of public health departments. To demonstrate
the applicability of the ADA to communicable disease, I will analyze
the relevant definitions, legislative history, and standards.

PHYSICAL OR MENTAL IMPAIRMENT

Disability is defined broadly in the ADA to mean "a physical or mental
impairment that substantially limits one or more of the major life
activities, a record of such impairment, or being regarded as having
such an impairment." Physical or mental impairment includes (1) any
physiological disorder or condition, disfigurement or anatomical loss
affecting any of the major bodily systems; or (2) any mental or physiological disorder such as mental retardation or mental illness. The legislative history,[5] as well as the prior case law,[6] reveal that "disability"
includes diseases and infections that are communicable (e.g., tuberculosis,[7] hepatitis,[8] and HIV[9]) as well as those that are not (e.g., heart
disease,[10] cerebral palsy,[11] arthritis,[12] diabetes, and epilepsy[13]).

The legislative history of the Rehabilitation Act barely mentions
infectious disease.[14] In *School Board of Nassau County, Florida v.
Arline*, the question arose for the first time in the Supreme Court[15]
whether discrimination on the basis of contagiousness constitutes discrimination "by reason of . . . handicap." The Court held that a teacher
who had been hospitalized with tuberculosis that affected her respiratory system had a "record" of substantial physical impairment. The fact
that a person with a record of impairment is also contagious does not
remove her from protection as a person with disability.

The *Arline* Court observed that, in defining a person with disability,
the contagious effects of a disease cannot be meaningfully distinguished from the disease's physical effects. "It would be unfair to allow
an employer to seize upon the distinction between the effects of a
disease on others and the effects of a disease on a patient and use that
distinction to justify discriminatory treatment."[16] Citing the example of
cosmetic disfigurement, the Court argued that Congress was as concerned about the effects of impairment on others as it was about its
effects on the individual.[17]

The inclusion of contagious conditions in the definition of disability
was, according to *Arline*, consistent with the basic purpose of disability
law to protect people against the prejudiced attitudes and ignorance of
others. "Society's accumulated myths and fears about disability and

disease are as handicapping as are the physical limitations that flow from impairment. Few aspects of handicap give rise to the same level of public fear and misapprehension as contagiousness."[18]

"RECORD" OF OR "REGARDED" AS BEING IMPAIRED

A person is disabled if he or she has a "record" of or is "regarded" as being disabled or is perceived to be disabled, even if there is no actual incapacity.[19] A "record" indicates that the person has had a history of impairment, or has been misclassified as having had an impairment. This provision is designed to protect persons who have recovered from a disability or disease that previously impaired their life activities.[20] By including those who have a record of impairment, Congress acknowledged that people who are no longer suffering the effects of conditions such as epilepsy or cancer still face discrimination based upon prejudice and irrational fear.[21]

The term "regarded" as being impaired includes individuals who do not have limitations in their major life functions, but are treated as if they did. This concept protects people who are discriminated against in the false belief that they are disabled. It would be inequitable for a defendant who intended to discriminate on the basis of disability to raise successfully the defense that the person was not, in fact, disabled. This provision is particularly important for individuals who are perceived to have stigmatic conditions that are viewed negatively by society. It is the reaction of society, rather than the disability itself, that deprives the person of equal enjoyment of rights and services. Persons with infectious diseases are particularly prone to irrational fears by those who are misinformed about the modes and relative risks of transmission. Persons with disfiguring conditions such as leprosy or severe burns may also suffer from negative attitudes and misinformation because they are perceived to be disabled.[22]

ASYMPTOMATIC INFECTION AS A DISABILITY

The fact that a record or perception of disability is included within the ADA is vitally important in determining whether pure asymptomatic infection can be regarded as a disability. The abiding interest at the time of *Arline* was whether an asymptomatic carrier of a contagious infection such as human immunodeficiency virus (HIV) could be regarded as having a disability. A Justice Department memorandum in June 1986 concluded that although the disabling effects of AIDS may constitute a disability, contagiousness—the ability to transmit infection to others—is not covered within the Act.[23] The *Arline* court, in its widely studied footnote 7, stated that the facts of the case "do not present, and we therefore do not reach, the question whether a carrier of a contagious disease such as AIDS could be considered to have a physical impairment."[24]

The Presidential Commission on the HIV Epidemic recommended that all stages of HIV infection should be covered under disability law.[25] On July 29, 1988, C. Everett Koop, the surgeon general, wrote to the Justice Department seeking a fresh opinion in light of *Arline* and the growing scientific understanding that HIV infection is the starting point of a single disease process.[26] In response, the Justice Department withdrew its previous opinion, concluding that "section 504 protects symptomatic as well as asymptomatic HIV-infected individuals against discrimination." The person is protected only if he or she "is able to perform the duties of the job and does not constitute a direct threat to the health or safety of others."[27]

The applicability of asymptomatic infection to disability status had already been clarified in amendments to the Rehabilitation Act. The Civil Rights Restoration Act of 1987[28] states that a person with a contagious disease or *infection* is disabled if he or she does not "constitute a direct threat to health or safety" and is able to "perform the duties of the job."[29] Since *Arline*, the courts have consistently held that HIV-related diseases, including asymptomatic HIV infection, are covered disabilities.[30]

DIRECT THREAT: AN EVOLVING QUALIFICATION STANDARD

The antidiscrimination principle in the ADA applies only to "qualified individuals."[31] A "qualified" person must be capable of meeting all of the performance or eligibility criteria for the particular position, service, or benefit.[32] There is, moreover, an affirmative obligation to provide "reasonable accommodations"[33] or "reasonable modifications"[34] if they would enable the person to meet the performance or eligibility criteria. Employers are not required to provide reasonable accommodations if they would impose an undue hardship on the operation of the business.[35]

The key concepts of "qualification" and "reasonable accommodations" or "modifications," on their face, apply only to a person's ability to do a job or participate in public programs, with or without adaptations or modifications by the employer or public entity. A ban specifically of discrimination against persons with disabilities who are "qualified," without better established limits, might require covered entities to integrate persons in jobs, accommodations, and services, even if they posed a risk of transmission of disease. This prospect led some Congressmen to ask whether employers could be required to employ persons with AIDS if they risked "exposing others to tuberculosis, cytomegalovirus, and other AIDS-associated illness?"[36]

It does defy established public health practice to suggest that persons with readily transmissible airborne conditions such as measles, influenza, or active tuberculosis could not be excluded from a particular job or from enclosed public spaces such as movie theaters; that persons with foodborne diseases could not be prevented from working in kitchens or as waiters in restaurants; or that public health departments could not set reasonable rules for the control of sexually transmitted disease in bathhouses. In short, the essence of public health regulation is that persons may be treated differently based upon a rigorous scientific assessment of the risk of transmission.

Congress anticipated this problem as it affected employment and public accommodations. Titles I and IV of the ADA state expressly that qualification standards can include a requirement that a person with a disability "not pose a direct threat to the health or safety of others"[37] if reasonable accommodations or modifications will not eliminate that direct threat. The ADA clearly provides a right to take action to protect the health and safety of all persons in employment and public accommodations.[38]

The question arises whether the same standard is similarly applicable to title II, as the concept of "direct threat" is not expressly extended to public services. Title II is of seminal importance in the regulation of public health because it is concerned with activities of state and local government. If taken at face value, title II could appear to undermine rules, regulations, and practices of public health departments that exclude persons from services, programs, or activities because of a communicable disease. A defense of direct threat is not expressly available under title II. Congress clearly did not intend to impede valid public health measures based upon rigorous scientific determinations of a significant risk to the public. In the words of one court, "It would be unreasonable to infer that Congress intended to force institutions to accept or readmit persons who pose a significant risk of harm to themselves or others."[39] Accordingly, future regulations should specifically apply the "direct threat" standard to title II.

Title II applies only to "qualified" individuals. Although that term is not defined in title II, it can reasonably be taken to have the same meaning as in title I. Indeed, in discussing the qualification standards for public services, the House Committee on Energy and Commerce referred to the Rehabilitation Act principle that a person must meet "the basic eligibility requirements of the program," and could not pose "a significant risk to the health or safety of others that could not be eliminated by reasonable accommodation."[40]

REASONABLE ACCOMMODATIONS FOR PERSONS WITH COMMUNICABLE DISEASE

The ADA follows a long tradition[41] in disability law by requiring reasonable accommodations or modifications for otherwise qualified individuals, unless they would pose an undue hardship.[42] The need for accommodations for persons with physical disabilities is straightforward: adaptation of facilities to make them accessible, modification of equipment to make it usable, and job restructuring to provide more flexible schedules for persons who need medical treatment.[43]

The kinds of accommodations reasonably necessary to assist persons with communicable diseases, however, are not self-evident. The concepts of reasonable accommodations and "direct threat" are related.[44] A person who poses a significant risk of communicating an infectious disease to others is qualified if reasonable accommodations will eliminate that risk.[45] Employers may, for example, be required to provide infection-control training and equipment to prevent bloodborne diseases in order to accommodate persons infected with hepatitis B virus (HBV). An employer, however, is not forced to endure an undue hardship that would alter the fundamental nature of the business or would be disproportionately costly.[46,47] The Eighth Circuit Court of Appeals held that a school for persons with mental retardation was not obliged to vaccinate employees in order to reasonably accommodate a student who was an active carrier of HBV. The vaccination program that had been ordered by the lower court was unduly costly and unable to eliminate the significant risk of transmission.[48]

The Eighth Circuit's decision to uphold the exclusion from school of students with mental retardation who were active HBV carriers is directly at odds with the Second Circuit's decision in a case with essentially the same set of facts.[49] Each court had a different perception of the meaning of "significant risk" and "reasonable accommodation." The standards proposed below should clarify how the ADA ought to be applied in the public health realm.

THE ADA AND THE FUTURE OF PUBLIC HEALTH REGULATION

HOW SIGNIFICANT MUST HEALTH RISKS BE?

By utilizing the Supreme Court's term "direct threat," Congress codified *Arline*.[50] Although the direct-threat criterion was limited to persons with contagious disease in the Senate bill, it was extended in conference to all individuals with disabilities.[51] The ADA defines direct threat consistently with the *Arline* decision: "a significant risk to the health or safety of others" that cannot be eliminated by reasonable accommodation in employment,[52] or reasonable modification of policies, practices, or procedures, or by the provision of auxiliary aids or devices in public accommodations.[53]

"Significant risk," therefore, becomes the standard against which public health regulation must now be measured. The question now becomes which risks are significant? It is possible to arrive at a rather sophisticated jurisprudential and public health understanding of the concept of significant risk by piecing together the language in *Arline* and the ADA's rich legislative history.

First, the determination of significant risk is a public health inquiry.[54] Relevant evidence must be provided by the multiple disciplines of public health, including medicine, virology, bacteriology, and epidemiology. The science of public health provides the sole basis for determining modes of transmission, probability levels for transmission, efficacy of policies and practices for avoiding transmission, and the likelihood and severity of risk. Disability law has been thoughtfully crafted to replace reflexive actions based upon irrational fears, speculation, stereotypes, or pernicious mythologies,[55] with carefully reasoned judgements based upon well-established scientific information.[56]

Second, significant risk must be determined on a case-by-case basis, and not under any type of blanket rule, generalization about a class of persons with disabilities, or assumptions about the nature of disease. This requires health officials to conduct a fact-specific, individualized inquiry resulting in a "well-informed judgement grounded in a careful and open-minded weighing of risks and alternatives."[57] A specific determination must be made that the person is in fact a carrier of a communicable disease and that the disease is readily transmissible in the environment in which he or she will be situated. In the context of behavioral risks, health officials must identify the specific conduct and provide credible evidence that the person is likely to engage in dangerous behavior. For example, if a person with mental illness or mental retardation were to be excluded from school or a job because he or she posed a "direct threat," health officials must present objective evidence that a recent dangerous act was committed.[58] If a person with a needle-borne or sexually transmitted infection were to be denied equal employment or housing opportunities, evidence that the person is likely to share needles or engage in sexual activity in that setting must be offered.

Third, the risk must be "significant," not speculative, theoretical, or remote. The ADA sets a "clear, defined standard, which requires actual proof of significant risk to others."[59] This is derived from the highly regarded footnote 16 in *Arline*: "A person who poses a significant risk of communicating an infectious disease to others in the workplace will not be otherwise qualified for his or her job if reasonable accommodation will not eliminate that risk."[60] The court illustrated its point by observing that a school board would not be required to place a teacher who has active, contagious tuberculosis with elementary-school children.

Several distinct issues emerge from the concept of significant risk: what is the standard of proof, who bears the burden of proof, and what level of risk is required? These are critically important questions that ought to be clarified in regulations on the ADA and comparable state statutes.

The *standard of proof* goes to the issue of the weight of evidence required. The standard of proof is not specified in the ADA, but should be based upon clear and convincing evidence. The public health position taken should be consistent with the clear weight of scientific evidence. Restrictions on liberty ought not be based upon a minority medical opinion. A single physician's view, for example, that HIV might be transmitted casually or from a bite is not sufficiently persuasive when compared with all the accumulated data based on scientific evidence. The proof of risk, on the other hand, need not be conclusive or decisive. "Little in science can be proved with complete certainty, and section 504 does not require such a test."[61]

The *burden of proof* should fall on the entity seeking to demonstrate significant risk. This is consistent with the fact that "direct threat" is a defense in title I.[62] Thus, an employer, public health department, or public accommodation must be able to offer evidence substantiating its decision to treat persons with disabilities inequitably because they pose a threat to others. It would be difficult, if not impossible, for a person with a communicable disease to prove that transmission cannot occur or is unlikely to occur.

The *level of risk* varies depending upon the severity of the harm and the probability of it occurring. For example, minor or inconsequential infections might require a higher risk of transmission than lethal or fatal infections. Significant risk is not a remote risk, possibly not even an "elevated risk."[63] There must be a material, real, or substantial possibility that the disease can be transmitted.

The factors to be used in determining significant risk are increasingly well understood.[64] The decision maker must determine significant risk based upon reasonable medical judgments and current scientific understanding as outlined below:

1. Mode of Transmission. The mechanism of transmission of most diseases is well established by epidemiologic research. A significant risk should be based upon a primary mode of transmission, not an unestablished or highly inefficient one. A bloodborne disease, for example, could conceivably be transmitted through a bite,[65] through rough play among children,[66] or by bleeding into food.[67] Yet the "significant risk" test would not be met if personal restrictions were based on such speculative mechanisms of transmission.

2. Duration of Risk. A person can be subject to compulsory public health powers only if he or she is actually contagious, and only for the period of time of contagiousness. A fundamental principle of public health law,[68] often breached in early cases,[69] is the requirement that the subject must be proven by medical examination or testing to be carrying an infectious agent. "The mere possibility that persons may have been exposed [to a disease] is not sufficient . . . They must have been exposed to it, and the conditions actually exist for a communication of contagion."[70] The person must also be actively infectious. The key factual determination in *Arline* was whether a teacher was actively contagious and currently capable of transmitting tuberculosis through casual contact.[71]

3. *Probability of Risk.* The authority of the public health department to impose restrictions grows as the probability of the risk of transmission increases. The probability that a person will transmit disease is a scientific calculation that can be made with relative degrees of confidence. The range of probability that a person will contract HBV or HIV from a percutaneous exposure (e.g. a needle stick or cut), for example, is well established by prospective studies.[72] The level of risk from a single sexual relationship is much more difficult to calculate. Substantial probabilities of transmission based upon firm scientific calculations provide the best justification for public health powers.

4. *Severity of Harm.* The seriousness of harm to third parties represents an important calculation in public health regulations. In assessing the validity of public health powers, a rough inverse correlation exists between the seriousness of harm and the probability of it occurring. As the seriousness of potential harm to the community rises, the level of risk needed to justify the public health power decreases.

Central to the understanding of the "significant risk" criterion is the fact that even the most serious potential for harm does not justify public health regulation in the absence of a reasonable probability that it will occur. Parents of school children, for example, have difficulty comprehending why courts would uphold the exclusion of children from school who are infested with lice, but not those infected with HIV. The reason is that a very high probability exists that other children will become infested with lice, whereas the risk of contracting HIV in that setting is highly remote.

5. *Human Rights Burdens.* Although human rights burdens are often missing from public health calculations,[73] they are of central importance. The nature, severity, and duration of the personal restrictions must be weighed against the efficacy of the public health power. Substantial public benefit would be required to justify restrictions of great severity and/or duration. A requirement to report an infectious condition to a public health department that maintained strict confidentiality would not usually impose significant human burdens. A short period of exclusion from school due to measles or influenza might similarly be reasonable. On the other hand, isolation for a disease

without a finite period of infectiousness would be burdensome both in the degree and the duration of human deprivation. A decision to indefinitely separate a child or adult with mental retardation from the rest of her classmates would be stigmatic and would psychologically wound her.[74]

Courts must first determine if the health risk is significant. This ought to be followed by a careful weighing of efficacy (will the public health power reduce a serious health threat?) and burdens (at what human, social, and economic cost will the public health benefit be achieved?).[75] Wherever possible, public health officials should use the least restrictive or invasive power capable of achieving the public health goal. The concept of the "least intrusive alternative" is consistent with the ADA's duty to provide reasonable accommodations for modifications. By providing services for education, prevention, or treatment, the public health frequently can be protected without discrimination against persons with disabilities.

PUSHING THE ADA TO ITS LIMITS: THE CASE OF THE HIV-INFECTED HEALTH-CARE PROFESSIONAL

Although the foregoing proposed standards provide a clear framework for judicial decision making, they can be pushed to their limits in the most troublesome cases. Consider the application of the "direct threat" test to an HIV-infected health-care professional (Gostin 1989c). Although the risk of transmitting infection to the patient is highly remote, the consequence for any patient is grave.

A powerful argument can be made for the ADA to prohibit compulsory HIV testing or limitations in practice for infected professionals. Certainly, professionals engaged in noninvasive procedures would not pose a meaningful risk of infection for patients because comingling of the blood is virtually impossible. Thus, testing or restrictions on the right to practice for professionals engaged in noninvasive procedures would be inconsistent with the ADA. Still, the Fifth Circuit Court of Appeals in Leckelt[76] held that a hospital could compulsorily test a nurse suspected of being infected with HIV. The court found that Mr. Leckelt was "regarded" as having a disability, but was not qualified for his job because of his refusal to submit to an HIV test. Turning the obligation to provide reasonable accommodations on its head, the court concluded that the hospital was prevented from enforcing a program of infection control, monitoring, and counseling by Leckelt's refusal to disclose his HIV status.

The U.S. Centers for Disease Control (CDC) may be on the verge of recommending that professionals infected with HIV could be tested and restricted in the practice of seriously invasive procedures such as surgery and perhaps even dentistry (Cimons 1990). One case of probable transmission from a dentist to his patient has already been identified (Centers for Disease Control 1990), and several health-care facilities have dismissed HIV-infected surgeons or dentists (Gostin 1990). Would CDC guidance, board of licensure standards, or health-care-facility practices that discriminated against HIV-infected surgeons or dentists violate the ADA? The ADA has transformed the legal and public health questions. Instead of asking whether restrictions on practice of invasive procedures would protect the patient's health, the courts may ask whether health-care facilities are depriving persons with disabilities of employment opportunities.[77]

Applying the criteria proposed above, it is possible to conclude that limitations on the practice of seriously invasive procedures by HIV-infected health-care professionals would be lawful. A surgeon or dentist has her hands in a bodily cavity where there can be direct blood exposure, and studies show a high rate of torn gloves and cut hands (Cruse 1980). Thus, the mode of transmission is well established. The duration of risk is also long term, as one supposes the surgeon will practice for many years and on many patients. Although the risk that any one patient will be exposed to HIV is very low, the cumulative risk is within a range that the ADA would allow some reasonable public health regulation. The probability of the risk, to be sure, remains low, but the severity of the harm is high. The human rights burden on the individual is significant because, in the absence of retraining and reassignment, an entire career can be lost.

The ADA may sensitively handle even this perplexing case by requiring reasonable accommodations in order to allow the professional to continue practicing noninvasive medicine. This may require the health-care provider to offer the surgeon or dentist retraining to perform noninvasive or administrative functions and to provide reasonable compensation. Providers may also be required to accommodate HIV-infected professionals in the practice of non-invasive procedures by requiring counseling and monitoring of strict infection-control techniques.

THE FOOD-HANDLERS CONTROVERSY AND THE
PREEMPTION CLAUSE: A FEDERALIST APPROACH

A dissenting view in the House Judiciary Committee stated that a person with AIDS should not be transferred to another job out of a food-handling position even if the employer continued to pay the same wages. This would be the "ultimate undue hardship." "Unfortunately, there are many Americans who panic at the mention of the AIDS and would refuse to patronize any food establishment if an employee were known to have the virus." This policy will "translate to no customers and no business at all."[78]

Congress, therefore, was not simply concerned with the potential danger to the public of airborne disease, but also with the business interests of the food establishment. The argument that customer preference can justify discrimination has been thoroughly repudiated by the courts. Employers cannot accede to the prejudices of customers who prefer white people to black people, men to women, or able-bodied people to those in wheelchairs. Nor can the "repulsive" face of a person with neurofibromatosis ("elephant disease") or hatred of persons with drug dependency and AIDS justify discrimination.

The House amendment (the "Chapman Amendment") to the ADA, but not the Senate bill, specified that it shall not be a violation of the ADA for an employer to refuse to assign or continue to assign any employee with an infectious or communicable disease of public health significance to a job involving food handling, provided the employer makes reasonable accommodation to offer a comparable alternative employment opportunity.[79] The House acceded to the Senate with the following amendment: The Secretary of Health and Human Services must publish a list of infectious and communicable diseases that are transmitted through handling of the food supply, specifying the methods by which such diseases are transmitted, and widely disseminating the information about the dangers and their modes of transmission.[80]

The ADA authorizes employers to refuse to assign individuals to a job involving food handling if they have a presently infectious condition that is listed as transmissible through the food supply.[81]

The Chapman Amendment contained a misconception of disability law that it is permissible to fire an employee if the reason for the discrimination is not the employer's biases, but protection of the business from the irrational fears of patrons. The courts do not allow employers to succumb to customers' wholly unsubstantiated fears as a justification for discrimination, even if this involves picketing the establishment,[82] a large increase in health insurance or other benefits costs,[83] or adverse publicity.[84] Exclusion of HIV-infected food handlers was not condoned under the Rehabilitation Act and state disability law because there was no evidence that infection could be transmitted through food.[85]

The purpose of the food-handlers compromise was to ensure the American public that "valid scientific and medical analysis, using accepted public health methodologies and statistical practices regarding risk of transmission" will be brought to bear in analyzing foodborne transmission of disease.[86] This is the same standard that ought to be applied to future public health decision making.

What emerged as a problem of significant import was the interaction between the ADA and state or municipal public health statutes. Federal laws, unless they specify otherwise, preempt state and local statutes with comparable coverage. The ADA specifies that state or local law that creates "*greater* protection for the rights of individuals with disabilities" is not preempted.[87] The question arises whether public health laws that *restrict* the rights of a person with a disability more than the ADA allows is preempted. The simple answer is that all state and local public health law restricting the rights of persons with communicable diseases in ways that are inconsistent with the ADA will be invalidated by federal courts. Although the preemption provision in section 103(c)(3) applies only to food handlers, it illustrates clearly the interaction of the entire ADA with public health law. That section specifies that state, county, or local law or regulation designed to protect the public health from individuals who pose a significant risk of contamination of the food supply is not overruled or modified by the ADA.

The House Conference Report emphasizes that section 103(c)(3) "clearly defines certain types of existing and prospective state and local public health laws that are not preempted by the ADA."[88] The public health law must be designed to protect the community from significant public health risks that cannot be eliminated by reasonable accommodation. This preemption strategy supports legitimate state and local laws and regulations designed to protect the public from communicable disease, thus carrying out "both the letter and the spirit" of the ADA,[89] and promising a future of a more enlightened public health regulation.

A superficial examination of the ADA might lead to the conclusion that it interferes with the classic constitutional principle that the state has sole police-power authority to preserve the public health. True federalism, however, provides states with ample authority to regulate public health, but only within national guidelines ensuring that decisions are based upon rigorous public health evidence, rather than on false perception, unsubstantiated fears, or pure prejudice. Properly understood, the ADA strikes a constitutional balance that can only generate better and more consistent public health decision making.

CONCLUSION AND IMPLICATIONS FOR REGULATION WRITERS

The Americans with Disabilities Act emerges as far more effective than deferential constitutional analysis in reviewing public health powers. The standard of review proposed here should be reflected in future regulations on the ADA and comparable state statutes. The concept of direct threat should be expressly extended to include public services (title II). In construing "direct threat," regulations should explicitly place the burden of proof on public health authorities. Public health officials would have the burden of demonstrating significant risk by rigorous scientific assessment. The following elements would have to be established:

1. The mode of transmission is well established.
2. The person is currently contagious and is likely to remain so for the duration of the control measure.
3. A reasonable likelihood exists that the person will actually transmit the disease if the control measures are not applied.
4. The transmission of disease may result in serious harm.
5. The costs and human rights burdens are not disproportionate to the public health benefit to be achieved.

This regulatory standard is exacting and requires the public health department to have a clear basis for the exercise of its powers. The reason for the more focused review is that the ADA re-states the fundamental question that courts must ask of public health regulators. No longer must the courts ask what risks an uninformed, perhaps prejudiced, public is prepared to tolerate; or whether some loose nexus exists between the compulsory power and the public health objective.

Instead, courts must search for scientifically convincing evidence of harm to the public to justify depriving persons with disabilities of equal opportunities. Once the issue is framed as coming with the corpus of anti-discrimination law, rather than the vague and undifferentiated traditions of the police powers, a whole new way of thinking about public health law becomes possible.

NOTES

1. P.L. 101–336, 104 Stat. 327, 42 U.S.C. 12101 et seq. 101st Cong.: an act to establish a clear and comprehensive prohibition of discrimination on the basis of disability.
2. The ADA does not repeal the body of antidiscrimination legislation that preceded it. The Federal Rehabilitation Act of 1973 proscribes discrimination against persons with "handicaps" (defined almost identically to "disability") by entities that are in receipt of federal financial assistance and does not reach into the purely private sector. The principal application of the Rehabilitation Act in the post-ADA era will be to protect those employees of the federal government who have disabilities because they are not covered by the ADA (§101[5][B][i]).

   Discrimination against persons with disabilities in housing is dealt with under the Federal Fair Housing Amendments of 1988. See *Baxter v. Belleville*, 1989 U.S.D.C. LEXIS 10298 (S.D. Ill. 1989).

   The Education for All Handicapped Children Act, 20 U.S.C. para. 1400 et seq. gives all school-aged handicapped children the right to a free public education in the least restrictive environment appropriate to their needs. See *Martinez v. School Board of Hillsborough County, Florida*, 861 F.2d 1502 (11th Cir. 1988), reversing 711 F. Supp. 1293 (M.D.Fla. 1989); *Community High School District v. Denz*, 124 Ill. App. 3d 1291, 463 N.E.2d 998 (2d Dist. Ill, 1984) (legislation and the judicial decisions construing them are referred to as the corpus of antidiscrimination law).
3. P.L. 101–336, §2(a)(8),(9).
4. See *Jew Ho v. Williamson*, 103 F.10 (C.C.N.D. Cal. 1900).
5. Id. at 22. Indeed, the House Energy and Commerce Committee rejected an amendment offered by Congressman Dannemeyer that would have expressly excluded currently contagious and sexually transmitted diseases or infections from the definitions of "disability." U.S. House of Representatives, May 15, 1990: *The Americans with Disabilities Act of 1989: Report of the Energy and Commerce Committee*, no. 101–485, part 4 (to accompany H.R. 2273), Washington. (Hereafter called Energy Report.)
6. See, e.g., *Strathis v. Department of Transportation*, 716 F.2d 227, 232–234 (3d Cir. 1983); *Doe v. New York University*, 666 F.2d 761, 775 (2d Cir. 1981).
7. *School Board of Nassau County, Florida v. Arline*, 480 U.S. 273 (1987) (school

teacher with tuberculosis was handicapped within the meaning of section 5.4 of the Rehabilitation Act).

8. *New York State Association for Retarded Children v. Carey*, 612 F.2d 644 (2d Cir. 1979) (mentally retarded children who are carriers of serum hepatitis B could not be excluded from public school because they were handicapped and did not pose a health hazard); *Jeffrey S., a minor by Ernest S., his father v. State Board of Education of Georgia*, 896 F.2d 507 (11th Cir. 1990) (ordered trial on the merits in case involving alleged exclusion from school because, inter alia, child was a carrier of hepatitis B); *Lussier v. Dugger*, 904 F.2d 661 (11th Cir. 1990) (Civil Rights Restoration Act of 1987 applied to corrections officer who alleged discrimination because he had infectious hepatitis disease); *Kohl v. Woodhaven Learning Center*, 865 F.2d 930 (8th Cir. 1989), reversing in part 672 F. Supp. 1221 (W.D. M.O. 1987) (inoculation of school staff for hepatitis not a "reasonable accommodation.")

9. See, e.g., *Doe v. Centinela Hospital*, 57 U.S.L.W. 2034 (C.D. Cal. 1988); *Chalk v. United States District Court*, 840 F.2d 701 (9th Cir. 1988).

10. *Bey v. Bolger*, 540 F. Supp. 910 (E.D. Pa. 1982).

11. *Alexander v. Choate*, 469 U.S. 287 (1985).

12. The Supreme Court in *Arline* cited remarks of Senator Mondale describing a case in which a woman "crippled by arthritis" was denied a job *not* because she could not do work, but because "college trustees [thought] 'normal students shouldn't see her.' " 118 Cong. Rec. 36761 (1972).

13. U.S. Senate, August 30, 1989: *The Americans with Disabilities Act of 1989: Report of the Labor and Human Resources Committee*, no. 101–116 at 24, Washington. (Hereafter called Labor Report.) This report cited examples of individuals with controlled diabetes or epilepsy "often denied jobs for which they are qualified. Such denials are the result of negative attitudes and misinformation." In an appendix to the regulations on the Rehabilitation Act, the Department of Health and Human Services specifically listed a number of diseases to which the Act applied, including epilepsy, cerebral palsy, muscular dystrophy, multiple sclerosis, cancer, heart disease, and diabetes. 45 CFR, part 84, App. A, at 310 (1985).

14. *School Board v. Arline*, 107 S.Ct. 1123, 1134 (1987), Rehnquist J., dissenting.

15. Lower courts had already found that contagious diseases were handicaps. See, e.g., *New York State v. Carey*, 612 F.2d 644 (2d Cir. 1979).

16. *School Board v. Arline*, 480 U.S. 273, 282 (1987).

17. Id. at 318.

18. Id. at 284.

19. This concept derives from *Southeastern Community College v. Davis*, 442 U.S. 397 (1979).

20. Labor Report at 23, supra note 13.

21. *School Board v. Arline*, 480 U.S. 273, 284 (1987).

22. Labor Report at 24, supra note 13.

23. Opinion of Charles J. Cooper, Assistant Attorney General, Office of Legal Counsel, for Ronald E. Robertson, General Counsel, Department of Health and Human Services, June 23, 1986.

24. Id. at 282, note 7.
25. Report of the Presidential Commission on the Human Immunodeficiency Virus (June 24, 1988).
26. Letter from C. Everett Koop to Douglas Kamiec, Acting Assistant Attorney General, July 29, 1988.
27. Memorandum for Arthur B. Calvahouse, Jr., Counsel to the President, from Douglas W. Kamiec, Acting Assistant Attorney General, Office of the Legal Counsel, re Application of Section 504 of the Rehabilitation Act to HIV-Infected Individuals, September 27, 1988. The concept of "direct threat" as a qualification standard is discussed below.
28. P.L. 100–259.
29. Civil Rights Restoration Act of 1987, P.L. 100–259, para. 557 (March 22, 1988).
30. See, e.g., *Doe v. Centinela Hospital,* 57 U.S.L.W. 2034 (D.C. Cal. 1988). See also Gostin (1990).
31. P.L. 101–336, §§102, 202.
32. Title I requires qualification standards, employment tests, or other selection criteria to be "job related" and "consistent with business necessity." See P.L. 101–336, §102 (b)(6). Title II requires the disabled person to meet the "essential eligibility requirements" for the receipt of services or the participation in programs or activities.
33. P.L. 101–336, §102 (b) (5).
34. Id., § 201 (2).
35. Id., §102 (b)(5)(A).
36. See Barton, Dannemeyer, and Ritter in Energy Report at 126, supra note 5.
37. P.L. 101–336, §§103(b), 302 (b)(3).
38. See U.S. House of Representatives, July 12, 1990: *The Americans with Disabilities Act of 1989: Conference Report,* no. 101–596 (to accompany S. 933) at 11, Washington. (Hereafter called Conference Report.)
39. *Doe v. New York University,* 666 F.2d 761, 777 (2d Cir. 1981).
40. Energy Report at 37, supra note 5.
41. See *Southeastern Community College v. Davis,* 442 U.S. 397 (1979).
42. P.L. 101–336, §§102(b)(5), 302(b)(2)(A)(ii).
43. P.L. 101–336, §101(9); Committee on Labor and Human Resources (to accompany S.933), August 30, 1989, at 31.
44. *Kohl v. Woodhaven Learning Center,* 865 F.2d 930 (8th Cir. 1989).
45. *Arline,* 107 S.Ct. at 1131, note 16.
46. P.L. 101–336, §101(10).
47. Supra, note 41.
48. Supra, note 44.
49. *New York State v. Carey,* 612 F.2d 644 (2d Cir. 1979).
50. See U.S. House of Representatives, May 15, 1990: *The Americans with Disabilities Act of 1989: Report of the Judiciary Committee,* no. 101–485, part 3 (to accompany H.R. 2273), at 26, 51, 52, Washington (hereafter called Judiciary Report); U.S. House of Representatives, May 15, 1990: *The Americans with Disabilities Act of 1989: Report of the Education and Labor Committee,* no. 101–485, part 2 (to accompany H.R. 2273) at 121, Washington (hereafter

called Education Report). The term "direct threat" is also found in the Civil Rights Restoration Act of 1988 and the Fair Housing Amendments of 1988.

51. Conference Report at 11, supra note 38. In the House, the standard of "direct threat" was extended by the Judiciary Committee to all individuals with disabilities, and not simply to those with contagious diseases or infection. U.S. House of Representatives. May 15, 1990. Judiciary Report at 51, supra note 50.

52. P.L. 101–336, §101(3). The report of the Senate Labor and Human Resources Committee suggests that direct threat to property may also be sufficient. Labor Report, at 27, supra note 13.

53. P.L. 101–336, §302(b)(3).

54. See, e.g., Judiciary Report at 51 (direct threat must be based on objective and accepted public health guidelines). Supra, note 50.

55. The legislative history is replete with statements that reject decision making based upon ignorance, misperceptions, and patronizing attitudes. See Labor Report at 27, supra note 20; Judiciary Report at 52, 153, supra note 50; Energy Report, at 38, supra note 5; Education Report at 77, 121, supra note 50.

56. *School Board v. Arline*, 480 U.S. 273, 285 (1987).

57. *Hall v. U.S. Postal Service*, 857 F.2d 1073, 1079 (6th Cir. 1988), quoting *Arline*. See also *Mantolete v. Bolger*, 757 F.2d 1416 (9th Cir. 1985); *Strathe v. Dept. of Transportation*, 716 F.2d 227 (3d Cir. 1983).

58. See Judiciary Report at 52, supra note 50; Labor Report at 27, supra note 20; Education Report at 77, supra note 50.

59. See Judiciary Report at 53, supra note 50.

60. *School Board Arline*, 480 U.S. 273, 287 (1987).

61. *Chalk v. U.S. District Court*, 840 F.2d 701 (9th Cir. 1988).

62. Although the "direct threat" standard is not framed as a defense in title III, it is reasonable to conclude that Congress intended that the public accommodation should bear the burden of substantiating a direct threat.

63. Judiciary Report at 53, supra note 50 ("the decision to exclude cannot be based on merely 'an elevated risk of injury' ").

64. The following discussion is based upon the amicus curiae brief of the American Medical Association in *Arline*, and the discussions in several of my previous works. (See Gostin 1986a; 1989a,b.)

65. See, e.g., *United States v. Moore*, 846 F.2d 1163 (8th Cir. 1988), *affirming*, 669 F. Supp. 289 (D. Minn. 1987) (holding that the mouth and teeth of an HIV-infected person could be regarded as a "dangerous" or "deadly weapon"); *Indiana v. Haines*, 545 N.E. 2d 834 (Ind. App. 2d Dist. 1989) (reinstating a conviction for "attempted murder" for splattering emergency workers with HIV-contaminated blood).

66. See, e.g., *Thomas v. Atascadero Unified School District*, 662 F. Supp. 376 (C.D. Cal. 1986) (unlawful to exclude HIV-infected kindergartner who bit another child and was labeled "aggressive").

67. See, e.g., *People v. Dunn*, Florida Criminal Case, Associated Press release, September 28, 1987 reported in Gostin, Porter, and Sandomire (1990): prisoner convicted of introducing "contraband" into a state facility by lacing

guards' coffee with HIV-contaminated blood. See further discussion of food workers in the section on the food-handlers controversy below.

68. This principle is discussed and a line of cases cited in Gostin (1987, at 467).

69. Id., at 80–483; ex parte Company 106 Ohio St. 50, 139 N.E. 204 (1922).

70. *Smith v. Emery*, 11 A.D. 10, 42 N.Y.S. 258 (1896).

71. *Arline*, 480 U.S. at 287, note 16.

72. The range of risk for HIV transmission following a needle stick is between 0.03 to 0.9 percent, compared with 12–17 percent for HBV transmission. See Gostin (1989a).

73. The AMA amicus brief in *Arline* is silent as to the impact of public health regulation on individual rights.

74. *Martinez v. School Board of Hillsborough County, Florida*, 861 F.2d 1502 (11th Cir. 1988).

75. This balancing of benefits and burdens is further explained in Brandt, Cleary, and Gostin (1990).

76. *Leckelt v. Board of Commissioners of Hospital District 1*, 714 F. Supp. 1377 (E.D. La. 1989), aff'd, 909 F.2d 820 (5th Cir. 1990).

77. Association of the Bar of NY City, letter to William Roper, Nov. 26, 1990; NY State AIDS Institute, letter to James Curran, Sept. 24, 1990.

78. See Judiciary Report, at 146–47, supra note 50 (dissenting views of Hon. Chuck Douglas).

79. See Conference Report, at 12–13, supra note 38.

80. P.L. 101–336, §103(d)(1).

81. P.L. 101–336, §103(d)(2).

82. *Mosby v. Joe's Westlake Restaurant*, Cal. Super. Ct., San Francisco County, No. 865045, reported in Gostin (1990).

83. *State Division of Human Rights v. Xerox Corporation*, 480 N.E. 2d 695, 697098 (Ct. App. N.Y. 1985).

84. *Shannon v. Charter Real Hospital*, Human Rights Commission, Dallas, April 28, 1986.

85. See, e.g., *Little v. Bryce and Randall's Food Market*, 733 E.2d 937 (Tex. App. Hous. 1st Dist. 1987); *Wolfe v. Tidewater Pizza*, Sup.Ct. of VA: January 1988.

86. Conference Report at 14, supra note 38.

87. P.L. 101–336, §501 (b) (emphasis added).

88. Conference Report at 17–18, supra note 38.

89. Id.

REFERENCES

Bayer, R. 1989. *Private Acts, Social Consequences: AIDS and the Politics of Public Health*. New York: Free Press.

Brandt, A. 1985. *No Magic Bullet: A Social History of Venereal Disease in the United States since 1880*. New York: Oxford University Press.

Brandt, A., P. Cleary, and L. Gostin. 1990. Routine Hospital Testing for HIV:

Health Policy Considerations. In *AIDS and the Health Care System*, ed. L. Gostin, 125–42. New Haven: Yale University Press.

Burris, S. 1985. Fear Itself: AIDS, Herpes, and Public Health Decisions. *Yale Law and Policy Review* 3:479.

———. 1989. Rationality Review and the Politics of Public Health. *Villanova Law Review* 34:933–82.

Centers for Disease Control. 1990. Possible Transmission of HIV to a Patient during an Invasive Dental Procedure. *Morbidity and Mortality Weekly Reports* 39:489–93.

Cimons, R. 1990. U.S. 'Leaning' toward a Plan to Test Surgeons for AIDS. *Los Angeles Times* (December 6): 1A.

Cruse, F. 1980. The Epidemiology of Wound Infection. *Surgical Clinics of North America* 60:27.

Gostin, L. 1986. The Case against Compulsory Casefinding in Controlling AIDS: Testing, Screening and Reporting. *American Journal of Law & Medicine* 12(1):7, at 21–24.

———. 1987. The Future of Public Health Law. *American Journal of Law and Medicine* 12:461.

———. 1989a. Hospitals, Health Care Professionals, and AIDS: The "Right to Know" the Health Status of Professionals and Patients. *Maryland Law Review* 48(1):12 at 17.

———. 1989b. The Politics of AIDS: Compulsory State Powers, Public Health and Civil Liberties. *Ohio State Law Journal* 49(4): 1017 at 1020–26.

———. 1989c. HIV-infected Physicians and the Practice of Seriously Invasive Procedures. *Hastings Center Report* 19:32–39.

———. 1990. The AIDS Litigation Project: A National Review of Court and Human Rights Commission Decisions. Part 2: Discrimination. *Journal of the American Medical Association* 263:2086–93.

Gostin, L. L. Porter, and H. Sandomire. 1990. *The AIDS Litigation Project*. Washington.

Merritt, D.J. 1986. Communicable Disease and Constitutional Law: Controlling AIDS. *New York University Law Review* 61:739.

Musto, D. 1973. *The American Disease: Origins of Narcotic Control*. New Haven: Yale University Press.

Parmet, W. 1989. Legal Rights and Communicable Disease: AIDS, the Police Power, and Individual Liberty. *Journal of Health Politics, Policy & Law* 14:741–71.

ACKNOWLEDGMENTS

The author is grateful to Renee Solomon, Theo Kennedy, and Ann Gamertsfelder for research assistance, and to San Juanita Rangel for technical and editorial assistance.

IV. Reinforcements for the Mandate

The ADA is not only affordable, we literally cannot afford not to have it. It is the status quo discrimination and segregation that are unaffordable that are preventing persons with disabilities from becoming self-reliant, and that are driving us inevitably towards an economic and moral disaster of a giant, paternalistic welfare bureaucracy.

Justin Dart, chairperson of the President's Committee on Employment of People With Disabilities, testifying before Congress on May 9, 1989.

Tax Incentives

Daniel C. Schaffer

EDITOR'S NOTE

Some commentators have claimed that the Americans with Disabilities Act (ADA) is "morality on the cheap" — that Congress has mandated behaviors that will cost money, but has avoided finding money to foot the bill. With the enactment of the new access credit, Congress acknowledged that compliance with ADA could cost businesses, particularly small businesses, and moved to provide some relief, through the tax code, for compliance.

Daniel C. Schaffer examines the new access credit as well as two other provisions of the tax code (the section 190 deduction and the Targeted Jobs Tax Credit), which are related to the goals of the ADA. He suggests that an examination of the impact of these provisions would be an opportunity to examine the fundamental question of the efficacy of using the tax code to promote social policy. He proposes that monitoring the utilization of these provisions could provide valuable information about how the ADA is being implemented.

Schaffer is a tax lawyer, professor of law at Northeastern University Law School, and a member of the section on taxation of the American Bar Association. He is the author of numerous articles that have appeared in the American Journal of Tax Policy, *the* Tax Law Review, Taxes, *the* Tax Lawyer, *and the* Journal of Health Politics, Policy and Law.

Congress has often used the Internal Revenue Code as a means of promoting social and economic goals. Since 1976 Congress has reduced the tax burden of businesses that remove barriers to persons with disabilities (section 190 of the Revenue Code), and since 1978 it has reduced the taxes of businesses that hire certain subgroups of persons with disabilities (the Targeted Jobs Tax Credit—TJTC). In 1990, shortly after the enactment of the Americans with Disabilities Act (ADA), a new tax credit, the "access credit," was enacted to provide tax relief to small businesses that incur eligible costs when complying with the ADA. This article examines these provisions of the Revenue Code —provisions that complement the key policy goal of the ADA: full participation of persons with disabilities in the mainstream of American life.

THE DEDUCTION AND CREDIT FOR ADA-RELATED COSTS

Soon after Congress enacted the ADA, it turned its attention to providing relief for small businesses that incur expenses in complying with the Act. The Revenue Reconciliation Act of 1990 added an "access credit" (section 44) to the code, which enables small businesses to claim credit against taxes for one half of the first $10,000 of eligible costs of complying with the ADA.[1] The addition of the credit was offset by a reduction of the existing section 190 accessibility deduction from $35,000 to $15,000, making the change revenue neutral.[2]

TERMS OF THE DEDUCTION AND CREDIT

Section 190 of the Internal Revenue Code, first enacted in 1976,[3] allowed a business to deduct in the year incurred any "barrier removal expenses . . . for the purpose of making any facility or public transportation vehicle . . . accessible, and usable by handicapped and elderly individuals."[4] The deduction was limited to $25,000 per year when first enacted; in 1984 Congress raised the limit to $35,000 per year,[5] where it remained until the 1990 legislation.[6]

The reason for the 1976 enactment was expressed as follows:

In spite of previous federal legislation to contend with the problem of architectural and transportational barriers to the handicapped and elderly, such barriers remain widespread in business and industry . . . [C]reating a tax incentive for a limited period could promote more rapid modification of business facilities and vehicles. [The removal of barriers had to meet the standards promulgated] by the Secretary [of the Treasury] with the concurrence of the Architectural and Transportation Barriers Compliance Board. . . . [7]

The Treasury regulations interpret the statute to mean the deduction may be taken only for the cost of adapting existing premises. "It does not include any part of any expense . . . in connection with the construction or comprehensive renovation of a facility or . . . vehicle."[8] This is a reasonable interpretation because section 190 speaks of "removal" of barriers,[9] and the legislative history just quoted refers to "modification."

The 1990 Act changed this statutory scheme in four ways.

1. It added the new section 44 to the Code, providing a credit against tax for 50 percent of eligible expenditures that exceed $250 but are not greater than $10,250. (For the difference between a tax deduction and a tax credit see the discussion below.)
2. This credit is allowed only to small businesses, unlike the section 190 deduction, which is allowed to firms of any size.[10]
3. It reduced the limit on the section 190 deduction from $35,000 to $15,000. Thus, for larger firms, the 1990 legislation lowered the section 190 deduction and did not add a credit as it did for small businesses.
4. The expenses for which the new access credit may be taken ("eligible access expenditures") are defined more broadly than the expenses for which section 190 allows a deduction. They include not only the removal of physical barriers (as under section 190), but also "all amounts paid for the cost of enabling [the taxpayer] . . . to comply with applicable requirements under" the ADA.[11] This extends tax relief for the first time to the kind of expenses the ADA calls "auxiliary aids and services": interpreters for individuals with hearing impairments, readers and taped texts for individuals with visual impairments, acquisition or modification of equipment or devices, and other similar services and actions.[12]

There are two restrictions on the kind of expenses for which the credit may be taken. First, no credit is allowed for the cost of removing "architectural, communication, physical or transportation barriers" in connection with "any facility first placed in service after the date of enactment" of the Revenue Reconciliation Act of 1990.[13] The credit, like the section 190 deduction, is not allowable for costs incurred when making new construction accessible to persons with disabilities. The reason is that the cost of retrofitting existing facilities is significantly higher than the cost of making new construction accessible to persons with disabilities. (For a further discussion of the cost of making new construction accessible, see the article by Burgdorf in this volume.)

Second, only "reasonable" costs, not "unnecessary" ones can be used in computing the credit.[14] Because section 44 extends only to expenses incurred for the purpose of enabling a business to comply with the ADA,[15] a requirement that expenses be reasonable and necessary will probably not have a significant effect on the expenditures eligible for the credit.

Representatives of persons with disabilities joined with representatives of small businesses in support of the new access credit, which had originally been discussed during congressional consideration of the ADA. Both the House and Senate determined that the credit would be considered separately from the ADA, and after its passage. The final credit that was enacted represents the merger of a number of bills introduced to provide tax relief for ADA-related expenditures.[16] The credit was enacted as part of the Revenue Reconciliation Act of 1990, three months after the ADA was enacted.

Although all provisions of the ADA did not take effect at the time of enactment (firms are given time to comply by phasing in the Act's effective dates of requirements), the access credit took effect on November 5, 1990, the date of enactment of the 1990 Revenue Act. This timing was deliberate. The sponsors of the credit wanted to give a benefit to small businesses that complied with the ADA even before they were under a legal obligation to do so.[17]

In summary, small businesses have both the access credit and the deduction available to them for ADA-related costs. The access credit can be utilized for a wide range of expenditures ("eligible access expenditures"), whereas the deduction is only available for the removal of physical barriers. Big businesses have only the deduction available to them. When claimed for the removal of physical barriers, both the

TABLE 1
Comparison of Credits and Deductions

	1[a] No deduction or credit	2[a] Deduction	3[b] Credit	4[c] Deduction at 15%
1. Income	$2.00	$2.00	$2.00	$2.00
2. Deduction	– (.0)	– (1.00)	– 0	– (1.00)
3. Taxable income	2.00	1.00	2.00	1.00
4. Tax at 34%	.68	.34	– .68	$ 0.5 (tax at 15%)
5. Tax credit	—	—	– (.50)	—
6. Tax after subtracting tax credit	.68	.34	.18	$0.15
7. Tax saving from deduction or credit	—	.34	.50	.15

Note: In all columns, the income before deductions is assumed to be $2.00. Column 1 shows result with neither a credit nor deduction, column 2 with a deduction, and column 3 with a credit for 50% of the $1.00 spent, as in §44. Notice that the subtraction of the deduction occurs before multiplying the tax rate times taxable income (lines 2, 3, and 4), whereas the credit is subtracted from the tax (lines 5 and 6).
[a]Tax rate = 34%.
[b]Tax rate = irrelevant.
[c]Tax rate = 15%.

deduction and the credit are available only for existing facilities, not for facilities that are new or undergoing extensive renovation.

DIFFERENCE BETWEEN A TAX DEDUCTION AND A TAX CREDIT

Both deductions and credits reduce income tax, but in different ways. The difference between a deduction (section 190) and a credit (new section 44) is that a deduction is subtracted from taxable income, whereas a credit is subtracted from tax. Allowing a firm a deduction for an expenditure of $1.00 reduces its taxable income by that amount, and reduces its tax by its tax rate (for corporations today, usually 34 percent) times the amount of the deduction: in this example, 34 percent of $1.00 or 34 cents. A credit of 50 percent of the $1.00 spent would reduce the firm's tax by 50 percent of $1.00, or 50 cents. (Compare columns 1, 2, and 3 of table 1.)

The advantage of taking a 50 percent credit instead of a deduction is even greater if the tax rate is lower. The rate is only 15 percent on corporate taxable income up to $50,000 and 25 percent on taxable income from $50,000 to $75,000. For a corporation with a taxable income below $50,000, deducting an expenditure of $1.00 reduces its tax by 15 cents. The change to a 50 percent credit increases the tax benefit to fifty cents. (Compare columns 3 and 4 of table 1.)

In summary, the amount of a deduction depends upon the tax rate, whereas the amount of a tax credit does not. (Column 3 of table 1 remains the same no matter what the tax rate, whereas columns 2 and 4 are quite different.) In general, the lower the income, the more advantage the credit has over a deduction. Thus, for small businesses, which are likely to have less income than large businesses, a credit is often more beneficial.

DIFFERENTIAL IMPACT ON SMALL BUSINESSES

The enactment of the new access credit in section 44 was the Congressional response to the concerns of small business about the costs of complying with the ADA. Small businesses eligible for the access credit are defined as those whose gross receipts are under $1 million or that have 30 full-time employees or less. Congressional sponsors of the tax credit crafted it to favor small business. Senator Pryor (D-Ark) noted that small business could "most use help and . . . will be called upon most often to accommodate the disabled. . . . Large businesses that may have benefitted slightly more under the $35,000 deduction . . . are already in a better position to comply with the ADA since most already employ or serve disabled persons."[18] In commenting on one of the access credit bills, the Small Business Legislative Counsel noted that "we are gravely concerned about the burden . . . [of ADA] upon small business. The . . . potential costs of compliance are significant. Your initiative will provide a positive incentive to comply with the law, and this may reduce the likelihood of chaos on Main Street and confrontations in the court house."[19]

In order to keep the new section 44 credit revenue neutral, Congress reduced the maximum deduction under section 190 from $35,000 to $15,000.[20] With both the credit and the deduction available to small businesses and only the deduction available to large businesses, Congress was clearly directing relief to the small businesses.

Small businesses with a low taxable income are favored most. Recall that under a credit for 50 percent of an expenditure, spending $1.00 reduces a firm's tax by 50 cents (50 percent of $1.00). If a corporation's income is less than $50,000, its tax rate is only 15 percent, and a deduction of $1.00 reduces its tax by only 15 cents (15 percent of $1.00). The corporate tax rate rises to 25 percent for taxable income above $50,000 and 34 percent for taxable income above $75,000. Even in the 34 percent bracket, the credit is better than a deduction: the credit for an expenditure of $1.00 reduces tax by 50 cents, while deducting $1.00 reduces tax by 34 cents.

Finally, the 1990 legislation increased the reward for small expenditures and reduced the reward for larger expenditures. This is the result of limiting the credit to $10,000 of costs while reducing the deductible amount from $35,000 to $15,000. This formulation benefits small businesses the most because their expenditures are likely to be small. A payment of $35,000 deducted under old section 190 would reduce tax by $11,900, assuming a tax rate of 34 percent. The 1990 Act offers a credit that reduces tax by $5,000 and a deduction that reduces tax by $5,100, for a total tax benefit of $10,100[21]

EFFECTIVENESS OF THE DEDUCTION AND CREDIT AS INCENTIVES

The most important question about the deduction and credit is whether they provide a benefit for persons with disabilities. In particular, do businesses provide more access to customers and employees with disabilities than they would if there were no such tax incentive? Currently, there are no data available to answer that question. We do not know how many business firms used the section 190 deduction in past years, nor the amount of the average deduction. The Internal Revenue Service does not break out these numbers in its annual Statistics of Income, and the Department of the Treasury has never published them.

One reason there is so little information about section 190 is that there have never been congressional oversight hearings at which the Department of the Treasury might have presented information. The Department of the Treasury has neither favored nor opposed it. There are no reports on its efficacy from the General Accounting Office, congressional committee staff, or in the secondary literature. The history of this bit of tax law confirms the observation of the late Stanley Surrey, who stated: "It can generally be said that less critical analysis is paid to . . . subsidies [delivered through tax law] than to almost any direct expenditure program one can mention."[22]

As far as we know, this deduction has never been expensive for the government, which suggests that it has not been widely used. When it was first enacted in 1976, it was expected to cost $11 million annually.[23] When Congress reinstated it in the Tax Reform Act of 1984 after a brief period of expiration and increased the deductible amount to $35,000, the Joint Committee on Taxation estimated the annual revenue loss as $16 million in 1985 and $7 million in 1986.[24] These are small amounts considering the number of business firms in the United States. In 1990, the National Federation of Independent Business asserted: "The credit was proposed because smaller businesses do not have enough taxable income to take full advantage of a deduction."[25] In predicting that the 1990 legislation would be revenue neutral, however, congressional revenue estimators seem to have expected that relatively few firms will use the credit. If, for example, the average credit claimed was $2,500 (half the maximum), no firm claimed a section 190 deduction, and the revenue loss from section 44 was $10 million (a hypothetical number based on the estimates published for the 1984 Act), only 4,000 firms would have claimed the credit. Considering that there may be over 16 million firms eligible for the credit, this is a small number indeed.[26]

One explanation of why the deduction has apparently not been widely used is that businesses have done little to provide access to persons with disabilities. If so, this may change with the enactment of the ADA, which was indeed the expressed reason for enacting the new credit. Other explanations for the apparent minimal usage of the deduction are that (1) it is unknown to businesses and (2) it is too much trouble to claim the relatively small amount deductible. These explanations seem unlikely because many small businesses retain accountants to prepare their tax returns — and accountants are generally well versed in the various deductions available to businesses.

Any evaluation of the deduction under the original section 190 and of the credit and deduction under new section 44 and revised section 190 will require an examination of criteria against which the provisions will be measured. Is it enough if they help small business, or must there be a concomitant rise in the employment and/or participation rate of persons with disabilities? Is it acceptable if they provide windfalls for what businesses would have done anyway? The legislative history indicates that the credit and deduction are intended to shift some of the financial burden of complying with ADA from small businesses to the government.[27] Wide usage of the credit and deduction would indicate that this goal was being met. However, data revealing wide usage of these provisions may or may not indicate movement toward the full participation goal of the ADA.

Determining whether usage of the credit and deduction are correlated to increased participation by persons with disabilities will require a detailed analysis. The purpose for which the claimed expenditures were made needs to be examined for its direct impact on persons with disabilities. For example, if the credit was utilized to provide reimbursement for a portion of the cost of purchasing equipment for an individual who was hired by a firm, it would be clear that claiming the credit was directly correlated with participation of a person with a disability. However, claiming the credit to add a ramp to a building may or may not be correlated with increased participation. In other words, the existence of the ramp does not necessarily mean that persons with disabilities entered the building and/or participated in the program or utilized the services.

Many factors need to be considered in examining the relationship of claims and participation. Time is one such factor. For example, people who use wheelchairs might not use the ramp in the first year (perhaps because they are unaware of it), but might use it in subsequent years.

An analysis of the nature of the claims would offer a revealing picture of the types of expenditures and accommodations taking place in a range of settings. Such an analysis could be quite useful in assessing the overall implementation of the ADA.

THE TARGETED JOBS TAX CREDIT AND PERSONS WITH DISABILITIES

DESCRIPTION OF THE TARGETED JOBS TAX CREDIT

The 1990 tax legislation also renewed another provision of the tax code intended to promote the participation of persons with disabilities — the Targeted Jobs Tax Credit (TJTC). Renewed until December 31, 1991 in the Revenue Reconciliation Act of 1990, this provision is intended to promote employment for persons with disabilities, among others.[28] As with the new credit and revised deduction under sections 44 and 190, enactment of the ADA may result in wider usage of TJTC for persons with disabilities. Like the deduction and credit, TJTC is a tax benefit available to employers, and not directly to persons with disabilities.

The TJTC was first enacted in 1978,[29] and has been periodically renewed since then.[30] In 1977, Congress had experimented with a tax credit for employers who increased the number of persons they employed, as a remedy for general unemployment. The TJTC was a shift to a credit for hiring members of specific disadvantaged groups with high levels of unemployment. The Senate Finance Committee's explanation for the change was that "the unemployment rate has declined sufficiently so that it is appropriate to focus employment incentives on those individuals who have high unemployment rates, or on other groups with special employment needs."[31] Most of the cost of the program derives from lost tax revenue, estimated at $81 million for 1991 and $104 million for 1992.

For reasons that I will review later in the article, the Department of the Treasury has opposed renewal of the credit since 1985. However, a coalition of businesses that use the credit and representatives of targeted beneficiaries has prevailed upon Congress to retain the credit. Although the efficacy of the credit in terms of increasing employment for the targeted groups is a subject of debate, the program holds considerable political appeal. Among the reasons for its appeal are that it addresses unemployment by subsidizing businesses directly and it targets the "hard core" unemployed, especially unemployed youth.[32]

An employer's credit against tax is 40 percent of the wages paid to an employee (up to $6,000) during the first year of employment. This would give a maximum tax credit of $2,400 per person hired; however, a deduction for wages paid is denied to the employer to the extent of the credit,[33] reducing the maximum tax benefit by about $800 ($2,400 times the rate of tax, usually 34 percent for corporations). Therefore, the actual maximum tax credit available under the TJTC per person per year is about $1,600. The first year of employment will usually extend over two of the employer's taxable years. If, for example, an employer who uses the calendar year as the taxable year hires an employee on July 16, 1990, and employs him through the end of 1991, the employer's tax return for 1990 would claim a credit based on wages paid from July 16, 1990 to the end of that year, and its return for 1991 would claim a credit based on wages paid from January 1, 1991 through July 15, 1991.

The TJTC is available to an employer who hires members of any of ten statutorily delineated groups that are vulnerable to high unemployment.[34] Although persons with disabilities may be in a number of the targeted groups, they are represented most often in the categories of "vocational rehabilitation referrals," defined to mean persons with a "disability which, for such individual, constitutes . . . a substantial handicap to employment" and who has completed or is receiving vocational rehabilitative services.[35] A second targeted group with a substantial proportion of persons with disabilities is the group of recipients of supplemental security income (SSI).[36] SSI is a cash-assistance program, administered by the federal government, which provides a minimum income to needy persons who are aged, blind or have disabilities.

CONCERNS ABOUT THE IMPACT AND UTILIZATION OF TJTC

Unlike the deduction under section 190, the efficacy of the TJTC as a method of yielding benefits for targeted groups has been discussed by Department of the Treasury officials, employers, representatives of the targeted groups, and in the secondary literature. In this section, I examine the information available related to the usage and efficacy of TJTC and the extent to which TJTC may benefit persons with disabilities.

Impact of TJTC. A frequently cited shortcoming of the TJTC is that it reaches only a small fraction of those whom it is intended to benefit. Economically disadvantaged youth (aged 18 to 24) form the largest of the groups for which TJTC is claimed (58.5 percent or 332,712 individuals in 1987).[37] Yet, in 1989 the Department of the Treasury reported that employers had claimed the credit for only about 8 percent of the disadvantaged youth who had found employment in 1981.[38] (The 1986 report on the credit by the Department of Treasury and the Department of Labor called this "lack of penetration.")[39] The Treasury interprets this to mean that for 92 percent of the disadvantaged youth hired, the TJTC was irrelevant.[40]

Persons with disabilities, as far as we can determine, constitute a relatively small proportion of those certified as members of TJTC targeted groups. In 1987, 6.9 percent of the total of TJTC-certified persons (39,448 individuals) were certified as members of the targeted group of "vocational rehabilitation referrals." Only 0.8 percent of the total (4,449 individuals) were in the target group of SSI recipients.

There is no study available that examines the impact of TJTC on the subgroup of persons with disabilities, nor on most other subgroups targeted by TJTC. Often the analyses and examinations of the group of economically disadvantaged youth are used as a surrogate for the whole program because this group has had the largest number of persons certified for TJTC.[41]

Another concern about the effect of the credit is that even if employers do hire members of the targeted groups whom they would not have otherwise hired, there may be no net increase in net employment of targeted workers (or, in another variation, workers generally). "If newly hired . . . targeted employees replace previously employed targeted employees who are no longer eligible for the credit or are hired in place of [other] targeted workers, targeted employment will not increase on a net basis."[42] The Congressional Budget Office speculated that net job creation occurred under TJTC,[43] but other commentators have noted that "little evidence exists to determine whether employers substituted TJTC eligible workers for other employees rather than creating additional jobs" (Levitan and Gallo 1987, 647).

THE TJTC: A WINDFALL TO EMPLOYERS?

Unlike most tax programs, the TJTC is not run by the Internal Revenue Service alone, but in conjunction with the Department of Labor and state job-security offices. An employer gets a tax credit if the state job-security agency "certifies" that the person to whom the employer pays wages is a member of a targeted group.[44] The employer must apply for a certificate on or before the first day the new employee starts work.[45]

Under this system firms may hire the applicants they prefer, later inquiring whether any bring with them the tax credit. An employer who finds that some of the new employees qualify, then asks the state employment security agency to certify those persons, making sure to submit the request on or before the day the employees begin work. This practice is called "retroactive certification."

Some employers go a step further. They use specialized firms to screen new employees, after they have been hired, to determine which of them will bring the tax credit. (These firms are said to be paid a fee contingent on the number of certifications they obtain.) A 1985 study of large users of the TJTC found that three quarters of them relied on this method.[46] A variation on this method was to send requests for certification of every new hire, letting the local state employment security agency sort out who qualifies and who does not.[47] (The Revenue Reconciliation Act of 1989 amended the statute to forbid this practice.)[48]

For employers who use retroactive certification, the tax credit functions as a windfall, in the sense that it pays them to do what they would have done in the absence of the credit. At this point, it seems to be

generally recognized that "requesting TJTC eligibility after hiring con-
tradicts the Act's intent of increasing job opportunities for those who
otherwise might not be hired" (Levitan and Gallo 1987, 645). Congress
attempted to forbid this practice in 1981, but the statutory language
used proved to be ineffective.[49]

In 1989 the Department of the Treasury recommended a prohibition
against retroactive certification.[50] If the retroactive certification were
prohibited, advance certification of eligible individuals by the state
job-security agencies would be the only avenue of certification. The
agency issues a "voucher" to the job seeker as a preliminary determination that the seeker is a member of a targeted group. The job seeker can
present the voucher when applying for a job, assuring an employer that
the agency will certify him or her as a member of a targeted group. The
TJTC would be allowed only where the state employment security
agency has issued a voucher to the person hired before that person
applied for a job. This proposal was not adopted by Congress, and the
issue of "retroactive certification" is still problematic for the TJTC.

The many questions raised about the efficacy of TJTC have led to
calls for repeal and reform from a range of quarters. The debate is often
highlighted when the credit expires and is considered by Congress for
extension, which will next occur at the end of 1991.

THE ADA AND THE TJTC

The interplay between the mandate of the ADA and the TJTC has
positive potential. As we move toward implementing ADA, we anticipate that employers increasingly will hire more persons with disabilities. Employers may also take greater advantage of TJTC, either as a
"windfall" (or subsidy for a behavior they would have engaged in without the credit), or as an effective incentive to change their behavior and
hire a person with a disability, perhaps even seek out a person with a
disability, which they might not have done otherwise.

Of course, the persons with disabilities who are targeted by the TJTC
comprise a smaller universe, probably considerably smaller, than the
persons with disabilities who are protected by the ADA. In addition,
the TJTC is available to an employer for only one year, whereas the
ADA antidiscrimination mandate is ongoing.

It is worthwhile to consider how these two statutes, in their implementation, may differ and be in need of reconciliation. An employer
who utilizes the TJTC by inquiring in advance whether a potential

employee is certified for TJTC may be in violation of the ADA. The ADA specifically prohibits preemployment "inquiries of a job applicant as to whether such an applicant is an individual with a disability."[51] One can imagine situations in which the closer a job interview comes to satisfying this clause of the ADA, the more a tax credit for hiring a person with a disability becomes a windfall to the employer.

Of course there are ways in which no conflict would exist because an employer may know about the TJTC certification of a potential employee without asking that employee. That information would be volunteered by the potential employee, the state employment-security agency, or, when it is making the referral to the employer, the vocational rehabilitation agency. In addition, it may be acceptable for the employer to inquire whether the person is certified for TJTC in general, and this might not be a violation of the ADA prohibition against preemployment inquiry regarding a disability. Because persons with disabilities make up such a small percentage of the total TJTC-certified population, an inquiry related to TJTC status would not serve as a proxy for an inquiry about disability status.

Although the use of a voucher that could be presented by the job applicant may be an appealing way to resolve this dilemma, vouchers bring their own set of drawbacks. At least one study indicates that employers discriminate against applicants who present TJTC vouchers. In 1985, an experiment was conducted whereby two groups were sent out to apply for jobs. One group presented TJTC vouchers to prospective employers and the control group did not. Members of the control group were hired about twice as frequently as applicants with vouchers (Burtless 1985). The result is striking, and has been interpreted by some to mean that a TJTC voucher is stigmatizing and results in the exact opposite of what is desired: discrimination and rejection from employment. For persons with disabilities, who already encounter discrimination on an all-too-regular basis, the addition of a TJTC voucher may have particular liability.

Although the extent of the benefit TJTC provides to persons with disabilities is unclear, nevertheless at least some employers are using it. With the addition of the ADA anti-discrimination mandate, employers may use the credit more widely. Close monitoring of the interaction of these two statutes will facilitate a better understanding of exactly how TJTC works for persons with disabilities and how it might be improved.

RECOMMENDATIONS AND CONCLUSION

It will be necessary to gather and analyze data to answer basic questions about the use and efficacy of the section 190 deduction, the new access credit, and the TJTC for persons with disabilities. In the case of the Section 190 deduction, it would be informative to know how many firms used the deduction each year, the amount of the average deduction, the amount of tax saved by the average firm using the deduction, and the industries that most widely claimed the deduction. These data could be obtained by examining tax returns that claim the deduction and the data should be made available as well for the new access credit as it begins to be used by employers.

Other questions would require empirical study that goes beyond data in the files of the Internal Revenue Service. What proportion did the credit or deduction represent of the average firm's cost of removing barriers or otherwise providing access to persons with disabilities? Did the firms claiming the credit or deduction experience increased participation by persons with disabilities? The Department of the Treasury should begin to monitor both the new access credit and the revised deduction, collecting and publishing information for a future evaluation of the statute.

The questions raised by critics of the TJTC should continue to be explored and more data about the utilization of the credit should be collected.[52] An in-depth examination of the interplay of TJTC and ADA would be instructive in terms of how it could be more effective in accomplishing increased employment for persons with disabilities.

Finally, an examination of the efficacy of these three provisions in the tax code would be an opportunity to consider the advantages and disadvantages of promoting social policy through the tax code, as opposed to direct appropriations. (This practice has been called "tax expenditure" [Surrey 1973].) Provisions in the tax code appear to receive less scrutiny in terms of their impact than programs funded through direct appropriations (for example, the vocational rehabilitation program). The section 190 deduction has been in place for over 14 years, apparently without any analysis of its utilization or impact. On the other hand, the vocational rehabilitation program, like many other programs that receive appropriated funds, is examined in depth through the reauthorization process every three to five years, and in the appropriations committees every year.

Congress clearly intended to lessen the financial burden of complying with ADA by enacting the new access credit. The section 190 deduction is available to firms that remove physical barriers. The TJTC is intended to result in increased employment for eligible persons with disabilities (among others). Clearly all three of these provisions in the tax code complement the ADA goal of full participation in the mainstream of American society by persons with disabilities. The challenge for implementation is to see that these provisions work in synchrony — the tax code and civil-rights law — as a powerful blend applied toward the fulfillment of a long-awaited promise.

NOTES

1. Revenue Reconciliation Act of 1990, P.L. 101–508, §11611 (a).
2. Id. at §11611 (c).
3. Tax Reform Act of 1976, P.L. 94–455, §§22 (a) & (c), 90 Stat. 1914.
4. I.R.C. §190 (b)(1).
5. Deficit Reduction Act of 1984, P.L. 98–369, §1062 (b), 90 Stat. 1047.
6. As a matter of financial analysis, section 190 is not about the deductibility of the cost of removing barriers. It is about the timing of the deduction. As a business expense the cost would be deductible under general principles of tax law even without section 190. It would, however, be capitalized and deducted over the remaining life of the structure modified. Section 190 changes this timing to allow more of the deduction to be taken in the year of expenditure. The advantage to the taxpayer is that taxable income is reduced in the year of the section 190 deduction, at the cost of not having the deduction in the later years in which it would ordinarily be taken. Tax is deferred by shifting from the year of the expenditure to later years. The benefit is purely a matter of the time value of money: it is better to pay later than to pay now because one can invest the unpaid tax until the time comes when it must be paid.
7. I.R.C. §190 (b)(2). Large parts of the obligatory prolix regulations were drawn from the American National Standards Institute (1971): American National Standard Specifications for Making Buildings and Facilities Accessible to, and Usable by, the Physically Handicapped. Treas. Reg. §1.190–2 (b)(1) (1979).
8. Treas. Reg. §190–2 (b) (1979).
9. I.R.C. §190 (a) & (b).
10. I.R.C. §44 (a) & (b).
11. I.R.C. §44 (a) & (c).
12. ADA, §3(1); I.R.C. §44 (c)(2).
13. I.R.C. §44 (a) & (c)(4).
14. I.R.C. §44 (a) & (c)(3).
15. I.R.C. §44 (a) & (c)(1).
16. E.g., S. 1661, 101st Cong., 1st Sess. (1989); H.R. 3500, 101st Cong., 1st Sess. (1989).

17. "Many small businesses will not be required to comply with the ADA for several years. The tax credit in this . . . bill, however, will immediately offer those businesses an incentive to make access expenditures . . . In this way the ADA tax credit . . . will reward small business for making those expenditures before they are required." Statement of Sen. Herb Kohl (D.Wisc.), 136 Cong. Rec. S 17520 (daily ed. Oct. 27, 1990).
18. 135 Cong. Rec. S 11710 (daily ed., Sept. 22, 1989).
19. Letter to Senator Pryor from Small Business Legislative Council dated Sept. 19, 1989, inserted in Congressional Record (daily ed., Sept. 22, 1989 at S 11711).
20. "Mr. Kohl: . . . Finally my proposal for an ADA tax credit follows what must become every politician's first commandment: Thou shall not deficit spend. The tax credit I propose can be paid for completely by placing a . . . cap on the current $35,000 annual deduction allowed [by section 190]" 136 Cong. Rec. 312851 (daily ed. Sept. 12, 1990).
21. The following are illustrative examples:
    a. A corporation that is a small business spends $40,000 in 1989 for making its premises accessible to persons with disabilities. It could deduct $35,000 of this amount, without regard to whether it was a small business or a large one. The deduction reduced its tax by 34 percent of $35,000, or $11,900. If its taxable income before the section 190 deduction had been less than $50,000, the deduction would have reduced its tax by only $5,250 (15 percent of $35,000).
    b. A corporation that is a small business spends $40,000 in complying with the ADA in 1991. It may take a credit against tax of $5,000 (50 percent of $10,000), under new §44 of the Code. This reduces its tax by $5,000. It may also deduct another $15,000 under the revised §190; this reduces its tax by another $5,100 (34 percent of $15,000), for a total tax reduction of $10,100.
    c. If the taxable income of the corporation in example 2 had been less than $50,000 before the §190 deduction, the deduction would reduce its tax by only $2,250 (15 percent of $15,000), and the total tax reduction from deduction and credit would have been $7,250.
    d. A corporation that is not a small business spends $40,000 in complying with the ADA in 1991. It may not use the credit under new §44, and its deduction under §190 is limited to $15,000, reducing its tax by $5,100.
    e. A corporation spent $11,000 in 1989 for making its premises accessible to persons with disabilities. It could deduct all of this, for a tax reduction of $3,740 without regard to whether it was a small business. If its taxable income was below $50,000 (before the §190 deduction) its tax reduction would be only $1,350.
    f. A corporation that is a small business spends $11,000 in 1991 in complying with the ADA. It may take a credit against tax of $5,000 (50 percent of $10,000) and a deduction of the remaining $1,000 under revised §190. Its tax reduction is $5,000 plus $340 (34 percent of $1,000), or $5,340.
    g. A corporation that is a small business spends $9,000 in 1991 for compliance with the ADA. It is allowed a credit against tax of $4,250 (50 percent of [$9,000 less $250]). Senator Kohl explained that the purpose of denying

the credit for the first $250 of costs "represents the commitment of both business and the Federal Government to the goals of the ADA—a commitment demonstrated by willingness of both the private and public sectors to spend the money needed to make those goals a reality." 136 Cong. Rec. S 12151, S 12852 (daily ed. Sept. 12, 1990).

22. Hearings before the Subcommittee on Priorities and Economy in Government of the Joint Economic Committee, 92d Cong., 1st Sess. 48 (1972) (statement of Stanley S. Surrey).

23. S. Rep. No. 938, 94th Cong., 2d Sess. 439 (1976).

24. Staff of Joint Committee on Taxation, 98th Cong., 2d, Sess., *General Explanation of the Revenue Provisions of the Deficit Reduction Act of 1984* 1177 (Comm. Print 1984).

25. Statement of Michael Roush, National Federation on Independent Business, before Senate Small Business Committee, Sept. 19, 1990, reprinted in *Tax Notes Today*, 194-25.

26. The Internal Revenue Service reports that for 1986 it received 16,639,000 returns from businesses with annual receipts of less than $1 million. (U.S. Department of Commerce, Bureau of the Census, 1990: *Statistical Abstract of the United States, 1990*, 110th ed, 521.) Although this figure does not take into account the number of employees of a firm, it provides a useful guide to the number of business that might be eligible for the access credit.

27. Revenue Reconciliation Bill of 1990, S. 3209, as approved by the Senate Finance Committee on October 13, 1990, 1990 Stand. Fed. Tax Rep. (CCH).

28. I.R.C. §51, as renewed by P.L. 101–508, §11405 (a)(1990).

29. Revenue Act of 1978, P.L. 99–600, §321, 92 Stat. 2830.

30. The credit expired at the end of 1985, and was retroactively renewed in October 1986.

31. S. Rep. No. 1263, 95th Cong., 2d Sess. 125 (1978).

32. For example:

Mr. Stark [Rep. Fortney H. (Pete) Stark, D-Calif]: As you may recall, I was lukewarm to cautious about this program last year. But now I am a convert. . . . I do not like tax credits . . . But I dislike these tax credits least because they do help . . . those who are most helpless. . . . I support the continuation of the job credits because of the cuts being made in other spending programs at a time that I think most people consider unemployment unacceptably high. This has become the only game in town. It is certifiably the most help to the most disadvantaged and handicapped in our society.

Extension of the Targeted Jobs Tax Credit: Hearing before the Subcommittee on Select Revenue Measures of the Committee on Ways and Means, 99th Cong., 1st Sess. 7 (1985).

33. I.R.C. §280C (a).

34. The groups are: (1) a vocational rehabilitation referral; (2) an economically disadvantaged youth; (3) an economically disadvantaged Vietnam-era veteran; (4) an SSI recipient; (5) a general assistance recipient; (6) a youth participating in a cooperative education program; (7) an economically disadvantaged ex-convict; (8) an eligible work-incentive employee; (9) an involuntarily terminated CETA employee; (10) a qualified summer youth employee.

35. I.R.C. §§51 (a), (b), (d)(1)&(2).
36. I.R.C. §51 (d)(5).
37. Joint Committee on Taxation, 1989: *Present Law and Issues Relating to the Targeted Job Tax Credit (H.R. 452, H.R. 815, and H.R. 2098)*, 22.
38. *Revenue and Spending Proposals for Fiscal Year 1990: Hearings Before the Senate Committee on Finance*, 101st Cong., 1st Sess. 195, 205 (1989) (statement of Dana L. Trier, Tax Legislative Counsel, Department of the Treasury) [hereinafter referred to as 1989 Treasury Statement]. This number was apparently taken from the Department of Treasury and Department of Labor, 1986: *The Use of Tax Subsidies for Employment* [referred to hereafter as the Joint Report].
39. Joint Report, supra note 38 at 90.
40. 1990 Treasury Statement, supra note 38 at 205.
41. A study by the Congressional Budget Office of the TJTC, for example, looked at the effect of the largest of the targeted groups (disadvantaged youth) because sufficient data existed only for that group. Congressional Budget Office, The Targeted Jobs Tax Credit 22, 20, 1984, reprinted in *Targeted Jobs Tax Credit Extension: Hearing before the Subcommittee on Select Revenue Measures of the Committee on Ways and Means*, 98th Cong., 2d Sess. 30, 57, 55 (1984) [hereafter cited as CBO report].
42. *Targeted Jobs Tax Credit: Hearings before the Subcommittee on Select Revenue Measures of the committee on Ways and Means*, 101st Cong., 1st Sess. 18, 26 (1989) (Statement of Thomas S. Neubig, Director, Office of Tax Analysis, Department of the Treasury) [hereafter referred to as 1989 OTA Statement].
43. CBO report, supra note 41 at 55–56.
44. I.R.C. §51 (d).
45. Id.
46. Joint Committee on Taxation, 1989: *Present Law and Issues Relating to the Targeted Jobs Tax Credit*, 18.
47. National Commission for Employment Policy, 1989: *The Targeted Jobs Tax Credit in Maryland and Missouri: 1982–1987* 73. This is an unusually rich and revealing study of the TJTC as it actually worked in two states.
48. I.R.C. §51 (d) (16) (c), enacted by P.L. 101–239, §7103(c) (1), 103 Stat. 2305.
49. I.R.C. §51 (d)(16), enacted by the Economic Recovery Tax Act of 1981, P.L. 97–34, §261 (c), 95 Stat. 172.
50. 1989 OTA Statement, supra note 42 at 18, 20.
51. ADA, §102 (c)(2). I am grateful to Daniel M. Fox for suggesting this point to me.
52. One observer has suggested the following: Congress should require the collection, dissemination, and analysis of data that would allow for better insights into TJTC operations. At a minimum, the following information is necessary to assess the effectiveness of TJTC: (a) job characteristics (including type of job, duration and wage rate); (b) firm characteristics (including type and size); (c) characteristics of vouchered individuals; (d) number eligible for TJTC and total requests for vouchers; (e) time required by public employment offices to respond to employer requests; (f) collection and analysis of post-hiring voucher requests and (g) more accurate estimates of revenue loss resulting from TJTC.

The General Accounting Office should be instructed to analyze the data and assess the program's effectiveness. *Targeted Jobs Tax Credit: Hearing before the Subcommittee on Select Revenue Measures of the Committee on Ways and Means,* 101st Cong., 1st Sess. 38, 41 (1989) (Statement of Sar A. Levitan).

REFERENCES

Burtless, G. 1985. Are Targeted Wage Subsidies Harmful? Evidence from a Wage Voucher Experiment. *Industrial and Labor Relations Review* 39:105–14.

Levitan, S., and F. Gallo. 1987. The Targeted Jobs Tax Credit: An Uncertain and Unfinished Experiment. *Labor Law Journal* (October): 641–49.

Surrey, S. 1973. *Pathways to Tax Reform*. Cambridge: Harvard University Press.

The Role of Technology in Removing Barriers

John C. De Witt

EDITOR'S NOTE

Technology is a powerful presence in our society, mediating how we work, play, and communicate. In the last decade the application of technology to the particular needs of persons with disabilities (generally called "assistive technology") has slowly gained momentum so that it is developing as a field in its own right. The combination of the emergence and development of assistive technology and the maturation of civil-rights protections for people with disabilities yields a depth and breadth of unique opportunity as we proceed with the implementation of the Americans with Disabilities Act (ADA).

John C. DeWitt examines "assistive technology" in the context of the ADA, other recent federal mandates, and daily application in businesses and public accommodations. Holding that the creative use of technology is a key to the success of the ADA, DeWitt offers considerable practical advice for implementation.

DeWitt is president of DeWitt, Mendelsohn & Associates, a private consulting firm in New Jersey specializing in assistive technology and related disability issues. A charter member of AT&T's Consumer Advisory Panel, DeWitt has evaluated a range of technologies from closed-circuit televisions to synthetic speech-computer products. A 1989 National Institute on Disability and Rehabilitation Research Switzer scholar, DeWitt has testified before Congress a number of times.

The success of the ADA as civil-rights legislation will depend
upon the creative use of technology, especially by American
businesses and public institutions, as much as upon the good
will of the general public. Technology is a powerful force throughout
American society. For people with disabilities the application of technology is particularly powerful. It may enable a person who previously
could not talk to do so, or a person who could not walk to become
otherwise mobile.

In this article, I consider the limitations of hearing, seeing, moving,
speaking and interpreting, especially in employment and public
accommodations. I examine the contribution technology can make to
the removal of barriers to equal opportunity and meaningful participation for people with disabilities.

For entities covered under the ADA, the essential questions, in terms
of technology are:

- In the workplace or public facility, is access or participation
  restricted for an individual with a disability?
- Would use of technology reduce or eliminate that individual's
  limitations for essential job tasks or participation in the use of a
  public facility?

Solutions abound that could meet the needs of most individuals with a
disability much of the time, especially for employment and education.
However, there remain challenges not yet fully addressed, especially in
places of public accommodation and transportation. Communication
barriers exist almost everywhere.

Within the disability community and among companies manufacturing and distributing technologies useful to persons with disabilities,
the term "assistive technology" has gained widespread use. Terms such
as "rehabilitation engineering" or "adaptive technology," which are less
inclusive, appear to be fading from use. Assistive technology can be
low-tech or high-tech. The term will be used throughout this article
and discussed more fully later. When the ADA refers to "auxiliary aids"
and "reasonable accommodations," it implicitly includes assistive
technology.

Assistive technology is a recently coined term. Shortly after World
War II, the term "tools and equipment" was used in vocational rehabilitation for veterans. In the blindness field, "aids and appliances" was
used from the late 1930s until 1979. About this same time, 1978,

"sensory and communications aids" were being provided through vocational rehabilitation services. With the passage of the 1986 amendments to the Rehabilitation Act of 1973, the term "rehabilitation engineering," already used in academia, was added to the lexicon.[1]

By 1988, when Congress passed the Technology-Related Assistance for Individuals with Disabilities Act ("Tech Act"), a coalition of disability-related organizations worked with Congress to develop a definition of "assistive technology devices and services" commonly called assistive technology.[2] Although the term "assistive technology devices and services" does not appear in the ADA, it should be thought of as a component of both "reasonable accommodation" and "auxiliary aids and services."

The Tech Act defines an "assistive technology device" as "any item, piece of equipment, or product system, whether acquired commercially off the shelf, modified, or customized, that is used to increase, maintain, or improve functional capabilities of individuals with disabilities."[3] A corollary concept is also defined: "Assistive technology service . . . means any service that directly assists an individual with a disability in the selection, acquisition, or use of an assistive technology device."[4] Later in this article, I shall discuss the important role "services" play in assistive technology. For now, it is useful to bear in mind that knowledge about how to find, select, acquire and use devices is *critical* to their successful deployment for persons with disabilities, American business, and public institutions.

TECHNOLOGY AND DISABILITY INEVITABLY LINKED

Society is increasingly impacted by technology. When a device assists us in functioning either physically or mentally, we are employing technology. Technology often makes the performance of tasks easier, but is sometimes itself a barrier. Imagine that you want to:

- *Hear* the sound of a stadium sports announcer or fire alarm in a hotel
- *See* the signs in a shopping mall or the screen of a PC
- *Move* from home to work on public transportation or ascend an escalator
- *Speak* into a telephone

- *Interpret* the array of buttons and switches on a photocopy machine

Similarly, imagine yourself doing these common everyday tasks without technology if you had a limitation in functioning:

- *Hearing* a normal conversation
- *Reading* print
- *Walking* across the room
- *Speaking* to someone
- *Interpreting* instructions

For centuries simple technologies have helped some individuals with disabilities gain access to the world about them: for instance, a walking stick, eye glasses, an ear trumpet, or a wooden leg, and more recently, prosthetic hands or wheelchairs.

To overcome barriers, including those created by technology itself, assistive technology devices are frequently employed to provide an alternative way of doing things. Some of these are:

- *Hearing* with use of a hearing aid, amplified telephone handset, infrared system in a theater
- *Reading* with the aid of large print, taped materials, synthetic speech added to a PC
- *Moving* in a wheelchair over curb cuts, onto a bus with a lift or into a building's elevator; using an alternative keyboard for data entry, or an implement to permit feeding oneself
- *Speaking* with use of an artificial electric larynx, amplified telephone transmitter, or augmentative communications board
- *Interpreting* through pictographs on a computer, a telephone auto-dialer, simple diagrams, concise language, or consistent symbol sets

How assistive technology is used differs from setting to setting. Telecommunications deployed for dual-party relay services and TV captioning under title IV of the ADA, requires a more limited range of assistive technology. However, within workplace settings and places of public accommodation, many of the same assistive technology solutions will be found applicable. Before providing many more examples, let's more closely define the term "assistive technology."

Assistive technology devices are not simple to define in practice. Removing the casters from a chair may make it easier for an individual with balance difficulties to rise more easily and stand. Is that assistive technology or merely a technique? An operator-style telephone headset makes it convenient for an individual to take notes with one hand and use the other to operate an artificial larynx. Is this assistive technology or merely using common sense? Is a pacemaker assistive technology or a life-sustaining medical procedure? Most practitioners will agree that the first two examples are assistive technology, even though the "device" also has nondisability applications. As for the third example, some might argue that a medically based device is not assistive technology.

Assistive technology appears in many guises. Individuals with disabilities may be enabled in the performance of actions or tasks with:

- an off-the-shelf general market product without any modification
- a general market product that has been modified or adapted for specific tasks
- a product developed and manufactured specifically for its "assistive" application
- a customized device fabricated to meet the needs of a particular individual

What constitutes assistive technology is not always clear cut. A device that assists an individual in detecting the ringing of a telephone by visual rather than the body's natural hearing mechanism is clearly assistive technology. A work-station modification that permits an individual with a cardiovascular condition to sit rather than stand while working is clearly assistive in nature, even if the individual is also waering a pacemaker. It is less clear that one could contend that such medical devices as pacemakers or cochlear implants are assistive technologies, or that it is the responsibility of an employer or public institution to provide them. In general, assistive technology includes devices that enhance the ability of an individual with a disability to engage in major life activities, actions, and tasks. It is helpful to distinguish between life activities and actions taken or tasks performed in relation to them. Major life activities include hearing, seeing, moving body parts, speaking, and interpreting information. Assistive technology currently exists to assist in the performance of actions (or tasks) associated with each of these major life activities.

For example, tasks associated with seeing, like reading or writing, can be assisted in a variety of ways. Some of these enhance seeing itself; for example, a closed-circuit TV magnification system. Others substitute the function of seeing with another function. For instance, a person who cannot see a computer's monitor can hear its contents using synthetic speech or feel the text via an electronic braille display.

Table 1 illustrates many major life activities and actions where substantial limitations in performing them exist due to disability. Assistive technology might be used to augment or substitute for the activity and thereby eliminate or modify the effects of a functional limitation. A significant contribution to our understanding of the connection between major activities and specific tasks, especially the moving of body parts, has been made by James Mueller (1990).

The assistive-technology solutions cited in the table are by no means exhaustive. Rather they are examples that have a track record of success in a variety of settings: employment, educational institutions, and places of public accommodation.

Many assistive technologies must be used differently in different settings. In employment they must always be matched to an individual's needs, preferences, capabilities, and comfort. Sometimes the solutions need time to evolve and mature. The individual with a disability is usually best qualified to figure out the appropriate technological solution cooperatively with the employer and, perhaps, an outside expert.

In contrast, assistive technologies for telecommunications and places of public accommodation need to address as broad a group of potential users as possible. Detailed attention to very specific individual needs would not be cost effective. The maximum level of accessibility for the broadest range of actions associated with disability must be part of any comprehensive design configuration. There will be many instances where individuals will choose personal assistance over an assistive-technology solution. A hard-of-hearing individual might prefer an aural interpreter to an assistive listening device during a meeting. A visually impaired person might prefer a personal reader to an optical scanner/PC with text-to-speech capability. Personal interaction may foster better overall acquisition of information.

Personal-assistance services should not be substituted for assistive technologies because they are *easier* for the employer or business, or they are *assumed* to be preferred by the individual with a disability. Use of assistive technology often enables a person to take responsibility for

TABLE 1

Major Life Activities, Consequences of Functional Limitations, and Assistive Technology Solutions

Major life activity	Consequences of functional limitation	Assistive technology solution
Hearing	Difficulty in understanding usable speech, identifying sounds, discriminating between sounds—with or without amplification; deafness—inability to process auditory information in both ears	Unambiguous labels, signs, written communications, electronic mail/Fax means less need for verbal communication; maximize face-to-face communication; lower ambient noise in restaurant, terminal, work station; telephone handset receiver amplifier, signal light for incoming calls, visual displays of call status, TDD; vibrator for paging—PA, intercom, phone message; additional amplification for face-to-face communication, pocket-size transmitter/receiver, body aid; inductive loop, infrared or FM systems for meetings, large-group situations; captioning of audiovisual materials to capture spoken dialogue
Seeing	Difficulty reading, writing or printing, recognizing objects or faces, distinguishing between colors—with or without corrective lenses or glasses; total blindness, inability to process visual information in both eyes	Even, nonglare lighting to provide sufficient lumens, maximum contrast; large-print labeling, signs with high-contrast letters (white or yellow on black or dark blue); tactual labels, signs with raised characters and braille; reduce sole reliance upon written/printed information—closed-circuit TV magnification for reading print, enhancing handwriting; redundant audio signals for visual displays such as machine gauges, shopping-mall directories, room numbers, exits, restrooms, ATMs; optional voice prompts for telephone system, Fax, photocopier; synthetic-speech output, large print or electronic braille access to PCs, mini-computers, and mainframes; electronic mail, local area networks, optical document scanning to reduce reliance upon print media, especially dot matrix; telephones with large LED rather than LCD arrays, raised "nibs" for important keys; voice prompts and/or audible status signals

319

Speaking	Capability of only soft, indistinct, or very slow speech; nonverbal or nonvocal communication	Unambiguous labels, signs, written communications, electronic mail/Fax means less need for speaking; maximize face-to-face communication; PC with synthetic speech output; speech-amplified telephone handset; speaker phone or operator headset for artifical larynx users facilitates writing with free hand; portable speech amplifier, other augmentative communications—boards, cards for common words/messages/symbols, laptops with LED, speech output, built-in printer; continuous-loop tape recorder for short messages; TDD for telephone conversations
Interpreting	Impaired ability in perception of visual, auditory, or tactual information; impaired memory ability; difficulty in sequencing; impaired ability in reasoning or understanding spoken or written information	Maximize use of multisensory information paths, e.g., audible and visual signs; confirming beep tones for telephone-programming features; unambiguous labels, signs, written communications; minimize distractions, e.g., high ambient noise, clutter; telephones with single-button dialing using pictures or familiar symbols to aid identifying person/use; sufficient time to respond to electronic messages, e.g., voice mail, computer-error messages; optional large print for PCs, with or without programmable font styles; optical document scanning to PC; macros, spell checking, word prediction, grammatical software; voice-recognition input for PC; mouse, joystick, pull-down menus, clear graphics
Moving	Head—difficulty in looking up, down, or to the side	Swivel chair with adjustable recline feature; maximize face-to-face communication without need for turning head; limit need to reach, stretch, bend; reach extenders, grabbers where appropriate; fish-eye lenses, mirrors to improve field of view

Upper extremities — absence of limbs, complete paralysis, severe incoordination, impaired mobility of arms, hands or fingers (range, strength, lack of control in placing or directing, spasticity)	Rocker switches, large-handle slide controls, push-action door latches decrease twisting, gripping motions; large handles on drawers; nonslip surfaces; concave surfaces for areas to be depressed, e.g., telephone keypads, computer keyboards, office and machine-equipment controls; gloves with gripping surfaces, e.g., velcro; printer with single-sheet feeder rather than tractor; store computer data on hard rather than floppy disks; key guards to avoid accidental keystrokes; adjust keyboard sensitivity; expanded keyboard or emulator; software to enhance multiple keystroke functions, word abbreviation/prediction; mouse, alternatives key mapping; copy holder with electric scrolling, page turner; optical document scanning to PC; go/no-go gauges for precision measuring; speaker phone, gooseneck cradle switch, headset, single-digit or voice-activated dialing; portable note taker; limit force required for activating, e.g., force-2 use levers; powered letter openers, staplers
Upper body — impaired mobility, range of motion of strength for reaching, lifting, or carrying	Lazy Susans, pull-out shelves, suspended storage; mechanical reachers; powered lift tables for positioning heavy work; extensions for hard-to-reach controls; environmental control units; telephone headset, speaker phone, gooseneck for holding handset and cradle switch, "sip and puff" switches/other alternative switches; back pack, shoulder bag, wheeled cart for carrying
Lower body — impaired mobility, range of motion of strength for turning, bending, balancing, or sitting	Appropriate chair for individual, e.g., height size, arms, angle, castors (on/off); seat belts, cushions; increase angle of work surfaces, raised edges to prevent slippage; also, many items listed above for upper-body limitations such as shoulder bag/back pack, reach extenders, telephone/PC-assistive technologies
Lower extremities — absence of limbs, complete paralysis, slowness of gait, impaired ability to kneel, rise, walk, stand, or climb stairs	Wheelchair, walker, supports while standing; rising assist devices, cushions, grab bars, lap trays; room for wheelchair under desk/table, public telephone, work area (including footrest); also many items listed above for upper-body limitations such as shoulder bag/back pack, reach extenders, telephone/PC-assistive technologies

him/herself and maintain high self-esteem. The valued and meaning-ful involvement of persons with disabilities in decision making will result in the most effective solutions.

AN ACCESSIBLE WORLD IS INCLUSIVE

Virtually everyone benefits when products, services, and their underly-ing technologies are designed and deployed with persons with disabili-ties in mind. If a task is made easier for a person with a disability, those without disabilities also often find the same task easier for them. This is not to say that every product and service can or must be designed to accommodate every individual combination of functional limitation. Individuals with severe mental or multiple disabilities may require customized approaches. Generally, design approached from a broad perspective will help a broad range of people, with and without disabil-ities. Here are three examples:

CURB CUTS

Sidewalk curb cuts were originally believed to be of benefit only to those in wheelchairs. Just observe: mothers pushing baby carriages, shoppers with carts, children with bikes find the gradual slope easier to navigate. Even travelers who are blind and use canes find that the gradual slope serves as a tactile warning of the sidewalk's end. Many benefit from this accessibility feature; no one is inconvenienced because of it. This is a concrete example of simple technology in action.

ELEVATORS

Building architects and engineers met, so the story goes, to figure out a way to keep elevator doors open long enough for people in wheelchairs to move to the open door and enter. Designing new buildings with additional elevators would reduce rental space. Retrofitting the build-ings with additional elevators would be infeasible as well as costly. Keeping doors open would increase waiting time on all floors. A soft-ware engineer came up with the simple low-cost solution: reprogram the lights and bells at each floor to indicate sooner which elevator would stop next at the floor. Given more time to move to an elevator, the person in a wheelchair would be able to enter in the same time required by anyone else. This technological innovation also helped travelers with suitcases in hotels, mail clerks with carts, and many others.

VOLUME-AMPLIFIED TELEPHONE HANDSETS

Many public telephones contain volume controls built into the handset, installed for people who are hard of hearing. However, the volume control is useful to everyone wishing to hear better when the ambient noise level is high. For very little extra cost, everyone benefits.

There are three elements to consider when planning for accessibility. What is the nature of the facility? What barriers restrict access? Which assistive technologies might help reduce these barriers?

The suggestions given below may be matched with the potential assistive technology solutions outlined in table 1. As with all examples given in this article, they are illustrative rather than exhaustive.

SIGNS

- avoid hard-to-read scripts, unusual fonts
- avoid small print, less than three to four inches high at five feet from observer
- include braille *and* large print in elevators, adjacent to room entrances, and with other points of orientation
- provide aural equivalents for frequently encountered information (cash registers, mall directories)

LIGHTING

- eliminate harsh fluorescent colors/tints
- cover bare bulbs
- relocate lamps away from eye level
- provide minimum of 300 lumens in public areas

DECOR

- provide definitive color contrast between adjoining areas (walls and doorways, floors and walls, columns and floors, etc.)
- avoid dark color schemes exclusively throughout area
- avoid single color throughout area

- avoid busy or changing patterns (especially on floors/
carpeting)

SOUND

- augment public address system with visual equivalent
- offer paging-system alternatives to clients, patrons (visual or
tactual)
- decrease multiple sound sources, confusing sounds
- provide "quiet spaces" in high ambient-noise environments

ALARMS

- include both aural and visual methods for all systems, i.e., fire,
smoke, danger (vehicles backing up, electric carts in airports,
etc.)
- include audible as well as visual "exit" signs

AISLES/COUNTERS/DISPLAYS

- provide space between aisles, near counters for wheelchairs/
walkers
- provide lower surface at counter area to accommodate wheelchairs, persons of short stature
- provide reachable display areas for persons with motion
impairments

TELEPHONES

- install systems with built-in volume controls (preferably return
to normal setting on public phones)
- provide TDD capacity for some public phones, assure availability for hotel/motel guest rooms
- provide both aural and visual methods for ringing and message-
alert functions

TV/VCR IN LODGING

- provide accessible switches for motion impaired (remote control, membrane pad)
- provide nonvisual method for selecting stations/functions
- provide captioning equipment

A/V PROJECTION SYSTEMS

- provide alternative listening method (inductive loop, infrared)
- provide captioning for audio portions of presentations, films
- provide "descriptive narration" for visual aspects of presentations, films, plays, operas

For anyone thinking about improving accessibility there are two essential steps to take. First, try it yourself. Close your eyes, wear ear plugs, sit in a wheelchair (if available). Then try to see, hear, or move throughout your facility.

Second, consult with clients, patrons, patients and customers with a broad range of disabilities. They can help identify specific barriers and suggest particular assistive technology solutions. In addition, consult with organizations and consultants having expertise with particular disabilities *and* assistive technology.

DETERMINING WHICH ASSISTIVE TECHNOLOGIES TO USE

Which products will address which disability? How can their performance be evaluated? This is a special concern for small businesses that may not have had experience making accommodations for people with disabilities. Assistance is available and more is forthcoming.

Each of the federal agencies responsible for implementing titles of the ADA will also be providing technical assistance. For assistive technology, the most relevant federal agencies are the Architectural and Transportation Barriers Compliance Board (ATBCB), the Department of Justice (DOJ), Equal Employment Opportunity Commission (EEOC), the President's Committee on Employment of People with Disabilities, and the U.S. Department of Education's National Institute of Disabilities and Rehabilitation Research (NIDRR).

ATBCB has already established minimal standards for communications and architectural accessibility. The ATBCB, the DOJ, and the EEOC have instituted technical-assistance programs. The President's Committee, through its long-standing Job Accommodation Network, is expanding its services, especially to small businesses. They have thousands of examples on file of successful accommodations. A toll-free 800 number is answered by trained personnel. NIDRR is setting up regional technical-assistance centers to facilitate the implementation of the Act.

In addition, each major type of disability is being addressed by Rehabilitation Engineering Centers (REC) funded by NIDRR. Twenty-four
states now have Technology Assistance Programs (TAPs) focusing specifically upon assistive technology. Soon every state will have its own
program. Many other government and nongovernment regional, state,
or locally based initiatives are in place. A number of well-qualified
consulting firms are in the assistive-technology arena.

Persons with disabilities often know what they need to make their
jobs accessible. The same principle applies to places of public accommodation. Frequently, the individual's suggested accommodation is
simpler and less expensive than the accommodation the employer,
business, or public entity might have devised. Several companies
involved with telecommunications and transportation have consumer
advisory panels to counsel them.

Here are some guidelines for persons wishing to use assistive technology properly:

- Accommodation is best understood as a process in which barriers to opportunity are removed.
- A problem-solving approach should be used to identify the
  particular tasks or actions related to employment or use of public facilities.
- Assistive technology that can lead to meaningful access should
  be identified.
- Any assistive technology device should be effective for the specific application. Factors to be considered include its suitability,
  reliability and potential for timely delivery.
- Acquire the assistive technology.
- Provide for appropriate training of personnel who will use or
  show others how to use the assistive technology device(s).
- Establish a program of maintenance, upgrading and
  replacement.

These guidelines are similar to the ones suggested by the U.S. Congress in a House Committee report accompanying the ADA,[5] and meet
the definition of assistive technology services in the Tech Act.[6] The
process fosters cooperation between employee and employer, customer
and business, or patron and public facility. It generates solutions
acceptable to each and creates a basis for changing stereotypical attitudes about disability.

BENEFITS OF ASSISTIVE TECHNOLOGY

Assistive technology has extended horizons in education and employment, for personal independence and social integration. The sheer volume of devices in use and the number of companies that develop, manufacture, and distribute them are evidence of a lively marketplace. In addition, the American business community, especially the retail trade, is likely to find strong incentives to provide assistive technology. Creating public good will is one such incentive. A more powerful force is the quest for new customers.

Assistive technology is still not widely deployed, however. Knowledge about and appreciation of its value in places of public accommodation, transportation, and telecommunications is limited. Although persons with disabilities know a great deal about technology, they are not universally aware of the variety of devices available or how to obtain them.

The extent to which assistive technology is being used is not clearly understood. Many devices are purchased and later laid aside. Some simply never worked right; others became obsolete.

Moreover, little systematic research supports the anecdotal evidence of the benefits of assistive technology. Much of this research is several years old and does not address the more recent infusion of newer technologies. However, the most frequently quoted studies have set the foundation upon which future research may be built (Berkeley Planning Associates 1982; U.S. Congress 1982).

Data gathered more recently about assistive technology for visual impairment might be extended to other disabilities. In 1986, the National Technology Center of the American Foundation for the Blind embarked upon a project to capture information about the use of electronically based devices by people who are visually impaired. To date, about 1,200 persons have volunteered information.

From the interviews, some significant data have emerged.[7] Eighty-three percent of respondents were employed, more than 90 percent full time. By contrast, only 30 percent of the overall population of visually impaired persons of working age are employed. Fifty-one percent of respondents used a computer with assistive technology components as an accommodation to their disability a minimum of five days per week. Overall, about 70 percent of respondents used computers.

COSTS OF ASSISTIVE TECHNOLOGY

The deployment of assistive technology in the workplace and places of public accommodation will not be a burden on American business and public institutions. The cost of assistive technology is frequently quite small. Offsetting tax and accounting treatments might reduce its impact upon tight budgets. Most important, the economy benefits as Americans with disabilities become integrated more fully into society as employees, customers and taxpayers. Moreover, work productivity increases with the use of assistive technology. In addition, the customer base increases when people with disabilities can spend their larger disposable income to reach and use accessible business establishments. Finally, the general taxpaying public contributes less to programs of support and aid.

Testimony before Congressional committees demonstrates that the cost of most accommodations and auxiliary aids is usually minimal. For instance:

> "Sears and Roebuck made their whole national headquarters accessible for $7,600 with TDDs, ramps, this and that and the other thing. It is hard to believe that they could do it for that cheap a price. But if a person wants disabled people, the accommodations really don't become a burden. If they don't, they always do."[8]

> "Jay Rochlin, former Executive Director of the President's Committee testified that a 1982 study showed that a majority of accommodations provided by Federal contractors involved little or no cost."[9]

> "Charles Crawford, Commissioner for the Massachusetts Commission for the Blind, stated: ' . . . I think that the application of technology for disabled persons will bring down the cost of a number of accommodations. For example, with the blind community, it is possible through microcomputer networks and braille production to produce accessible materials with very little cost . . . ' "[10]

The cost of assistive technology is frequently limited to an "add-on" for existing equipment. Prime examples are assistive technologies for personal computers: synthetic-speech or alternative data-entry modules are added to existing equipment. Similarly, Go/No-Go switches can be added to existing workplace machines. Gooseneck clamps that hold telephone handsets are only an add-on.

The funding of assistive technology is a key issue for persons with disabilities. Solutions can be expensive and prohibitive in times of tight budgets and limited funds. Furthermore, there is no systematic funding or reimbursement for the purchase of assistive technology. The National Council on Disability has initiated a study on the financing of assistive technology, as mandated by Congress in the Tech Act. Businesses and public entities subject to the ADA must pay for required accommodations or auxiliary aids. However, there are limits, which are addressed in other articles in this volume.

Both tax credits and tax deductions are available for entities making expenditures in order to comply with the ADA. Another article in this volume examines ADA-related tax incentives in depth.

In weighing the costs and benefits of utilizing assistive technology, consider the following two hypothetical examples.

- Many patrons of the Good Times Restaurant who are deaf really like the food, ambiance and service. However, making reservations is a pain! The restaurant has never had a TDD connected to its telephone line. The Better Times American Bar & Grill is also excellent. Having installed a TDD as well as a public pay phone with TDD capabilities, they have geared up to attract customers with disabilities, including family and friends.
- The Palace Shopping Plaza and Capitol Mall Shopping Center traditionally engage in fierce competition for customers. When the Capitol Mall management decided to refurbish all its public areas, store entrances, and other facilities, they consciously tried to make it accessible. Not only were architectural barriers removed, but also many communications barriers. Entrances to the center have convenience kiosks nearby. Customers with visual impairments can pick up special receivers, about the size of a garage-door opener, to use while in the mall. With this assistive technology device, each store could be identified through Talking Signs™ transmitters placed above their entrances. In addition, the mall directory includes optional synthetic-speech output to assist shoppers with visual or perceptual impairments.

In both examples, the incremental cost of providing assistive technology can be quickly offset by increasing the customer base. The cost of the TDD (about $250) can be recouped from only a few extra meals. The same principle applies to the Capitol Mall scenario. Accessibility design features were integrated into plans for renovations. Increased mall traffic would soon have offset the costs. Both examples might be eligible for a tax subsidy.

CONCLUSION

The role of technology will be especially important in the successful implementation of the ADA. A particular branch of technology, assistive technology, will be key to persons whose physical or mental impairments substantially limit one or more of their major life activities. Hearing, seeing, speaking, interpreting information, or moving are essential for performing a wide variety of actions or tasks. Many of these tasks are made possible, or enhanced, through appropriate assistive technology.

I have stressed a common-sense approach to incorporating assistive technology. Simple low-tech solutions often work well for some tasks. When higher-tech solutions are called for, several products are frequently available from which to choose. The task of an individual with a disability and his or her employer, is to analyze the job to be done and match it with available options. The critical question changes for public institutions, transportation carriers, telecommunications companies or places of public accommodation. It becomes, What solutions will work best for the greatest number of persons with disabilities in the greatest number of situations?

The Americans with Disabilities Act is part of an evolutionary process. Its goal is inclusion. Its promise is opportunity, enlightened attitudes and social integration. Its rewards will be realized as persons with disabilities become coequal, as students, colleagues, taxpayers, customers and contributors to society, with their peers. A key to its success is the infusion of appropriate assistive technology: access to books, information, and the tools of learning; access to transportation; accommodations for employment; elimination of architectural and communications barriers in retail and service businesses, telecommunications, and in places of leisure and enlightenment.

NOTES

1. P.L. 99–506 §103.
2. P. L. 100–407 codified at 29 U.S.C. §2201 et seq. Subsequent references are to P.L. rather than U.S.C. sections.
3. P.L. 100–407, §3(1).
4. Id., §3(2) (A-F).
5. H. Rep. no. 101–485, part 2 at 65–67.
6. P.L. 100–407, §3(2) (A-F). Condensed, the points are: "(A) . . . evaluation of the needs of an individual . . . in [his or her] customary environment; (B) . . . the acquisition of assistive technology devices by individuals with disabilities; (C) selecting, designing, fitting, customizing, adapting, applying, maintaining, repairing, or replacing of assistive technology devices; (D) coordinating and using other . . . interventions or services with assistive technology devices . . . and programs; (E) training or technical assistance for an individual, or where appropriate, the family; and (F) training or technical assistance for professionals who provide services to, employ, or are otherwise substantially involved in the major life functions of individuals with disabilities."
7. Careers in Technology and Information Base (CTIB), National Technology Center at the American Foundation for the Blind, October 1990.
8. Testimony before the House Subcommittees on Select Education and Employment Opportunities, September 13, 1989, no. 1010951 at 20.
9. Id. at 35.
10. Testimony before the House Subcommittee on Select Education, October 24, 1988, no. 10009109 at 29.

REFERENCES

Berkeley Planning Associates. 1982. *A Study of Accommodations Provided for Handicapped Employees by Federal Contractors.* Washington: U.S. Department of Labor, Division of Employee Administration.

Mueller, J.L. 1990. *The Workplace Workbook: An Illustrated Guide to Job Accommodation and Assistive Technology.* Washington: The Dole Foundation.

U.S. Congress, Office of Technology Assessment. 1982. *Technology and Handicapped People.* Washington.

ADDITIONAL READING

Anderson, S.L., J.H. Stevens, and L.H. Trachtman. 1990. *A Guide to Funding Resources for Assistive Technology in South Carolina.* West Columbia, S.C.: Center for Rehabilitation Technology Services.

Assistive Technology. RESNA. New York: Demos Publications.

Closing the Gap. Henderson, Minn.

Davies, T., and K. Beasley. 1988. *Design for Hospitality: Planning for Accessible Hotels and Motels*. New York: Nichols.

De Witt, J. 1990. *Reading Print Electronically: A Guide to Optical Character Readers/Scanners*. Glen Rock, N.J.: Unpublished manuscript.

De Witt, J., and J. Leventhal et al. 1987a. A Guide to Selecting Digital Alarm Clocks/Clock Radios for Persons with Low Vision. *Journal of Visual Impairment and Blindness* (September).

————. 1987b. An Evaluation of Five Braille Printers. *Journal of Visual Impairment and Blindness* (June).

————. 1988a. An Evaluation of Eight Large Print/Enhanced Image Computer Products for Persons with Low Vision: A Guide to Their Selection. *Journal of Visual Impairment and Blindness* (December).

————. 1988b. An Evaluation of Four Closed Circuit Television Systems (CCTV) and Guide to Their Selection. *Journal of Visual Impairment and Blindness* (April).

De Witt, J., and S. Mendelsohn. 1990. *Establishing a Foundation to Pay for Assistive Technology*. Washington: Resna Technical Assistance Project.

Electronic Industries Foundation. 1987. Background papers from the *Proceedings of the Symposium on Rehabilitation Technology Service Delivery*. Washington.

Enders, A. Ed. *Assistive Technology Source Book*. Washington: RESNA Press.

Farmer, M. 1989. *Redefining and Rebuilding American Life*. New York: Marketing Institute.

Grandjean, E. Ed. 1987. *Ergonomics of Computerized Offices*. Bristol, Penn.: Taylor & Francis.

Mendelsohn, S. 1987. *Financing Adaptive Technology*. New York: Smiling Interface.

Mueller, J.L. 1979. *Designing for Functional Limitations*. Washington: George Washington University Rehabilitation Research and Training Center.

————. 1989. Toward Universal Design: A Project on the Ergonomics of Disability. In *Proceedings of the 12th Annual RESNA Conference*. Washington: RESNA Press.

Rehabilitation Service Delivery: A Practical Guide. Washington: RESNA Press.

Rehabilitation Technologies: 13th Institute on Rehabilitation Issues, ed. D.W. Corthell. Menomonie: University of Wisconsin-Stout Rehabilitation Research and Training Center.

Ringwald, E. 1984. On the Eve of Universal Design. *Home Magazine* 34(10).

Schwartz, G., S. Weston, D. Galvin, and E. Lipoff. 1987. *The Disability Management Sourcebook*. Washington: Institute for Rehabilitation and Disability Management.

Scott, N. 1987. *Computer Assistance for People with Disabilities*. San Francisco: Desktop Marketing.

Spectrum. West Columbia, S.C.: Center for Rehabilitation Technology Services.

Summing Up: Opportunities of Implementation

Jane West

At the White House signing ceremony for the ADA, President Bush ended his remarks by articulating one of the Act's most significant opportunities. He said, "Let the shameful wall of exclusion finally come tumbling down." The opportunity to remove barriers that have excluded and denied persons with disabilities from participating, developing their skills and talents, and contributing to the riches of our nation is one we have before us. It is a chance to recommit ourselves to a fundamental cornerstone of the American dream: equal opportunity.

The ADA presents an opportunity to turn the corner on policies promoting welfare-like dependence and to develop instead supports for independence in the context of working, living, and recreating in the mainstream. In this sense, implementing the ADA is an opportunity to contribute to an improved economy. When persons with disabilities give up public subsidies for jobs, they leave funds in the public coffers. When they become taxpayers, they contribute directly to the public treasuries. When persons with disabilities become consumers in the marketplace, they strengthen the economy.

The ADA offers opportunities for partnerships between the private and public sectors, between persons with disabilities and the business community, and between accessibility experts and industry. The generation of these partnerships will bring opportunities for creativity and ingenious problem solving as people with disabilities join government officials, proprietors of shops, business owners, industry leaders, unions, technical-assistance experts, and disability service providers to fashion accessible and inclusive situations, environments, and practices.

Finally, implementation of the ADA offers an unprecedented opportunity to advance our knowledge about effective practices in constructing an inclusive and integrated world for people with disabilities. We can learn more about what sort of technical assistance is effective, for whom, and in what circumstances. We can learn about how behaviors and attitudes toward persons with disabilities can change. Research undertaken while policy is put into practice is likely to be relevant to policy makers when they raise the inevitable questions about the success and impact of the ADA. In the rush to proceed with implementation, let us not overlook evaluation as an important component of our efforts.

The ADA is not the answer to all of the challenges faced by persons with disabilities—rather, it is a new beginning. Justin Dart, chairman of the President's Committee on Employment of People with Disabilities, articulated this thought lucidly when he said, "The ADA is only the beginning. It is not a solution. Rather, it is an essential foundation on which solutions will be constructed."

Appendices

A: ADA IMPLEMENTATION DATES

Title	Law's effective date	Regulations due by federal agency	Enforcement jurisdiction
Title I **Employment**	July 26, 1992, for employers with twenty-five (25) or more employees; July 26, 1994 for employers with fifteen (15) or more employees.	July 26, 1991, all regulations due from Equal Employment Opportunity Commission (EEOC).	Remedies identical to those under Title VII of the Civil Rights Act of 1964 which are private right of action, injunctive relief, i.e., job reinstatement, back pay, and EEOC enforcement.
Title II: Public Services All activities of local and state government	January 26, 1992	July 26, 1991, all regulations due from Attorney General.	Remedies identical to those under the Rehabilitation Act of 1973 Section 305 which are private right of action, injunctive relief, and some damages.
(Part I) Public transportation (buses, light and rapid rail including fixed-route systems, paratransit, demand response systems and transportation facilities).	August 26, 1990, all orders for purchases or leases of new vehicles must be for accessible vehicles; one-car-per-train must be accessible as soon as practicable, but no later than July 26, 1995; paratransit services must be provided after January 26, 1992; new stations built after January 26, 1992 must be accessible. Key stations must be retrofitted by July 26, 1993, with some extensions allowed up to July 26, 2020.	July 26, 1991, all regulations due from Secretary of Transportation.	Same as above.

(Part II) Public transportation by intercity Amtrak and commuter rail (including transportation facilities).	By July 26, 2000, Amtrak passenger coaches must have same number of accessible seats as would have been available if every car were built accessible; half of such seats must be available by July 26, 1995. Same one-car-per-train rule and new stations rule as above. All existing Amtrak stations must be retrofitted by July 26, 2010; key commuter stations must be retrofitted by July 26, 1993, with some extensions allowed up to 20 years.	July 26, 1991, all regulations due from Secretary of Transportation.	Same as above.
Title III: Public accommodations operated by private entities. A. Public accommodations (all business and service providers).	In general, January 26, 1992, except no lawsuits may be filed before July 26, 1992 against businesses with twenty-five (25) or fewer employees and revenue $1 million or less; or before January 26, 1993 for businesses with ten (10) or fewer employees and revenue	July 26, 1991 regulations due from Attorney General standards must be consistent with the Architectural and Transportation Barriers Compliance Board (ATBCB) guidelines. Due April 26, 1991.	For individuals, remedies identical to Title II of the Civil Rights Act of 1964 which are private right of action, injunctive relief: For Attorney General enforcement in pattern or practice cases or cases of general importance with civil penalties and compensatory dam-

B. New construction/alteration to public accommodations and commercial facilities.	January 26, 1992, for alterations, January 26, 1993 for new construction.	Same as above.	Same as above.
C. Public transportation provided by private entities.	In general, January 26, 1992, but by August 6, 1990 all orders for purchases or leases of new vehicles must be for accessible vehicles. Calls for a three (3) year study of over-the-road buses to determine access needs with requirements effective July 26, 1996 to July 26, 1997.	July 26, 1991, regulations due from Secretary of Transportation. Regulations will be based on standards issued by the Architectural and Transportation Barriers Compliance Board (ATBCB). Due April 26, 1991.	Same as above.
Title IV: Telecommunications	July 26, 1993, telecommunications relay services to operate twenty-four (24) hours per day.	July 26, 1991, all regulations due by the Federal Communications Commission.	Private right of action and Federal Communications Commission.
Title V: Miscellaneous	Effective dates of Title V are those determined by most of the analogous sections in Titles I through IV.	In general, this title depicts the ADA's relationship to other laws, explains insurance issues, prohibits state immunity, provides congressional inclusion, sets regulations by ATBCB, explains implementation of each title, and notes amendments to the Rehabilitation Act of 1973.	

Source: This table was compiled by Erica C. Jones and reprinted with permission of The President's Committee on Employment of People with Disabilities.

B: RESOURCE ORGANIZATIONS

Americans with Disabilities Act
  Information Line
(202) 514–0301
Answers general questions about the law; provides brochures and pamphlets as well as referral services.

Architectural and Transportation Barriers
  Compliance Board
Suite 501
1111 18th Street NW
Washington, DC 20036
(202) 653–7848 (voice and TDD)
Issued accessibility guidelines for the ADA; ensures compliance with standards issued under the Architectural Barriers Act of 1968.

Department of Education
Clearinghouse on Disability Information
Program Information and Coordination Staff
Room 3132 Switzer Building
Washington, DC 20202
(202) 732–1723 or 732–1241
Provides general information and referral services about disability programs and issues.

Department of Education
National Institute on Disability
  and Rehabilitation Research
400 Maryland Avenue SW
Washington, DC 20202
(202) 732–5066
The key federal research agency for disability issues. Funds research and training centers; administers the Technology Related Assistance for Individuals with Disabilities Act; funds research projects according to established priorities; administers regional ADA technical assistance centers.

Department of Education
Rehabilitation Services Administration
Mary E. Switzer Building
Room 3028
330 C Street SW
Washington, DC
(202) 732–1282
Administers state vocational rehabilitation programs as well as special projects to facilitate employment and independence of persons with disabilities, such as Independent Living Centers, Projects With Industry, and Supported Employment Programs.

Department of Justice
Civil Rights Division
Coordination and Review Section
Office on the Americans with
    Disabilities Act
320 First Street NW
Washington, DC 20530
(202) 307–2222
Responsible for enforcing the public accommodations requirements of the ADA; issues regulations for state and local services and public accommodations requirements of the ADA; funds technical assistance projects for the ADA. Responsible for overall government-wide ADA technical assistance plan.

Department of Transportation
Office of Chief Counsel
400 7th Street SW
Room 9316
Washington, DC 20590
(202) 366–4011
Contact person: Susan Schruth
Issues regulations for the transportation requirements of the ADA.

Equal Employment Opportunity
  Commission
Office of Communications
  and Legislative Affairs
1801 L Street NW
Washington, DC 20507
(202) 663–4900
Responsible for enforcing compliance with the employment provisions
of the ADA; issues regulations on employment; funds ADA technical
assistance activities.

Federal Communication Commission
The Common Carrier Bureau
Domestic Facilities Division
2025 M Street NW
Washington, DC 20554
Contacts:
Abe Leib   (202) 634–1816
Phil Cheilit   (202) 634–1831
Linda Dubroff   (202) 634–1808
Issues regulations for the telecommunications requirements under title
IV of the ADA; responsible for ensuring that the requirements are
enforced.

General Services Administration
Clearinghouse on Computer Accommodation
18th and F Streets NW
Room 2022
Washington, DC 20405
(202) 501–4906
Provides technical assistance and information to federal agencies and
companies making computer products to sell to the federal
government.

Job Accommodation Network
West Virginia University
809 Allen Hall
P.O. Box 6122
Morgantown, WV 26506
(800) 526-7234   (voice or TDD)
(800) 526-4698   (in West Virginia)
(800) 526-2262   (in Canada)
Provides information about accommodating jobs for persons with disabilities. Maintains a database of accommodations that have been successful.

National Council on Disability
800 Independence Avenue
Suite 814
Washington, DC 20591
(202) 267-3846
Advises the President and Congress on issues of concern to persons with disabilities. Issues annual reports and special reports on a range of policy issues.

President's Committee on Employment
   of People with Disabilities
1111 20th Street NW
Washington, DC 20036
(202) 653-5044
Promotes the employment of persons with disabilities; issues regular publications and brochures; holds annual conference.

Public Health Service
AIDS Hotline
(800)342-2437
Answers questions about AIDS.

Public Health Service
National AIDS Information Clearinghouse
(800) 458-5213
Provides information about AIDS services, educational resources, and sends out free publications.

ABLEDATA
c/o The Adaptive Equipment Center
Newington Children's Hospital
181 East Cedar Street
Newington, CT 06111
(800) 344–5405
(203) 667–5405
Maintains a database and provides information about assistive technology and adaptive equipment.

American Civil Liberties Union
ADA Education Project
132 West 43rd Street
New York, NY 10036
(212) 944–9800 ext. 545
Contact: Bill Rubenstein
Provides educational materials and technical assistance regarding the ADA.

American Civil Liberties Union
AIDS Project
132 West 43rd Street
New York, NY 10036
(212) 944–9800 ext. 545
Contact: Bill Rubenstein
Provides technical assistance, materials for employers and businesses, and policy analysis related to AIDS.

American Foundation for the Blind
National Technology Center
15 West 16th Street
New York, NY 10011
(212) 620–2080
Provides information about assistive technology products for persons who are blind.

American National Standards
  Institute Inc.
1430 Broadway
New York, NY 10018
(212) 354–3300
Provides information about accessibility standards for persons with
disabilities.

American Speech-Language-Hearing
  Association
10801 Rockville Pike
Rockville, MD 20852
(301) 897–5700
Provides information about audiology and speech/language
pathology.

Association for Retarded Citizens
  of the United States
500 East Border Street
3rd Floor
Arlington, TX 76010
(817) 261–6003
Promotes the interests of persons with mental retardation and provides
information.

Cerebral Palsy Research Foundation
  of Kansas
2021 North Old Manor
P.O. Box 8217
Wichita, KS 67208
(316) 688–1888
Conducts research activities related to assistive technology; provides
information about assistive technology.

Disability Rights Education
  and Defense Fund
2212 6th Street
Berkeley, CA 94710
(415) 644-2555
  and
1633 Q Street NW
Suite 220
Washington, DC 20009
(202) 986-0375 (voice and TDD)
Provides technical assistance and training related to the ADA and other
disability laws; monthly newsletter.

Disability Statistics Program
  Information Service
InfoUse
1995 University Avenue
Suite 215
Berkeley, CA 94704
(415) 644-9904
Provides statistical information related to disability in the United
States.

Electronic Industries Foundation
1901 Pennsylvania Avenue NW
Suite 700
Washington, DC 20006
(202) 955-5810
Develops and provides information about assistive technology for persons with disabilities.

Epilepsy Foundation of America
Suite 406
4351 Garden City Drive
Landover, MD 20785
(301) 459-3700
Promotes the interests of persons with epilepsy, provides information.

Gallaudet University
Gallaudet Research Institute
Technology Assessment Program
College Hall 409
800 Florida Avenue NE
Washington, DC 20002
(202) 651–5257
Assesses and develops technology for persons who are speech and hearing impaired.

Higher Education and Adult Training
    for People with Disabilities (HEATH)
Suite 800
1 Dupont Circle
Washington, DC 20036
(800) 544–3284
(202) 939–9320
National clearinghouse providing information and referral services related to postsecondary education for persons with disabilities.

IBM Educational Systems
National Support Center for Persons
    with Disabilities
P.O. Box 2150
Atlanta, GA 30055
(800) 426–2133
Provides information on computer-related products for persons with disabilities.

Mental Health Law Project
2021 L Street NW
Suite 800
Washington, DC 20036
(202)467–5730
Provides information about disability laws, with a focus on persons who have mental illness.

National Association for the
   Visually Handicapped
22 West 21st Street
New York, NY 10010
(212) 889-3141
Sells products for people with low vision; some publications.

National Association of the Deaf
814 Thayer Avenue
Silver Spring, MD 20910
(301) 589-3006 (voice or TDD)
Promotes the rights of persons who are deaf or hard of hearing.

National Alliance for
   the Mentally Ill
2101 Wilson Boulevard
Suite 302
Arlington, VA 22201
(703) 524-7600
Publishes information that promotes the interests of persons with mental disabilities.

National Association of Rehabilitation
   Facilities
P.O. Box 17675
Washington, DC 20041
(703) 948-9300
Provides information about rehabilitation services for persons with disabilities. Newsletters and publications.

National Association of Protection
   and Advocacy Systems
220 I Street NE
Suite 150
Washington, DC 20002
(202) 408-9514
Advocates for the rights of persons with developmental disabilities.

National Braille Press, Inc.
88 Saint Stephens Street
Boston, MA 02115
(617) 266–6160
Prints materials in braille.

National Center for Law and the Deaf
800 Florida Avenue NE
Washington, DC 20002
(202) 651–5373 (voice and TDD)
Provides technical assistance, legal analysis, and publications related to persons with hearing impairments and deafness. Also provides legal services and counseling to the deaf and hard-of-hearing community.

National Center for Learning
  Disabilities
99 Park Avenue
New York, NY 10016
(212) 687–7211
Provides information and referral services related to learning disabilities.

National Easter Seal Society
70 East Lake Street
Chicago, IL 60601
(312) 726–6200
Publishes information about assistive technology, and helps promote independence for persons with disabilities.

National Easter Seal Society
Project Action
1001 Connecticut Avenue NW
Suite 435
Washington, DC 20036
(202) 659–2229 (voice)
(202) 835–7393 (TDD)
Provides information about accessibility in transportation services; supports model projects.

National Federation of the Blind
Braille and Technology Center
   for the Blind
1800 Johnson Street
Baltimore, MD 21230
(301) 659-9314
Provides information about assistive technology products for persons
who are blind.

National Information Clearinghouse
   for Children and Youth
   with Disabilities (NICHY)
P.O. Box 1492
Washington, DC 20013
(800) 999-5599
(202) 893-6061
National clearinghouse providing information and referral services
about disabilities issues, services, and programs.

National Recreation and Park
   Association
3101 Park Center Drive
12th Floor
Alexandria, VA 22302
(703) 820-4940
Provides information about accessible parks and recreation services for
all ages throughout local, state, and federal areas.

National Rehabilitation Association
633 South Washington Street
Alexandria, VA 22314
(703) 836-0850 (voice)
(703) 836-0852 (TDD)
Provides information about ADA and accommodations for people with
disabilities.

National Rehabilitation Hospital
Rehabilitation Engineering
   Program
102 Irving Street
Washington, DC 20010
(202) 877–1932
Conducts research and evaluates the effectiveness of assistive
technology.

National Rehabilitation Information Center
Suite 935
8455 Colesville Road
Silver Spring, MD 20910
(800) 346–2742 (voice and TDD)
(301) 588–9284 (MD only)
Maintains a database of rehabilitation information; conducts literature
searches.

Paralyzed Veterans of America
801 18th Street NW
Washington, DC 20006
(202)872–1300
Promotes accessibility and provides information about accessibility.

RESNA Technical Assistance Project
Suite 700
1101 Connecticut Avenue NW
Washington, DC 20036
(202) 857–1140
Provides technical assistance and publishes information related to technology and people with disabilities.

Self Help for Hard of Hearing
7800 Wisconsin Avenue
Bethesda, MD 20814
(301) 657–2248 (voice)
(301) 657–2249 (TDD)
Promotes the interests of those who cannot hear well but who are
committed to living in a hearing world.

Telecommunications for the Deaf, Inc.
814 Thayer Avenue
Silver Spring, MD 20910
(301) 589-3006 (voice and TDD)
Promotes the use of TDDs, text telephones, telecaptioning, and visual alerting systems in the public and private sector.

Tele-consumer Hotline
1910 K Street NW
Suite 610
Washington, DC 20006
(202) 223-4371 (voice or TDD)
(800) 332-1124 (voice or TDD)
Provides information and referral services on telecommunication services and equipment for persons who are deaf and persons with other disabilities.

The Association for Persons
    with Severe Handicaps
1511 King Street
Alexandria, VA 22314
(703) 683-5586
Represents the interests of persons with severe handicaps; provides information.

United Cerebral Palsy
    Association, Inc.
1522 K Street NW
Suite 1112
Washington, DC 20005
(202) 842-1266
Represents the interests of persons with cerebral palsy; conducts research projects (e.g., on technology), and provides information.

Index

Accessibility
  building modification for, 160, 191–2, 196
  and environmental impact, 197–8
  to historic buildings, 201
  of parks and recreational facilities, 197–8,
    200–1
  and reasonable modifications to permit, 190
  and small building elevator exemption, 193,
    194, 196, 204, 207*
  and social participation, 32, 186
  and standards: for new construction, 19, 188,
    193, 221; for ready accessibility, 204–5,
    207
  tax incentives for, 295
  technical assistance for, 199–200
  and topological problems, 196
  See also Transportation
Activities
  as actions, 59–60
  and assistive technology, 317
  limitation of: demographics, 62, 65; highest
    prevalence, 67; substantial, 57–58
  ranked by life importance, 60
ADA industry, xiv
Affirmative action, 16
AIDS (auto immune deficiency syndrome), see
  HIV infection
Air Carriers Access Act (1986), 18
Alcoholism, 35–6, 41, 44, 86, 107n

American National Standards Institute (ANSI),
  199–200, 210n
American Public Transit Association, 217
American Sign Language, 242–3
Americans with Disabilities Act (ADA), xi–xii,
  xiv–xviii, xix–xxii, 3–5, 14, 21–2, 25–9, 30–2,
  69–70, 73–5, 92, 94, 104–6, 112, 120, 126,
  129–31, 150–4, 187–93, 199, 201, 203–8,
  214, 293, 295, 300–1, 305–8, 313–14, 330,
  335–6
  and accommodation imperative, 3, 7–9
  ambiguities of, 41–8
  Chapman Amendment to, 282–3
  compliance with, xiii, 154
  and coverage of Congress, 29, 40–1
  definitions in: of disability, 50n, 55–8, 60, 63,
    163–4, 170, 271; of essential functions, 36,
    89–90, 108n, 287n; of public entity, 37; of
    qualified person, 88–90, 273–5
  and direct threat, 103, 269, 273–6, 287n, 288n:
    from HIV, 280–1
  and discrimination prohibition, 90–2, 151, 154,
    189, 258, 270, 274, 305–6: applied to public
    health risk, 270–1, 280
  economic analysis of, 157–8, 174n, 175n
  economic benefits of, xxiv–xxv
  employment protections and requirements of,
    xxii–xxiv, 34–7, 81–106
  and equal employment opportunity mandate,
    81, 145–6

---

*Number in italic indicates a table; n indicates a note.

353

evaluation of, 73, 129–31, 138–41, 143–45,
    159, 169–73, 301, 307–8
and the future, 48–9, 126–7, 206–8, 335–6
goals of, 4, 6
health insurance and, 100–2
individualized approach to, 32, 36–7
as insurance for entire society, 206
and medical exams: for applicants, 98–100; for
    employees, 99–100
opportunities offered by, 335–6
overview of, 32–42
phase-in of, 104, 214, 221–6
population covered by, 64
and public accommodations access, xxv, 38,
    183–5, 187–93: alternative methods for, 192,
    197, 205, 207; auxiliary aids for, 190–1,
    203–4, 207; coverage and scope of, 187–8;
    facility, defined in, 194; fundamental
    alteration for, 190; exemptions from, 188; to
    historic properties, 201; and prior legislative
    standards, 193–4; and readily accessible
    standard, 204–5, 207; reasonable
    modifications of, 190, 195–6, 203, 209n;
    topological problems of, 196–7
and public health powers, 269–70, 283–5
and reasonable accommodation provisions, xvii,
    xix, 17, 25, 35–6, 44–5, 47–8, 89–91, 93–7,
    108n, 150–1, 154, 175n, 209n, 270, 275–6,
    280; see also Assistive technology
significant health risk defined by, 276–80
and site-specific coverage, 44–5, 192
and small business, 109n, 150, 183, 203–5,
    207
social and policy context of, 3–22
and Targeted Jobs Tax Credit, 305–7
telecommunications requirements of, xxvii,
    38–40, 238: enforcement, 254–6; evaluation,
    261–2; reasonable accommodation, 257–8;
    telephone relay services, 239, 241–53, 262
and universal service mandate, 239
transportation requirements of, xxvi, 37–9,
    214–15, 219–27
and demand responsive systems, 221, 223,
    226–7; and demonstrated good faith efforts,
    225–6; fixed-route systems in, 220, 225–7;
    for over-the-road buses, 223–4, 231; for
    paratransit, 224–5, 229–30; and private
    entities, 223, 225, 226; and rail transit,
    221–3; regulatory implementation of,
    224–31; and UMTA recipients, 224–5; vehicle
    acquisition for, 225–7
and undue burden, hardship provisions of,
    xix–xx, 17, 25, 35–8, 44–7, 91, 94–5, 151–2,
    154–5, 175n, 191, 203–4, 207, 220–1, 230,
    273, 282
Architectural Barriers Act of 1986, xxv, 16, 195,
    210n

Architectural and Transportation Barriers
    Compliance Board, xxv, 16, 40, 195, 199,
    202, 211n, 224n, 228, 325
Army Corps of Engineers, 198
Arthritis, 61, 66, 67, 142, 144
Assistive technology, xxx–xxxi, 47–8, 313–31
    and ADA, 314, 330
    benefits of, 327
    costs of, 328–30
    defined, 314–15, 317–18
    and disability, 315–22
    examples of, 322–5
    guidelines for use of, 325–6
Asthma, 67
American Telephone and Telegraph (AT&T), 116,
    248, 264n
Austin, Texas, 233
Barrier-free environments, xv, xx, xxv
Barriers, xvii, 7–9, 70–1
    to employment, 114–15
    to public accommodations, 186
    removal: readily achievable, 38, 191–2, 195–6;
        as reasonable accommodation, 161; tax
        incentives for, 295
Bartlett, Representative, 28
Bell Telephone companies, 248, 253
Berkeley, California, 123
Berkeley Planning Association, 116, 161–3
Berkowitz, Edward, Disability Policy, 21
Blindness, see Vision, impaired
Braille, xxi, 192, 196, 318, 319, 323, 328
Brennan, William, 30
British Columbia Transit (Canada), 233
Bureau of National Affairs, 116
Bush, George, 29, 79, 112, 186, 206, 219, 335
Business and industry, xiii, xvii, xix, xxiii–xxv,
    xxix, 34–7, 81
    and contractual arrangements, 90–1, 100
    and costs: under ADA, 124–6, 202, 217; under
        section 504, 111, 125
    and customer preference, 45–6, 282–3
    and definition of employer, 34, 44–5
    discrimination by, 90–2, 101–4, 146, 152,
        167–9
    and eligibility criteria for public access, 189
    and employee benefit plans, 47, 100–2, 109n;
        see also Health insurance
    and jobs: essential functions of, 89, 108n,
        109n; pace and schedules, control of, 142–4,
        148n; screening for 91–2, 98–100, 109n
    and manufacturing, sales decline in, 135,
        137–8
    networks of, 96
    partnerships among, 126–7
    parent companies in, 191–2
    and phase-in of ADA coverage, 161–2
    and persons with disabilities: positive

experiences with, 116, 168; negative reactions toward, 71, 82

and service organizations, demands of, 117, 109*n*

and service sector growth, 129–30, 135, 137–8

and small business, 109*n*, 150, 183, 202–6, 207, 295–6, 298–9, 309*n*, 310*n*

and tax incentives: for access, 293–301; for employment, 301–7

and transit, 217, 225, 231

workplace accommodations by, 71, 89–91, 93–7, 111, 124–6, 142–4, 151–79, 172–3: costs recouped of, 169; process of, 95–6

and undue hardship: for employers, 94–5, 125, 151–4; for public accommodations, 159

Canadian Health and Activity Limitations Survey, 61–2

Canadian Health and Disability Survey, 216, 232

Cancer, *68*, 142, 272

Cardiovascular disease, *see* Heart disease

Case law, 92, 286*n*, 288*n*, 289*n*

   ADAPT v. Skinner, 218–19

   American Public Transit Association v. Lewis, 230

   Forrisi v. Bowen, 43

   Kohl v. Woodhaven Learning Center, 275–6, 286*n*

   Leckelt v. Board of Commissioners of Hospital District 1, 280–1

   Tudyman v. United Airlines, 44

   Nelson v. Thornburgh, 47–8, 94

   See also U.S. Supreme Court

Cerebral palsy, 66, *68*

Cerebrovascular disease, 67, *68*

Chapman, Representative, 28

Census Bureau, 138, 232

   and 1980 Census, 69–70

Centers for Disease Control, 281

Chronic disease

   from disability, 64–7, 74–5

   and withdrawal from work, 166

   and work schedules, 142

Civil rights,

   access to public accommodations and, 184–5

   and financial benefits, 48–9

   and the disabled, 83

   and employment legislation, 130

   and the legislative arena, 26–7

   movement, 26, 184

   and section 504, 30

Civil Rights Act of 1964, xix, 16, 26, 37–9, 44, 46, 49*n*, 83, 104

   Title VII of, 83, 104, 130, 184, 187–8

Civil Rights Act of 1990, 51*n*

Civil Rights of Institutionalized Persons Act (1980), 18

Civil Rights Restoration Act (1988), 17, 27, 147*n*, 273

Coelho, Anthony, 28

Cognitive impairment, *see* Developmental disabilities

Communicable disease

   asymptomatic, 273

   defined: as disability, 269, 270–73, 285*n*; as handicap, 30–1, 33

   direct threat language and, 17, 35, 38, 86, 269, 273–5

   fear and misapprehension of, 272

   food handling and, 28, 35, 45–6, 274, 282–3

   See also Persons with communicable diseases

Computer, personal, 316, 318, *319–21*, 327–8

Costs

   of accommodations, xviii, xxiv, xxvi, 35–7, 93–5, 111, 124–6, 150–63, 169, 172–73: correlation of with employment levels, 157–8; determinants of, 156–8; to families, 172; health-related determinants of, 171–2

   of assistive technology, xx, 47–8, 328–30

   of building alterations, 193, 201–3

   of civil rights benefits, 48–9

   of damages, 37–9, 104–5

   of employability benefit programs, 117–19, 123, 153, 157

   of liability insurance, 160

   of paratransit, 217

   redistribution of, 150–1, 155, 173, 175*n*

   site-specific, 44–5

   of Telecommunications Devices for the Deaf, 205–6

   of telephone relay services, xxvi, 245

   of transportation, xxvii, 217–18, 231

Crawford, Charles, 328

Current Population Survey, xxiv, 138–40, 144–6, 170, 176*n*

Dart, Justin, 291, 336

Dayton, Ohio, 233

Denver, Colorado, 70, 217, 233

Developmental Assistance and Bill of Rights Act (1975), 18

Developmental disabilities, 18, 186, 192; *see also* Mental retardation

Developmental Disabilities Councils, 18

Diabetes, 67, 286*n*

Disability,

   in childhood or youth, 166–67

   definition of, xx–xxi, 17, 25, 30, 33–4, 42–4, 55–8, 83–6, 163–4, 170: by disability-rights advocates, 62–3; by persons with disabilities, 63–4; by researchers, 58–60; by World Health Organization, 60

   demographic estimates of, 60–2, 74

   discrimination and, 70–2, 167–9

   and high-risk conditions, *68*

and jobs: occurring on, 115, 159; restricting
    performance of 30, 148*n*, 166–7
language of, 14–15
and major life activities, 57–8, 60
types of, 65–8
variations in prevalence of, 69–70
See also Persons with disabilities, listings for
    specific disabilities
Disability Rag, 11, 14
Disability rights,
    activists, xvii, xix
    advocates, 62–3, 124, 192
    financial support for, xx
    movement, 3–4, 11–14
Discrimination, xi, xxii–xxiii, xxv, 6–9, 70–2, 74
    ADA mandate against, 33
    basis of, 30
    burden of proof and, 86, 102–3
    and communicable disease, xxviii, 270–1
    and customer preference, 46, 282–3
    and defenses to charges of, 35, 102–4
    disconfirmation and, 10
    dual, 6
    and eligibility criteria, 189
    in employment, 82, 102–4, 113, 146, 153,
        167–9
    and facility accommodation, 39
    forms of prohibited by ADA, 90–2
    and gender, 168
    in health insurance, 100
    and job applicants, 97–8
    motivation for, 30
    and occupational segregation, 167
    in public accommodations, 189
    prejudice and, 6–7, 30
    and the private sector, 19, 21
    and the Rehabilitation Act, 16, 31–2
    remedies for, 104–5
    research into, 143–5
    statistical theory of, 168
    wage, 167–9, 176*n*
Disfigurement, 272, 282
Disk disorders, 67, *68*
Dog, service, 93
Dole, Robert, 28
Douglas, William, 184
Down's syndrome, *see* Developmental disabilities
Drugs
    addiction and use of, 35–6, 41, 44, 86–7, 106*n*
    and rehabilitation, 87
DuPont, 116
Dyslexia, 93
Education for All Handicapped Children Act
    (1975), 52*n*, 285*n*; *see also* Individuals with
    Disabilities Education Act
Emphysema, 67, *68*
Employability, 141–3

Employability programs, xxiv
    and Allied Services, 109*n*
    coordination of, 117, 121
    and costs of accommodation, 156, 159
    funding of, 121–2
    and Goodwill Industries, 117, 120
    job matching in, 121
    and Just One Break, 112, 121
    and Projects with Industry (PWI), 121–2
    and rehabilitation, xxiii, 19, 96, 118, 120–1,
        164
    and sheltered workshops, xxiii, 118–20
    and supported employment, 122–3
    and technical assistance for employers, 109*n*,
        117
    and transitional services, 159
    and Vocational Rehabilitation, xxiii, 96,
        118–19, 120, 159
Employers, *see* Business and industry
Employment, of persons with disabilities
    barriers to, 114–15
    costs and benefits of, 117–19, 123, 151–9, 173
    discrimination in, prohibited by ADA, 34–7,
        82, 89–90, 151, 154, 159
    and essential functions of jobs, 36, 89
    evaluation of, 117–18, 123, 138–49, 159
    by federal agencies, 20, 136–7
    of the hearing impaired, 258
    increasing employability and, 112–13
    limitations of, 71, 74
    and medical exams, 99–100
    protection of, xxii, 81–106, 113–14, 116–24
    reasonable accommodations and, 93–7, 108*n*,
        142–3, 151–63, 175*n*; *see also* Assistive
        technology
    statistical database for, xxiv
    of targeted jobs groups, 303–7
    and tax incentives for, 301–7
    trends in, 132–6, 164–9
    See also Labor market; Persons with disabilities
Epilepsy, 286*n*, 272
Equal Employment Opportunity Commission, xiii,
    xxiv, 37, 104–5, 140–1, 143–6, 325
    data collection by, 141, 145–6
Equal protection analysis, 26
Evaluation and monitoring, 72–5, 138–41, 151,
    159, 169–73, 261
    of accommodation costs, 160–3, 169–73
    augmentation of, 131, 139–41, 169–73
    baseline and current data for, 73, 117, 145–6
    costs of, 140–1, 152–4
    definitional issue in, 73, 170
    diversity of population and, 73, 117, 170
    of employability programs, 117–18, 123
    of employers' need for, 117, 144, 169
    of employment, ADA impact on, 129–31
    and quantification of discrimination, 73

research needs for, 143–5
of state and local estimates, 74
structural limitations of, 138–9, 162–3, 169–72
of tax incentives, xxix, 307–8
See also specific surveys and projects
Fair Housing Act Amendments of 1988, 19, 21, 195, 107n, 196, 210n, 285n
Federal Communications Commission, xiii, 39, 241–5, 248–50, 254–5, 260, 262, 263n, 264n, 265n, 266n
Funding
  for disability rights, xx, 52n
  effects of recession on, 115
  for employment mandates, 21, 125, 150–1
  for programs and services, 19, 121–2
Funding Partnership for People with Disabilities, xiii
Gaullaudet College, 249
General Accounting Office, 201, 203, 299, 308
General Services Administration, 199
Genetic traits, 43–4, 52n
Goldberg, Arthur, 184, 208
Goodwill Industries, 117, 120
Great Britain, survey of functional limitations in, 61–2
Greensboro, North Carolina, 184
Greyhound Bus Lines, 217
Handicap
  defined, 60, 107n, 167
  and vocational rehabilitation, 118–19
Harkin, Thomas, 14, 28
Harris, Louis, and Associates, 20, 116, 160, 166, 171, 185–6, 216
Hatch, Orrin, 28
Hawking, Stephen, 11
Health insurance, 25, 40, 46–7, 63, 100–2
Hearing, impairment of, 67
  and communication access, 186, 192
  demographics of, 249–50, 261
  discrimination against, prevented by TDD use, 258
  interpreters for, 93, 155–6, 191, 318
  technological aids for, 316–17, 319
  telephone amplifiers for, 87, 93, 323
  telephone relay services for, xxvii–xxviii, 245–6, 249–50: consumer monitoring of, 254–5, 262
Heart disease, 68, 166, 317
Hepatitis B, 275–6, 286n
HIV infection, 17, 28–9, 64, 86, 107n, 142, 272–3, 278–9, 280–1, 288n, 289n
Homosexuality, 41, 87–8, 107n
Houston, Texas, 233
Hoyer, Representative, 28
Hypertension, 61, 67
Impairments
  and activity limitation, 66, 68, 50n

defined, 56, 58–9: by ADA, 33–4, 57–8, 270–1; when visible as handicap, 167
demographics of, 60–1, 159
persons regarded as having, 85
record of, 85
types of disabling, 65–8
See also Disability; Limitations
Independent living
  centers, 125
  movement, 123–4
  philosophy, 12–14
Individuals with Disabilities Education Act, xx, 17–18, 25, 48
Internal Revenue Code, 294–5
International Center for the Disabled, 63–4, 70–1, 73, 160, 166, 171
International Standards Association, 229
J. M. Foundation, 120, 123
Jordan, I. King, 1
Kennedy, Edward, 28
Kohl, Herb, 309n, 310n
Koop, C. Everett, 273
Labor market, 114–16, 130–5
  changes in, 131–5, 141–2
  and economy, 114–15, 147n
  and service sector expansion, 129–30, 135, 137–8
  supply and demand in, 153, 174n, 175n
Larynx, electronic, 316, 317, 320
Legislation, federal, 15–21, 27–9, 40; see also specific laws
Legislation
  for building codes, 195, 202
  state, 100–1, 105, 198
Lewis, David, 216
Lewis, Jerry, 14
Lifts, for buses, 217, 221, 225, 228, 233
Limitations
  as barriers, 71, 72
  defined by ADA, 59
  demographics of, 61–2
  functional, 60
  of major life activities, 57–8, 72, 85
  See also Disability; Impairments
Local governments, xiii, xv, 19, 37, 39, 218
  building codes of, 195
  and employment of persons with disabilities, 147n
  mass transit systems of, 217–22, 224–7
  public health activities of, 274
Mainstreaming, 18, 20, 105
Marshall, Thurgood, 32
Massachusetts Commission for the Blind, 328
McDermott, Representative, 28
Medicaid, 32, 165–6
Medical examinations, 97–100
Medicare, 165

Mental illness, 65, 67, 87, 277
Mental retardation, 65–6, 67, 68, 162, 280; see also Developmental disabilities
Mobility devices, see Wheelchairs and mobility devices
Mondale, Walter, 286n
Multiple sclerosis, 68
Nagi, Saad, 58, 60
National Association of Rehabilitation Facilities, 120
National Center for Health Statistics, 62, 64–5, 69–71, 138–9, 144–6
National Council on Disability, 14, 16, 27, 40, 329
National Cristina Foundation, 14
National Easter Seal Society, 14 and Project ACTION, 216, 232
National Federation of Independent Business (NFIB), 202–3, 209n, 300
National Health Interview Survey, xxiv, 62–4, 73, 147n, 138–40, 173
National Highway Traffic Safety Administration, 229
National League of Cities, 201
National Park Service, xxvi, 197–8, 200–1
National Railroad Passenger Corporation, 37, 220
National Restaurant Association, 28
National Technology Center, 327
Nervous disorders, 67
New Jersey, 186
Nixon, Richard, 112
Obesity, 43, 51n
Office of Management and Budget, 160, 202
Office of Technology Assessment, 39, 223–4, 231
Oregon, 233
Oregon State University, 233
Orthopedic impairments, 61, 66, 67, 68
Osteomyelitis and bone disorders, 67
Pennsylvania, 94, 233
Personal assistance services, 318, 322
Persons with communicable diseases, xxviii, 17, 268
    accommodations for, 274–6
    attitudes toward, 272
    defined: as disabled, 269; as handicapped, 30–1, 33
    direct threat language and, 17, 35, 38, 86, 269, 273–6
    discrimination against, 274
    employment of, 274–5
    food handling and, 28, 35, 45–6, 274, 282–3
Persons with disabilities, xi, xvi–xviii, xxi–xxviii, 3, 56–7, 117
    associates and families of, 88, 107n, 172, 220
    attitudes toward, 4, 9–12, 21, 30, 34
    barriers to work faced by, 70–1
    and consumer advisors, 326

demographics of, xxi, 5, 55–75, 117, 147n, 170–1, 216
desire to work by, xxii, 5, 71, 82, 113, 115–16, 166: as affected by transfer income, 163–6; need for better analysis of, 171
discrimination toward, 5, 6–7, 10, 19, 21, 30, 33, 70, 90–2, 146, 153, 167–9
education of, 5, 70, 152, 166–7
effects of federal laws on, 20, 165
employability of, 112–16, 141–3, 153: self-prognosis by, 144; of persons with severe disabilities, 150, 153, 157, 159, 166
employment of by federal agencies, 20, 136–7, 161–2, 302–7
health-care utilization by, 171–2
and identification of disability: for control over work scheduling, 142–4, 148n; to employer, 125, 318, 326
income, 5, 70: recent decline in 151–2; from transfer payments, 163–6
inferior status of, 5
labor force participation by, xxiii, 130–1, 148n, 151–54, 164–7: and race, age, and gender, 132–5, 133; in service sector, 135–6, 141–2; and supply and demand, 156–9, 175n
qualified, definition of, 88–90
section 504 definition of, 30, 83–5
self-perception of, 63–4, 70–2, 165
social participation by, 5, 70, 183, 185–6
and terminology, 174n
transportation services for, 231–3: lack of access to public; 214–16, views on, 216
as unique individuals, 8–9
unemployment of, 113, 118, 129–31, 135–6, 151
work aids for, 163
work performance of, xxii, 113
Persons with record of impairment, 85, 272
Physical appearance, as disability, 43
Presidential Commission on the Human Immunodeficiency Virus, 16, 27, 273
President's Committee for the Employment of People with Disabilities, 14, 126, 145, 291, 325, 334
Programs and services, xxiii, 19
    coordination of, 19, 117, 121
    funding for, 19, 21–2
    for protection and advocacy, 18, 21
    types of, 19
    See also Employability programs
Pryor, Senator, 298
Public accommodations, xx, xxv, 38, 183–208
    alternative methods for access to, 192–3, 197, 205, 207
    and auxiliary aids for access to, 190–1, 203–4, 207, 295; see also Assistive technology
    environmental impact of, 197–8

fundamental alteration to, 190
in historic buildings, 201
and new construction or alteration, 193, 202–3
in parks and recreation facilities, 197–8, 200–1
and reasonable modification requirements, 190:
    costs of, 202–3; for ready accessibility 204–5;
    for ready achieveability, 195–8, 203, *207*
removal of barriers to, 191–2
TDDs in, 258
topological problems in, 196–7
Public health law and powers, xxvii–xxix, 46, 268
and compulsory HIV testing, 280–1
as least intrusive alternative, 280
significant risk, determination of, 276–80,
    284–5
statutory review of, 269
See also Persons with communicable diseases
Rehabilitation Act (1973), xix, xxiii, xxv, 16–17,
    20, 37, 40–2, 82–5, 95, 103, 118, 121–6,
    151–2, 154, 161, 190, 283, 315
accessibility requirements of, 32, 190, 194–5,
    197, 200
discrimination prohibited by, 31–2, 285*n*
and employment in federal agencies, 136–7
enforcement of, 20
extension of to private sector, 29, 151
qualified handicapped person defined by, 31,
    83–4
and reasonable accommodation provision, 31–2
section 504 of, 17, 20–1, 25–7, 29–32, 40–2,
    50*n*, 52*n*, 57, 81, 83–4, 92, 107*n*, 125,
    129–30, 147*n*, 194–5, 197, 200, 209*n*, 218
and transportation, 218
Religious entities
employment preference and, 35
exemptions of, 33, 188
job requirements and, 104
Revenue Reconciliation Act of 1990, 294, 296,
    301, 304–5
Rheumatoid arthritis, *68*
Rochlin, Jay, 328
San Bernardino/Riverside, California, 70
San Francisco, California, 214, 217, 232
Sears, Roebuck, 328
Seattle, Washington, 217, 233
Sexual behavior disorders, 41, 44, 87
Sinusitis, chronic, 61
Small Business Legislative Council, 298
Smoking, 40, 43, 44
Social Security Act, 165
Social Security Disability Insurance (SSDI), 142,
    146, 148*n*, 164–6, 176*n*, 303
Social Security surveys, 143, 146, 167
Society of Automotive Engineers, 229
Sprint Services, 242
Stark, Fortney, 310–11*n*

State governments, xiii, xix, 18, 19, 21, 27, 39,
    40, 119, 195, 202
cooperation with federal government, lack of,
    21
employment of persons with disabilities by,
    147*n*
and employment security offices, 304–5
public health activities of, 274, 283–4
See also Legislation, state
Statue of Liberty, 198
Surrey, Stanley, 299
Survey of Income and Program Participation
    (SIPP), 61, 73
Tacoma, Washington, 186
Tax incentives, xxix–xxx, 115, 126, 293–308
and access credit, xxix, 150, 293–301, 307,
    309*n*, 310*n*
and deduction analysis, xxix
monitoring of, 307–8
and section 190 deduction, 293–301, 307,
    308*n*, 309–10*n*
and Targeted Jobs Tax Credit, xxix–xxx, 293,
    301–7, 311*n*, 312*n*
Tax Reform Act of 1984, 300
Technology assistance programs, 52*n*, 315, 326,
    329
Telecommunications, xx, xxvii, 39–40, 238
assistive technology for, xxx, 316
and closed captioning, 39, 316, 324
emergency calls in, 258
future technology of, 260–1, 266*n*
and state telephone relay services, 240–8:
    funding for, 250–3; outreach and education
    for, 253–4; monitoring and evaluation of,
    254–5, 262; restrictions on, 246–7; structure
    of, 248–9
and telecommunication devices for the deaf
    (TDDs), xxvii, 205–6, *207*, *319–20*, 324,
    328–30: costs of, 249; 260, defined; 239–40;
    distribution of, 260; formats for, 259–60; and
    dual party relay, 240, 262
and telephone relay services, xxvii–xxviii, 39–40,
    205–6, *207*, 238, *319*: automated, 242;
    blockage of, 243–4, 264*n*; confidentiality in,
    241–3; consumer involvement in, 254; costs
    of, 245, 265*n*; demand for, 245–6; defined,
    239–40; operators for, 242, 245, 264*n*;
    and technological features of, 256–7
television, 39, 318, *319*
Teleconsumer Hotline, 263*n*, 266*n*
Toronto Transit Commission, 232–3
Transportation, xix–xx, xxvi, 37–9
and effective mobility, 215, 218
full accessibility to, xxvi–xxvii, 37, 214, 215,
    218–19, 233
and mass transit, 217–22, 224–7

and paratransit services, xxvi–xxvii, 37, 216, 219–21, 229–30, 232–3
research on, 231–3
security of wheelchairs on, xxvi, 217, 227–8, 233
and training of personnel and discrimination, 225, 233
transit access, xxvi–xxvii, 37, 214, 233
Transportation Research Institute, 233
Transsexualism, 87
Transvestitism, 41, 87
Tuberculosis, 271, 277, 279
Uniform Federal Accessibility Standards (UFAS), 196, 199–201, 210n
U.S. Congress, 84–5, 92, 101, 125, 206, 218, 239–40, 243, 254, 274–6, 282, 288n, 294, 296, 298–9, 302, 326
Congressional Budget Office, 141, 202, 232, 304
Joint Committee on Taxation, 300
House of Representatives, 27–9, 32, 34, 41, 193–4, 252, 256, 282–3, 285n: committees—Education and Labor, 27–8, 41; Energy and Commerce, 259; Judiciary, 196, 288n
Senate, 28–9, 32, 41, 204, 244, 249, 252, 256–7, 264n: committees—Finance, 302; Labor Relations, 288n; subcommittee—Disability Policy, 14, 192, 194
U.S. Circuit Courts of Appeals, 218–19, 224, 275–6, 280–1
U.S. Department of Education, xiii, 119, 325–6
U.S. Department of Health, Education, and Welfare, 83, 84, 201; see also U.S. Department of Health and Human Services
U.S. Department of Health and Human Services, xxviii, 35, 163, 282, 286n
U.S. Department of Housing and Urban Development, 195, 199, 201–2
U.S. Department of the Interior, 198
U.S. Department of Justice, xiii, 199, 273, 325
Attorney General of, 38, 39, 193–5
U.S. Department of Labor, 116, 119, 143, 161, 303, 304
Bureau of Labor Statistics, 137–41

U.S. Department of Transportation, xiii, xxvii, 18, 38, 39, 199, 216–17
regulation under 504, 218–19, 230: of vehicle acquisition, 224–7, 228–9; of research, 217, 231–2, Secretary of, 38, 39, 220, 221, 223, 224
U.S. Department of the Treasury, 294, 299, 302, 303, 305, 307
Internal Revenue Service, 304, 307
U.S. government agencies, see individual agencies
U.S. Postal Service, 199
U.S. Supreme Court, 17, 18, 30–3, 190, 276
Alexander v. Choate, 31
Bell v. Maryland, 184, 208
Civil Rights Cases, 184
Grove City College v. Bell, 17, 147n
School Board of Nassau County, Florida v. Arline, 17, 33, 43, 103–4, 271–3, 276–7, 279, 286n
Southeastern City College v. Davis 31, 190
UAW v. Johnson Controls, Inc., 43–4
Urban Mass Transportation Act of 1970, 218, 224
Vision, impaired, 68
and blindness in both eyes, 68, 161, 162
and public access, 186, 192
readers and other aids for, 93, 191, 318, 319, 328–9
Voting Access for the Elderly and Handicapped Act (1984), 18
Wall Street Journal, 14
Washington, D.C., 214, 217, 232
Washington Post, 186
Weicker, Lowell, 14, 16, 208n
Wheelchairs and mobility devices
access and accommodations for, 97, 162, 186, 222
assistive technology for, 316, 320–1, 323–4
ramps for, xxi, 89, 157, 192, 195–6, 202, 301, 328
security of, xxvi, 217, 227–3, 233
in wilderness areas, 40
White House Conference on Handicapped Individuals (1977), 16
Wilderness Act, 40
Workforce 2000: Work and Workers for the 21st Century, 114
World Health Organization, 60